THE POSER 4
HANDBOOK

THE POSER 4
HANDBOOK

R. Shamms Mortier

CHARLES RIVER MEDIA, INC.
Rockland, Massachusetts

Publisher: Jenifer Niles
Production: Publishers' Design and Production Services, Inc.
Cover Design: The Printed Image, Sherry Stinson
Cover Image: R. Shamms Mortier
Printer: Inter City Press, Inc.

CHARLES RIVER MEDIA, Inc.
P.O. Box 417
403 VFW Drive
Rockland, Massachusetts 02370
781-871-4184
781-871-4376(FAX)
chrivmedia@aol.com
http://www.charlesriver.com

This book is printed on acid-free paper

The Poser 4 Handbook
by R. Shamms Mortier
  ISBN 1-886801-93-2
  Printed in the United States of America

99 00 01 02 03 7 6 5 4 3 2 1

CHARLES RIVER MEDIA titles are available for site license or
bulk purchase by institutions, user groups, corporations, etc. For
additional information, please contact the Special Sales Department
at 781-871-4184.

DEDICATION

FOR STEVE COOPER,
THANKS

ACKNOWLEDGMENTS

Many thanks are owed to the following individuals for their participation in making this book a reality:

To all of those who contributed content for the book and the CD.

To the guidance and feedback of all the respondents on the MetaCreations' Poser List.

To everyone at MetaCreations, especially Larry Weinberg, Steve Cooper, John Ladle, and Dorothy Eckel.

To Jenifer Niles and the staff at Charles River Media.

To David Fugate and Maureen Maloney at Waterside Productions.

Thank you all so very much . . .

CONTENTS

FOREWORD vx

INTRODUCTION. xv

SECTION I   **THE BASICS** 1

CHAPTER 1   **NEW FEATURES** 3
IMPORTANT ADVANCEMENTS. 4
MOVING ALONG. 18

CHAPTER 2   **NAVIGATING THE INTERFACE**. 19
FIRST THINGS FIRST. 20
THE POSER 4 INTERFACE 22
IMPORTANT POSER 4 DATA SITES. 46
MOVING ALONG. 46

CHAPTER 3   **POSING AND CUSTOMIZING THE HUMAN BODY** 47
PAYING ATTENTION 48
BASIC POSING. 49
CUSTOMIZING THE HUMAN FORM 60
CUSTOMIZING WITH DEFORMERS. 65
MOVING ALONG. 70

CHAPTER 4   **POSING AND CUSTOMIZING HANDS** 71
A SHOW OF HANDS 72
CUSTOMIZING HANDS. 76
USING DEFORMERS ON A HAND 79
MOVING ALONG. 81

CHAPTER 5   CREATING EXPRESSIVE FACES 83
                   EMOTIVE POWER 84
                   THE NEW RACIAL MORPHS 99
                   MOVING ALONG 106

CHAPTER 6   POSING AND CUSTOMIZING ANIMAL MODELS 107
                   INTERNAL ANIMAL MODELS 108
                   EXTERNAL ANIMAL MODELS 121
                   ASSIGNING HUMAN CHARACTERISTICS TO ANIMALS 133
                   DEFORMING ANIMAL MODELS 144
                   MOVING ALONG 148

CHAPTER 7   COMPOSITED FIGURES 149
                   WHAT IS A COMPOSITED FIGURE? 150
                   INTERNAL AMALGAMATED COMPOSITES 151
                   USING THE HIERARCHY 174
                   POSEABLE CLOTHES 174
                   PROP MORPHING 176
                   SPAWNING PROPS 177
                   MOVING ALONG 178

CHAPTER 8   BACKGROUNDS, PROPS, AND RENDERING 179
                   THE GROUND PLANE 180
                   BACKGROUNDS 191
                   PROPS 193
                   CD CONTENT COLLECTIONS 205
                   CREATIVE RENDERING 207
                   TRANSPARENT FIGURE TEXTURES 212
                   MATERIAL GROUP PAINTING 216
                   MOVING ALONG 218

SECTION II   POSER 4 ANIMATION 219

CHAPTER 9   ANIMATION CONTROLS 221
                   THE IDEA BEHIND KEYFRAMING 222
                   TWO ANIMATION CONTROL ENVIRONMENTS 223
                   THE ANIMATION MENU 230

IK. 233
PREPARATORY MOVEMENTS 234
MOVING ALONG 234

CHAPTER 10   ANIMATING ARTICULATED HANDS 235
PRE-ATTACHED HANDS 236
STANDALONE HANDS 238
ANIMATED HAND PROJECTS 239
HAND JEWELRY 240
STUDY YOUR BODY 242
NEW IN POSER 4 242
MOVING ALONG 242

CHAPTER 11   FACIAL, MOUTH, AND EYE MOVEMENTS 243
ANIMATING THE MOUTH 244
ANIMATING THE EYES. 249
TWO APPROACHES TO ANIMATING FACIAL CHARACTERISTICS. . 253
MOVING ALONG 255

CHAPTER 12   ANIMAL ANIMATION 257
WHERE ARE THE POSER ANIMALS?. 258
EADWEARD MUYBRIDGE 259
TIPS ON THE POSER ANIMALS. 270
MORE ANIMALS 276
MOVING ALONG 276

CHAPTER 13   COMPOSITE CHARACTER ANIMATION 277
MULTIPLE COMPOSITE POSER MODELS. 278
PROP COMPOSITES 281
MIXED COMPOSITE COMBINATION ANIMATIONS 283
MOVING ALONG 290

CHAPTER 14   THE WALK DESIGNER 291
THE WALK DESIGNED CONTROL DIALOG 292
WALK DESIGN PARAMETERS. 295
WALK DESIGN PARAMETER COMBINATIONS. 298
PATHS. 298

TRANSITIONAL WALKS 299
ANIMALS AND THE WALK DESIGNER 299
USING BVH MOTION FILES 302
MOVING ALONG 303

CHAPTER 15   MORPHING MADNESS 305
CREATING YOUR OWN MORPH TARGETS 306
MOVING ALONG 317

SECTION III   ADVANCED TOPICS 319

CHAPTER 16   HIERARCHIES 321
BASIC HIERARCHY DEVELOPMENT 322
A PRIMITIVE TOY BIRDOID 327
AUTOMATED HIERARCHIES 343
MOVING ALONG 345

CHAPTER 17   HANDSHAKING 347
RAYDREAM STUDIO 348
OTHER 3D APPLICATIONS 353
2D PAINTING APPLICATIONS 368
GREAT 2D F/X PLUGINS 370
POST-PRODUCTION EDITING 372
3D PAINTING APPLICATIONS 377
BVH MOTION CAPTURE 379
FASHION STUDIO 385
MEDIA CONVERSION AND COMPRESSION 385
METASYNTH, METATRACKS, AND XX. 387
CONTENT YOU GOTTA HAVE 388
MOVING ALONG 392

CHAPTER 18   CUSTOMIZING TEMPLATES 393
FILE NAMING CONVENTIONS 394
CREATING TEXTURES WITH PAINTER 394
CREATING TEXTURES WITH PHOTOSHOP 403
MAPPING A PHOTOGRAPHIC FACE 406
POSER FORUM WEB RING 408
MOVING ALONG 408

CHAPTER 19   **CAMERAS, LIGHTS, AND MORE RENDERING TIPS**. . . . **409**
CAMERAS 410
NEW LIGHTS AND LIGHTING 416
MORE ON RENDERING 418
MOVING ALONG. 421

CHAPTER 20   **HINTS AND TIPS FROM MASTER USERS**. **423**
CHRIS DEROCHIE. 424
MARTIN TURNER 429
PHONEMES, A QUICK BUT IMPORTANT NOTE. 429
FAST AND DIRTY LIP-SYNCING 430
CECILIA ZIEMER. 436
ROY RIGGS 444
JACKIE LEWIN 448
STEPHEN L. COX 453
RICK SCHRAND 457
MORPH MANAGER 464
THE OBJ FILE FORMAT 465
MOVING ALONG. 468

CHAPTER 21   **FIGURE DEVELOPERS**. **469**
THE ZYGOTE MEDIA GROUP 470
bioMECHANIX 480
WHITECROW 3D 483
THE POSER PROPS MODELER'S GUILD 485
MOVING ALONG. 486

CHAPTER 22   **ADVANCED POSER PROJECTS**. **487**
THE CAROUSEL 488
THE CENTAUR 493
MAKING VAMPIRE MORPHS 496
BRYCE BEACH AND RIVER SCENES FOR POSER FIGURES 505
PHYSICAL MANIFESTATIONS OF TERROR 515
MOVING ALONG. 529

CHAPTER 23   **COLOR PLATE DETAILS**. **531**
COLOR PLATE 1: THE POOL OF SECRETS 532
COLOR PLATE 2: GREENING 533

COLOR PLATE 3: (TOP) VERDICT........................535
COLOR PLATE 4: (TOP) MEDUSA.......................538
IN CLOSING 539

APPENDIX A   ABOUT THE CD 541

APPENDIX B   CONTRIBUTOR BIOGRAPHIES 543

APPENDIX C   VENDOR CONTACT DATA.........................549

APPENDIX D   POSER WEB RESOURCE SITES....................551

               INDEX...557

FOREWORD

Why Poser?

Sometime in the late 1980s I had notions of finding out how much of a cartoonist I could be. I quickly discovered that the process of visualizing the human form in pose and in perspective—without reference—was quite difficult. I knew what I wanted to portray, but I couldn't "see" the pose. It wasn't the details of drawing that scared me, it was the overall form.

So I went out and bought one of those wooden mannequins and quickly discovered that it was good for about six poses. Why are they built the way they are? They don't have anywhere near the range of motion of a human being—and forget about pushing beyond that. So I set out to design and build a better mannequin. My research led to some very interesting materials that produced a number of odd-looking creatures. The closest I got to a usable mannequin involved using some modular tubing parts I discovered at a machine shop in Ohio. I think I eventually designed a better Bunsen Burner, but the human form kept eluding me.

Then one day it struck me. I had been animating and programming professionally for several years in Hollywood (mostly with Rhythm & Hues Studios). I had all this built-up 3D math knowledge and first-hand experience with the difficulties and complexities of creating computer-generated artwork as well as traditional artwork. So, why not combine my knowledge with my needs and make a simple but better "digital" mannequin?

My initial goals were very modest. I just wanted something representational of the size and proportions of a human body, and I wanted it to be extremely easy to use and pose. Direct 3D manipulation of the figure was essential. If I could simply represent directional lighting, that would be great. That was all I wanted to do. I wasn't planning to write a 3D renderer or create detailed human models that could bend. I wasn't planning to allow for animation or props or clothed models or textures or lighting or bump maps. But Poser had a mind of its own, and sometimes things just can't be stopped.

Now years have passed. Fractal Design took an interest, adding some talented programmers, artists, writers, and managers. Then came the merger with RayDream and MetaTools, adding even more programmers and designers. The end result is now the fourth release of Poser for digital artists and animators. Poser still maintains its roots as a tool for traditional artists and sculptors, but has grown significantly over the years.

I am continually amazed at the varied users and surprising uses people find for Poser—from home hobbyists to fashion designers to architects to scientists to sculptors to professional animators to fine artists. For me, it has been especially exciting to help foster the creativity of developing artists. Art is a very healthy expression of humanity. I am still hoping that one of these days I can take a break from programming and put Poser to use on my own cartoons as I had originally planned!

Larry Weinberg
Poser Master Programmer

INTRODUCTION

Welcome to the awesome animated world of MetaCreations' Poser 4. Poser 4 is a morphing and animation system, a place where you can design and move human, animal, and alien 3D models and Props. With a little study and experimentation, this book will allow you to master all of Poser 4's capabilities.

Preparations

To be able to use this book effectively, you must be working-familiar with Poser 4. That means that you will have, at the very least, worked through the tutorials and references in the Poser 4 documentation, so you have an understanding of the basic parameters of the Poser 4 tools and processes. Chapters 1 and 2 of this book reference Poser 4 tool usage, and can be used to reinforce your learning, but not to supplant information in the documentation. Most references to Poser 4 tools and their associated icons or menu listings in this book are meant to stretch your working knowledge of Poser 4 beyond the basic information presented in the documentation, and to build upon the basics. So read the documentation at least once, and work through *all* of the associated tutorials. You should also sign up for the Poser List, an Internet site that allows you to learn from and speak with hundreds of other Poser users. Go to:

poser-owner@onelist.com

and get instructions there. You will find that in doing all of these things, your appreciation and understanding of what is contained in this book will be many times more valuable.

METACREATIONS' MAILING LISTS

The OneList list is run by MetaCreations and is an official mailing list of the company. The list is solely for the discussion of MetaCreations software and other software products as they relate to MetaCreations software. It is not a general art discussion list, so please try to keep the topics centered around the aforementioned subjects. You should respect the Listmaster's requests to take threads or discussions off this list whenever the Listmaster deems them inappropriate. Flames and "trolls" are not permitted on this list.

A flame is defined as publicly berating or belittling someone. A troll is defined as someone who posts messages intended to disrupt discussion on the list, or to enrage other list members en masse. If you have personal problems with another list member, please discuss them with that person via private mail. If a person on this list is harassing you via private mail, please contact that person's Internet Service Provider for resolution of the issue.

Please do not use obscene language on the list. Also, if you want to share an image that contains nudity or content that is generally considered to be obscene or pornographic, it is requested that you state that fact when posting the link so nobody is unpleasantly surprised. Posting links to pornographic images on the Onelist Bookmarks page for this list is expressly prohibited. Also, posting links to commercial services not directly related to MetaCreations or its products is also prohibited on the Onelist Bookmarks page.

Commands

Please refer to the Onelist Help Center for detailed help on using Onelist mailing lists. The Help Center can be reached at:

http://www.onelist.com/info/helpcenter.html

Please review the links at the top of your Member Center page for more information.

Some Helpful Email-Based Commands for Onelist

- listname-subscribe@onelist.com—Subscribe to a list.
- listname-unsubscribe@onelist.com—Unsubscribe from a list.
- listname-digest@onelist.com—Switch your subscription to digest mode.

- listname-normal@onelist.com—Switch your subscription to normal mode.
- Where listname is the name of the list (KPT or poser).

Where to Get Help

To send email to the moderators of the list, send the message to the address <listname-owner@onelist.com>, where listname is the name of the list (KPT or Poser). You may also communicate with the MetaCreations Listmaster at <lists@metacreations.com>. You can get help with using Onelist via the Help Center:

http://www.onelist.com/info/helpcenter.html

YOU MUST HAVE THE FOLLOWING

The following items are essential if you are to get as much value out of this book as possible:

MetaCreations' Poser 4 (Mac and/or Windows Version)

Obviously, without the software, your appreciation of the contents of this book will be either nonexistent or severely limited. It is suggested that you purchase a copy of Poser 4 or upgrade your existing Poser 1, 2, or 3 version (piracy is illegal, and hurts everyone). Check with your local or mail-order vendor for current prices and upgrade policies.

An Appropriate Computer Platform to Run the Poser 4 Software

You will need a PowerMac or Pentium system to make creative use of Poser 4. The systems used in the creation of this book were both major platforms: PowerMacs (a 100-MHz PowerComputing 100 and an Apple 233-MHz G3) and a PentiumPro 300-MHz system. The author found these to be adequate for both creating the illustrations in the book and rendering the animations on the CD-ROM. Faster is always better when it comes to generating computer art and animation, and Poser 4 is a very demanding application when it comes to memory and speed. If you can afford an acceleration card, that's better yet. If your computer runs at less than 100 MHz, your Poser 4 renderings are going to be pretty slow.

RAM

The more RAM (Random Access Memory) your computer can access with Poser 4, the better. More RAM allows for larger scenes, which in turn render faster. The systems used in the creation of this book contained 172MB and 128MB (PowerMacs) and 256MB (PentiumPro) of RAM, respectively. Running Poser 4 with less than 48MB of RAM is not advisable.

CD-ROM Drive

CD-ROM drives are so commonplace today, that one is probably already installed on your system. A 4X speed CD-ROM is the lowest speed drive you should be using, with 24X and higher CD-ROM drives now becoming commonplace. Since all of the animations referenced in the book are also included on the accompanying CD-ROM, you have to have a CD-ROM drive to utilize the book's CD added goodies.

System Requirements	**MACINTOSH PPC PROCESSOR**

System 8+ (the software will run under System 7.5.5 and 7.6, but this is not recommended), Color Display with a minimum 800 x 600 pixel resolution (24 bit recommended), CD-ROM Drive, 32MB of available RAM (64MB recommended), 240MB Hard Disk Space*.

WINDOWS

Pentium, Microsoft Windows 95/98/NT4 (with Service Pack 3 or later), Color Display, True-Color recommended, Hard Disk, CD-ROM Drive, 32MB of system memory (RAM), 240MB Hard Disk Space*.

No matter what platform you have installed Poser 4 on, disk space is an important consideration. The Poser 4 applications used to create this book took almost a gigabyte of storage space, because a lot of additional modeling, texturing, and other content was added. 240MB of storage space would be a minimum requirement.

The Book's Structure

This book has been carefully laid out into three comprehensive sections: Covering the Basics, Animation, and Advanced Topics. Depending on your level of skill as an experienced Poser user and/or as a digital animator, you may desire to skip one section or another. Please do not do so. The reason for working through this whole book, no matter what your experience level with Bryce or computer animation techniques, is that each section contains new and useful material for maximizing your Poser 4 encounter.

SECTION I: COVERING THE BASICS

This is the first section of the book. It includes the following chapters:

Chapter 1: New Features

This chapter details the new features contained in Poser 4, and what they mean to your creative options. Please note that a number of new and exciting features have been added since the previous book, the *Poser 3 Handbook*, was placed on the market. Review this section carefully.

Chapter 2: Navigating the Interface

The Poser 4 interface has been upgraded since Poser 3, but most of the tools and tool/menu locations will be familiar to Poser 3 users. Learning to intuitively navigate the Poser 4 interface will greatly enhance your Poser creations.

Chapter 3: Posing and Customizing the Human Body

Learn to pose the human body models in believable and humorous ways.

Chapter 4: Posing and Customizing Articulated Hands

Poser 4's hands are exquisitely modeled, and every joint can be moved into any required position.

Chapter 5: Creating Expressive Faces

Combining emotions and phonemes produces faces that can express all of the human emotions needed for any situation.

Chapter 6: Posing and Modifying Animal Models

From the Dolphin to the Velociraptor in the Poser 4 libraries, and from the Chimp to the Zebra in the Zygote Extras CD collections, posing animal models continues to be one of the most exciting features of Poser 4.

Chapter 7: Composited Figures

Poser 4 allows you to mix and blend figures of various types, so creatures that are based in mythology and fantasy can easily be brought to life.

Chapter 8: Backgrounds, Props, and Rendering

Working with Backgrounds and Props allows you to create complete worlds that act as environments for your characters, and also to generate new and novel creature parts.

SECTION II: ANIMATION

This is the second section of the book. It includes the following chapters:

Chapter 9: Animation Controls

You have to master Poser 4's animation controls and techniques in order to choreograph your models at selected keyframes on the timeline. Using IK (Inverse Kinematics) can be a big help.

Chapter 10: Animating Articulated Hands

Because of their articulated complexity, hands have to be treated with care to evoke believable choreography.

Chapter 11: Facial, Mouth, and Eye Movements

This chapter tells you how, when, and why to animate faces, and also walks you through the use and development of phoneme targets and other facial morphing cycles.

Chapter 12: Animals In Motion

A reference is included in this chapter for the *Muybridge Animation Books*, and other techniques used to create animals in motion.

Chapter 13: Composite Character Animation

This chapter is devoted to fantasy and mythological character choreography.

Chapter 14: The Walk Designer

Here's a detailed look at one of the most spectacular features in Poser 4. The Walk Designer has been upgraded from the Poser 3 version.

Chapter 15: Morphing Madness

One of the oldest myths in the world concerns the ability of sorcerers and mythic animals to shape-shift, to change from one form to another. Poser 4 gives you access to this capability by allowing you to shape-shift your characters.

SECTION III: ADVANCED TOPICS

This is the third section of the book. It includes the following chapters:

Chapter 16: Hierarchies

Understanding hierarchy development is vital if you want to bring your own models into Poser 4.

Chapter 17: Handshaking

How to Import/Export Poser 4D object and animation files, and why and when to do it. An important chapter for RayDream, 3DS, Bryce 3D and other 3D application users. Also covers mapping Poser animations to a plane in any 3D application: Painter 3D and Poser, ArtMatic, Dance Studio, and more.

Chapter 18: Customizing Templates

Preparing content in bitmap painting applications, including Painter, Photoshop, and other applications. How to map photographic faces on Poser models.

Chapter 19: Camera, Lights, and Rendering

Vital tips for creating great Poser art and animation.

Chapter 20: Hints and Tips from Master Users

Hints and tips from three exemplary Poser 4 masters. Larry Weinberg is the parent and creator of Poser. Steve Cooper is the Poser 4 product manager at MetaCreations. Cecilia Ziemer is a Poser master user, whose work has been published in *3D Artist Magazine*, in the *Ray Dream 5 f/x* book (Coriolis), and in the *Bryce 3D Handbook* (Charles River Media).

Chapter 21: Poser Content Creators

An exclusive reference written by the master modelers at Zygote Media Group. The Zygote Media Group was responsible for crafting all of the new high-quality animatable models in Poser 3 and 4. Also included is an article written by Keith Hunter of Rhythm and Hues, the developer responsible for the articulated robot models included with Poser 4.

Chapter 22: Poser Projects

The development of some original Poser 4 projects.

Chapter 23: Color Plate Details

Here are details that walk you through the creative thinking and Poser techniques used to generate the color plates shown in the color section of the book.

END MATTER

Appendix A: About the CD-ROM
Appendix B: Contributor Bios
Appendix C: Vendor Contact Data
Appendix D: Poser Resources on the Web

THE BOOK'S CD-ROM

Movies, extra props and backgrounds, new templates, poses, and more. The Companion CD-ROM is loaded to the top, and adds hundreds of dollars' worth of Poser 4 extras.

How to Use This Book

The way that you use this book will necessarily depend upon how much experience you have had with both Poser and computer art and animation in general. Here are some basic categories that describe various classes of users. If one of these categories seems to closely resemble how you define yourself, you might find it helpful to use the underlying text as a guide for the way to explore this book's contents.

THE EXPERIENCED POSER USER AND COMPUTER ANIMATOR

If you are an experienced Poser 1, 2, or 3 user, and have also invested a good amount of time mastering your computer animation skills in other applications, you will find Poser 4 easy to understand. Because Poser 4 has tools and options not contained in other 3D applications, however, you should read this whole book. If you have studied the documentation, you can spend less time on Section I of this book, and most of Section II will be an easy read. Section III will probably be your main focus, since it explores details more suited to professional approaches. You should look at all of the animations and other material on this book's CD-ROM, and customize elements according to your needs.

THE POSER USER WITH LITTLE OR NO ANIMATION EXPERIENCE

If you are an experienced Poser 1, 2, or 3 user, but have little or no animation experience, then here is how you might benefit best from this book. Skim Section I, except where the new Poser 4 tools and options are discussed. Spend most of your initial time reading through and working from Section II (after you have, of course, worked through the Poser 4 animation documentation thoroughly). Since you are new to computer animation, save your study of Section III until later, after you feel comfortable creating basic animations in Poser 4. After you have reached that comfort level, you can study and customize the material contained on the CD-ROM.

THE EXPERIENCED COMPUTER ANIMATOR WITH NO PREVIOUS POSER EXPERIENCE

If you feel that this user category describes you best, then you can use this book to your best advantage by doing the following. Spend time learning Poser 4 first, both from its documentation and from Section I of this book. When you have a good feel for how the general tools and options work, move on to Poser 4's animation capabilities in the documentation and as detailed in Section II of this book. Remember that although your previous experience as a computer animator may have already given you a good understanding of the necessary vocabulary of the trade, Poser 4 does some things differently than other 3D applications. Compare Poser 4's animation and configuration options and methods with those you are already familiar with, and if necessary, jot down the differences and similarities for continued exploration and study.

THE EXPERIENCED 2D COMPUTER ARTIST WITH NO POSER OR 3D ANIMATION BACKGROUND

The great thing about Poser 4 for 2D artists ready to move into 3D, is that you can use the Poser 4 presets to create astounding 3D graphics and animations with ease. For the 2D artist, creating (and printing out) Poser 4 pictures is the best way to familiarize yourself with the interface design and the tools. This is suggested before you move on to various 3D and animation options. In terms of your best way to work with this book, spend a lot of time with Section I. Reread it a couple of times, and with the Poser 4 documentation at your side, create a series of single images. When you feel ready to move on to 3D and animation, move slowly, so you can appreciate the options and power of each succeeding step along the way. You should also study as much animation as possible, on TV, in the movies, and on the Web. Also notice and pay attention to your own movements as you go about the day. At that point, you will be ready to work through and customize the projects listed in Section III of this book and to gain more advanced knowledge.

THE NOVICE USER, WITH NO PREVIOUS EXPERIENCE IN COMPUTER ART OR ANIMATION

If you were attracted to this book without knowing why, you have made a wise choice. Before you can make good use of it, however, you will have to get accustomed to computer basics. This includes a familiarity with your system and its components. You may be an artist or animator whose experience includes art and/or animation with noncomputer media. Poser 4 is a great way to move from "traditional" to electronic media, since you can create amazing graphics and animations with a minimum of study. More advanced projects will take deeper study and concentration, but that comes in time. When you are ready, purchase Poser 4 for your computer. After you have worked through the Poser 4 documentation, work at a steady and comfortable pace through the examples presented in this book. You will be amazed at how quickly your efforts will result in professional images and animations.

POSER 4 CONQUERS THE MOVING WORLD

MetaCreations' Poser 4 is one of the most innovative and exciting pieces of software to ever be developed for desktop systems, rivaling in many cases the capabilities and output of systems and software costing hundreds of thousands of dollars. You can choreograph human and animal figures of every type, and populate your electronic worlds with animated beings. When completed, the results can be printed on paper for gallery presentations, sent to videotape or CD-ROM for animated productions, or output to removable disk media and to the Web for presentation to the world.

Welcome to Poser 4, where your animated characters can bring the computer screen to life.

THE BASICS

CHAPTER

1

NEW FEATURES

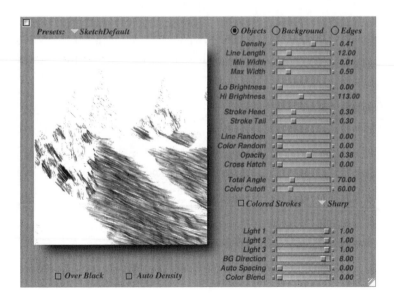

Important Advancements

Poser 4 is loaded with new features, as well as fixes and upgrades to features added in Poser 3. The interface is basically the same as that seen in Poser 3, but there are some important changes here too. In Chapter 2, "Navigating the Interface," we'll take a detailed tour of the interface, its tools, and its effect on the way its design and components influence your work. This chapter is a general overview of the brand new Poser 4 features. In Chapter 2, we fly closer to the ground, giving you a more enhanced and detailed view of the Poser 4 landscape, and how you can best interact with it.

POSER: A BRIEF HISTORY

To really appreciate where Poser 4 is today and what it does, it's necessary to understand how and why it came into being in the first place. Poser was originally conceived as a way to provide fast and accurate reference models for drawing the human figure, to be used as copy for 2D artists to trace over. Poser was developed as a utility for MetaCreations' Painter software. Poser was based on the idea of a model posing in an artist's studio, and also on the Mannequin models that many artists have that suffice for that purpose. Almost immediately after Poser's release, however, users started to clamor for more 3D and animation features. It is the constant pressure from Poser's user base that has driven its development toward a professional 3D art and animation target, and that pressure continues to inspire each new version.

Poser 4 is the result and embodiment of both the 2D and 3D artists' needs. The creation of posable Human and Animal models for the 2D artist has never been so easy or accurate, as well as affordable. 3D artists and animators, on the other hand, are presented with a huge array of options and functionality in Poser 4. Many of these features could only be found in very expensive workstation-based 3D applications just a few years ago, and many of Poser 4's features have never been seen before on any platform at any price.

BRAND NEW TO POSER 4

OK. With some observance and respect for history having been given, it's time to list the features that are propelling Poser 4 to the forefront of the Human and Animal model art and animation arena.

New Features

As you read through this list of new Poser 4 content, pay special attention to the features that are most interesting to you. That will give you a better idea of how to use this book to enhance your Poser 4 learning curve by zeroing in on the specific chapters that attend to those topics.

- **Sketch Designer**. This new rendering feature in Poser 4 rivals the creative power found in MetaCreations' Painter, although not even Painter has such an intuitive interface. If you have ever found yourself in need of a way to generate the kind of animations that appear to have been created with hand media (pens, pencils, charcoal, felt pens, and more), then you will love this new Poser 4 rendering option. An interesting sidelight of this new feature is that it treats any imported background image just as it treats the Poser content. That means you can use Poser as a utility to create media variations of any of your stored bitmaps (as long as they are in a format Poser can import as a background image). See Figures 1.1 and 1.2.

- **Interchangeable and Posable Clothes**. Poser users cried out for this feature, and Poser 4 implements it. Posable Clothes cover a wide range of included selections, with more on the way from other content providers. Although meant to be used on the Nude models, they can be retrofitted to any model, since you can always make the model's original body parts invisible. You can even develop cross-dressed characters if it pleases you. Over 40 models of 3D clothes are included on the Poser 4 CD. Be sure to read Chapter 3, "Posing and Customizing the Human Body." See Figure 1.3.

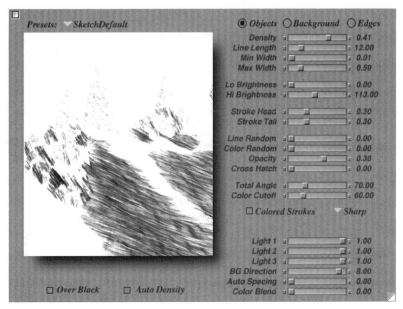

FIGURE *The Sketch Designer interface is loaded with controls for customizing your Poser*
1.1 *media looks.*

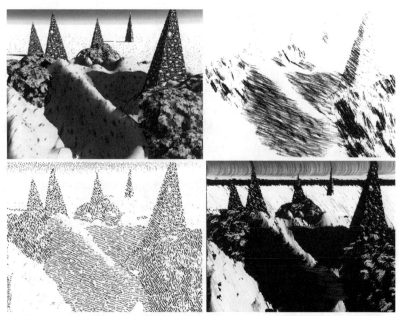

FIGURE **1.2** *The image in the upper left was imported into Poser 4 as a background. Using the media controls in Sketch Designer, the variations on the background image were created.*

FIGURE **1.3** *You'll find a wide selection of male and female Posable Clothes in the Poser 4 Figures Library.*

- **Magnet and Wave Deformers.** These deformation options can be used to create effects like animated warping of any selected figure element, or to cause wave and ripple effects on any figures or props. Used on the Ground Plane, you can create terrain and moving water effects. You manipulate the parameters of the Deformer and the area of influence it addresses. Also see Chapter 9, "Animation Controls." See Figure 1.4.
- **Polygonal Grouping and Picking.** This new feature greatly increases the potential for modifying your selected elements in Poser. Using the Grouping tool, you can select any portion of a model or prop for assigning a different texture or for deformations. For instance, you can select any part of a face before a deformation is applied, and have the deformation applied to just that part instead of the whole face. This leads to a higher variety of Morph Target development. Using the Grouping tool to create new texture areas allows you to colorize Poser models in some unique ways, and also allows you to apply bitmap labels to props. See Chapter 15, "Morphing Madness," for more on the use of the Grouping tool. See Figure 1.5.

Be aware that the Grouping operation leaves jagged edges on the area selected in many cases, so you have to use it with care.

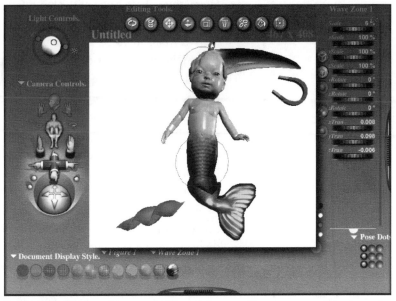

FIGURE   *Using the new Magnet and Wave Deformers adds even more modification and*
1.4   *animation effects.*

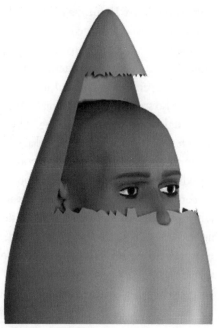

FIGURE
1.5   *Using the Grouping tool, you can select any area of a Prop and apply a different material to it. In this case, a transparent material was applied to the Teardrop prop, creating a window to see inside to the head.*

- **Hierarchies.** This is one of the most useful new features in Poser 4. A new Hierarchy list has been added that allows you to select and multiselect everything in a scene for Parenting and other operations. The Hierarchy Window is also essential when you import your own models for use in Poser, since it lists everything that will be linked in the chain of elements. Having this capability in Poser will convince many developers to create add-on models, since the hierarchical linking process is now so intuitive. The new Hierarchy Editor is essential for bringing in new models and for developing IK configurations. Be sure to read Chapter 16, "Hierarchies." See Figure 1.6.
- **Transparent and Reflecting Materials.** The revamped Surface Materials Window has two new parameters for assigning transparency and reflection to any selected element. This allows you to create metallic surfaces and windows, among other effects. Be sure to read Chapter 8, "Backgrounds, Props, and Rendering," for detailed discussions on these new material features. See Figure 1.7.
- **New Lighting Options.** Poser 4 is no longer limited to the three unconfigurable light sources found in Poser 3. Not only are you allowed as

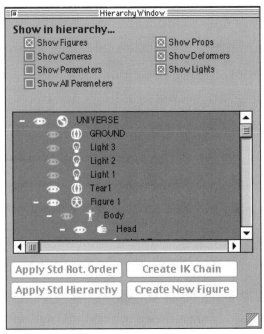

FIGURE   *The new Hierarchy Editor displays all of the elements in a scene, as well as*
1.6   *their linked chains.*

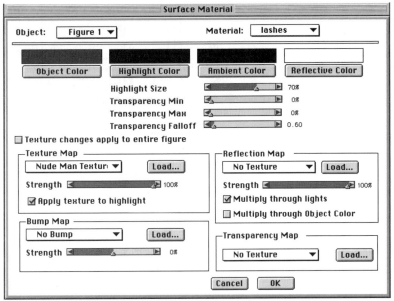

FIGURE   *Transparency and Reflectivity, including their respective bitmaps, can be*
1.7   *targeted in the Surface Materials window.*

```
┌─ Light Properties ─────────────────────────┐
│                                            │
│   Name:      Spot 1|                        │
│                                            │
│   ☑ On              ☑ Visible               │
│                                            │
│   ☑ Animating       ○ Infinite              │
│                                            │
│   ☑ Casts Shadow    ● Spot                  │
│                                            │
│   Light Color:    ▢▢▢▢▢▢▢▢▢                 │
│                                            │
│   [ Set Parent ]                            │
│                                            │
│                    [ Cancel ]  [ OK ]       │
└────────────────────────────────────────────┘
```

FIGURE *The new Light Properties Window.*
1.8

many lights as you like, but they can also be configured as Spotlights, creating more dramatic Poser scenes. Read Chapter 19, "Cameras, Lights,
and Rendering." See Figure 1.8.

- **Full Figure Morphs.** Are you old enough to remember the Superman
  episodes, the ones where he went into a phone booth and reappeared in
  full Superhero regalia? Poser now allows you to develop full-figure
  morphs that may not be able to do all of that (yet), but they are neat to
  work with. A Full Figure Morph is composed of all of the separate
  morphs and deforms that you develop for a model, and then save out as
  one Full Figure Morph file. With the turn of one Parameter Dial, your
  figure changes into that selected full-morphed targeted model. A Superhero Full Figure Morph is included on the Poser 4 CD. Be sure to read
  Chapter 15. See Figures 1.9 and 1.10.

- **New BioVision Motion Capture Files.** If you are one of the 100 million or so individuals who saw the film Titanic, then you have already

FIGURE *With the twist of one Parameter Dial, Mr. Thin Guy becomes Mr. Carved-and-*
1.9 *Cut, using the Superhero Full Figure Morph.*

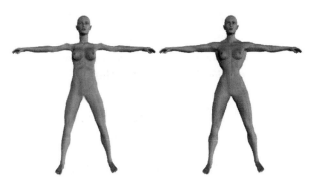

FIGURE   *The Woman model can also be transformed into a Superhero using her own Full*
1.10   *Figure Morph Parameter Dial.*

seen Motion Capture files in use. As the camera flew over the deck from stem to stern, hundreds of people were visible, going about their holiday and travel tasks. Attention! These were not human actors, but digital proxies. The reason they looked so real was that their motion was captured from real human models, and mapped to the digital models. This capability is present in Poser 4, so you can begin scripting your own Titanic movie (though perhaps with a somewhat smaller budget). The capabilities of Poser 4 to access and save Motion Capture files pushes it into the realm of a movie-maker's application, and a professional user's dream. Fifty Motion Capture files are included on the Poser 4 CD-ROM, and more are available from third-party developers.

BVH motion capture data is an industry standard motion format. To create ultra-realistic, highly kinetic animation, motion capture hardware is used every day by scientists and movie-makers alike to record complex human motion. Dance, sports, and medical data motions are just some examples of typical usage. Poser 4 imports BVH motion data files and allows you to apply it to a Poser figure. The final animation that is generated is remarkably lifelike, and would be virtually impossible to achieve any other way. You can also save out BVH Motion files, so that your Poser 4 animated moves can be read by any other application that can import this animation format. You will also want to pay attention to Credo's LifeForms and MetaCreations' Dance Studio (read Chapter 17, "Handshaking").

• **Deformable Props.** The new Props library that ships with Poser 4 is just the start. You are expected to add your own props as well, beyond the basic group contained here. Any prop can also be deformation animated, or just plain deformed with either or both the Magnet and Wave tools. For more ways to use Props, be sure to read Chapter 8 and Chapter 13, "Composite Character Animation."

- **The Copy/Paste Function.** Using the Copy/Paste function in Poser 4, you can select the choreography of any body part on any model and apply it to any body part on any other model, even across both gender and species lines if desired. This leads to exacting symmetry, which in some cases can be very humorous. See Figure 1.11.

- **New Hair Models.** With all due respect to readers who may have witnessed, as I have, that it's "hair today, gone tomorrow" (sorry), Poser 4 contains a new library of Hair objects so that all of your models don't need look like a radical rock singer anymore (unless you want them to). These hairpieces are not just blocky models either, but sport such niceties as stray strands of hair. Hair, like any object, can be rotated, resized, and even retextured. Hair objects come in already attached to the heads of any of the People models, though it has to be moved into place most times. The textures already mapped to them, however, are truly spectacular, adding even more personality traits to your models. Not only that, but there is also a collection of morphed and animatable Hair models for

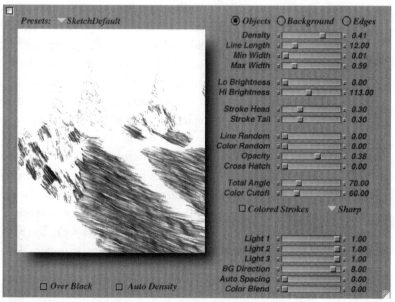

FIGURE *Any posed element or figure can be copied and pasted to any other, no matter*
1.11 *the model.*

even more realism. See Chapter 5, "Creating Expressive Faces," and Chapter 7, "Composited Figures," for more on Hair options and uses. Figure 1.12 illustrates some of the Hair objects.

THE CONTENT CD

Poser 4 ships with two CDs. One holds the application, and the other is jam-packed with content. If you install all of the content on your hard drive, be prepared to have a few hundred MB of extra space. The Poser 4 Content CD contains over 500MB of images, sounds, BVH motion files, props, free software, demos, and animations. The Texture Templates, in a separate folder on the content CD, are useful to import into Painter 3D (contained on the CD) as a reference image map. The included Canoma props were exported as Poser

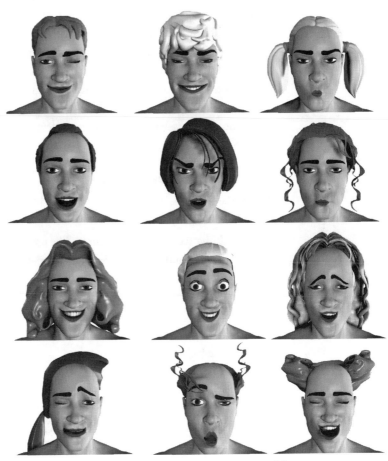

FIGURE   *Here are just a few examples from the Poser 4 Hair library.*
1.12

props and then resaved as Poser files. Each of these Poser files sits in a separate directory that contains not only the Poser file but all the necessary texture files. When either importing or opening these files, be sure to show Poser 4 where the textures are located. Poser 4 should find the textures automatically if the Poser file is in the same directory with those textures.

In the 3rd Party Developers folder are four items that are well worth checking out. LIPSINC: This self-running multimedia demo speaks for itself—literally. The future for Poser is very bright. CREDO: Their HTML demo comes with 12 BVH motion files that we hope you'll find very useful Hunyes Publishing: Great robots from a talented creative team that works in the special effects production world outside LA. FORGE STUDIOS: Chris at Forge is very active in the Poser community and has created some great examples of animation for you to use and hopefully learn from. These include sound files and exemplify what a talented animator can create within Poser. Chris's PoseAmation Trailer movie is also in the Movies folder.

In the Motion Capture folder are a good number of BVH motion files from the House of Moves. Dance Studio BVH motion data is also included (see Chapter 17 for more on MetaCreations' Dance Studio).

Also included on the CD, for Windows users, is a demo Motivate from the Motion Factory. Motivate allows game developers to assign "intelligent behaviors" to Poser figures.

UPGRADED FOR POSER 4

There are a number of elements in Poser 4 that have been seriously upgraded from their counterparts in Poser 3.

- **Enhanced Custom Textures.** The textures designed for the new People models and the Animal models are detailed and realistic, and each one can be further customized in a 2D bitmap application (Read Chapter 18, "Customizing Templates"). The ability to modify the textures of any model increases your personal creativity. The standard Template size is 9.7 × 9.7 inches at 72 dpi, and it takes up about 1.4MB of drive space. See Figures 1.13 and 1.14.

- **Upgraded Walk Designer.** There are new options in the Walk Designer so that you can create more original walk parameters for any selected bipedal model. As in Poser 3, you can also design your own Walk Styles and save them out for later use. Using the Figure Type control, you can preview the walk as applied to any Poser bipedal model. Be sure to read Chapter 14, "Walk Designer." See Figure 1.15.

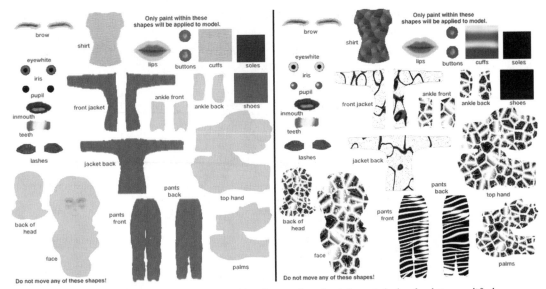

FIGURE *On the left is the Business Woman texture Template, and on the right, as it looks after being modified.*
1.13

FIGURE *When the modified texture is mapped to the Business Woman model, a whole*
1.14 *different character emerges, as shown in the right-hand model.*

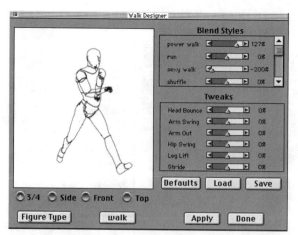

FIGURE *The Walk Designer has been upgraded, providing more animation options.*
1.15

- **Interface and Speed Upgrades.** As you read through Chapter 2, "Navigating the Interface," you will discover that the Poser 4 interface features some new and enhanced tools. Poser 4's basic models have also been redone to upgrade anatomical accuracy, and the overall rendering speed has been improved as well.

PROXY MODELING ENHANCEMENTS

As in Poser 3, any of these models can also be a temporary proxy for other Figure types, simply by selecting that Figure from the Figure Height item on the Figure menu. Alternate Figure Height types include Baby, Toddler, Child, Juvenile, Adolescent, Ideal Adult, Fashion Model, and Heroic Model. All that is adjusted is the proportions of the figures' anatomical geometry. Otherwise, all costuming remains intact. Selecting a male Business figure for instance, and then selecting the Baby Figure Height, will result in a baby that is attired in a business suit. The speed of this operation has been increased dramatically in Poser 4. See Figure 1.16.

If you use the Baby to Juvenile Figure Heights, and globally resize the figure to that of an adult, you will have a very unique adult with different proportions than the standard adult figure. See Figure 1.17.

In Chapter 3, you'll read about ways to customize standard characters, so that each model leads to infinite variations. You can take a Baby Figure Height, for instance, and use it as an adult character.

FIGURE   *The Business Man model looks very different when alternate Figure Heights are chosen. From left to right: Baby,*
1.16   *Toddler, Child, Juvenile, Adolescent, Ideal Adult, Fashion Model, and Heroic Model.*

FIGURE   *The Baby Figure Height globally resized to adult proportions with a wig on*
1.17   *creates a unique adult character. See Chapter 3 for more figure modifications.*

A METACREATIONS EXCLUSIVE

Poser 4 incorporates MetaCreations' exclusive SREE-D acceleration technology. This built-in high-speed 3D renderer allows unprecedented real-time performance, eliminating the need for platform- or OS-specific 3D software. Faster redraw of 3D models on screen allows for more realistic, shadowed previews, easier positioning of models, faster playback of keyframed animation, and higher resolution models with much more physical detail. In computer graphics and animation, this increase in speed results in a more natural creative approach by the 3D artist.

Moving Along

In this chapter, we've looked at Poser 4's new feature list. Each new feature was introduced and detailed. In the next chapter, we'll take a detailed walk through the Poser 4 interface, paying special attention to techniques that allow you to optimize your work.

CHAPTER

2

NAVIGATING THE INTERFACE

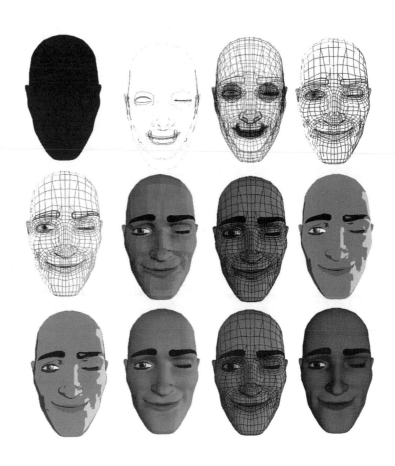

**First Things
First**

The very first action you should take before starting your Poser 4 work sessions is to make sure that you're working in a screen size that allows Poser 4 enough elbow room. Poser 4 will work on a screen set to 640 × 480, but it will present you with some space problems at this size. The reason for this is that the actual working area in Poser 4 is differentiated from the surrounding tools and utilities. A 640 × 480 screen size will mean that your actual workspace can't be set a whole lot larger than 320 × 240. This is fine for some multimedia work, but not much else.

So, if you have the capacity to do so, change your monitor size to 1024 × 768, with the option of 800 × 600 as the lowest size (if you have to). This will allow you a working area of 640 × 480, and even larger when needed. A 17-inch monitor or larger is necessary when working at this screen size so that you can read the text. If your system doesn't allow you to work at this screen size (because you don't have a suitable monitor or enough RAM), then you'll have to get by at a screen size of 640 × 480. In all cases, you should be working with 16 million colors.

CHANGING THE SCREEN SIZE ON THE MAC

To change the screen size on the Mac, do the following:

1. Go to the Apple menu at the top left of your screen, and move down to Control Panels. Once the Control Panels list opens up, double-click Monitor.
2. Once in the Monitor dialog, click the Options button. This will display a list of monitor size options. Select 1024 × 480 if it's listed, or 800 × 600 if that's the largest setting displayed. See Figure 2.1.
3. After selecting the enlarged monitor size, your screen will be replaced by that option.

Poser 4 loves RAM. On the Mac, be sure to increase Poser 4's memory allocation as much as possible, given the amount of RAM you're working with. Do this by selecting Poser 4 and bringing up its INFO window, then increasing the Preferred Memory as much as possible.

CHANGING THE SCREEN SIZE IN WINDOWS 95/98/NT

To change the screen size in Windows 95/98/NT, do the following:

1. Open "My Computer" and double-click the Control Panel directory. Once it opens, double-click Display. When the Display dialog opens, click the Settings tab.

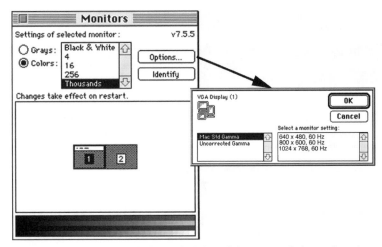

FIGURE   *The Mac Monitor dialog on the left, and the Options dialog on the right with*
2.1   *the screen sizes displayed.*

2. Move the slider until 1024 × 768 is displayed. Select Large Fonts from
   the Fonts list unless you are working with a 19-inch monitor or larger.
   You may be asked to insert your original Windows 95/98/NT CD so the
   new fonts can be loaded. Press the TEST button to see the new size, and
   then click OK. The screen will change to the new size. See Figure 2.2.

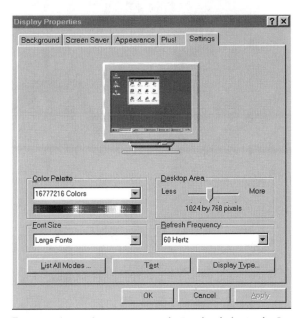

FIGURE   *Change the screen size in the Display dialog in the Control Panel directory to*
2.2   *the new size for Windows 95/98/NT.*

The Poser 4 Interface

Okay. Now that you have enlarged your monitor settings, it's time to explore the Poser 4 interface. Open Poser 4. You will be presented with the Poser 4 interface once the splash screens have disappeared. See Figure 2.3.

Although this chapter is devoted to exploring and detailing the new Poser 4 interface, it is not meant to replace the Poser 4 documentation. You should make sure that you read the Poser 4 documentation in its entirety, and work through all of the tutorials. Then you can use this chapter, and indeed this whole book, as a handy reference to expand your knowledge and to fill in some of the needed details.

Referring to Figure 2.3, the key letters point to the following Poser 4 menus, tools, and options.

A. Menu Bar

This area is Poser 4's Menu Bar, where the File, Edit, Figure, Object, Display, Render, Animation, Window, and Help menus are accessed. Read the documentation to learn about all of the features contained in these menus. Here's a synopsis of each menu's items:

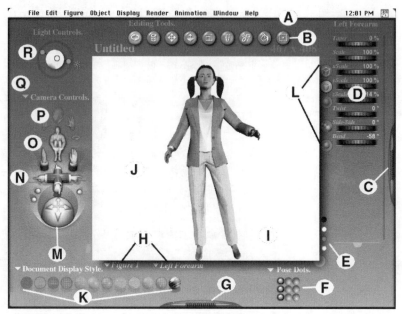

FIGURE **2.3** *This is the Poser 4 interface. All of the key letters point to various elements on the interface that we will detail in the following text. Refer to this interface schematic for locating the placement of the options pointed out in the text that follows.*

File Menu

Besides the standard load/save selections, there are two very important listings in the File Menu that you should pay attention to at the start: Import and Export.

Import lists a number of different types of file format data that can be read into Poser 4. This can be separated in background data (movie files or graphics used as a backdrop for your Poser 4 choreography), 3D Object Data (Poser 1 and 2 documents and libraries, and 3D props in the following formats: 3DMF, 3DS, DXF, OBJ, and Detailer/Painter 3D Texture files), and BVH Motion Capture files. You can also load Sound files, either music sequences or sound effects. The Import option is where you go when it's time to enhance your Poser 4 world with more content.

Export is important because it allows Poser 4 to handshake with other applications. Poser 4 allows you to export the following types of data: Image files (PICT for Mac user, and BMP or TIFF for Windows users); 3D Object data (RIB, 3DMF, 3DS, DXF, OBJ, and Detailer/Painter 3D Texture files); Painter Script, Detailer Text, and BVH Motion files. Image file exports allow you to read the Poser graphic into a bitmap paint application (like MetaCreations' Painter), where it can be customized and composited with other images (this is how the cover to this book was created, compositing Poser 4 images in Adobe Photoshop and MetaCreations' Painter). Exporting objects is important because other 3D applications may have a larger set of 3D tools for putting the final touches on a Poser 4 scene. Motion file export is important because other 3D applications can also read motion files.

At a number of places in this book we'll have reason to discuss and illustrate the ways that Poser 4 output can be redirected to a number of alternate 3D applications. When it comes to the sheer beauty of applying a texture or material to a Poser 4 object, Bryce is an optimum choice. Poser 4 does not export animation files to Bryce, but Bryce can be used to place origin points on Poser 4 elements for keyframe animating. You will be astounded at the quality of Poser 4 models exported to any of your favorite 3D applications. Applications that allow "boning" are especially suitable for Poser 4 imports, since boning allows you to animate a figure's parts without visible seams or breaks in the model. This is especially important to 3D Studio and Studio Max users.

Edit Menu

There are several options in the Edit Menu that you must pay special attention to.

Undo. This is a standard UNDO feature, reversing whatever the last operation was.

Cut/Copy/Paste. If you use Cut, the item is placed in the system buffer. Copy/Paste operations allow you to copy all of the parameters from any Human or Animal model and paste them to any other. This is a quick way to get symmetrical figure choreography elements.

Copy Picture. This option copies the image content in the Document Window to the system buffer, and is useful when you want a quick image to customize in a 2D bitmap application.

Restore. Although the UNDO option erases the last operation you have performed, using Restore allows you to return any Element, Figure, Light, or Camera (or All) to its original state with one click.

Memorize. If you use this option on any Element, Figure, Light, or Camera, using Restore will return that item to its Memorized state. Use Memorize every once in a while so you can continue to explore without worrying about returning to some set condition if things take a wrong turn.

General Preferences. Why is the Preferences dialog so important? Because you can configure Preferences to the way you work best in Poser 4. First, set your screen size and menu placement the way you like them. Place the Poser figure on screen that you want to be there when you first start Poser 4. Then, simply go to the Preferences dialog and click Set Preferred State, and wait while all of your settings are read. Make sure Launch to Preferred State and Use Previous State are on, and quit the dialog by pressing OK. Now quit Poser 4, and start it up again. You will find that all of the settings you adjusted will still be there. See Figure 2.4.

Figure Menu

A number of the items in this menu are carry-overs from Poser 2, so experienced users will take comfort in the familiarity of the listings. Included are:

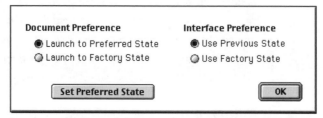

FIGURE **2.4** *The General Preferences dialog allows you to configure and save the Poser 4 workspace to your liking, which becomes the new default when Poser 4 starts up the next time.*

Figure Height. Just as in Posers 2 and 3, Figure Height options are available. Simply select an option, and watch your figure assume that specific physique. The options are Baby, Toddler, Child, Juvenile, Ideal Adult, Fashion Model, and Heroic Model. Although the option reads "Figure Height," that doesn't mean you can't use any one of these selections and resize it. A Toddler, for instance, can be resized to adult proportions in order to create a strange-looking Adult. Likewise, a Heroic Model can be resized to create a rather bizarre -looking baby model.

Set Figure Parent. Any element in the scene may become the Parent of another element. Parent actions set the movement, rotation, and sizing actions of the Child. This is handy when you've developed a Walk Cycle, and assigned it to one figure, and need the exact same choreography to be emulated by another figure(s), or when a Child figure is to emulate the Parent's behavior.

Conform To. Be sure to read Chapter 7, "Composited Figures" for details on this item. Using Conform To, you can substitute other clothing for that presently worn by a figure.

Create Full Body Morph. Be sure to read chapter 15 on "Morphing Madness" to get a detailed understanding of this exciting new feature.

Use Inverse Kinematics. IK (Inverse Kinematics) is a carry-over from Posers 2 and 3. In IK, you have to move the element at the end of a connected chain, like the foot or the hand, to move those elements farther up the chain. I would advise that you turn IK off until you've had a lot of experience animating body parts without it; then you can explore its uses. See Chapter 9, "Animation Controls."

Everyone works differently, and sets up defaults to accommodate personal comfort levels. For me, that means leaving IK off in most circumstances. The first thing I do in Poser 4 after importing a figure is to switch its IK settings off for all parts. I find that I can pose figures more accurately and quicker without IK. You will discover whether using IK is suitable for your approach, and take the appropriate action.

Use Limits. Any figure model element can have its movements limited, allowing it to bend only so many degrees. For more realism in your figure's movements, it's advisable to leave this checked. For maximum control, however, leave it off.

Genitalia. Male genitalia in Poser 4 has been completely remodeled, and is now very realistic. Since there may be situations where this might be considered inappropriate (when the audience is too young, or it is deemed otherwise inappropriate), you may select to leave this option unchecked.

Auto Balance. Auto Balance is an advanced posing feature. When it's on, it attempts to realign the figure according to the calculated weight of each of the body parts. The results are very subtle, but if you're looking for maximum realism, leave it on. It is a good idea to check this option when using BVH Motion Files. See Chapter 3, "Posing and Customizing the Human Body."

Lock Figure. This is a new Poser 4 feature that allows you to lock an entire figure so it can no longer be manipulated. It is most useful when you have a scene with multiple figures, so you can work on one selected figure at a time without disturbing the rest.

Lock Hand Parts. Poser 4 hands have articulated fingers and finger/thumb joints. When a figure is being posed, it's sometimes difficult to select a hand without selecting one of the finger/thumb joints. This option can be used to prevent that from happening.

Drop to Floor. Dropping a figure to the "floor" is especially useful when shadows are on, so the shadows that are cast seem more realistic. For maximum effect, make sure the Ground Plane is also visible.

Symmetry. Poser 4 allows both left and right symmetry. Just pose half of the body, select Symmetry for that posed half, and the same pose is applied to the other half of the body. See Chapter 3.

Delete Figure. Any figure in a Poser 4 scene can be eliminated from the Document Window. Props are deleted by selecting "Delete Object" in the Object menu.

Hide Figure/Show All Figures. When you have so many figures in a scene that it becomes hard to pose the one you want to, hide the rest. Selecting the Show All Figures command brings them all into view again.

Create Walk Path. A Walk path is associated with Walk Designer, so read Chapter 14, "The Walk Designer," for details on its design and use.

Object Menu

This menu is new to Poser 4, and contains many items previously located in other menus. Note that Properties applies to both anatomical models and Props.

Properties. The Properties dialog is important because it tells you at a glance the parameters of any selected object. In Chapters 3 through 7, this book covers various types of figure creation, so knowing how and when to bring up a selected element's Properties dialog is important. The three central attributes that can be accessed from the Properties dialog are Visibility, Bending, and Morph Target selection. More on Morph Targets in Chapter 15, "Morphing Madness." See Figure 2.5.

Lock Actor. Locking can be applied to any part of a model and to any Prop. Once locked, that element will not respond to Parameter Dials or other editing tools or alterations until it is unlocked.

Change Parent. This command is meant for Props, because you cannot change the Parent of a figure element.

Point At. Any selected element in your scene, including a body part, can be forced to Point At any other element. This includes Lights and the Camera.

Replace Body Part with Prop. As we will explore in Chapters 7, 8, 13, and 22, there are powerful consequences when you replace a Poser 4 figure element with a Prop, expanding your creative options.

Load Morph Target. Selecting this option allows you to retrieve any saved Morph Target from storage. More and more Poser sites on the Web are offering free Morph Target downloads. See Appendix D, "Poser Resources on the Web," for a listing of Poser sites.

Spawn Morph Target. This option creates a Morph target, taking into account all of the Deformations you have applied. All of these Deformations are placed under the control of one Parameter Dial. This is one of the most spectacular controls in Poser 4, and it can't be matched by any other application around. When you Spawn a Morph Target and then save the object, it is saved with the Morph as a Parameter Dial.

Create Magnet. A Magnet is one of the two Deformation tools in Poser 4. Depending on the size and position of the Magnet's Zone of Influence,

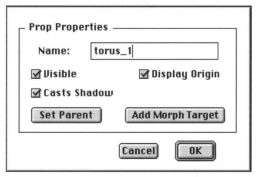

FIGURE   *The Properties dialog lists specific attributes for each part of a Poser 4 figure,*
2.5   *and also for any selected Props.*

all or part of a targeted object or figure is distorted in accordance with the Magnet's position and rotation. See Figure 2.6.

It is important to note that the Zone of Influence for either a Magnet or a Wave deformation has important properties, which can be seen when you bring up the Zone's Properties Window. See Figure 2.7.

The Properties of a Zone of Influence for the Magnet and Wave Deformers, as seen in Figure 2.7, display two new options. The first is that the Falloff of the Deformer's power can be altered. Clicking this option brings up the Falloff Graph, which can be interactively altered. The only way to understand how the shape of the graph changes the Deformer's power is to alter it, select OK, and move the Deformer in the Document Window to get a feel for the difference. Read Chapters 3, 4, and 6 for examples of Deformers in action. See Figure 2.8.

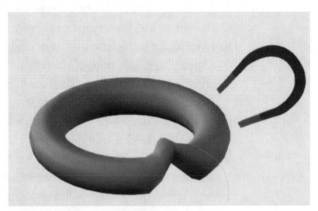

FIGURE **2.6** *A Magnet is a Deformation object that alters the parameters of the targeted element it is connected to. It appears with a Zone of Influence that can be sized and positioned, so the Magnet affects only that part of an object you want it to.*

Sphere Zone Properties

Name: Mag Zone 1

☑ Visible

[Edit Falloff Graph]

[Set Parent]

☐ Group: [▼]

[Cancel]   [OK]

FIGURE **2.7** *The Properties for a Magnet and a Wave Deformer's Zone of Influence display special features.*

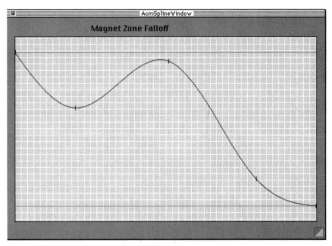

FIGURE *The Falloff Graph can be altered to affect the power of the Deformer on the*
2.8 *object.*

The second item you can alter in the Properties window of a Deformer is that its influence can be targeted to a separate Group. To have this happen, you must first identify that Group by using the Grouping Tool. Read Chapters 3 and 6 for examples of deforming groups.

Create Wave. The Wave is the second Poser 4 Deformer. It attaches itself to any object or figure element selected in the scene, and appears as a wavy object. See Figure 2.9. You can alter the same parameters of this Deformer as with the Magnet Deformer, by bringing up its Properties Window (see Figures 2.7 and 2.8 again). As you move and/or rotate the

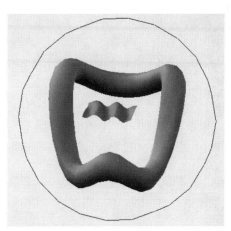

FIGURE *The Wave Deformer appears as a wavy object when added to the scene.*
2.9

Wave Deformer, you warp the object or element it is associated with. One of the best ways to create a Full Figure Morph is to use Magnet and Wave Deformers on different elements of a figure, and then save the whole thing by selecting Spawn Morph. The Wave Deformer has a list of parameters associated with it that you can tweak to create different effects. These parameters are displayed in the Wave Deformers Parameter Dials. See Figure 2.10.

It is important to understand how each of the following Parameters affects the Wave Deformer. The way to do this is to tweak a parameter while the Wave Deformer is stationary, and watch what effect that has on the associated object or element. The important parameters include:

- **Phase** (–10,000,000 to +10,000,000). This parameter shifts the peaks and valleys of the Wave, and when animated, produces moving ripples.
- **Amplitude** (.001 to 100,000). This is the Wave's power. You will seldom use values above 1 because the resulting warping will be too severe.
- **Wavelength** (0 to 100,000). This value determines the size of the ripples. Smoother ripples result from higher values.
- **Stretch** (–1 to 1). This value acts as a multiplier.
- **Amplitude and Frequency Noise** (0 to 1,000). Noise adds a random factor into the deformation.

FIGURE   *A detailed list of options that influence the way the Wave Deformer behaves*
2.10   *appears in its Parameter Dials.*

- **Wave Type** (Sinusoidal, Square, Triangular). Each of these parameters can be adjusted on a scale from 0 to 1, creating different wave shapes.
- **Turbulence** (0 to 100,000). Turbulence introduces spikes into the wave shape. You will seldom want to use values above .5.
- **Offset** (–100,000,000 to 100,000,000). This value pushes the targeted object away, and has to be used with care. Values in the range of –.5 to .5 are the most common.

Create Spot Light. This selection creates a Spotlight. Selecting the Properties option (either from the Objects menu or from the light bulb icon in the Light Controls) brings up the light's Properties window. Here, you can set the various attributes of the selected light. See Figure 2.11.

Delete Object. Any selected object can be deleted. Elements that are linked in a hierarchical model cannot be deleted, but only made invisible.

Display Menu

The Display Menu lists items that control what you see on your screen. Because you have diligently read the Poser 4 docs before opening this book, we'll touch on just a few of the important options in this menu.

Camera View. See Chapters 9 and 19 for a detailed look at Poser 4 camera use. In general, the cameras you'll be using most in Poser 4 animations are the Main, Posing, and especially the Dolly Camera. Other cameras are more useful in the design phases of your productions.

Styles. Poser 4 features a new list of Style options. A Style indicates the way that Poser 4 renders to the Document display in front of you. The Styles you may select from include Silhouette, Outline, Wireframe,

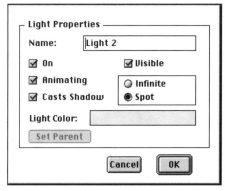

FIGURE   *A Light's Properties attributes.*
2.11

Hidden Line, Lit Wireframe, Flat Shaded, Flat Lined, Cartoon, Cartoon With Line, Smooth Shaded, Smooth Lined, and Texture Shaded. A Style can address the whole document and all of its elements, just the selected figure, or just separate targeted elements. On the last point, this means that you could have a hand on which every finger renders in a different display style.

The most important thing to remember about Styles is that although they are geared primarily toward the display screen, they can also be rendered in a final animation by selecting "Render From Display" in the Rendering output options.

Read Chapter 8, "Backgrounds, Props, and Rendering," and Chapter 19, "Camera, Lights, and Rendering," for more details on Display Styles. See Figure 2.12.

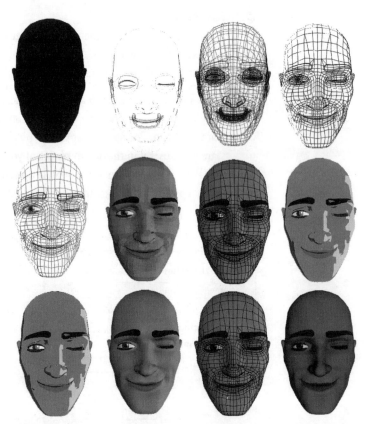

FIGURE   *The Styles (upper left to lower right): Silhouette, Outline, Wireframe, Hidden*
2.12 *Line, Lit Wireframe, Flat Shaded, Flat Lined, Cartoon, Cartoon With Line, Smooth Shaded, Smooth Lined, and Texture Shaded.*

Depth Cued. When this feature is on, elements farther from the camera look more faded.

Tracking. Use these menu items to select a Tracking type, or use their associated controls next to the Document Window.

Deformers. This control allows you to Show All, Hide All, or Show only the Deformer currently selected.

Ground Shadows. Toggle ground shadows on and off.

Figure Circle. Toggle the reference circle on or off.

Bend Body Parts. Always leave this attribute on in Poser 4. When off, the figure will show ugly separations between its elements.

Foreground/Background Color. Set these colors here or from their icons next to the Document Window.

Paper Textures. Here's another new item. Paper textures add a little personality to your rendered output, but can also serve as posing guides. The Grid option is especially useful when it comes to aligning and measuring onscreen elements in your Poser 4 compositions.

Show/Clear Background Picture. After loading a background image, you can use these options.

Paste Into Background. This is not a new Poser 4 attribute, but is nevertheless extremely valuable. Each time you activate this command, a snapshot of every item in the scene is taken and a replica is pasted onto the background. This is not a keyframe option, so the background holds for the entire sequence. Using this feature, it's very easy to create a non-moving background group of figures, a crowd, or even a more abstracted background design. Once the background is created, you can erase the elements that created it, and use the background for whatever new foreground material you like.

Show/Clear Background Footage. After loading background footage, (movie) you may select these options.

Guides. Use any of the optional Display Guides (Ground Plane, Head Lengths, Hip-Shoulder Relationship, Horizon Line, and Vanishing Lines) as posing aids.

Render Menu

Rendering can mean any of several possibilities in Poser 4. You can render to the Display for previewing purposes, to a file, or you may select to render a movie. As far as movies go, Mac users render QuickTime animations, while Windows users can select either AVI or QuickTime formats (as long as Quick-

Time for Windows is installed). You can also render single-frame sequences on either platform.

Sketch Style Render. Selecting this option renders the scene in whatever settings you have used in the new Poser 4 Sketch Renderer (see the Sketch Renderer details later in this chapter).

Antialias Document. Selecting this option antialiases the Document Window contents. This holds until you move any of the Parameter Dials.

Render Options. This is the most important item in the Render menu, since it's where you select and determine all of the rendering parameters for Preset rendering. In order not to be confined to your display setting size, check the New Window button, and set the size and dpi of the finished rendering. Rendered output for publishing normally requires a dpi of 300 or more. You can also select the Surface material dialog from here, or choose it separately from the Render menu. The Surface material dialog is where all of the elements in your scene get their color, texture, and other material assignments. See Chapters 8, 9, 17, and 19 for more rendering details. See Figure 2.13.

Materials. This Window is all new in Poser 4, replacing the Surface Materials Window used in Poser 3. The most important additions concern the new Reflection and Transparency options. Be sure to read Chapter 8. See Figure 2.14.

Animation Menu

The listings in this menu allow you to set your preferences for making movies, and to accomplish several complex interactions to customize your settings. The details are covered in Chapter 9, "Animation Controls." As far as rendered out-

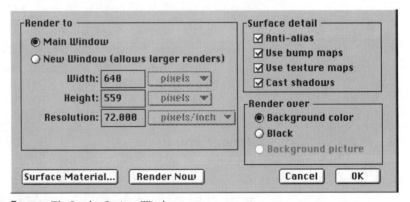

FIGURE *The Render Options Window.*
2.13

Surface Material			

Object: [Figure 1 ▼]   Material: [skin ▼]

[Object Color]   [Highlight Color]   [Ambient Color]   [Reflective Color]

Highlight Size   ◄□▬▬▬△▬► 70%
Transparency Min   ◄□▬▬▬▬▬► 0%
Transparency Max   ◄□▬▬▬▬▬► 0%
Transparency Falloff ◄□△▬▬▬▬► 0.60

☐ Texture changes apply to entire figure

┌─ Texture Map ──────────────────┐   ┌─ Reflection Map ─────────────────┐
│ [Nude Man Texture ▼] [Load...] │   │ [No Texture ▼] [Load...]   │
│ Strength ◄□▬▬▬▬▶ 100%   │   │ Strength ◄□▬▬▬▬▶ 100%   │
│ ☑ Apply texture to highlight   │   │ ☑ Multiply through lights   │
└───────────────────────────────┘   │ ☐ Multiply through Object Color   │
┌─ Bump Map ─────────────────────┐ └─────────────────────────────────┘
│ [No Bump ▼] [Load...]   │ ┌─ Transparency Map ──────────────┐
│ Strength ◄□▬▬△▬▬▶ 0%   │ │ [No Texture ▼] [Load...]   │
└───────────────────────────────┘ └─────────────────────────────────┘

                                    [Cancel]   [OK]

FIGURE   *The revamped Surface Materials Window.*
2.14

put, this is the location of the Animation Setup Window and the Make Movie dialog. See Figures 2.15 and 2.16.

Window Menu

This menu has been completely redesigned for Poser 4, though some of the items from Poser 3 remain. The Walk Designer itself is detailed in Chapter 14, "The Walk Designer." See Figure 2.9.

> **Animation Palette (toggle).** This is an alternate way to bring the Animation Palette into view, instead of using its click-on control below the Document Window. Read Chapter 9.

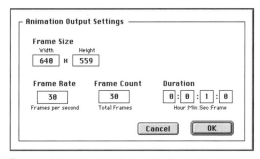

FIGURE   *The Animation Setup Window, where the parameters of the animation are*
2.15 *placed.*

FIGURE   *The Make Movie dialog.*
2.16

Graph (toggle). This is an alternate way to bring the Graph into view, as opposed to using the button on the Animation Keyframing Window. Read Chapter 9.

Libraries (toggle). This is an alternate way to pop out the Poser library, and to remove it from view.

Hierarchy Editor. The Hierarchy Editor and its use are vital when striving to master Poser. This is a new Poser 4 feature, designed to give you far more interactive control over all of the elements in your scene. Read Chapter 16, "Creating Hierarchies." See Figure 2.17.

Joint Editor. Be sure to read Chapter 16. The Joint Editor allows you to edit the manner in which any selected joint is configured. See Figure 2.18.

Sketch Designer. See Chapter 19 for details on the use of the new Sketch Designer. See Figure 2.19.

Walk Designer. Be sure to read Chapter 14, to learn how to use the Walk Designer. Poser 4 adds new walk parameters to this spectacular animation module. See Figure 2.20.

Tool Control Toggles/Show-Hide Tools. Using any of the items on this list, you can show or hide any of the interface features.

Document Window Size. Set the pixel size of the Document Window here, or simply click and drag the resizing control at the bottom-right of the Document Window.

Help Menu

There are important new features listed here. This is where you access the Poser Help Files, and also connect to the Web via a number of listed Links.

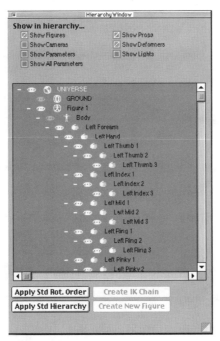

FIGURE *The new Hierarchy Editor lists every element in the scene, and also how*
2.17 *everything is linked.*

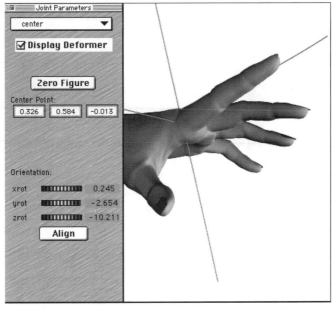

FIGURE *The Joint Editor allows you to do very fine editing of all joint parameters.*
2.18

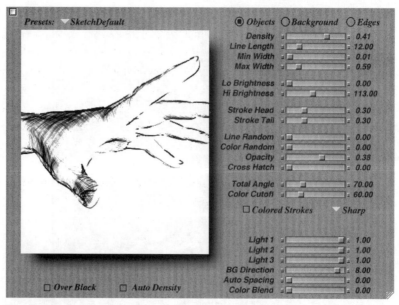

FIGURE *The new Sketch Designer allows you to create rendered looks for Poser scenes*
2.19 *that rival an array of fine art media.*

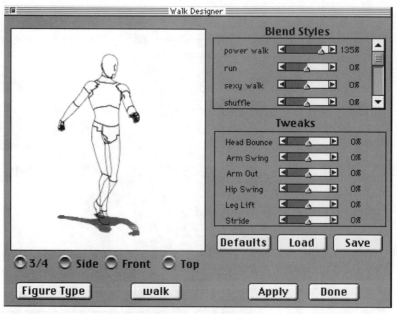

FIGURE *The Walk Designer interface.*
2.20

B. Editing Tools (See Figure 2.3 for Keyletter Location)

You'll find that every chapter in this book makes some reference to one or more editing tools, so knowing where they are and how to use them is vital. Work through the Poser 4 documentation, and you should have them mastered in days, if not hours. Remember that they are dual-use controls. If you click and drag the cursor over them, they act on a figure globally. If you select a tool so that it lights up, and then click and drag on an element in the Document Window, only that element will be affected by the tool. See Figure 2.21.

C. Library Palettes Toggle (See Figure 2.3 for Keyletter Location)

Click this toggle, and the Library Palettes pop to the screen. Once activated, you can access any of the Libraries to add elements to the Document, or add/delete items from a library. There are libraries for every element in Poser 4, including figures, props, poses, lights, and cameras. See Figures 2.22 and 2.23.

FIGURE   *The Editing Tools Group (left to right): Rotate, Twist, Translate/Pull,*
2.21   *Translate/In-Out, Scale, Taper, Chain Break, Color, and the Grouping Tool.*

FIGURE   *The Library Palettes toggle on the right side of the screen.*
2.22

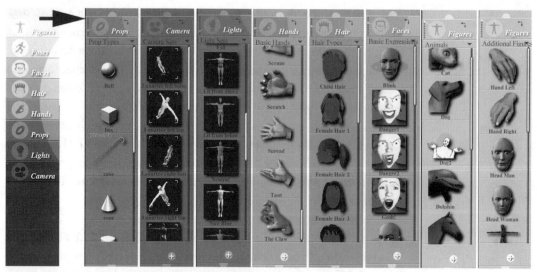

FIGURE *From the Main Library List, all of Poser 4's Libraries become available.*
2.23

D. Parameter Dials (See Figure 2.3 for Keyletter Location)

Parameter setting names differ, depending upon the object, figure element, camera, or Light selected. A human, for instance, has different parameters than a quadruped, so the settings that need to be adjusted are named accordingly. See Chapters 3 through 8. See Figure 2.24.

FIGURE *Parameter Dials are used to configure any of the selected item's adjustable*
2.24 *parameters.*

E. Color Controls (See Figure 2.3 for Keyletter Location)

The Color Controls give you instant access to global color settings for the Background, Foreground, Shadows, and Ground Plane. They are located on the bottom-right of the Document Window, just above the resizing control. See Figure 2.25.

F. Memory Dots (See Figure 2.3 for Keyletter Location)

Memory Dots can be a real time-saver when it comes to recalling previous settings and views. Bryce users will recognize this Poser 4 feature. They can be moved anywhere on the interface. See Figure 2.26.

G. Animation Controls Toggle (See Figure 2.3 for Keyletter Location)

See Chapters 9 through 15 for a detailed look at Poser 4 animation options and techniques. This toggle brings up the Animation Controls on the bottom of the interface. See Figure 2.27.

FIGURE **2.25** *These controls allow you to alter the Background, Foreground, Shadow, and Ground colors.*

FIGURE **2.26** *Memory Dots are used to return you to previously saved settings and views.*

FIGURE *Clicking on the toggle brings up Poser 4's Animation Controls.*
2.27

H. Selection Lists (See Figure 2.3 for Keyletter Location)

Knowing how to use the Selection Lists is vital for finding the exact Document item you need to alter. See Figure 2.28.

I and J. Document Window (See Figure 2.3 for Keyletter Location)

The Document Window is where you see the results of your alterations and modifications. See Figure 2.29.

FIGURE *The left control brings up the global selection, and the right control accesses the*
2.28 *itemized list.*

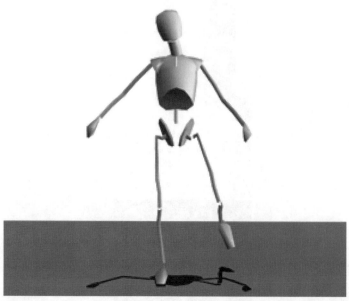

FIGURE *The bottom part of the Document Window shows the Ground Plane (I), if it's*
2.29 *switched on. The rest of the area behind your figures and props (J) shows either*
a background color, or the image/movie file loaded in.

K. Style Buttons (See Figure 2.3 for Keyletter Location)

Clicking one of the Style buttons changes the entire Document, the Figure, or the selected Element to any specific rendered Style. Using these buttons to accomplish this is quicker than using the respective menu commands. See Figure 2.30.

L. Depth Cueing, Tracking, Display Shadows (See Figure 2.3 for Keyletter Location)

These buttons activate or deactivate Depth Cueing, Tracking, and Shadows. In general, leave Depth Cueing off until you need it (though it's also a nice animation effect). Tracking indicates the rendered quality of your Document when previewed and animated. As a default, leave Tracking set to fast Tracking (the center button), and leave Shadows on. See Figure 2.31.

FIGURE *Clicking a Style Button changes the rendered Style in the display.*
2.30

FIGURE *These buttons toggle Depth Cueing, Tracking Options, and Display Shadows on*
2.31 *or off.*

M. Camera Controls 1 (See Figure 2.3 for Keyletter Location)

The Rotation Trackball allows you to rotate the camera left/right and up/down. It has no effect when you're in an orthogonal camera view. The button to the upper left controls the camera zoom. Below that is a button that controls the camera's focal length setting. To the upper right is a button that allows the camera to bank left and right. See Figure 2.32.

N. Camera Controls 2 (See Figure 2.3 for Keyletter Location)

The crossed arms control camera movements left/right and in/out of the screen. See Figure 2.33.

O. Camera Controls 3 (See Figure 2.3 for Keyletter Location)

Instantly alter the Camera View by clicking and dragging left or right over the Central icon in this group. The Hand icons allow you to move the camera on either the ZY or the XY planes. The Key icon is a switch that turns animation on or off, and the Looping Arrow icon switches on the Fly Around feature, so you can preview a scene from all sides. See Figure 2.34.

FIGURE *The Rotation Trackball will be the Camera Control you use the most.*
2.32

FIGURE *Camera movement is controlled left/right and in/out of the screen by these*
2.33 *crossed arms.*

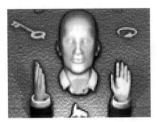

FIGURE *The Hand icons allow you to adjust movement up and down, while the Key icon*
2.34 *turns animation on or off. The Looping Arrow icon switches on the Fly Around*
feature. The Central icon shows you what camera view you're in.

P. Camera Controls 4 (See Figure 2.3 for Keyletter Location)

In this set of Camera Controls, the icons couldn't be clearer as to what they do. Clicking activates either the left or right Hand camera views, or the Head camera. Always use the Head camera when posing a face. See Figure 2.35.

Q. Camera Controls List (See Figure 2.3 for Keyletter Location)

The listing of the Camera Controls is new to Poser 4. It allows you to select a Camera quicker than using the menu list. See Figure 2.36.

R. Light Controls (See Figure 2.3 for Keyletter Location)

The Poser 4 lights offer many advantages over the light controls in Poser 3. Now, you can use as many lights as you like in a scene, including Spotlights. See Chapter 18, "Customizing Templates." See Figure 2.37.

FIGURE *The icons tell the story. Click to use either the left or right hand camera views,*
2.35 *or the Head Close-up camera.*

FIGURE *The Camera Controls List Arrow.*
2.36

FIGURE *The Light Controls.*
2.37

Important Poser 4 Data Sites

It's vital to stay in close contact with MetaCreations and all of the other developers whose work supports Poser 4 in one way or another, for additions and upgrades. Here are three important Web sites to visit. The first is the address of the MetaCreations page where you can download the Poser 4 Advanced Animation Guide (in PDF format). Following that are the sites for the Zygote Media Group, BioVision, and the House of Moves. A complete listing of Poser 4 data sites can be found in Appendix D.

> http://www.metacreations.com/products/poser3/resources2.html
> **Advanced Animation Guide- PDF**

> http://www.zygote.com/
> **Data on All Zygote Models**

> http://www.biovision.com/
> **BioVision Motion Capture Site and Freebies**

> http://www.moves.com/
> **House of Moves data Site and Freebies**

Moving Along

In this chapter, we have explored all of the items and their location on the Poser 4 interface. In the next chapter, we'll look at the posing and customization of the human body models.

3

POSING AND CUSTOMIZING THE HUMAN BODY

Paying Attention   In his famous book, *Island*, Aldous Huxley speaks about the large birds that inhabit the surrounding jungle. Every once in a while, when a character in the plot gets too far off track, the birds start yelling "Karuna, Karuna!" or "Attention, Attention!" You might think of Poser 4 as a Karuna bird, because it too calls for your attention. Attention to what? Attention to observing the bodies of humans and animals, with a specific attention to how bodies bend and twist, and (as we'll see in Section II of the book) how bodies move.

Artists and animators actually have a long history of paying attention to the human body and, when necessary or called for, the bodies of other creatures. It has long been considered that to emulate the movements of the body in sculpture, painting, and dance is to give special witness to realms of the sacred. To be able to shape a piece of art in a way that reminds the viewer of the body, especially the body in motion, is to call attention to the great mystery of life and time.

All visual art is the art of storytelling, of relating an unspoken narrative, a secret message. We can intuit more in a few seconds from a body pose or a facial expression than we can from hundreds of descriptive words. I can remember my early years as an art student in Chicago. I rode the elevated trains about two hours a day, back and forth from the Loop, Chicago's downtown. I used to carry a sketchpad, and make quick impressionistic drawings of people that I was standing or sitting across from. Sometimes, I'd spend weeks just observing a single feature, like noses. Other times, I'd try to capture the tableau of an entire group, and how their body statements unconsciously related one member to another. Karuna!

The first demand this book makes upon you is that you pay attention to all the life forms that surround you, human and nonhuman, day and night. If you purchased Poser with the intention of having an easy no-thought time generating instant animations with no real concern about the deeper implications potentially involved, then you are missing out on an opportunity to reinvigorate your appreciation of the world around you. Creating fast and easy populated scenes and movies in Poser 4 is certainly possible, but so is paying attention to the nuances and the finer points for an enhanced learning experience.

Karuna! Whether in your pocket or in your head, begin carrying a sketchbook. Notice how life forms dance through your day, and take that same information back to your work and play sessions in Poser 4. Always Karuna!

CAUTION

Basic Posing

Make sure that you understand how the Editing tools and Parameter Dials work before proceeding with these exercises.

OUR FIRST POSING EXERCISE

Okay. Get ready to take some mental notes, though you may write down what I'm going to ask you to do afterwards. At the end of reading this paragraph, put the book down. Either in the chair you're sitting in or another favorite chair, relax. Get your body in a comfortable position. Take note of how each part of your body is either bent or twisted. Where are your feet? Where are your hands? Are there noticeable angles between your torso and the rest of your body? Take a mental picture of every part and how it relates to every other part. Do it, and then come back to the book when you're ready.

Okay. Hopefully, you really did have a few moments of relaxation, as well as taking note of all of the things I asked you to. If you have to, while the memory of your body pose is still fresh, jot down whatever you can concerning the relationship of your body parts while you were relaxing. After that, when you're finished noting everything you can recall, open Poser 4.

Use whatever figure is on your screen at the start for this initial exercise. Do the following:

1. Import a basic Box prop from the Props library. Place it somewhere in the center of the scene. This will be a stand-in for the chair you were just sitting in.
2. Resize the Box with the Resizing tool in the Edit tools above the Document window. Hold the Shift key down while resizing so that the Box has relative proportions to substitute for a chair, as compared to the figure's size.
3. Turn off any Inverse Kinematics for your figure. Move your figure somewhere in proximity to the Box-chair. Use the orthogonal side camera view and the front view. Click Drop To Floor for both the Box-chair and the figure. See Figure 3.1.
4. Select and Bend both thighs at a value of –86, using each thigh's Parameter Dials. You should now have a model as depicted in Figure 3.2.
5. Bend each of the Shins at an angle of 72. Move the model so that it sits on the Box (use the Translate/Pull tool in the Edit toolbar, while keeping the mouse over the tool, and not in the Document window). See Figure 3.3.
6. This step is optional. I have added another box to act as the chair back, because that is more fitting for the chair I was sitting in. See Figure 3.4.

FIGURE **3.1** *The figure is moved so that it is in proximity to the resized Box-chair, as seen from a side view.*

FIGURE **3.2** *The model with its thighs angled after the Bend operation.*

FIGURE **3.3** *The model's shins are Bent, and she is placed on the Box-chair.*

FIGURE   *A back is added to the chair.*
3.4

7. From here on, I will adjust the figure according to the pose I was sitting in. Your pose may be quite different, but you'll get a good idea of how to make your own customized adjustments by following along. The next thing I did was to angle the Abdomen by using a Bend of –30, so that the model is leaning against the back of the chair. She looks a little stiff, but I'll make the final adjustments later. See Figure 3.5.

8. Now my relaxation pose turned out rather complex, since I placed both of my hands behind my head in a locked position, and rested my head on them. My next step was to get the Right Arm/Hand in place. If I was using Inverse Kinematics, I could just move the hand into place and the arm parts would follow, but I'm not. Therefore, I moved the Right Shoulder, followed by the Right Forearm, followed by the Right Hand. See Figure 3.6.

FIGURE
3.5

FIGURE   *The Right Arm and Hand are placed into position.*
3.6

 *When you are posing a model, switch views as necessary to get the best view for the task at hand. The orthogonal views are especially valuable in this regard.*
Important: When making global changes to a hand, always select Lock Hand Parts from the Figure menu. This allows you to select and rotate the hand without accidentally selecting the thumb or a finger joint.

9. Now for some Poser 4 magic. I used Figure/Symmetry/Right to Left to instantly snap the Left Arm/Hand into place, instead of arduously modifying it separately. See Figure 3.7.

10. At this stage, when you have the basic pose done, it's time to make small adjustments for reality's sake. First of all, destroy symmetry a little. Life forms are not completely symmetrical, not left to right or any other way. As you can see in Figure 3.8, I have adjusted my model's legs so they are

FIGURE   *The Left Arm/Hand is placed by using the Right to Left Symmetry command.*
3.7

not exactly at the same angle. It doesn't take a lot of movement to interrupt symmetry, just a little here and there. I also adjusted the model to fit the confines of the chair more accurately. I placed hair on her head for two reasons: to enhance reality, and to hide her hands a little. I wanted to hide her hands so that a close-up wouldn't reveal that I didn't spend the necessary time locking her hands exactly together. I could have done that, but for this pose, it wasn't necessary. See Figures 3.8 and 3.9.

Now that you have the pose you want, the first thing to do is to save it to the Poses Library. Just go to the Poses Library and press the Plus Sign, name your Pose, and press OK. Since you have the Pose, you can apply it to any selected figure. See Figure 3.10.

FIGURE **3.8** *The final pose has been accomplished.*

FIGURE **3.9** *A more interesting camera view.*

FIGURE *Here we've applied the same Pose to all of these Zygote models (available on the Zygote Extras CD).*
3.10

It is seldom wise to apply a Pose across species lines. This Zygote Bear model, for instance, dislikes having its forelegs placed behind its head. See Figure 3.11.

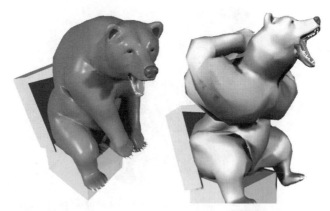

FIGURE *When the Pose was applied to the Zygote Bear, it complained loudly. We can see*
3.11 *that in the way that the Bear's polygonal mesh warps.*

CAUTION

Karuna! *A Bear has sharp teeth and claws. Do not force the Bear, or any being, into poses it doesn't appreciate.*

ANOTHER BASIC POSE

This time, we'll investigate another pose, one that displays emotion. It's true that you can use Poser 4's excellent facial controls to display a wide range of emotions, but there are times when your camera is not pointed at the face of a figure. It's also possible that the face of a figure is not large enough in certain shots to allow the face to tell the story. At those times, you have to figure out a way to allow the body pose to work as the narrator, so that the emotion is clearly understood by the body pose alone.

Karuna! One of the best ways to study body pose emotions is to watch silent films. The poses of the characters are often exaggerated in order to make up for the lack of audio, and for that reason the poses are easier to see. Body poses in a silent film often tell the story quite effectively.

For this exercise, instead of actually placing your body in a suitable pose, close your eyes and imagine the emotion of despair. Several pictures should appear before you. Perhaps some will be related to this emotion as you have witnessed it being played out on film, or perhaps even from moments in your memory. No need to linger on this feeling. What you're looking for is the ability to transfer your imagined sense of how a body might evidence despair to the Poser 4 figure. When you're ready, allow me to lead you through an appropriate pose as I might shape it. You can always add your own personal touches afterward.

Note that the figure illustrated is from the Zygote Extras CD collection: the Old Man. See Figure 3.12.

1. Despair is a crushing weight, felt by the soul and the body. Imagine the figure besieged by a weight above it, and shape the figure accordingly by bending its knees slightly, and rotating the neck so that the shoulders hunch. See Figure 3.13.
2. Use a bend of 90 to drop the right shoulder. See Figure 3.14.
3. Now we'll use an old painter's trick (though nobody knows exactly who the old painter was) to emphasize the weight of the situation. When despair hits, we feel as if our extremities have suddenly grown larger. To re-

FIGURE *Here is the figure before any customized posing.*
3.12

FIGURE **3.13** *The weight of despair has affected the model. The knees are bent and the shoulders hunched. The figure is also Bent (20) at the abdomen slightly.*

FIGURE **3.14** *The Right Shoulder hangs limp from the emotional weight.*

late this feeling ever so slightly, select the Left Hand and use the Scale dial to resize it to 125%. Then do the same with the Right Hand. See Figure 3.15.

4. The next part's a little tricky. You have to maneuver the figure's right arm and hand so it hides part of his face. Use the Head Camera for close-ups. The idea is to get the hand close, but not to poke any fingers into the head. See Figures 3.16 and 3.17.

ONE FINAL POSE

Let's do one more pose before moving on to the customizing section. This time, just in case the despair exercise left you down in the dumps, we'll opt

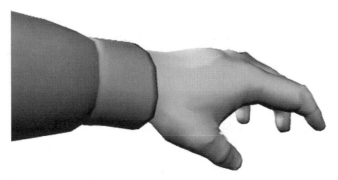

FIGURE *The hands are enlarged 125%.*
3.15

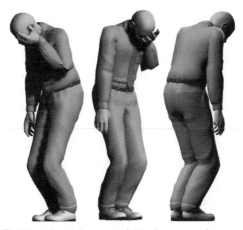

FIGURE *The Right Arm and Hand are rotated into position so the figure's face is*
3.16 *partially hidden.*

FIGURE *A close-up of the pose.*
3.17

for pure joy. If despair is a weight that drives us down, then joy can be described as an emotion that lifts us up, sort of an anti-gravity response. Where despair makes us fold up and cave in on ourselves, joy opens us to the world and literally lifts our spirits. With all of that in mind, load a figure and follow along.

The figures illustrate the Zygote Old Woman model, but you can use any figure you like for this posing example.

1. Load in your figure from the Library. It can be any figure you will enjoy working with.
2. Use the Bend dial to bend the neck at –25. Go to the Hands Library, and double-click the Reach hand. When the dialog appears, select Right Hand. Repeat this operation for the Left Hand. Raise the Right Shoulder to a bend of –20, and the Left Shoulder to a Bend of 20. See Figure 3.18.
3. We could stop right here, but we want a more ridiculous joy. Use a Side-to-Side parameter of –16 on the Abdomen. Then turn the Chest Parameter dial to 15. The model bends at the middle. See Figure 3.19.
4. Use a Twist of 77 and a Side-to-Side of 61 on the Right thigh. Then use a bend of 108 on the Left Shin. See Figure 3.20.
5. We want our model to literally "click her heels," so the Left Leg has to be brought into position. Use a Twist of –53 and a Side-to-Side of –5 on the Right Thigh. Then use a Bend of 90 on the Right Shin to complete the pose. See Figure 3.21.

FIGURE *The model beams joy.*
3.18

FIGURE *The model bends in the middle.*
3.19

FIGURE *The Right Leg is posed.*
3.20

FIGURE *The pose is completed, and the model skips into the sunset.*
3.21

Customizing the Human Form

Take one look at Figure 3.22, and you'll realize that Poser 4 figures can be sculpted to take on looks not quite familiar to everyday observation. If you're an admirer of Bosch or Dali, you will want to explore ways to add a touch of surrealism to your Poser 4 creations. The techniques we'll describe will require your familiarity with both the Editing tools and the Parameter Dials.

GLOBAL RESIZING

Global Resizing refers to scaling a selected element of a figure (model) while holding the Shift key down with the Resize tool positioned over the selected element, or by using the Scale Parameter Dial. Either of these operations resizes the selected element in all XYZ directions at the same time. It sounds like a pretty basic function, and it is. The results, however, can be quite interesting. In these exercises we'll move from some simple customizing alterations to more radical examples.

The Heads Have It

Let's apply a simple resize to the head of a selected figure. Do the following:

1. Load the Business Man figure from the People Library. Resizing a head looks all the more bizarre on the business-suited figures. See Figure 3.23.
2. Click the Resize tool in the Edit toolbar. Place the cursor over the head of the model, hold down the Shift key, and click-drag the cursor upward to the right. See Figure 3.24.

FIGURE *A bizarre humanoid parades in ecstasy.*
3.22

FIGURE   *The Business Man model at the start.*
3.23

FIGURE   *The head of the model becomes enlarged, almost like a strange human balloon.*
3.24

3. Now do the opposite. With the same Resize tool highlighted, place it over the head and click-drag down and to the left, with the Shift key held down. See Figure 3.25.

Bomber Man

Using the same model as depicted in Figure 3.25, with its head shrunk, click on the Abdomen element. Using the Scale Parameter Dial, select a Scale of 40. See Figure 3.26.

Now we'll globally resize more of the model's elements. Resize the Left/Right Shins, Shoulders, and Forearms to 50. Resize the Left/Right Thighs to 125. I call this fella Bomber Man, since it looks like all he needs is a WWII flying cap and a scarf blowing in the wind. See Figure 3.27.

FIGURE **3.25** *Now the figure has a pinhead, and the suspicion is that its intelligence suffers a blow.*

FIGURE **3.26** *Scaling the Abdomen down gives the model the appearance of a wasp.*

FIGURE **3.27** *Bomber Man to the rescue!*

AXIAL RESIZING

You can also use either the Resize tool or the Parameter Dials to resize a model's elements on any selected axis. It's a lot easier with the Parameter Dials, because you have more control over each dimension. In standard computer graphics terms, this operation is called a "stretch."

The Ostrich Lady

Import the Casual Woman from the People Library. Select her Neck, and use the Parameter Dial for a Y-Scale value of 950. See Figure 3.28.

Now it's time to apply a more radical series of Axial Stretches. Set the Parameter Dials to the following values: Y-Scale for Left/Right Thigh, Abdomen, and Chest = 50; X-Scale for Left/Right Shoulder = 182; Y-Scale Neck = 1200; Head globally resized to about 300% with the Resize tool. Your finished biogenetic engineering experiment should look similar to Figure 3.29.

TAPERING

The Taper operation in Poser 4, whether initiated through the use of the Taper tool in the Edit toolbar or by the Taper Dial in the Parameters module, is the single most powerful way to add radical customized elements to your models inside of Poser. Heads are a special case for tapering, since there is no Taper Dial in the parameters module. To Taper a Head, you have to use the Taper tool in the Edit toolbar.

FIGURE   *They say she can see over any obstacle.*
3.28

FIGURE *The famous Ostrich Lady.*
3.29

Taperhead

The Head of a model can be tapered small to large, or large to small. The axis of tapering is always vertical for a Head. See Figure 3.30.

Pushing the Taper to extra large, so that the head is wider at the top than at the bottom, and the width of the head is as wide as the outstretched arms, creates a very bizarre situation. The head flattens out into a circular plane that can be rotated against the body. All of the head parts are still fully articulated and animatable! See Figure 3.31.

CAUTION

Karuna! Use the flattened head for a Sun face. Just make all of the other parts of the body invisible.

FIGURE *Left to right: Normal Head, Head with large taper at bottom, and head with*
3.30 *large taper at top.*

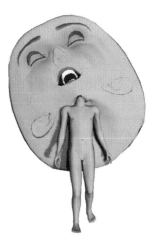

FIGURE *When pushed to the limits, the Tapered head can become a flat plane. All the*
3.31 *parts still move.*

Taper, Taper Everywhere

Except for the Head, all other figure elements have a special Parameter Dial devoted to customizing the Taper. You should explore the look of Tapers on all
body elements. When used on body parts, Tapers can create a very cartoony
character. See Figure 3.32.

FIGURE *Tapers were used on all of this model's body parts.*
3.32

**Customizing
with Deformers**

In this tutorial, the Zygote Heavy Man from the Zygote People collection will
be used as the target model. You can use any model you like if you don't have
this one, since it's the process that's important. Do the following:

1. Load the model to the Document Window, and size it appropriately in the Pose View. See Figure 3.33.
2. Select the Head, go to the Head View, and select the Wireframe Display mode. See Figure 3.34.

FIGURE *The Zygote Heavy man as he appears in the Pose View.*
3.33

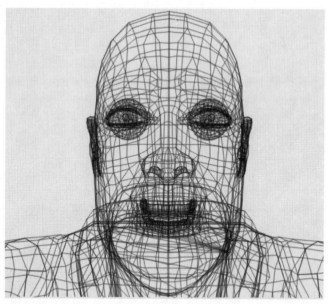

FIGURE *The model as seen in the Head View in Wireframe Display mode.*
3.34

3. Use the Twist Tool to make the head face to your right. Click the Group Tool, and select New Group from the dialog. Name the New Group

Nose_1. Using the mouse, click and drag to select just the nose. Exit the Group process by closing the window. You have just set up a Deformation Zone. See Figure 3.35.

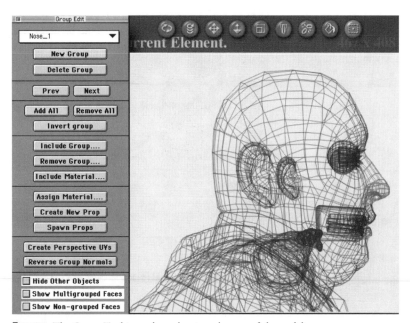

FIGURE   *The Group Tool is used to select just the nose of the model.*
3.35

4. With the Head still selected, go to the Object Menu and select Create Magnet. When the Magnet appears, resize it and move it away from the Head so you can see it clearly. Don't worry if the whole head distorts. Select the Magnet's Zone. With the Zone selected, go to its Properties window. Click Group. Your Nose_1 item should now be selected. Close the Properties window. Adjust the position and size of the zone so that it rests over the nose alone. Just the nose should distort when you move the Magnet. Move the Magnet until the nose distorts in some interesting fashion. See Figure 3.36.

5. Select the Head, and from the Object Menu, select Spawn Morph Target. Name the Morph target Nosey_01 when the window pops up. See Figure 3.37.

6. Select the Magnet and delete it—you don't need it anymore. If you look at the top of your Parameter Dials for the Head, you'll see that you have

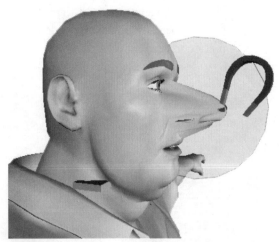

FIGURE   *The Nose distorts when you move the Magnet.*
3.36

Morph name:	Nosey_01|
	Cancel OK

FIGURE   *The Morph is named.*
3.37

a new dial called "Nosey_01." This controls the morphing of the nose. Try it out. See Figure 3.38.

7. With the Head selected, apply a Wave Deformer from the Object menu. Select the Nose_1 Group in the Wave Zone's Properties Window. Place the Wave Deformer and its associated Zone as displayed in Figure 3.39. Set the Wave's Parameters as follows: Phase 0, Amplitude .1, Wavelength 1, Stretch .5, Noise 0, Sinusoidal 1, square 0, Triangular 1, Turbulence .5, and Offset .5. The nose now exhibits a Rhino Horn.

Just as you did with the Magnet Deformer, create a Morph Target Parameter for this new deform operation. Delete the Wave, and the new deform parameter (I called mine "Rhino") appears as a Parameter Dial. You can use this same technique to create hundreds of variations for any single human figure.

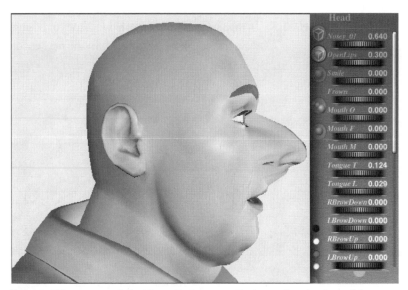

FIGURE *When you tweak the Nosey_01 Parameter Dial, you alter the shape of the nose.*
3.38

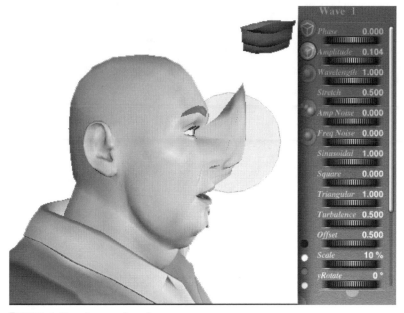

FIGURE *A Horn is created on the nose.*
3.39

Moving Along

In this chapter, we've explored methods of posing a figure, and also discovered ways that it can be customized. In the next chapter, we'll look at hands in the same way.

FIGURE *A pair of Northern Sqonks wish you happy Poserizing.*
3.40

4

POSING AND CUSTOMIZING HANDS

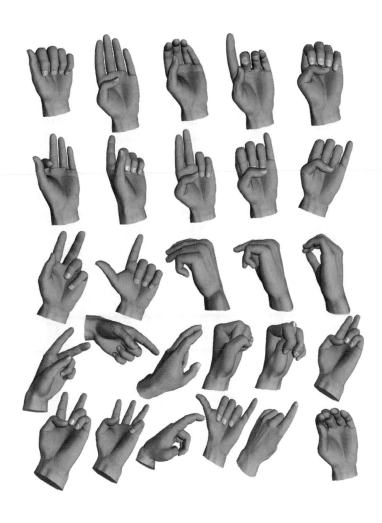

A Show of Hands   No longer do you have to shy away from close-up camera views of a model's hands, afraid that your audience will be presented with a gnarled and misshapen appendage. Instead, you can zoom in as close as need be, with a super-realistic Hand model as your reward. To emphasize this fact, there are two camera icons in the Camera Controls at the left of the Document window that display a left and a right hand. Click on either, and the Camera zooms in on the model's appropriate hand. The Hand models in Poser 4 have been further upgraded from those in Poser 3. See Figure 4.1.

Important Hand-associated items are contained in a number of places in Poser 4:

- *The Lock Hand Parts command in the Figure menu.* When selecting a Hand on a model, or a standalone Hand model, it's important to have this option. Otherwise, it can be difficult selecting the hand instead of a finger or thumb joint.
- *The Properties dialog in the Edit menu.* Properties are as important for Hand models as for any other model. Remember that you can selectively turn any element's visibility off, which we'll see is important when it comes to customizing Hands (later in this chapter).
- *The Additional Figures library list.* There are two Hand models, Left and Right, contained here. They are very important because they are disembodied hands, so that you can add them to a scene as standalone items. This leads to all sorts of possibilities, as we will see in this chapter and Chapters 7, 10, 17, and 22.

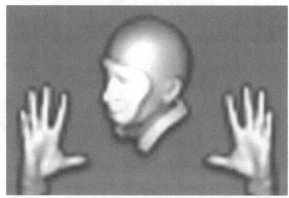

FIGURE   *The Left and Right Hand icons in the Camera Controls module zoom to a view*
4.1   *of either hand.*

- *The Joint Parameters dialog and the associated Use Limits command.* These are important for Hand poses because they lock in the standard values for resizing and other modifications. They may, however, prevent you from doing things like altering a Hand to achieve an alien or monstrous appendage.
- *The Pose Hands libraries.* Hand Poses are listed under five separate collections in the Hands library: Basic Hands, Counting, Hand Puppets, Poser 2 Figure Hands, and Sign Language. See Figures 4.2 through 4.5.

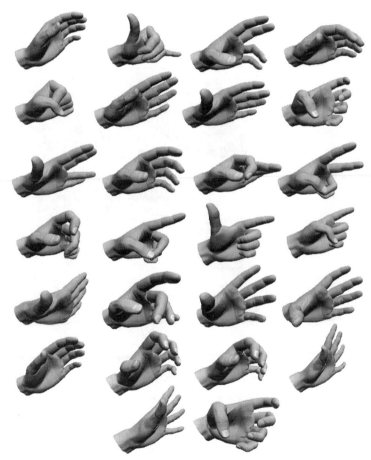

FIGURE
4.2
Basic hand poses: Basic, Call Me, Coupled, Cupped, Fist, Flat Out, Fully Extended, Gnarly, Greetings, Limp, OK, Peace, Pick, Point, Pointer, Pointer 2, Pusher, Quirky Relaxed, Reach, Reaching, Relaxed Basic, Scrape, Scratch, Spread, Taut, and The Claw. Although there are some minor differences in the Poser 2 library of Hand poses, you can use this figure as an example of the Poser 2 poses as well.

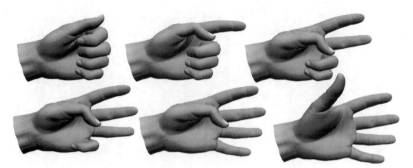

FIGURE **4.3** *Counting Hand poses: 0 to 5.*

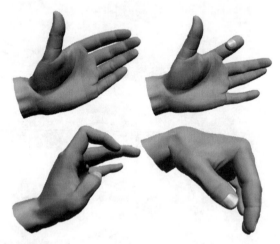

FIGURE **4.4** *Hand Puppets poses: Bird, Dog, Duck, and Swan.*

 *A project you might want to try is to access the Hand Puppets library and to render a Hand casting a shadow of one of the animals represented.*
Note that the Poser 2 poses are slightly different from those included in the Poser 4 Basics library.

GENERAL RULES FOR POSING THE HAND

The articulated hands in Poser 4 can be positioned into any needed pose in two ways. The first is to simply target a hand for a pose from the Hands library. You can either accept the library pose completely, or use it as a basis for making further modifications. This is the easiest way to get a hand posed. The second method, though a little more time consuming, serves best when the pose you

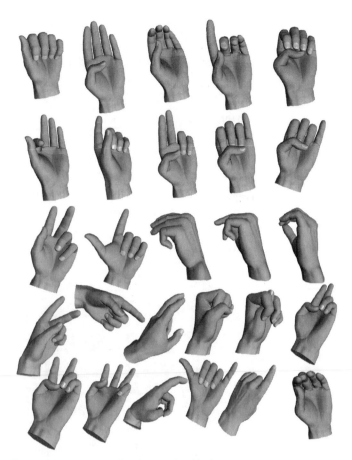

FIGURE   *Sign Language hand poses: A to Z, &.*
4.5

desire is nowhere to be found (or anything even close to it) in the Hands library. In that case, you'll need to go in and pose each digit yourself. When that becomes necessary, follow these rules:

- Always use the Hand Camera view (either left or right) to zoom in close to the Hand so you can see exactly what you're doing.
- Instead of trying to click on the appropriate digit with the mouse, use the elements list under the Document window to select the exact part of the hand needed to be moved into position.
- For a more natural and realistic pose, make sure Use Limits is checked in the Figure menu. This sets a boundary on possible movements, and prevents you from doing things that might cause deformations in the Hand's geometry.

Karuna! If your Hand has to be holding an object, like a spear, a hammer handle, or some other prop, you can use a fist pose as the easiest way to get the Hand into a general position, and then tweak the pose with the Parameter Dials.

PARAMETER DIAL ALTERATIONS FOR THE HAND

The three most important hand controls that can be manipulated by the Parameter Dials are Grasp, Thumb Grasp, and Spread. These three operators offer you global control over a selected hand. The Parameter Dials associated with selected finger and thumb joints are specific to those elements, and not to the overall hand. Grasp, Thumb Grasp, and Spread are important when you want to show some hand movement from frame to frame in an animation, but you aren't interested in the fancier poses offered by specific items in the Hand Poses library. See Figure 4.6.

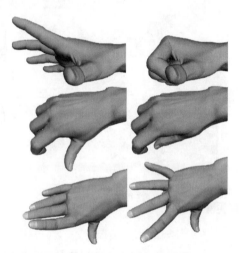

FIGURE *Grasp closes the fingers, Thumb Grasp closes the thumb, and Spread splays*
4.6   *open the fingers. Top: Grasp open and closed; Middle: Thumb Grasp open and closed; Bottom: Spread closed and open.*

**Customizing
Hands**

The general process for working through a Hand customizing process is as follows:

1. Apply the modifications.
2. Save the new model to the Additional Figures library.
3. Save the new Pose (if there is one) to the Hands library, preferably in a new folder named for your collection (such as MyHands or another appropriate name).

TYPES OF HAND CUSTOMIZING OPTIONS

There are some modifications that can be applied easily to a Hand in Poser 4, and some that require more planning and work. In general, the two simplest modifications you can apply to a Hand or to any of its parts are resizing and tapering. Each of these has its limits, beyond which the targeted Hand will start to warp and deform uncontrollably.

 *It's always a good idea to rotate the Hand after applying any modifications, since this allows you to see if any anomalies were caused by your efforts. If deformations are caused, then you have to decide to either retrace your steps and to correct them, or to accept them as part of the new model.*

When you customize Hands, there are two ways to engage in the process. The first is to load one of the standalone Hands from the Additional Figures library folder. This is a good option when you want to apply the hand either as a singular floating object, or to have it replace a Hand (or any other body part) on a figure already in your scene.

If you need to replace both hands of a model already in your scene, however, you may wish to take another route. In that case, use one of the Hand Camera views to zoom in on a Hand that you would like to customize. Apply the necessary modifications. When you're through, you can simply elect to use the Symmetry command to apply the same modifications to the other hand. If that completes the model, then save the model out with a new name, or save it out when all modifications are completed.

THE MOST DIFFICULT MODIFICATION

It's enticing to think that because Poser 4 contains a visible/invisible option in the Properties dialog, that you could easily just make some selected fingers invisible to create a two-, three-, or four-digit hand. You can do this, as long as you also address some attendant issues. When you make an element of a model invisible, you expose a hole where it once was. In the case of a Hand, the hole is most visible in the front and top views of the Hand. The hole will render, unless you do something to mask it.

You can place and size an elongated sphere (from a Ball Prop) to mask the hole, or use another imported object to do the same thing. But that's only part of it. From that point, the Hand (or the whole body of the model) will have to be glued to the patching object by making that object the Parent (set Figure Parent in the Figure menu). This can present big problems when animating, because only the patching object can be set to animate. Solution? Do not make any elements of the Hand invisible to achieve an alien or cartoon Hand—it isn't worth it. Besides, if you really need an alien Hand, you can model it in RayDream 5 or another 3D application (see Chapter 17, "Handshaking"), and import it for placement in Poser 4.

ALIEN HANDS

If you want to stay in Poser 4, and still need to create alien-looking Hands, you have some leeway to do so. Raising the Scale value on the tip of the fingers can create bulbous or padded looking finger tips. Decreasing the Scale of the fingertips to 10, and then lengthening the X Scale to 300 creates sharp, knife-like fingertips. Playing with the Taper values for the Hand and all of its elements can also lead to some interesting looks. See Figure 4.7.

FIGURE *A series of Alien hands, customized by using different Scale and Taper values*
4.7 *from the Hand's Parameter Dials.*

WRITHING SNAKES

One neat effect you can perform on a Hand is to use the Side-to-Side and Bend operations on the finger and thumb parts with Limits off. This allows you to bend the joints in relation to each other by angles of 90 degrees or more. When animated, this has the appearance of writhing snakes. See Figure 4.8.

TWISTED REALITY

If you apply a Twist of 1000 or more to a Hand element, it will display a contorted twist that looks like the element is being wound up like a rubber band. Apply this same twist to the base of all of the fingers, and the rest of the fingers will go along for the ride. Twisting is also an interesting way to create alien looking hands. When colored with a bluish green, the fingers look like coiled steel bands. See Figure 4.9.

FIGURE *By turning Limits off, you can shape the finger parts into unreal contortions.*
4.8

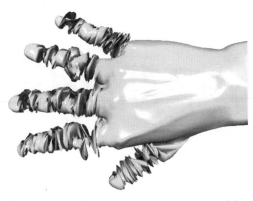

FIGURE *Twisted fingers reshape the very nature of the Hand.*
4.9

Using Deformers on a Hand

Although you may be attracted to using the Magnet and Wave Deformers on the head of a model first, there's no reason that you can't apply them to other parts of a human model like the hand or arm.

FLEXING A MUSCLE

Explore this technique by doing the following:

1. Place one of the Hand models from the Additional Figures Library into your Document. If you like, you can select one of the new Poser 4 Female hands.

2. Select the Forearm. Go to the Objects menu, and select the Create Wave item. Place the wave as shown in Figure 4.10. Set the Wave parameters as follows: Phase .256, Amplitude .092, Wavelength .394, Stretch 0, Noise 0, Sinusoidal 1, Square and Triangular 0, Turbulence 0, and Offset .5. Congratulations! You have just created a bulging forearm muscle. You can save it as a Morph Target if you like. See Figure 4.10.

Note that you can use this same technique on every muscle on the body, creating a totally realistic pumped-up being. The Superhero Total Figure Morph that ships with Poser 4 is based on a technique similar to this.

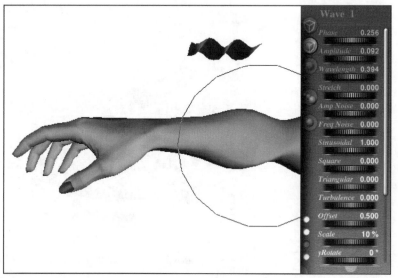

FIGURE *A bulging forearm muscle results from the Wave Deformation.*
4.10

THE ALIOD HAND MORPH

I remember a science fiction film that played in theaters in the 1950s. I don't remember its name, but there were little green aliens in it with super-long fingernails. They poked cows and drank their blood through their fingers (yech!). Here's a way to create that Aliod hand:

1. Place any Hand model on the screen, or use a Hand Camera to get a close-up of any human model's hand. Shape the hand with the "Five" Hand from the Hands/Counting Library. This splays the fingers so you can work on them.

2. You are going to use five Magnet Deformers, one for each finger and another for the thumb. Each will be targeted to the tip of that appendage. Move each Magnet Zone so that it covers just the upper half of the respective tip. Move the Magnet away from each finger and the thumb until you get a Morphed shape like that shown in Figure 4.11.

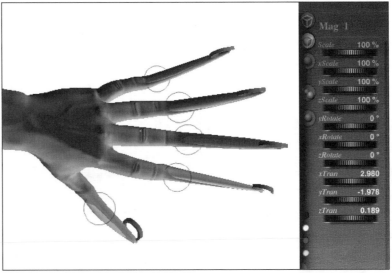

FIGURE *The fingertips and tip of the thumb are extruded by each Magnet Deformer.*
4.11

Note that you could also use the Grouping Tool to select just the fingernails, one at a time, before applying a Magnet Deformer.

Moving Along   In this chapter, we focused on posing and customizing Hands. In the next chapter, we'll explore the fascinating topic of posing and customizing Heads.

5

CREATING
EXPRESSIVE
FACES

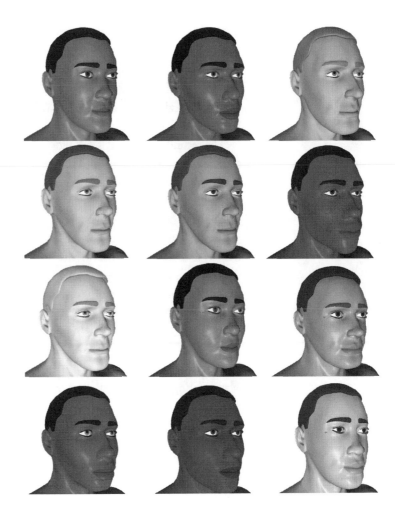

Emotive Power

If the eyes are the window to the soul, as philosophers tell us, then the face is the house that surrounds those windows. The human face is the central subject of the majority of works of art. The face is so powerful, that we look for signs of faces in the natural world, as omens and symbols of life. Driftwood, rocks, trees, mountain sides, anything that emulates the features of a human face is revered and given special suspected powers. The faces on Mount Rushmore are just one example of how the structure of the face overwhelms our senses, and touches upon our ancient symbol systems. It is said that the most present and powerful element in the world for human children is the shape and power of eyes and mouths, first the mother's, and later others.

THREE METHODS FOR FACE MODIFICATION

Poser 4 allows you to mold the expressions of a face in three ways. First, you can select either eye and scale it or rotate it. Scaling the eye is usually accompanied by moving it along the Z axis, in or out of the surrounding face. Otherwise, it will just be scaled inside of the head, with no noticeable alterations unless the scaling approaches zero or is very large.

The second way that Poser 4 allows you to adjust the seeming emotional content of the face is to alter the Parameter Dials associated with the Head. The dials are separated into two major areas, controls for the mouth and controls for the eyebrows. In concert, these two capabilities allow you to cover a wide range of expressive options, as we will see.

A third way, new to Poser 4 and detailed later in this chapter, is to use the Magnet and Wave Deformers to alter the facial geometry itself. Associated with this is the creation and development of Morph targets for the face, as represented in the new Racial Morphs included with Poser 4 and also covered later.

For the following exercises, you should know how to load either the Man or Woman Head from the Figures/Additional Figures library.

The Eyes Have It

Manipulating the Eyes in a Poser 4 face is a simple process to master, adding a good amount of emotion and personality content to a face. Do the following:

1. Load either the Man or Woman head to the Poser 4 Document window from the Additional Figures library. View the scene through the Head Camera, and zoom in as needed so that the Head fills the Document space. See Figure 5.1.

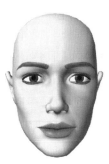

FIGURE   *The Woman Head as it appears when brought into the Document window.*
5.1

2. Click on the Left Eye. When the Left Eye's Parameter Dials appear, use the Side-to-Side dial to set a value of –40. Do the same for the Right Eye. See Figure 5.2.

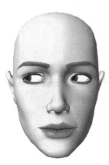

FIGURE   *The eyes look to the left in response to Parameter Dial Side-to-Side settings.*
5.2

3. Repeat the same exercise, but this time, set both Left and Right Side-to-Side dials to 40. See Figure 5.3.

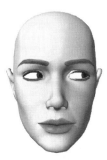

FIGURE   *Now the eyes shift their view to the opposite side of the face.*
5.3

4. To cross the eyes, set the Right Eye Side-to-Side to 40, and the Left Eye Side to Side to –40. See Figure 5.4.

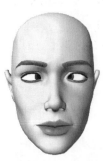

FIGURE *The Side-to-Side Parameter Dials can be used to create crossed eyes.*
5.4

5. Move the eyes in the opposite direction as their cross-eyed values to create extreme wall-eyed behavior. See Figure 5.5.

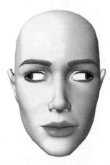

FIGURE *The wall-eyed look.*
5.5

6. The eyes can also be rolled up or down, either together or opposite each other. Just adjust the values on the Up-Down Parameter Dials for the effect you want. See Figure 5.6.

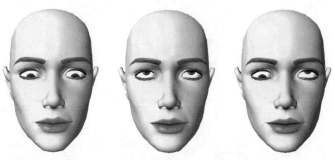

FIGURE *The eyes adjusted to look down, up, and opposite each other.*
5.6

Size Matters

When you enlarge the size of the eyes (or just one eye), you won't see any results until you move the eye out from the face. Do the following:

1. Select the Left Eye. Set the Scale at 270, and Z Translation at 0.006. Do the same with the Right Eye. See Figure 5.7.

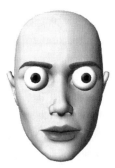

FIGURE   *The eyes bulge out from the confines of their sockets.*
5.7

2. If you increase the Z Translation too much, the eye will jump out of the Head. Then it can even turn back to look at the place it came from. See Figure 5.8.
3. Use the X, Y, and Z Translation dials to place the enlarged eye in the center of the head. See Figure 5.9.

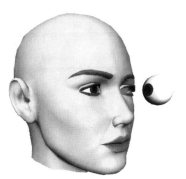

FIGURE   *Who's looking at whom?*
5.8

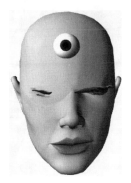

FIGURE   *The Cyclops lives!*
5.9

HEAD PARAMETERS

The Mouth and Eyebrows give the head its emotive capability, and both features can be altered and animated in Poser 4. It is suggested that you leave Limits off when exploring these features, though you've got to watch the distortions of the face to make sure you haven't gone so far as to warp out the geometry beyond what you need.

Load either the Woman or Man Head (from the Additional Figures library) to your Document window, and let's explore the Parameter Dial settings for the Head. Make sure the Head is selected, and not one of the eyes.

The Eyebrow Dials

Let's look at the Eyebrow Dial settings first. There are three Eyebrow settings types for the Left and Right brows separately. They are Left/Right Brow Down, Left/Right Brow Up, and Left/Right Worry. The dials can be turned in both negative and positive directions, and the settings can be applied to each brow separately.

Karuna! *Note that all Brow settings create emotions by degree and extent, so that smaller variations can make very major differences as far as the emotions perceived. Explore a wide range of alternatives, other than the examples presented here.*

Left/Right Brow Down

Using negative Brow Down settings tends to create a look of investigation or even a kind of haughty openness. Using positive Brow Down settings creates a look that ranges from extreme concentration to a hint of physical discomfort, or even a touch of sadness. See Figure 5.10.

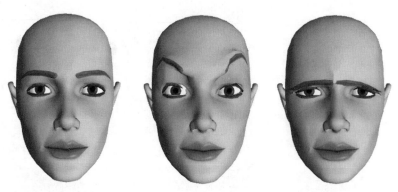

FIGURE *left: Default Brows at 0. Center: Left/Right Brow Down to –4. Right:*
5.10 *Left/Right Brow Down to 3.*

Note that when both the Left and Right Brow settings are equal, you may not get perfect symmetry on the face. Each brow setting stretches the skin and causes wrinkles. You may have to use unequal settings to get a more symmetrical look.

Pushing the Left and Right Brow Down settings to –10 or less creates a severe warping of the skin, and horn-like projections on the head. It also pulls open the eyelids much more, creating a strange, menacing appearance. This may be useful information for the creation of certain character types. Setting the Left and Right Brow Down settings to positive values over 4 creates spiky projections that poke through the face. See Figures 5.11 through 5.13.

FIGURE **5.11** *Meet Princess Bizarro. Her Right Brow Down setting is –33, while the Left Brow Down setting is –27. The "horns" look symmetrical, even though the settings are different.*

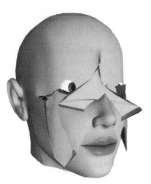

FIGURE **5.12** *No, she isn't very pretty, but could these high settings for the Left and Right Brow Down parameters (17 and 22) suffice for some alien being in one of your scenes?*

FIGURE *In this image, the Left Brow Down setting has been set to 1000. The result is a*
5.13 *wall with a face at the upper right. The mouth and other parameters still move.*

CAUTION

Karuna! *If you need to export and render a model that has been radically warped,
like that shown in Figure 5.13, you may have to triangulate the polygons and/or
adjust the normals. Otherwise, it may not render correctly. Refer to the documentation in the 3D application you plan to use.*

Left/Right Brow Up

Do not make the mistake in thinking that moving the Left/Right Brow Down
settings is opposite that of controlling the Left/Right Brow Up settings. They
are not related in that manner. In fact, applying variations of both will create
unique Brow looks that cannot be achieved by either one alone. Like the Brow
Down parameters, the Brow Up parameters can be moved in either negative or
positive directions. Positive values lend a look of surprise, while negative values
tend to give the model an appearance of active listening. See Figure 5.14.

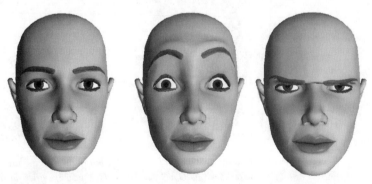

FIGURE *Left: The default eyebrow positions. Center: Left/Right Brow Up of 3. Right:*
5.14 *Left/Right Brow Up of –3.*

A more radical warping of the skin occurs when the Brow Up values are pushed below –2 or above 4. This can be useful in creating alien or monstrous characteristics. See Figures 5.15 and 5.16.

FIGURE **5.15** *A Right Brow of 10 and a Left Brow of 9 were used to generate this head. Note how the Brow Up parameter pulls on the eyes at higher values.*

FIGURE **5.16** *Changing the Left/Right Brow Up values to –10 creates a strange result that pulls the skin away from the eyes, and weds it to the cheeks, exposing the eyeballs.*

CAUTION

Karuna! *If you radically warp the skin on the Head, think about adding a patterned texture to hide the warped anomalies. A reptilian texture works well. See Chapter 17. See Figure 5.17.*

FIGURE *Displaced areas of skin look more natural when the head is textured.*
5.17

Open Lips

This is the first mouth parameter control. It can be used to define standard parameters, or pushed farther to create stranger results. See Figure 5.18.

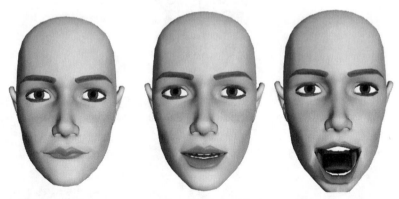

FIGURE *A variety of Open Lips settings: −1.1 (pursed lips), .5, 3 (maximum without*
5.18 *warping).*

Opening the Lips with settings below −1.1 or above 3 pokes parts of the mouth through the face, so this may not be too useful for standard models. See Figure 5.19.

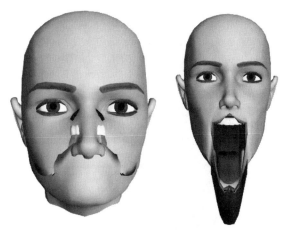

FIGURE   *Left: With an Open Lips setting of −6, the teeth poke through the face above the*
5.19   *bottom of the nose. Right: At a setting of 11, the bottom lip pokes through the*
chin.

Smile

Karuna! *The Smile and Frown parameters are not opposites. Each deforms very*
different muscle groups on the face.

CAUTION   The Smile parameter adds a smile at positive values, and a sort of droopy
look at negative values. Pushing the Smile parameter below 1.5 or above. See
Figure 5.20.

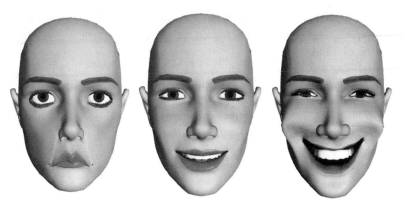

FIGURE   *Alternate Smile values create different looks. Left to right: −1.5, 1, and 3.2.*
5.20

Pushing the Smile value above 3.2 creates strange deformations. See Figure 5.21.

FIGURE *The Smile setting at 8.5. The severe warping might serve for the creation of a*
5.21 *character like the Joker.*

Frown

The Frown Parameter Dial allows you to create everything from a kissy face (at negative values) to sadness and anger (positive values). See Figure 5.22.

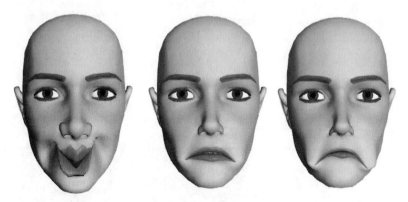

FIGURE *From left to right, the Frown values are –4, 2, and 3.3 (notice the jowls that*
5.22 *are caused).*

Mouth "O"

Poser 4 allows you to shape the mouth as if it was pronouncing specific vowel sounds, so you can create lip-synching attributes. The Mouth-O Parameter Dial creates a number of different mouth shapes. See Figure 5.23.

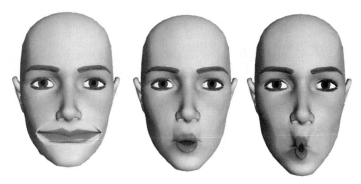

FIGURE *From left to right, the Mouth "O" Parameter Dial settings are –1.2*
5.23 *(horizontally elongated mouth), 1 ("oh"), and 1.8 ("ooh").*

Mouth "F"

The Mouth "F" controls mouth shapes from a thicker bottom lip to a visual representation of the "F" sound. "F" settings above 1 tend to be rather useless by themselves, since it pokes the bottom teeth through the lower lip. See Figure 5.24.

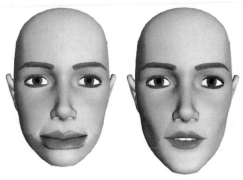

FIGURE *From left to right, Mouth "F" parameter settings: –2 (a thicker bottom lip),*
5.24 *and 1.*

Mouth "M"

The Mouth "M" settings create looks from a larger mouth to the visual pronunciation of the letter "M." See Figure 5.25.

Tongue "T"

Phonemes are shaped by a combination of tongue and mouth alterations. This is the first of two Tongue Parameters, the "T" sound. Say the letter "T," and feel what your tongue does. See Figure 5.26.

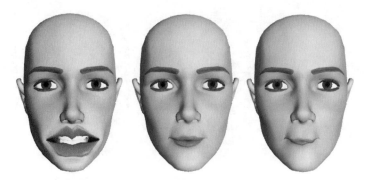

FIGURE *Mouth "M" settings of –4, 2.2, and .3.6.*
5.25

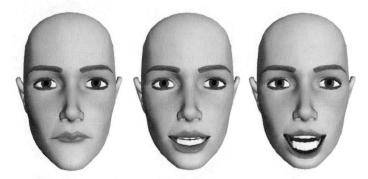

FIGURE *From left to right, the Tongue "T" settings are –1.7, 1.2, and 3.*
5.26

Tongue "L"

This is the second of two Tongue Parameters, the "L" sound. Say the letter "L," and feel what your tongue does. See Figure 5.27.

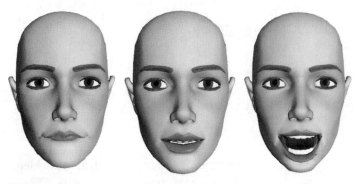

FIGURE *From left to right, the Tongue "L" settings are –1.3, .4, and 2.6 (singing the*
5.27 *sound "La").*

Worry

This is a special Parameter that can be applied to either the left or right brow. It's the only Parameter defined as a specific emotion instead of a facial feature. Settings below –2 or higher than 2.5 interfere with the placement of the eyes. See Figure 5.28.

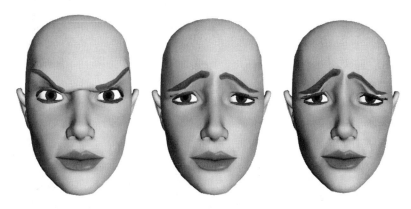

FIGURE   *From left to right, the Worry Parameter Dials were set to –2., 2, and 2.5.*
5.28

That completes a look at all of the Parameter Dials for the Head as single events. If you were to use any of the settings described, you could create hundreds of unique facial looks. But that is only the start of facial shaping possibilities. The real expressive fun begins when you use different Parameter settings in combination with each other. As the next section shows, your options then become limitless.

PARAMETER DIAL COMBINATIONS

If this book were to detail and display all of the Head Parameter Dial combination settings you can achieve in Poser 4, it would have to have hundreds, if not thousands, of extra pages. What we can do, however, is give you some idea of just how variable the Head Parameter settings can be, when used in combination with each other, and what different combinations lead to. To do this, we've devised a table (Table 5.1) that lists the settings as keyed to the faces represented in Figure 5.29. Apply these settings as detailed to develop the intended looks, and also be sure to explore settings not represented here to develop your own library of different facial expressions.

Table 5.1 These Parameter Dial combinations detail how you can create specific emotional and personality styles for Poser 3 Heads. See Figure 5.29 for the visual display of the 25 key letter descriptions in this table.

Figure Key	Description	Open Lips	Smile	Frown	Mouth	Tongue	Brow Down	Brow Up	Worry
A	Antagonistic	1.26	.58	2.84	0	0	0	0	2.75 L&R
B	"Well, I never!"	0	0	0	O=1	T=1	0	0	-1.3 Right
C	"Not a good day today . . ."	0	-1.4	0	0	0	0	-1.4 L&R	2 L&R
D	"Yippie!"	2.5	1.9	0	0	0	0	3.5 L&R	0
E	Innocence	-3	2	0	M 3.7	0	0	3.8 L&R	0
F	Whistler 1	0	-1.5	-3	0	0	-.6 Left	1.4 Right 3 Left	0
G	Seasick (eyes rolled up)	.4	0	2.6	F -.28	L .37	0	0	1.7 L&R
H	Drunk (eyes rolled up)	.4	1.5	-2.9	F -2.8	L .37	0	0	1.7 L&R
I	"Gimmee a kiss . . ." (eyes closed by using a -.02 Z translation)	-1	-.2	-3	O .5 F .2	L .4	0	.2 L&R	0
J	"It's you!"	0	-1.1	-2.7	0	L 2.8	0	3.6 R	.9 R
K	"Heh-heh . . . guess I goofed"	0	.1	-2.7	0	-4.5 T 4.5 L	-1 L	3.6 R	.9 R 2.5 L
L	"Grrrrrr!"	0	0	2.19	0	0	0	2.8 L&R	2.8 L&R
M	Deformed by anger	0	-.7	3.8	0	0	-3.6 R 1.7 L	6.4 R 3.1 L	-4.9 R -3 L
N	Deformed by anger #2	0	-.7	3.8	-11 M	0	-3.6 R 1.7 L	6.4 R 3.1 L	-4.9 R -3 L
O	Snapper	0	4.9	-10	0	-6.5 T	0	-1.7 L&R	0
P	"Hello there."	0	.6	-2.3	0	-1.4 T	0	1.3 R	0
Q	Unilip	1.2	-1.5	-4.6	-1.5 O 2.2 F .5 M	-10 T 2.75 L	0	0	0
R	"Holy Moley!"	1.4	0	-2.8	1 O	2.5 L	0	8 L&R	0
S	"Golly Gosh."	-1.7	-1.9	-1.6	0	3 T 1.6 L	0	2.7 L&R	2.4 L&R
T	Canary Head	-.5	-1.9	-1.6	-3.7 F 4.8 M	3 T 1.6 L	0	2.7 L&R	2.4 L&R
U	Whacko Fatmouth	0	3.1	0	-7 M	0	0	-2.6 L&R	0
V	Ta'ak (taper added to head, and eyes adjusted at Y and Z Translations values of .004)	-.9	0	0	-1.6 F	1.8 T	0	11.6 R 10.2 L	0
W	Peter L. (Taper used on the Head, and eyes adjusted Z Translations values of .003)	.5	-1.2	0	.7 O 2.3 F	.6 L	0	3.5 L&R	0
X	Sad Clown	1	-1.2	0	-1.5 O -1.9 F	0	0	2.5 R -1 L	1.6 L&R
Y	Opera Singer	0	0	0	2.09 O -4.2 M	0	0	4.2 R	2.6 R .7 L

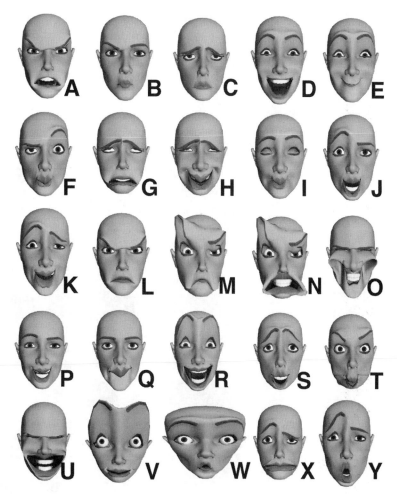

FIGURE   *These 25 keyed faces are detailed in Table 5.1.*
5.29

The New Racial Morphs

This feature alone is well worth the cost of the upgrade. It pushes Poser into a whole new realm of use, that of creating far more unique characters than can be crafted using just the standard Parameter Dials. The Racial Morphs are based upon a series of pre-crafted Morphs that affect those areas of a face normally associated with racial features. But that would be purely racial stereotyping if it didn't also allow you to reconfigure each feature involved to create a unique personal look within each racial group. If you see beauty in the diverse forms of the human face, then you will spend a good amount of time crafting unique facial characteristics using this new Morph collection. Each of the Racial Morphs is composited into a separate Male or Female Nude Figure, and they can be loaded into a Document from the Figures/Characters Male and Figures/Characters Female Libraries. Each of the separate figures has a first name, and comes with a Hair model attached (which can be deleted or replaced). See Figures 5.30 and 5.31.

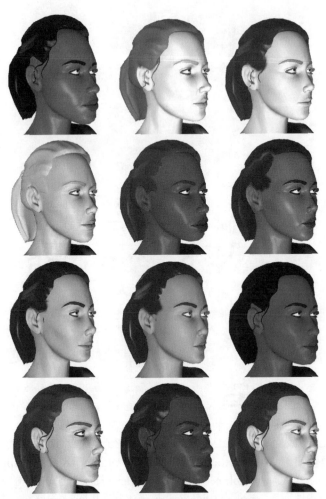

FIGURE *The new Female Characters (from upper left to lower right): (Default Figure*
5.30 *not shown), Carmen, Eve, Gabrielle, Greta, Holly, Luna, Marina, Masumi, Mercades, Monique, Mzuri, and Natsuko.*

Using the Parameter Dials for the Morph attributes, you can create your own Poser personalities. Five of mine are shown in Figure 5.32. The Parameter settings for these five Morphed models are detailed in Table 5.2.

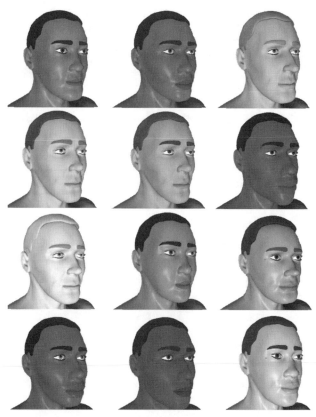

FIGURE
5.31
The new Male Characters (from upper left to lower right): (Default Figure not shown), Amane, Carson, Damien, Derek, Eddie, Geoph, Max, Naoki, Pablo, Peter, Shane, and Towa.

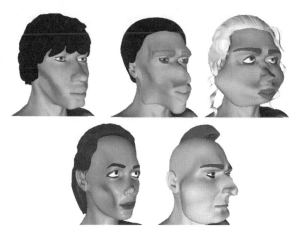

FIGURE
5.32
Left top to right bottom: Shamal. See Table 5.2 for the Morph Parameter Settings. Alternate Hair Props were used for more character variance.

Table 5.2 Morph Parameter details for the models displayed in Figure 5.32. Parameter Settings for Models in Figure 5.32

Params	Shamal	Jakur	Mandy	Marla	Red Bear
Round Face	–3.5	–3	1.1	–3.4	0
Long Face	–1.2	0.6	–2.3	–2.5	–0.8
Flat Face	–1.7	–0.7	–0.1	.0.4	0
Heart Face	0	–0.4	0.8	–0.7	0
Square Face	0	1.3	1.8	–0.3	2.3
Flat Bridge	0.75	0.7	1.1	0.3	–0.3
Jaw Strength	.6	1.9	1.2	–0.2	0
Eyes	0	0.9	–2.5	–0.8	1.7
Brow	0	1.9	1.9	0.6	1.5
Lashes	–.6	0.6	1.7	–0.6	0
Bump Nose	0	3.5	–5.2	–0.7	3.6
Flat Nose	0	–2.9	–2.4	1.3	–1.05
Pointed Nose	0	–1.3	1.7	1.8	–1.3
Round Nose	0	0	–1.0	–0.4	4.5
Cheeks	0	–0.7	0.7	–0.2	3.3
Chin	0	0.6	0.06	–0.9	0,4
Lips	0	0.065	1.3	1.1	0.9
Hair Model	Female Curly Curly Hair	Male Afro Hair	Zygote: Fem Hair w/Bun	Default Hair	Default Hair resized

ALTERNATE MORPH TARGETS FOR FACES

Instead of loading one of the preset racial types to the Document, there are three other methods you can use to input and use Morphs for facial attributes. The first is to select the morphs individually. Here's how.

Method Number One

1. Select either the P3 Male or P3 Female Nude. Avoid the P4 Nudes for this example, because the P4 Nudes have all of the Morphed Parameter elements already loaded in that are displayed in the Racial Types figures. The P3 Nudes do not, but the stored Morph racial geometry works.

2. With the Head selected, go to the Object/Properties selection. In the Properties window, select Add Morph Target. Load a Morph from your Poser4/Morph Targets/Male Head Morphs drawer, name it whatever

you like, and quit the Properties window. The Morph now appears in the Parameters list.

Why not select any old figure? Because the geometry is not correct for the Morphs stored in that location. Even though the Morph may load, just look at what happens when you try to use it. See Figure 5.33.

FIGURE
5.33 *A Morph from the Poser4/Morph Targets/Male Head Morphs drawer targeted to the male Businessman model, which has the wrong geometry. Not a pretty sight!*

When a Morph from the same drawer is used with the Poser 3 Nude Female geometry, however, everything works exactly as it should. See Figure 5.34.

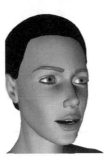  

FIGURE
5.34 *Left to Right: The Poser 3 Nude Female default; the same figure with the Afro-American Female Morph applied at 1.38; the Afro-American Morph applied at −1.5 produces an elderly Caucasian school marm caricature.*

Method Number Two

If you need to use Morph targets for either the Poser 3 or Poser 4 Nudes that are not present in the Poser4/Morph Targets/Male Head Morphs drawer, you can always look on the Web to see if anyone has created what you need. In Appendix D of this book, "Poser Web Resource Sites," we have listed a number of sites you can check out for free downloadable Morph Targets. One of my favorites is definitely MorphWorld, a site developed by Eric VanDycke at www.darksouls.com/traveler. Eric has placed dozen of morphs on the site, with new ones being added all the time. There are facial Morphs (Male and Female) and other examples for the kid models, clothes, and other Poser 4 content. All come as OBJ format files.

How to Apply Target Morphs Downloaded from MorphWorld:

1. Unzip them to any folder that you want to.
2. Open Poser.
3. Switch to the character that the Morphs were meant for.
4. Double-click on the body part that the morph goes to.
5. Click the Morph Target button when the Properties window opens.
6. On the new little window that pops up, search for your Morph Target.
7. Name it what you want to.
8. Press OK/Apply.
9. Now there should be a new Morph Target dial with the other usual ones.
10. Turn your dial to use the MorphWorld Morph Target.

See Figure 5.35.

The MorphWorld collections may need to be imported and exported again from RayDream Studio or another suitable application that reads and writes Poser-compatible OBJ files. This is especially true for Mac users. Also note that these Morphs will work on the Poser 3 and Poser 4 Male and Female Nudes, and especially well on the Morphman model from Zygote (which has to be purchased separately and is in the Zygote Characters drawer once you install it).

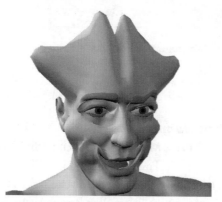

FIGURE *A selection of MorphWorld Target Morphs applied to a Poser 4 Male Nude*
5.35 *figure.*

Method Number Three: Morphman

To create models with Morphman, you'll have to purchase the Zygote Characters collection for Poser 4. Morphman comes ready loaded with facial Morph Targets that nobody else provides. Morphman is a Male Nude figure. Of course, you can always add MorphWorld or Racial Morphs to this collection, and save out the resulting figure as a separate file, or even as a Full Body Morph. See Figure 5.36.

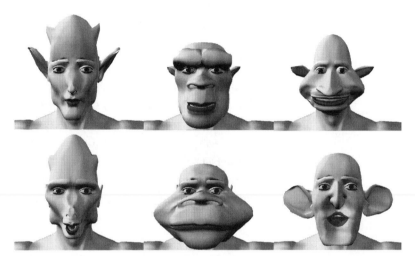

FIGURE   *Figures created with the Morphman facial Morph Targets.*
5.36

WHEN YOU NEED EVEN MORE...

There will come a time when you can't find the exact Morph target you need from the presets, or from MorphWorld or Zygote. In that case, you still have an option left. Roll your own. We have already walked through the use of the Grouping Tool and Spawning Morphs with the Magnet and Wave Deformers in previous chapters. That, coupled with your study of the documentation and time spent exploring the Deform option on your own, should make you more than ready to create and save your own Morph Targeted figures. See Figure 5.37.

FIGURE *Using the Grouping and Spawning methods described previously, you can*
5.37 *further extend your capacity for shaping Poser 4 faces.*

Karuna! *Although Poser 4 offers you the opportunity to stay within the software while customizing figure geometry with the new Grouping and Morph Target tools, these tools alone are no match for real down-and-dirty customization tools. For that you need an application, like MetaCreations' Ray Dream Studio or Carrara, that reads and writes OBJ files that Poser can interpret. You also need to make sure that the external application you use for this purpose doesn't arbitrarily add polygons while you are doing the customizing. For more on this topic, be sure to read Chapter 17, "Handshaking," and Chapter 22, "Poser Projects."*

Moving Along

If you have worked through this chapter, you have almost mastered the posing and customizing of facial geometry in Poser 4, and you're well on your way to mastery of the software. In the next chapter, we'll look at the posing and customizing of the Poser 4 Animals.

CHAPTER

6

POSING AND CUSTOMIZING ANIMAL MODELS

One of the most anticipated aspects of Poser 3 was the incorporation of Animal models, and Poser 4 continues that tradition. Poser's animals are fully articulated, so they can be interactively posed with ease. Five Animal models shipped with Poser 3: Cat, Dog, Dolphin, Horse, and Raptor. The Poser 4 additions include Angelfish, Frog, Lion, Rat, Rattler, and Wolf. The Zygote Media Group was responsible for the design of these models, and they also offer a larger addendum collection of Animal models on one of their extras CD-ROM collections. The extra Animal models for Poser 3 included Chimp, Lion, Frog, Cow, Zebra, Penguin, Grizzly Bear, Buck Deer, Gray Wolf, Killer Whale, and Shark, Triceratops, Bass, Butterfly Fish, Cow, Dragonfly, and more. In addition, Zygote provides a Doe model on their Sampler CD. In this chapter, we will explore the customization and posing of many of the Poser 4 Animal models, both those that ship with the software and the extras collection marketed by Zygote. We'll also explore customizing animals with the Deformers.

Internal Animal Models

The Parameter Dials for each Poser 4 Animal may be configured differently, especially for different species. The Horse, for instance, has controls for all four feet, while the Dolphin (which has no feet) has Parameter Dials for the fins. The Internal Animal models are found in the Animals directory in the Figures library. We'll look at the Posing of the Cat, Dog, Dolphin, Horse, and Raptor.

POSING THE CAT, DOG, DOLPHIN, HORSE, AND RAPTOR

There are two ways to think about posing the Animal models. The first is to pose them naturally, taking advantage of the ways that the targeted animal moves in real life. The second way is to think of the Animal models as cartoon figures, so that their poses become more related to humans than to the animals in question. Both of these alternatives are possible in Poser 4.

Real-Life Posing

Remember that the body can communicate emotion as well as the face can. This is certainly true of animals like the Poser 4 Cat, Dog, Dolphin, Horse, and Raptor. Each of these animals has certain features, controlled by specific Parameter Dials, that allow them to display basic (and sometimes quite subtle) emotions. Each Animal model is different in this regard, with some able to display a wider range of emotions, and some a more bounded range.

Posed Cat Bodies

The Poser 4 Cat is a house pet with possibility. See Figure 6.1.

You can body-pose the Cat model into any number of evocative positions. Here are just a few. See Figure 6.2.

A. **Angry**. Mouth 1.12; Waist Bend –19; Shoulders: Twist –5, Side to Side –12, Bend –44; Tail 1 Bend –47; Forearms: Y-Scale 121, Twist –18, Side to Side 14, Bend –17; Thighs: Bend –22.

B. **Begging**. Mouth .35; Neck Bend –10; Shoulders Bend –30; Forearms Bend –67; Wrists Bend 25; Hands Bend 24; Tail Bend (1 to 4) 67, 53, 61, 33; Thighs Bend 51; Legs Bend 23; Shins Bend 34; Feet Bend 2.

C. **Sleep Curl**. Eyes .6; LEar Turn .45; REar Back .28; Chest: Side to Side –48, Bend –2; Feet: Bend 11, Side to Side –9; Forearms: Twist 16, Side to Side –15, Bend –60; Hands Bend 78; Legs: Twist –2, Side to Side –6, Bend 23; Shins: Side to Side 49, Bend 14; Shoulders: Twist 11, Side to Side 14, Bend –21; Thighs: Twist 22, Side to Side –42, Bend –67; Wrists: Twist 10, Side by Side –2, Bend 144; Neck: Twist –6, Side to Side –21, Bend 107; Tail 1: Twist 10, Side to Side 45, Bend –3, Curve .9; Tail 2: Twist 3, Side to Side 14, Bend –48, Curve 1; Tail 3: Twist 0, Side to Side 0, Bend –34, Curve 1; Tail 4: Twist –1, Side to Side –2, Bend 13, Curve 1.

D. **Stretching**. LEar Turn .45; REar Back .28; Abdomen Bend 18; Chest: Bend –13; Feet: Bend –40, Side to Side 5; Hips Bend –5; Forearms: Twist 18, Side to Side –14, Bend –31; Hands Bend 31; LLeg: Twist –2, Side to Side –7, Bend 16; RLeg: Twist –2, Side to Side –7, Bend 23;

FIGURE *The Cat model in Poser 4.*
6.1

Shins: Side to Side 5, Bend 39; Shoulders: Twist 10, Side to Side 12, Bend –52; Thighs: Twist 0, Side to Side –8, Bend 54; Wrists: Twist –10, Side by Side 3, Bend 11; Neck: Bend –39; Tail 1: Twist 0, Side to Side 0, Bend 36, Curve .9; Tail 2: Twist 0, Side to Side 0, Bend 79, Curve 1; Tail 3: Twist 0, Side to Side 0, Bend 75, Curve 1; Tail 4: Twist –1, Side to Side –2, Bend 13, Curve 1.

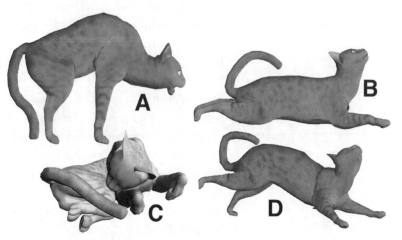

FIGURE *A. Angry. B. Begging. C and D. Stretching.*
6.2

Posed Cat Heads

The Cat model is somewhat limited when it comes to displaying emotions by customizing the Head parts. Aside from opening and closing the mouth, the Cat model can display a limited range of emotions by Eye open/close (no side-to-side eye movements), and Ear movement. Ear movements offer the most variation. If you have ever observed a cat, you realize that it shows a pretty full range of emotions or feeling by the way its ears move, if you watch carefully. See Figures 6.3 through 6.5.

Posed Dog Models

The Poser 4 Dog model is capable of a wide range of looks, (See Figure 6.6) and has a wider range of emotional possibilities than the Cat model. This is mainly due to the fact that the Mouth and Ears have many more options. Instead of Eye controls to open and shut the Eyes however (like the Cat has), the Dog model has moveable Eyebrows. Create the following Dog model poses by inputting the Parameters given. See Figure 6.7.

FIGURE   *Cat Eye settings, left to right: Wide open at –.5, partially open at .5, and closed*
6.3   *tight at 1.*

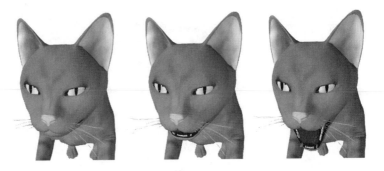

FIGURE   *Cat Mouth settings, left to right: Closed at 0, partially open at .7, and wide*
6.4   *open at 2.*

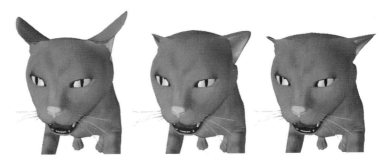

FIGURE   *Cat Ear settings, left to right: Ears turned at 1.5, Left Ear Back 1 and Right*
6.5   *Ear Side 1, Left Ear Back 1 and Right Ear Side 1 with both ears Turned .6.*

FIGURE *One variation of the Poser 4 Dog model.*
6.6

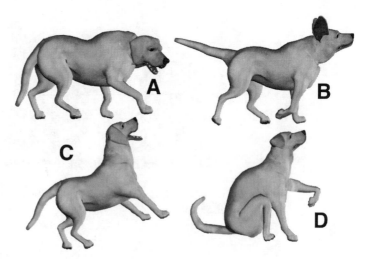

FIGURE *A. Ambling Along. B. Sniff Air. C. Bark Jump. D. Sit Beg.*
6.7

A. **Ambling Along**. Chest Bend –13; Head: Side to Side and Bend –34; Mouth .68; Hip Default; LEar (1,2,3) Default; REar (1, 2, 3) Default; Eyebrows Default; LFoot Bend 27; LForearm Bend –57; LHand Bend –35; LLeg Bend 27; LShin Bend –50; LShoulder Bend 46; LThigh Bend –13; LWrist Bend 56; RFoot bend 58; RForearm Bend –57; RHand Bend –2; RLeg Bend 28; RShin Bend –48; RShoulder Bend –1; RThigh Bend –52; RWrist Bend 56; Neck1 Bend 94; Neck2 Bend –21; Tail (1, 2, 3, 4) Bend –47, –25, –11, 19; Waist Bend 9.

B. **Sniff Air**. Chest Bend –13; Head: Bend –47; Mouth 0; Hip Default; LEar1 (Twist, Side to Side, Bend) 29, 15, 79; REar1 (Twist, Side to Side, Bend) 0, 8, –79; Eyebrows Default; LFoot Bend 66; LForearm Bend –24; LHand Bend –33; LLeg Bend 28; LShin Bend –48; LShoulder Bend 26; LThigh Bend –47; LWrist Bend 22; RFoot bend 28; RForearm Bend 20; RHand Bend –41; RLeg Bend 28; RShin Bend –17; RShoulder Bend 5; RThigh Bend –6; RWrist Bend 65; Neck1 Bend 64; Neck2 Bend –14; Tail (1, 2, 3, 4) Bend –13, 7, –2, 0; Waist Bend 9.

C. **Bark Jump**. Chest Bend –13; Head: Bend 0; Mouth 1.15; Hip Default; LEar (1, 2, 3) Default; REar (1, 2, 3) Default; Eyebrows Default; LFoot Bend 43; LForearm Bend –57; LHand Bend 19; LLeg Bend –57; LShin Bend –48; LShoulder Bend 34; LThigh Bend –34; LWrist Bend 15; RFoot bend 40; RForearm Bend 15; RHand Bend –2; RLeg Bend 28; RShin Bend –48; RShoulder Bend –34; RThigh Bend –46; RWrist Bend 23; Neck1 Bend –2; Neck2 Bend 0; Tail (1, 2, 3, 4) Bend –30, –25, –11, 19; Waist Bend –13.

D. **Sit Beg**. Chest Bend 61; Head: Bend 0; Mouth 0; Hip –79; LEar1 Bend 6; REar1 5; Eyebrows Default; LFoot Bend –6; LForearm Bend –10; LHand Bend 61; LLeg Bend 87; LShin Bend 68; LShoulder Bend –91; LThigh Bend –75; LWrist Bend 115; RFoot Bend –17; RForearm Bend 14; RHand Bend 27; RLeg Bend 112; RShin Bend 37; RShoulder Bend –19; RThigh Bend –74; RWrist Bend –5; Neck1 Bend 16; Neck2 Bend –25; Tail (1, 2, 3, 4) Bend 90, 35, 42, 55; Waist Bend 11.

Posed Dog Heads

The Poser 4 Dog model has a wider range of motion and emotion related to its Head than does the Cat. The Eyebrows do more than just open or close the eyes, they also add a range of expressions. The Ears are separated into three parts, and each can be manipulated separately. The mouth can open and close as expected, and it can also Snarl both front and back. See Figures 6.8, 6.9, and 6.10, and try these and other settings on your own.

FIGURE *A range of Eyebrow settings, left to right: –2, 0, 1.5.*

6.8

Karuna! *You should explore variation of the settings presented in Figures 6.8 through 6.10, keep track of new emotive possibilities you discover for the Dog model, and save out the best poses.*

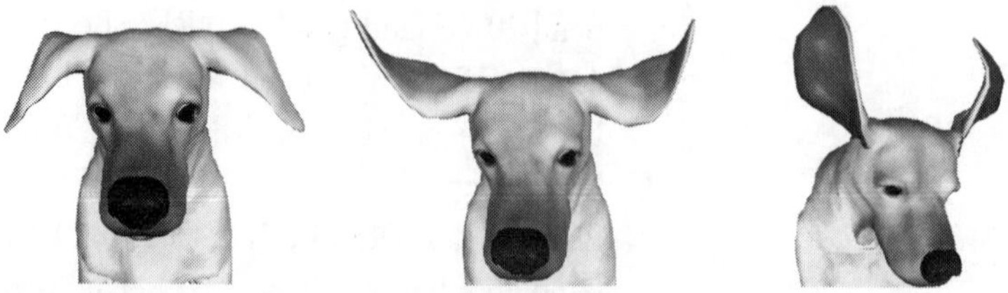

FIGURE 6.9 *Ear movements, left to right: REar and LEar #1 Bend 12 and –12, All three Ear sections Bent at the same angles, both Ear #1 sections Twist/Side-Side/Bend set to 50/15/50 and resized to 150%.*

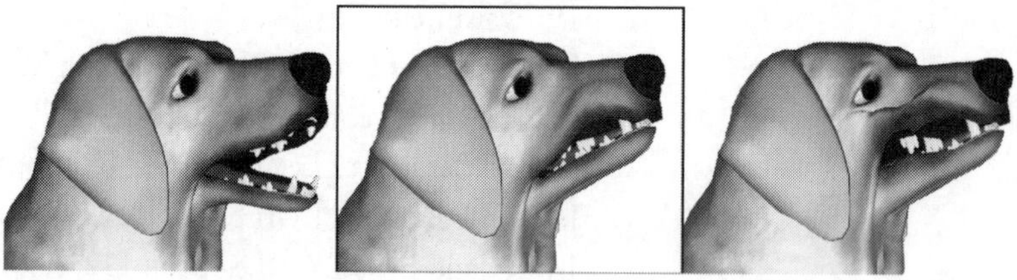

FIGURE 6.10 *Mouth options, left to right: Mouth Open .7, Front Snarl .9 with Mouth Open .05, REar Snarl of 1.9 added.*

Posing Dolphin Models

The Dolphin has always been a friend of the fisherman. See Figure 6.11.

Of all of the animals we share space with on the earth, the Dolphin remains one that evokes both mystery and admiration. It has always been a symbol of

FIGURE 6.11 *The Poser 4 Dolphin has been modeled with exacting detail.*

freedom, playfulness, and excitement. Dolphins actually have brains that exceed human brains in body weight ratio, and so their intelligence is also something we admire. The Poser 4 Dolphin model can be posed according to its moveable parts, which are far different from the Animal models we have explored thus far. The Dolphin model in Poser 4 communicates its personality through movements of its mouth and tongue, in addition to its body poses. See Figure 6.12.

Copy the settings to generate the poses in Figure 6.12, and then explore your own customized pose Parameters.

A. **Swim Fun.** Chest Bend 13; Head Bend 9; Mouth .5; Tongue .25; Hip Bend –38; Left Pectoral Fin: Twist –21, Bend –13; Right Pectoral Fin: Twist –15, Bend 8; Tail1 –5; Tail2 –10; Tail3 –10; Tail Fins Bend –18.

B. **Tail Up**. Chest Bend 50; Head Bend 9; Mouth .5; Tongue .25; Hip Bend –38; Left Pectoral Fin: Twist –21, Bend –13; Right Pectoral Fin: Twist –15, Bend 8; Tail1 30; Tail2 –30; Tail3 30; Tail Fins Bend 30.

C. **Loopy**. Chest Bend 13; Head Bend –40; Mouth .5; Tongue .25; Hip Bend –38; Left Pectoral Fin: Twist –21, Bend –13; Right Pectoral Fin: Twist –15, Bend 8; Tail1 40; Tail2 40; Tail3 40; Tail Fins Bend 40.

D. **Contortion**. Chest: Twist –33, Bend –56; Head Bend 68; Mouth .5; Tongue .25; Hip Bend –25; Left Pectoral Fin: Twist 31, Bend –42; Right Pectoral Fin: Twist 31, Bend –40; Tail1 40; Tail2 –57; Tail3 –41; Tail Fins Bend –60.

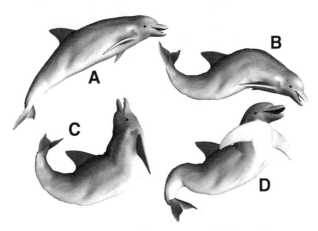

FIGURE *A. Swim Fun. B. Tail Up. C. Loopy. D. Contortion.*
6.12

Posed Dolphin Heads

Opening and closing the Dolphin model's Mouth and adjusting the height of the Tongue are the adjustable Parameters for the Dolphin's Head. See Figure 6.13.

FIGURE *Dolphin Mouth and Tongue settings, left to right: Mouth at 0, Mouth 1 and*
6.13 *Tongue .5, Mouth 1.6 and Tongue 1.5.*

Posed Horse Models

The Poser 4 Horse model is a magnificent steed. See Figure 6.14.

FIGURE *The Horse model is deftly crafted, and ready for placement in a pasture, race*
6.14 *track, or a mounted battle.*

The Horse model in Poser 4 cannot be altered as far as Head attributes, because no features on the Head are customizable. Except for Twisting, moving Side to Side, or Bending, the Head remains as it is. (Tapering and resizing is also possible, but we'll cover those alterations later). So posing the Horse model concerns itself with body poses alone. See Figure 6.15.

Explore the settings detailed for the poses in Figure 6.15, and then create your own poses for the Horse model. When you create poses that you like, be sure and save them to the Poses library.

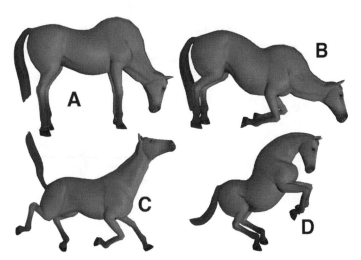

FIGURE *A. Munch. B. Kneel and Drink. C. Fast Trot. D. REar Up.*
6.15

A. **Munch**. Chest Bend –5; Lower Neck Bend –82; Upper Neck Bend –14; Head Bend –48.

B. **Kneel and Drink**. Abdomen Bend 33; Chest Bend –23; Head Bend –48; Ankles Bend 9; Feet Bend –18; Forearms Bend 109' Hands Bend –23; Shins Bend –47; Shoulder Bend 28; Thigh Bend –12; Upper Arms Bend –75; Wrists Bend 17; Lower Neck Bend 51; Tail 1 Bend –45; Upper Neck Bend –28.

C. **Fast Trot**. Abdomen Bend 13; Chest Bend –5; Head Bend –44; LAnkles Bend 67; RAnkle Bend 67; LFoot Bend –20; RFoot Bend –20; LForearm Bend 19; RForearm Bend 95; LHand Bend –38; RHand Bend –38; LShin Bend –82; RShin Bend –82; LShoulder Bend 32; RShoulder Bend 32; LThigh Bend –7; RThigh Bend 43; LUpper Arm Bend –86; RUpper Arm Bend –84; LWrist Bend 13; RWrist Bend 53; Lower Neck Bend –31; Tail 1 Bend 66; Tail 2 Bend 27; Upper Neck Bend –9.

D. **REar Up**. Abdomen Bend –33; Chest Bend –5; Head Bend 6; LAnkles Bend 67; RAnkle Bend 67; LFoot Bend –20; RFoot Bend –20; LForearm Bend 95; RForearm Bend 95; LHand Bend –38; RHand Bend –38; LShin Bend –82; RShin Bend –82; LShoulder Bend 32; RShoulder Bend 32; LThigh Bend –41; RThigh Bend –41; LUpper Arm Bend –84; RUpper Arm Bend –84; LWrist Bend 53; RWrist Bend 53; Lower Neck Bend –13; Tail (1, 2, 3, 4) Bend –45, –13, 23, 33; Upper Neck Bend –32.

Posed Horse Head

There are no controls that affect the Horse Head's features.

Posed Raptor Models

The Raptor is a nasty beast, with claws that tear and teeth that feast. See Figure 6.16.

FIGURE *Dinosaur lovers will spend a lot of time posing the Raptor model.*
6.16

The Velociraptor was unknown to the general public until Stephen Spielberg immortalized it in the film *Jurassic Park*. Now it's known the world over as an ancient dragon with a voracious appetite, and the means to get what it wants. The Poser 4 Velociraptor is extremely posable, with both Body and Head parts that can be moved to communicate all of the sinister messages you can think of. See Figure 6.17.

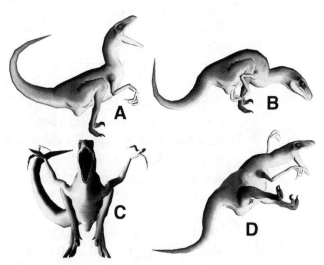

FIGURE *A. Haunch Sit. B. Sniff. C. Prepare Pounce. D. REar Up.*
6.17

Explore the settings detailed for the Raptor poses in Figure 6.17, and then create your own poses for this exquisite model. When you create poses that you like, be sure and save them to the Poses library.

A. **Haunch Sit**. (Claws and Fingers not altered for this example). Abdomen Default; Chest Bend 24; Head Bend –30; Mouth 1.2; Hip Default; LFoot Bend 9; LForearm Bend –121; LHand Bend 59; LShin Bend 124; LShoulder Bend 28; LThigh Bend –93; LToes (1 and 2) Default; RFoot Bend 9; RForearm Bend –121; RHand Bend 59; RShin Bend 124; RShoulder Bend 28; RThigh Bend –93; RToes (1 and 2) Default; Neck 1 Bend –53; Neck 2 Default; Tail (1, 2, 3, 4) Bend 27, 27, 60, 60.

B. **Sniff**. (Claws and Fingers not altered for this example). Abdomen Default; Chest Bend –67; Head Bend –30; Mouth 0; Hip Default; LFoot Bend 9; LForearm Bend –121; LHand Bend 59; LShin Bend 124; LShoulder Bend 28; LThigh Bend –93; LToes (1 and 2) Default; RFoot Bend 9; RForearm Bend –121; RHand Bend 59; RShin Bend 124; RShoulder Bend 28; RThigh Bend –93; RToes (1 and 2) Default; Neck 1 Bend –53; Neck 2 Default; Tail (1, 2, 3, 4) Bend –39, 27, 60, 60.

C. **Prepare Pounce**. Abdomen Default; Chest Bend 24; Head Bend –63; Mouth 1.35; Hip Default; LFoot Bend 9; LForearm Bend –121; LHand: Bend 59, Side to Side 26; LShin Bend 124; LShoulder Side to Side 41; LThigh Bend –93; LToes (1 and 2) Default; RFoot Bend 9; RForearm (Twist, Side to Side, Bend) –80, 40, 30; RHand: Bend –59, Side to Side –26; RShin Bend 124; RShoulder Side to Side –41; RThigh Bend –93; RToes (1 and 2) Default; Neck 1 Bend –88; Neck 2 63; Tail (1, 2): Bend 27, 27 and Side to Side of 60, 60.

Use the Right Hand Camera to open claws and fingers on the Right Hand, and then use Symmetry Right To Left to pose the Left Hand.

D. **REar Up**. (Claws and Fingers not altered for this example). Abdomen Bend –68; Chest Bend –47; Head Bend –68; Mouth 1.4; Hip Bend –18; Feet 0; LForearm (Twist, Side to Side, Bend) 45, 7, –81; LHand (Twist, Side to Side, Bend) –6, –2, 18; LShin (Twist, Side to Side, Bend) 0, –5, 20; LShoulder (Twist, Side to Side, Bend) –141, –42, 6; LThigh (Twist, Side to Side, Bend) 11, 29, –71; LToes (1 and 2) Default; RForearm (Twist, Side to Side, Bend) 45, –7, 81; RHand (Twist, Side to Side, Bend) –6, 2, –18; RShin (Twist, Side to Side, Bend) 0, 5, 20; RShoulder (Twist, Side to Side, Bend) –78, 14, 47; RThigh (Twist, Side to Side,

Bend) 0, –50, –83; RToes (1 and 2) Default; Neck 1 Bend 35; Neck 2 Bend –37 ; Tail (1, 2, 3, 4) Bend 42, 20, 48, 32.

Posed Raptor Heads

There aren't many controls that tweak the Raptor's facial options; in fact, there are just two: Jaw and Mouth. Jaw is a strange control. It causes the jaw to elongate and jut upward at negative settings, and at positive settings. Mouth controls the opening and closing of the mouth. See Figure 6.18.

Leave the Raptor Jaw setting at .5 to 1, because a little overbite displays the gnashing teeth much more clearly.

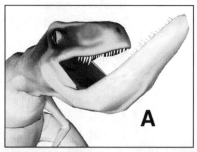

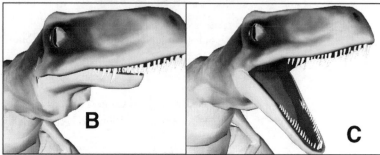

FIGURE **6.18**   *A. With the Jaw setting at –7; even though the Mouth setting is 0, the Jaw rotates upward and out. B. A Jaw value of 4 is just as strange, making the lower Jaw shorter, giving the Raptor a serious overbite. C. .75 is about the best large open mouth setting. Negative Mouth settings do nothing.*

Posed Raptor Hands and Feet

The Raptor is one of the few Animal models that has posable hands. There are three Claws and three Fingers on each hand that can be posed. Unfortunately, there is no control that allows you to Grasp, with all appendages working at the same time, so you have to pose each Finger and Claw separately. See Figure 6.19.

FIGURE *Three different poses of a Raptor Hand, with Fingers and Claws set to different*
6.19 *values.*

You should spend some time trying to create different poses for the Raptor's Hands, saving the ones that might be useful in later projects to the Poses library. You'll find that the Bend Parameter is the most useful control in posing the Fingers and Claws.

Although the Raptor has three toes on each Foot, the Parameter only lists two controls: Toe 1 and Toe 2. Toe one controls the two main toes, while Toe 2 controls the terrible tearing claw on the Foot. See Figure 6.20.

FIGURE *Here are three views of the Right Foot with its three clawed toes, set to different*
6.20 *Bend values.*

External Animal Models

The Zygote Media Group, the same developers responsible for the design of all of the Animal and Human models shipped with Poser 4, offer addendum CD collections bursting at the seams with alternate Poser 4 content. Animal models are included, greatly extending the professional capacity and the sheer enjoyment of working in Poser 4. That being the case, we would be remiss not to dwell on the Zygote Extra Animals in this chapter. I can't imagine any dedicated Poser 4 user not wanting to add the Zygote Animals and other Zygote content to their Poser 4 creative reservoir.

The Zygote CD contains Human and Animal Models, Motion Files, and Props and Accessories. The CDs allow you to unlock the libraries as you pay to do so and you receive a key code. For information on pricing and availability, contact Zygote at www.zygote.com. You can also contact Zygote at 801-375-0553, or 888-3DMODEL.

THE ZYGOTE ANIMALS

The Zygote Animal models we will dwell on here include the Bass, Bear, Buck, Chimpanzee, Cow, Doe, Frog, Killer Whale, Lion, Penguin, Shark, Wolf, and Zebra. This greatly expands the possibilities for Animal scenes and animations in Poser 4. It also adds a number of additional customized Animal options, as we shall detail later in this chapter.

CAUTION

Karuna! *If you have the Zygote Animal models, use the detailed posing information that follows as a guide for posing. After that, explore your own customized settings, saving out poses that look good to your Poses library, in a new folder you will create called Zygote Animals.*

Posing the Zygote Bass

The Zygote Bass model consists of five Fins, three Body parts, and the Head. The only Head features that can be manipulated are Mouth Open and Mouth Closed. Mouth Closed works like the Jaw parameter on the Raptor, elongating or shortening the lower jaw. To explore the poses for the Zygote Bass, adjust the Parameter Dials for each of these items. See Figure 6.21.

FIGURE *A. Mouth Open 1.0 (other elements at default). B. Body 3 Bend –38, Body 4*
6.21 *Bend –23, Tail Fin Bend –23, Head: Twist 40, Side to Side –34, Bend 56.;*
Mouth Open 3.5, Mouth Closed 4.7.

Posing the Zygote Bear

The Bear model can be both Body and Head posed. The Head includes Parameter Dials for controlling the Snarl and the openness of the mouth. You might be better off applying just a color instead of a texture map when posing the Bear with stretched-out limbs, since this can cause strange anomalies in the texture map. See Figure 6.22.

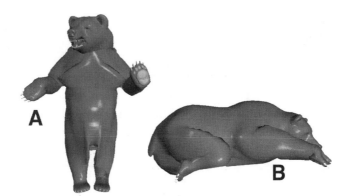

FIGURE *A. Bear Stand. B. Bear Sleep.*
6.22

CAUTION

Karuna! Use the following settings to pose the Zygote Bear model, and save the poses to the Poses library, in a new folder called Animals. Then customize the settings in order to form new poses of your own.

A. **Bear Stand.** Neck Bend 88; Head Side to Side –25; Snarl 2; Mouth 0; L&R Thigh Bend 65; R&L Shoulder: Side to Side and Bend are –37, 60 and 37, 60; L&R Forelegs Bend –62; LFrontFoot Bend 0 ; RFrontFoot Bend 125 ; Abdomen Bend 15. All other parts at defaults.

B. **Bear Sleep.** L&R Shoulder Bend –77; L&R FrontFoot Bend 83; Head Side to Side –12; Mouth Open –3; L&R Thigh –70; L&R Shin 122; L&R BackFoot Bend 52. All other parts at defaults.

Posed Bear Heads

The Bear's Head can be posed to communicate a small range of emotions by using the Parameter Dials to Open and Close the Mouth, and to set the value of the Snarl. See Figure 6.23.

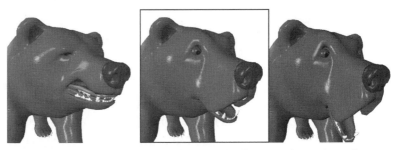

FIGURE *From left to right: Snarl 2 and Mouth Closed .75; Snarl –2 and Mouth Open*
6.23 *1; Snarl –3, Mouth Open 2, and Mouth Closed –1.*

The larger the Snarl Value, the more closed the eyes of the Bear. Negative value Snarls open the eyes and also drop the jowls.

Posing the Zygote Buck

The Zygote Buck model has legs and body sections that can be modified. As far as the facial features, only the ears and eyes can be altered. The Buck is perfect for adding interest to a Poser 4 woodland scene. See Figure 6.24.

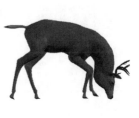

FIGURE **6.24** *From left to right: Close–up of the Buck's Head with a Bend of –50, and Ears altered by Side to Side of 30; Head Side to Side –50 and Bend –3, Ears Side to Side 30 and Bend 75; Front Legs bent naturally by leaving IK on, neck Low/Mid/Upper Bend 75, 20, 35. Head Bend 35.*

TIP

When you are bending the front of an animal, such as making it bend to drink or eat, leave Inverse Kinematics (IK) on for the front feet. This way, when you bend the front part of the body, the front legs will respond naturally. You can turn IK off later for more freedom in posing other parts of the body.

Posing the Zygote Chimpanzee

The Zygote Chimp is a model that many Poser 4 users will overuse, because it is crafted so realistically. The Chimp is also perfect for Walk Designer sessions, since its body shape so closely resembles the human shape and appendages (see Chapter 14, "The Walk Designer"). The Chimp has fully articulated hands and feet that can splay apart and grasp items. The Head can be posed by altering the Mouth Open and Closed settings, as well as by adjusting the eyes. See Figure 6.25.

Threatening. Leave IK on, and move body down from waist. The knees will bend automatically. Right and Left Shoulder, Bend –60 and 44. Right and Left Forearm, Bend –53 and 40. Mouth Open 4.2.

Knuckle Walk. Abdomen Bend 90. Head Bend –75. Right and Left Shoulder Front To Back 50 and –88. Right and Left Forearm Side to Side,

FIGURE *From left to right: Threatening, Knuckle Walk, and Sitting.*
6.25

–24 and –30. Left and Right Thigh and Shin Bend –15 and 70. Right and Left Foot Bend –44 and –12.

Sitting. Abdomen Bend 90. Right Thigh/Shin/Foot Bend –40, 70, –25. Left Thigh/Shin/Foot Bend –46, 77, –12. Right Shoulder: Twist –27, Front to Back 50, Bend 46. Right Forearm: Twist –47, Side to Side 54, Bend 30. Right Hand: Twist –117, Bend 47. Left Shoulder: Twist –72, Front to Back –64, Bend –122. Left Forearm: Twist 31, Side to Side –43, Bend –91. Left Hand: Twist –6, Side to Side 30, Bend 3.

Posing Chimp Hands

The Chimp's hands are super-posable, with all of the finger and thumb joints included. But the most startling feature concerning posing the Chimp's hands is that they respond suitably well to being automatically posed by assigning them Hands from the Hand Poses library. Because the Chimp has some finger and thumb dimensions that are different from human hand proportions, you may have to tweak the results after assigning a posed Hand. But that beats having to pose the Chimp's Hands one digit at a time. See Figure 6.26.

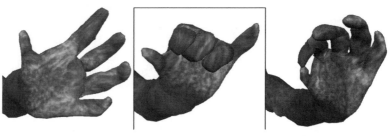

FIGURE *From left to right: Splayed Fingers using the Side to Side controls, "Call Me"*
6.26 *from the Hand Poses library, and "OK" from the Hand Poses library.*

Posing Chimp Heads

You don't have a lot to work with when you want to manipulate the Chimp's facial expressions. All that's possible is to open or close the Mouth, and to move the Eyes. Surprisingly, these limited alterations can still create a number of expressions. Try the settings in Figure 6.27, and then explore your own alternatives.

FIGURE *Left to right: Closed Mouth and Eyes rolled upward 23 degrees as if musing;*
6.27 *Eyes Side To Side −40, and Mouth Closed −2.7 creates a look of semi–surprise;*
         Left and Right Eyes Side to Side −40 and 40, Mouth Open 2.2, and Mouth
         Closed 2.4. The result is this rather silly look.

Posing the Zygote Cow

Being surrounded on all sides by farms where I live, I can attest to the fact that cows have two main poses: eating and standing around. The only other pose that sometimes intervenes is what they do when rain threatens, which is to lay down wherever they are. This being the case, you should work to master the three main cow poses: Eating, Standing Around, and Laying Down. See Figure 6.28.

Unique among the Poser 4 Animal models, the Zygote Cow has seven Tail sections. This allows for some fancy tail posing.

FIGURE *The three main cow poses: Eating, Standing Around (with the Tail in a strange*
6.28 *loop), and Laying Down. Using these images as an example, pose your Zygote*
         Cow model accordingly.

Karuna! *You can usually get away with stretching an Animal's neck on the Z axis up to 130%, if its Head has to be closer to the ground while foraging.*

Posing the Zygote Doe

Refer to Figure 6.24, the Zygote Buck, and the settings detailed in the caption, to pose the Zygote Doe. Most of the same settings are used here. See Figure 6.29.

FIGURE **6.29** *From left to right: Close–up of the Doe's Head with a Bend of –50, and ears altered by Side to Side of 30; Head Side to Side –50 and Bend –3, Ears Side to Side 30 and Bend 75; Front Legs bent naturally by leaving IK on, Neck Low/Mid/Upper Bend 75, 20, 35. Head Bend –60.*

Posing the Zygote Frog

The Frog is the only amphibian in the Zygote Animal Models collection. It's a big fat bullfrog, so make sure to place it on a lily pad, or maybe along the edge of a murky swamp. See Figure 6.30.

FIGURE **6.30** *The Zygote Frog, posed as detailed left to right: Head Bend –35, Mouth Open 3.6, Mouth Closed 3.9, Eyes resized to 150%; : Head Bend –35, Mouth Open 7, Mouth Closed 19, Eyes resized to 250%; : Head Bend –35, Mouth Open 0, Mouth Closed 5, Eyes resized to 75%.*

Input these settings for the Zygote Frog model to get these poses. Then alter them to explore other useful poses.

Be sure to explore posing the Frog's Hands and Feet, since fingers and toes can be manipulated.

- Use the Side to Side Parameter Dials when you need to splay the Fingers or Toes.
- Use the Bend Parameter Dials to open and close the Fingers or Toes.

See Figure 6.31.

FIGURE   *Using the Side to Side and Bend Parameter Dials, the Frog's Fingers and Toes*
6.31   *can be individually posed.*

Posing the Zygote Killer Whale

To pose the Killer Whale, you need only alter any of the four body sections: the Head, and three Fins. The Head has posable Mouth Open/Mouth Closed settings. Always use the Killer Whale's texture map, unless you want it to look like another creature altogether. See Figure 6.32.

FIGURE   *From left to right: Mouth Open 1.2, Mouth Closed –9.5, and a Body 3 Bend of*
6.32   *–21; Body 1 and Head Bend of 40, Mouth Open 2, and Mouth Close 6; Body 1*
Side to Side –24, Body 2 Default, Body 3 Side to Side –47, Body 4 default,
Head Bend 30 and Side to Side –50, Mouth Open 4, Mouth Closed 6, Tail Fin
Bend –45.

Consider using the Killer Whale in a composite scene with the Dolphin, or even with the Shark.

Posing the Zygote Lion

The Lion is indeed King of the Beasts, and the Zygote Lion is as regal as they come. The Head has open and closed Mouth Parameters, and a Snarl. The Tail has four sections, and a separate Parameter for the Tuft at the end. Use the settings detailed to pose the illustrated figures, and then explore your own Lion poses. See Figure 6.33.

Roaring. Head Bend –63. Mouth Open 3.

Sitting. Head Side to Side –38 and Bend 34. Mouth Open 3. L&R Thigh/Shin/Ankle/BackFoot –5, –52, 160, 0 and L&R Shoulder 18. (front and back appendages are Symmetrical).

Rear Up. Head Bend 2. Snarl 2. Mouth Open 3. Four Tail section Bends 31,34, 38, 40. Tuft Bend 30. Abdomen Bend –45. Chest Bend –33. Right Thigh Bend –32. Left Ankle Bend 34. Left RearFoot Bend –25. Right Shoulder Bend 35. Right Forearm Bend –8. Other settings at their default position.

FIGURE *From left to right: Roaring, Sitting, Rear Up.*
6.33

Posing the Zygote Penguin

The Penguin has gotten a lot of commercial attention recently, appearing in a number of TV ads as the spokes-animal for this or that product. The Penguin reminds us of ourselves because it walks upright, and looks like it's always wearing a tuxedo. See Figure 6.34.

FIGURE *From top left to bottom: Look Down, Look Up, and Sit.*
6.34

Look Down. Head Bend 63; LShoulder: (Twist and Side to Side) –138, 35 (LShoulder at Symmetry); Abdomen Bend 60.
Look Up. Head: (Side to Side and Bend) –46, 59; Abdomen Bend 39; LR-Shoulder Side to Side 26 (LShoulder at Symmetry).
Sit. Head Bend –49; Abdomen Bend 66; Chest Bend 72; LRShoulder: (Twist and Bend) –88, –105 (LShoulder at Symmetry).

Posing the Zygote Shark

The Shark is a symbol of aggression for human beings. The Zygote Shark has all of the frightening aspects of its real world counterpart, including the ability to snap its gaping Jaws. See Figure 6.35.

 *Input these settings for the Zygote Shark model to get these poses. Then alter them to explore other useful poses.*

FIGURE *From top left to bottom: Attack, Swimming, Bite Tail.*
6.35

Attack. Head Bend –31, Mouth Open 3.

Swimming. Tail Fin Side to Side ; Body (4, 3, 2) Side to Side 31, –9, –26, 27.

Bite Tail. Tail Fin Bend –56; Body (4, 3, 2, 1) Bend –39, –68, –60, –3; Head Bend 51; Mouth Open 1.75; Mouth Closed –1.

Posing the Zygote Wolf

The Zygote Wolf can't be manipulated as finely as the Dog model, but it can be posed enough to emote some powerful features. The Head offers only the Ears for posing. See Figure 6.36.

FIGURE *Top left to bottom: Grrrrr!, Howl, and Sniff.*
6.36

Input these settings for the Zygote Wolf model to get these poses. Then alter them to explore other useful poses.

Grrrrr! Neck 1 Bend 77. Head Bend 73, Tail 1 Bend –50, Mouth Open 1.

Howl. Neck 1 Bend –17. Head Bend –69, Tail 1 Bend –30, Mouth Open –.3, Mouth Closed .09, R Thigh Bend –30, L&R Shoulder Bend –2, –28.

Sniff. Neck 1 and 2 Bend 81, 31. Head Bend –66, Tail 1 Bend –30, Mouth Closed .8, R Thigh Bend –14, Waist Bend 6, Chest Bend 12 (IK on for L&R Front Legs).

Posing the Zygote Zebra

Karuna! *Without a texture applied, you can use the Zebra as another Horse model.*

The Zygote Zebra can be placed in a scene with the Lion, as long as it's far away enough not to become the Lion's breakfast. As with other Animals, its main Head posing feature are the Ears, which along with the Tail, can be forced to twitch to ward off the flies. See Figure 6.37.

Input these settings for the Zygote Zebra model to get these poses. Then alter them to explore other useful poses.

Looking Your Way. Tail bend (1, 2, 3, 4) –28, 0, –21, –29. Lower/Upper Neck Side to Side –39, –11. Head Twist/Side to Side/Bend –13, –29, –15. **Grazing**. Tail Bend (1, 2, 3, 4) 60, 60, 50, 40. Head Bend –63. Lower/Upper Neck Bend 83, –7. Increase the Z Scale of both the Upper and Lower Neck to 135, so the Head reaches closer to the ground. **Resting**. Tail Bend (1, 2, 3, 4) 60, 60, 50, 40. Head Bend –6. Right Shoulder/UpperArm/Forearm/Hand Bend 60, –117, –143, 58. Left Shoulder/UpperArm/Forearm/Hand Bend 2, –120, 75, 58. R&L Thigh/Shin/Ankle/Foot Bend 0, –79, 165, 0.

FIGURE *Left top to bottom: Looking Your Way, Grazing, and Resting.*
6.37

Assigning Human Characteristics to Animals

If you are creating a cartoon for a children's show, or art for a children's storybook, posing animals as if they were mimicking humans might be of high interest to you. In all cases, because of the way that the Animal model is articulated, there is no global guarantee that you can simply select a pose from the Poses library and apply it to an Animal. Sometimes this works, and sometimes it causes bizarre results.

In general, there are two ways to transform animal poses into a more human look:

1. Use a pose from the People Poses library on the animal. Note that you will have to tweak the results by hand, because animal anatomy is probably going to warp a bit in the attempt to fit the pose.
2. Resize or rescale one or more of the animal's appendages or extremities to mimic human arms and legs. This is sometimes very effective, though it works better for some animals and not for others.

Whatever human pose you assign to an Animal model, rest assured that you will have to fine-tune it by hand. See Figure 6.38.

FIGURE **6.38**   *Human poses assigned to the Chimpanzee model, and then fine-tuned a little by hand. From left to right, top to bottom: Model Stance, Superhero Landing, Yess Masster, Flying Kick, and Lunge.*

Animals that have some similarity to the human anatomy and that can be made to easily stand upright are the best choices for emulating human characteristics. These Poser 4 models include the Raptor, Chimpanzee, Penguin, and, to some extent the Bear, Cat, and Dog. The Dolphin is in a special category because of its historical symbol as a guide of the sea.

CUSTOMIZING ANIMAL MODELS

At first glance, even after purchasing the Zygote Animal Models, it seems that you will have a total of 18 Animal models to populate your Poser 4 scenes. You actually have a lot more than that, because each Animal model can be customized. In Chapter 7, "Composited Figures," we'll explore ways to customize models by compositing them with other models. However, there's even a simpler way to create customized models, as we already started to explore in Chapter 3, "Posing and Customizing the Human Body," with the human figure. Animal models can also be customized by using two basic Parameter Dial ranges or Editing Tools: Tapering and Resizing. Add some rotation when it's called for, and you can expand your Animal collection by a multiple of 10 or more.

Using these two parameter attributes, you'll be surprised at how many Animal model variants you'll be able to create. True, some will be fantasy creatures, but all will differ from the original Animal represented. As we present some examples for each of the 18 Animal models, we are not suggesting that our examples exhaust the possibilities. On the contrary, after following our illustrated examples, you should strike out on your own. Save your new creations to an Altered Animals library for future use.

All Poser 4 models, including Animals, can also be customized by mapping alternate textures to them, or using just a color map. See Chapter 17, "Handshaking," for more details on this and related possibilities.

In all of the customized Animal models shown in the illustrations that follow, we will use three modification tools in succession: Tapering, Resizing (globally or along a singular axis), and Rotation. The exact Parameter Dial values will not be given, because by now, you should be quite familiar with the principles involved. You should be able to look at the illustrated examples, read the basic caption, and apply the parameter changes shown for each customized Animal model. The object here is to test your knowledge of all of the material that we've covered so far, especially the Parameter Dial modifications. Look at the altered models, and see how well you can match them by adjusting the body part values. If you find something even more interesting along the way, so much the better. Save your new models to the Figures library in a new folder.

Karuna! *It is very important that you realize that setting extensive tapering, rotations, or resizing will deform your models. The trick is to do it just enough to get what you want without causing the model to become a chaotic jumble. You can only master this technique through experimentation, experience, and by watching the model views carefully.*

The Customized Cat

The Cat Animal model is very cute, representing a friendly tabby pet. Some of the modifications that can be applied, however, will definitely alter the Cat's personality. See Figure 6.39.

FIGURE *From left to right: Snagglefooted Catwallah, Snaprax, Tabbis (mapped with*
6.39   *Chimp texture).*

The Customized Dog

See if you can figure out how the standard Dog model was transformed into these other dog types. Save the customized Dogs you discover along the way. See Figure 6.40.

FIGURE *From top left to bottom: Poochus, Daaschund, Foohound.*
6.40

The Customized Dolphin

The Dolphin model is related to all of the strange fish shown here. Look at the illustrations, and try to emulate these forms. See Figure 6.41.

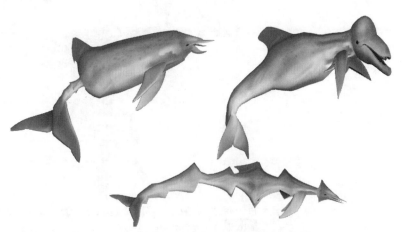

FIGURE *From top left to bottom: Wormtailed Thrasher, Gray Brainwhale, Cambrian*
6.41 *Rivergar.*

The Customized Horse

You might think that there's nothing much you can do with the horse, but take a look. Study these illustrations, and try to develop the figures. See Figure 6.42.

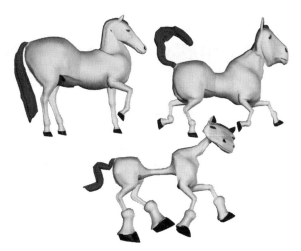

FIGURE *From top left to bottom: Trojanus, Hobart's Equimax, Horzee.*
6.42

The Customized Raptor

The Raptor may be one of our dim ancestors. At any rate, it has a definite disposition, and dislikes being ordered around. All manner of related beasties can be shaped from its parts. Look at the illustrations, and try to shape a Raptor like the versions represented. See Figure 6.43.

FIGURE *From top left to bottom: Scissorsaur, Spider-armed Spoonbill, Kangasaur.*
6.43

The Customized Bass

A lot of folks love to go Bass fishing, but few anglers would want to catch any of these bass cousins. See if you can tell which Parameters were altered to create these models, and apply the changes to your Zygote Bass. See Figure 6.44.

FIGURE *From top left to bottom: Jim's Gooberskark, Northern Clampmouth, Headerfish.*
6.44

The Customized Bear

Whether we think of the bear as a cave dweller in the deep woods, or as the more placid animal involved with the circus, there is little question that the bear demands our respect. The Bear models represented here are variations of the Zygote Bear model. Look at them carefully, and try to make your bear resemble what you see illustrated in these customized variations. See Figure 6.45.

FIGURE *From top left to bottom: Piggy-bear, Giant Bear-sloth, Miniature Shagbear.*
6.45

The Customized Buck

The Buck is a symbol of freedom in the forest. The variations we can create from the Zygote Buck model are numerous, with the illustrated figures being a few examples. Investigate customizing the Buck model, using these figures as a beginning blueprint. See Figure 6.46.

FIGURE *From top left to bottom: Beaver-Tailed Naxod, Pink-eared Sloof, Horned Ebex.*
6.46

The Customized Chimpanzee

The Zygote Chimp is the Animal model closest to the human form, and one of the most fun to customize. See if you can discover how the parameters were varied by looking at these figures, and then apply the same alterations to your Chimp model. See Figure 6.47.

FIGURE *From left to right: Gorillax, Bavarian Troll, Furry Hedrus.*
6.47

The Customized Cow

Perhaps these customized Cow models only appear in dream pastures, but they are interesting. Spend some time looking at the figures, and then apply what you see to the Cow model parameters. Save the creations you enjoy. See Figure 6.48.

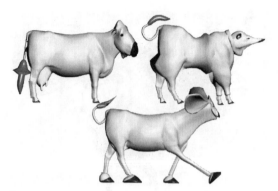

FIGURE *From top left to bottom: Monrovian Flat-faced Bovus, Mouse-nosed Harg,*
6.48 *Russian Mousecow.*

The Customized Doe

Even the gentle Doe can undergo a personality overhaul, when customized
with the Parameter Dials. See exactly how in these examples, and then apply
what you see to the Zygote Doe. See Figure 6.49.

FIGURE *From top left to bottom: Mule-faced Cameray, Upright Thamper, Wing-eared*
6.49 *Rooney.*

The Customized Frog

The deep-throated frog can be heard in the spring, croaking its song to the
night. But what does it really look like? We think we know, but maybe it resembles one of these Zygote Frog variations. After looking at these illustrations,
see if you can tweak the Parameter Dials to create similar creatures. See Figure
6.50.

FIGURE *From top left to bottom: Common Bulgix, Martian Sandfoo, Shapiro's*
6.50 *Egophibian.*

The Customized Killer Whale

The Killer Whale model from Zygote is as real as models can get, especially
with its texture applied. But there are other modified creatures waiting to be
born from this form. Here are a few. Look at them and try to figure out how
these results were achieved by altering the Parameter settings. See Figure 6.51.

FIGURE *From top left to bottom (with no Killer Whale texture applied): Bulbous-headed*
6.51 *Seapoot, Western Blobwhale, Torpedo Fish.*

The Customized Lion

If the Lion decides to wear another personality, who is going to argue with him?
Take a look at these customized Zygote Lion models, and see if you can create
them. See Figure 6.52.

FIGURE
6.52   *From top left to bottom: Irish Swamplion, Giant Lionarg, Lionette.*

The Customized Penguin

There are just a few animals that can live in the cold reaches of the planet. Polar bears and penguins come to mind as the two most well known. The penguin has always been seen as a proxy human being, since it walks upright with a decidedly Charlie Chaplin gait. The Zygote Penguin model for Poser 3 captures all of the lovable characteristics that the penguin possesses. We've taken more than a few liberties to customize the Penguin model into a wider range of creatures. See if you can tell how these new models were constructed from the standard Zygote Penguin, and then apply your learning to the Zygote Penguin on your system. See Figure 6.53.

FIGURE
6.53   *Note that the Penguin texture was not used on these customized models. From left to right: Wrenthrax, Eastern Blue Pigeon, Samoan Jily-Jily.*

The Customized Shark

The Shark rules the sea, intimidating most of the other inhabitants. Just look at the variety of customized creatures born from the Zygote Shark model. Try to customize your Shark model in the same ways that are illustrated here. See Figure 6.54.

FIGURE *From top left to bottom: Needle Shark, Bubblehead, Posersaurus.*
6.54

The Customized Wolf

The Wolf is a dog with a serious attitude. These canine cousins of the wolf were customized from the Zygote Wolf model. Investigate the illustrations, and when you're ready, customize your own Wolf model in the same manner. See Figure 6.55.

FIGURE *From top left to bottom: Bat-eared Lubock, Wild Fragdog, Brazilian Rock*
6.55 *Camel.*

The Customized Zebra

CAUTION

Karuna! Strong patterned textures, like that of the penguin and the Zebra, sometimes work against you when you're customizing a model. That's because we recognize these and other strong patterned creatures by their pattern as well as their shape. Explore other patterns as textures, or just use color. See Chapter 17.

The Zebra is known for its stripes. Underneath those stripes is a beautiful equine animal, a wild cousin of the horse. Customizing the Zygote Zebra model is similar to customizing the Horse. Try your hand at applying customization modifications that cause the Zebra to resemble the customized Zebra figures shown here. See Figure 6.56.

FIGURE *From top left to bottom: Longfaced Fragus, Two-footed Equiz, It-Ain't-Trigger.*
6.56

Deforming Animal Models

If you have read and worked through the Poser 4 documentation that concerns Grouping, Deformation with Magnets and Waves, and Spawning Morph Targets, and have read through the same material as presented so far in this book, then you have a good grasp already of the ways to modify any figure or prop in Poser 4. If you can deform human figures, you can deform animal figures—the techniques are the same. Just to recap the process, here's what it involves:

1. Select the body part of the figure you want to add a Deformation to.
2. If you want the Deformation to address just a section of that body part, then you have to set it up by using the Grouping process. If you want the Deformation to address the whole of that body part, no Grouping is necessary (in that case, skip step 3).

3. If you need to use the Grouping process, click on the Grouping Tool with the needed body part selected. Click on New Group and name it. Now take the mouse and click-drag a marquee around the area you want to target a Deformation to. When it lights up, you have defined the area, and can close the Grouping Window.

4. Add a Magnet or Wave Deformer from the Object menu. Select its Zone of Influence, and bring up the Properties window. In the Properties window, click Group, and find the name of the Group that is to be targeted. Close the Properties window, and configure the deform by adjusting the parameters for that Deformation object and tweaking it until you have achieved what you require.

5. Once the Deformation looks good, select the body part. Spawn a Morph Target, and name it as you like. It will appear as a Parameter Dial. You can now delete the Deformation object. Do this with as many deformations for the figure as you like, following the same procedure. When finished, save the figure to a Poser library or to another space on a disk. That's it. You are now a Deformation master of the Morphed Universe!

This exact process was used to create the following three customized Animal models in Poser 4.

THE ARCTURIAN RAT

This model starts with the Zygote Rat model. See Figure 6.57.

This is a rather basic model as models go. Its mouth doesn't open, but you get the creepy feeling that it is waiting for either cheese or your big toe. Okay, let's set about transforming it into another creature altogether, but one that still manifests some rat-like qualities. We are going to give it a horn on its snout, and a humpback. We'll make a few other alterations as well. Do the following:

1. For the horn, select the Head and go to the Grouping Tool. Create a separate Group called Horn that takes in just the tip of the snout. Create a Wave Deformer for that Group of polygons in the Wave's Zone Proper-

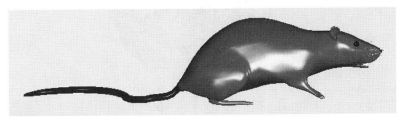

FIGURE *The Zygote Rat model is the starting point for our customized model.*
6.57

ties. Reduce the Zone so it covers just the top half of the Horn Group. You'll have to play around a bit here. Move the Wave object so that it starts to create a projection on top of the nose. Use a Triangular Waveform set at 1, with no Sinusoidal or Square components. Set Stretch to .5 or so. Move the Wave object until a horn-like feature starts to appear. Do a Spawn Morph for the Horn, and delete the Wave. You will now have the Horn Target Morph listed as a Parameter Dial for the Head. See Figure 6.58.

2. The Egyptians had a ceremony called "The Opening of the Mouth," and we are going to perform our own Opening Mouth ritual on the Rat. With the Head still selected, use the Grouping Tool to select just the lower lip of the Rat, naming the Group Mouth Open. Use a Magnet Deformer on the Mouth Group to rotate the Mouth open, and as before, Spawn a Target Morph and delete the Deformer. Voilà! Now you have a Parameter Dial called Open Mouth, and it works on a model that had no animated mouth possibilities. See Figure 6.59.

3. Select the Chest and create a Group for just the top 1/4 of it. Name it Hump, and use the Wave Deformer to create a smooth hump on the Rat's back. Use a Wavelength of 1.5, and experiment with the other set-

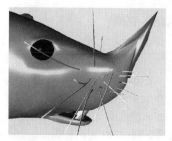

FIGURE *By moving the Horn Parameter Dial, the Rat gets a horn on its snout.*
6.58

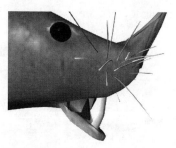

FIGURE *Now the Rat's Mouth can open and close, although the tooth stretches with it*
6.59 *because it was modeled that way. No matter, it still looks neat.*

tings. Spawn a Hump Target Morph, and delete the Deformer. See Figure 6.60.

4. For the rest of the model, we will use standard sizing operations instead of more Deformers. Scale the Right and Left Hand and the Right and Left Forearm to 200%. Make all but the first Tail section invisible, and use a Y Scale of 142 with a Taper of 490 on that Tail section. Pose this little bugger, and you will have created the famed Arcturian Rat. Save it. See Figure 6.61.

CAUTION

Karuna! *If you have to create Morph targets for smaller parts of a figure, and need to zero in on the geometry in a vertex-by-vertex way, then you should avoid using Poser 4's Deformation Tools. Instead, export the figure element to an external application (like RayDream), do what you have to do, and export it out of that application as an OBJ file. Import it as a Target Morph. This is the best way to do things like moving the eyelids or giving the lip a subtle twitch, things that the present version of the Deformation Tools are not equipped to handle. For more guidance on these procedures, be sure to read Chapter 20, "Hints and Tips from Master Users," and Chapter 22, "Advanced Poser Projects."*

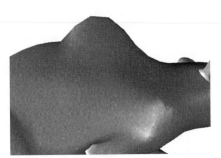

FIGURE **6.60** *Moving the Hump Parameter Dial creates a dromedary look for the Rat.*

FIGURE **6.61** *The fear-inspiring Arcturian Rat. Compare this to the original Rat model in Figure 6.57.*

MAKING CREATURES BREATHE

The Deformers are perfect for this task. Just select the Chest element of a human or beast. Create a Wave Deformer, and move it into place so that the Chest evidences a bulge (use a Waveform value of 1 and explore various Amplitudes to do this). Save it as a Morph Target. Now, by simply manipulating the Parameter Dial for that Morph Target, the Chest can heave rhythmically in and out.

MOVING THE IMMOVABLE

You can find a huge number and variety of nonarticulated Animal models in CD collections and on the Web in various places. These models were never meant to have animated parts, but you can use the Deformation options in Poser to create Morphs that make these creatures come alive. For things like rotating limbs, however, the model should be cut apart into its constituent elements in an external application and imported as a hierarchy. Using the cut-apart method for rotating limbs, and the Deformation Tools for more subtle movements, you can easily build a library of animatable creatures that your peers and audience will envy and admire.

Moving Along

If you have followed all of the examples presented in this chapter carefully, and have applied the detailed Parameters to each Animal's figure elements, then you are well on your way to mastering Animal poses and alterations in Poser 4. In the next chapter, we'll detail the compositing methods that you can apply to all sorts of models, creating some interesting hybrid characters in the process.

FIGURE *A trio of Zygote Gremlins astride their trusty Raptor steeds rides into the next chapter.*
6.62

CHAPTER

7

COMPOSITED FIGURES

What Is a Composited Figure?

When you were born, all of the genetic material that makes up the parts that are now you was taken from two sources, your mother and your father. That's how most of life works on this planet. Is it the same law for everywhere in the universe? We just can't be sure. Now imagine that you exist on a planet with a more multifarious life-generating law, one that admits multiple contributing parents in the procreation of the species. Well, that might mean that you would have father number seven's nose, mother thirteen's left eye, mother twenty's right eye, and so on. This is exactly what we mean by composited figures in Poser 4, because Poser 4 is its own planetary system with its own laws.

CAUTION

Karuna! Be sure to read the section on the Hierarchy Editor at the end of this chapter, since it can play an important role in your capacity to develop Composited Figures.

Composited Figures in Poser 4 can be created in several ways, including combining facets of all of these ways. In general, composites can be created by:

- Combining one or several parts from Poser figures into one amalgamated whole.
- Replacing elements of a figure with other figure elements, drawn from inside Poser. This is especially useful in creating cross-species composites.
- Replacing elements of a figure with other elements, drawn from outside of Poser and imported.
- Modifying elements of a figure with morphed elements (used mostly for Heads, but possible for their body parts as well).
- Completely replacing all of a figure's parts with either internal props or externally created imported objects.

Each of these compositing methods has rules and cautions, and moves from simple to complex. Let's look at each of them in turn.

CAUTION

Karuna! When you create a composited figure and want to save it out, DO NOT save it to the Figure library! All that will be saved is the selected figure, along with a misleading image of the composited whole, and not the composited figure(s) that is unselected. When you want to save out your Composited creations, save them as Poser 4 Project Files.

Internal Amalgamated Composites

In this composite method, items are added to the selected figure, without removing any of the elements of the figure itself.

SINGLE PROP COMPOSITES

What is a Prop? A Prop is any element in your Poser 3 scene that is not a part of any Poser figure. A Prop can be a sphere that acts as a ball, or a staircase that the figure navigates. There is also a more specific type of Prop, one which is attached via a hierarchy to a Poser 4 figure. If you attach the spherical ball to a figure's right hand for example, every time the figure moves its right hand, the ball will move with it. If you attach the figure to the stairway, other things are possible. You can set a walk motion in which the figure walks up the stairs without any problem. If the stairs are moved from one side of a room to the other, however, the figure will move along with them. All sorts of things are possible when Props are either the Child of a figure element, or the Parent. The first thing you need to do is to know how to add a Prop to the Document window.

To add a Prop to your Document window, do the following:

1. Go to the Props folder in the Library List (accessed by clicking on the list toggle at the right of the screen). See Figure 7.1.
2. Click on the Props item in the list. When the Props library folder appears, make sure the Prop Types listing is selected from the drop-down list. See Figure 7.2.

FIGURE **7.1**   *The Library List.*

FIGURE **7.2**   *The Prop Types listing shows the "Ball" as the first Prop object in the list.*

3. Double-click the Ball to add it to the Document window. After it's added, double-click the "Box" Prop below it to add it as well. Move the Box above the Ball in the Document window. Your Document window will now contain both Props, with the Box above the Ball, as displayed in Figure 7.3.

FIGURE *Your Document window now contains the Ball*
7.3 *and the Box Props.*

4. With the Box selected, bring up its Properties dialog (Edit/Properties). Click Set Parent, and make the Ball the Parent of the Box by selecting it in the Hierarchy list. See Figure 7.4.

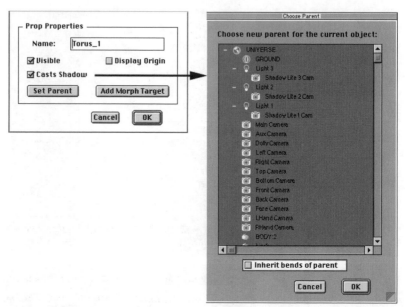

FIGURE *Make the Ball the Parent of the Box.*
7.4

The Ball is now the Parent of the Box. Rotate or Move the Ball, and the Box moves and rotates with it. Move or Rotate the Box, and nothing happens to the Ball, because it is not the Parent of the Ball.

You cannot cross-parent objects so that they are each other's parent. This would be highly incestuous anyway.

Congratulations! You have now mastered parenting a hierarchy, so anytime we simply say "Parent this object to that object," we will assume you know exactly what to do.

Basic Geometric Props

Basic Geometric Props include the Ball, Box, Cone, Cylinder, Square, Torus, and a selection of new Poser 4 items in the Prop Types folder inside of the Props library. Make sure you know how to access this location, and that all of these items are located there. With any human figure loaded in your Document window, do the following:

1. Add a Torus Prop to the Document window, and move it so that it rests over the waist of your human figure, like a belt. Resize the Torus as needed. See Figure 7.5.

FIGURE   *The Torus Prop covers the waist of the figure (in this case, the Zygote Baby) like*
7.5   *a belt.*

2. Now for parenting. What part of the figure's body should be the Parent of the Prop? What part of the body should control the Torus? That all depends on how you're going to manipulate the figure, and also on what

part of the figure is closest to the Prop. In this case, the Prop is closest to the Abdomen, so that might be the Parent to select. But the Abdomen is not the core element in the figure, the part that moves all of the other elements. That duty is left to the Hip. Parent the Torus to the figure's Hip. Now rotate or move the Hip, and the whole figure as well as the Torus should move and rotate along with it. See Figure 7.6.

FIGURE *Rotating and/or moving the Hip moves and rotates the whole figure, as well as*
7.6 *the attached Torus Prop.*

Now do this exercise all over again, but this time, move the Torus Prop over the Head like a hat. Parent the Torus Prop to the figure's Neck, because the Neck controls Head movements. We could also Parent it with the Head, but usually the Neck is adjusted to control the Head. Now, moving any other parts of the body that are Parents to the Neck (Chest, Abdomen, Hips) will also move the Torus Prop. See Figure 7.7.

FIGURE *The Torus Prop is now an attached Hat. The Torus moves and rotates with the*
7.7 *Neck.*

Any of the basic Props can be used in this same manner. You can even construct Prop "clothes" to encase most of a figure. See Figure 7.8.

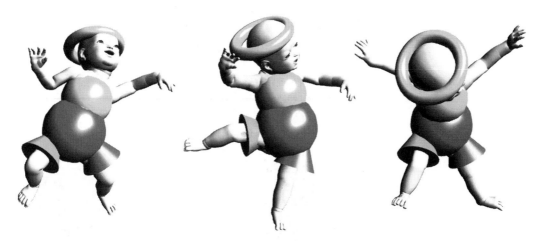

FIGURE   *Multiple basic Props used to encase the figure, with each one parented to appropriate parts of the body.*
7.8

Hair Library

Hair is a Prop that comes into the scene already parented with the figure's head. You can only add one hair Prop at a time from the Hair library, but hair Props in the Zygote "Hair and Hats" Props library allow you to add as many hair objects as you like. Note that Hair is automatically parented to the Head only when it is added from the Hair library, and not from the Zygote "Hair and Hats" Props library. Poser 4 adds new Hair models, and more can be found in the Zygote collections and CD collections from other developers. See Appendix D, "Poser Web Resource Sites," for a list of CD content developer information.

Karuna! It is highly recommended that you purchase the Zygote Extras libraries, so that you can add the new "Hair and Hats" Props, and also the new Hair folder to the Hair library.

Open the Hair library, and click on one of the Hair objects. In a matter of seconds, it will appear in your Document window, and may come in perfectly in place on the figure's head.

*The way to guarantee an instant placement of the Hair on the Head of your figure
is to avoid moving the figure around until after the Hair is placed. Use the Head
Camera to make fine-tuned adjustments to the position of the Hair.*

Each Hair Prop can be resized on any axis, so in effect, you have dozens of
unique hair styles made possible by these modification methods. See Figure 7.9.

Strange Modifications

You can try turning the Hair upside down, or tilting it on the side of a head for
some interesting personality transformations. See Figure 7.10.

FIGURE
7.9
*Any Hair element from the Hair library can instantly be altered to produce a
series of unique hair styles by simply resizing it on any axis, or globally. The
Zygote African American Casual model is depicted here.*

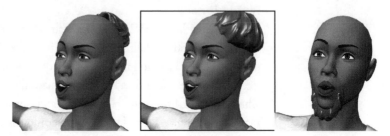

FIGURE
7.10
*Left to right: Hair sized at 30% and moved to the back of the head; Rotated
and placed over left ear; Flipped around and used as a beard.*

Hair from the Hair and Hats Folder in the Props Library

The main difference in using Hair from the Hair and Hats Props library, is that
you can use as many selections as you like. Not being limited to one clump of
hair makes the creation of all kinds of alternate looks and effects possible. See
Figure 7.11.

*You must manually make the Head the Parent of the Hair that comes from the
Hair and Hats folder in the Props library.*

FIGURE Left to right: Female Hair 3 from the Zygote Hair and Hats folder in the Props
7.11 library; Hair 3 and Hair 2 used together to create a double tinted look; Female
Hair 1, 2, and 3 used together for a triple tint.

Karuna! *Poser 4 also contains a number of Poseable Hair Props, allowing you to select a series of Parameter Dials to customize the look of the Hair by altering Morph
Target data.*

CAUTION

Zygote Hat Props

First, let's look at the Zygote Hair and Hats folder in the Props library again. If
you have not purchased the Zygote extras, then you can use a basic geometric
Prop as a stand-in. This time, instead of focusing on hair, we'll look at hats.
There are six hats in the Zygote Hair and Hats folder of the Props library: Baseball Cap, Baseball Helmet, Cowboy Hat, Helmet, Police Hat, and Top Hat.
Any hat you select has to be positioned in place, and the Head has to be selected as the Parent. See Figure 7.12.

FIGURE From left to right: A jaunty placement of the Baseball Helmet; The Cowgirl;
7.12 Law Enforcer.

Other Single Zygote Prop Composites

The difference between using a Prop and creating a Prop Composite is that the
Prop in a Composite has a Parent element that is one of the elements of a
model. A standard Prop might be a chair. A Prop Composite would be a hair or

hat object, or any other Prop attached by a Parental hierarchy to the selected figure. You can attach any Prop to a figure to make a Composite, although attaching a chair to a head may seem a little unusual to some viewers. A Zygote Mop Prop, on the other hand, can make a fine head of hair when turned upside down. See Figures 7.13 and 7.14.

You will often have to bury part of the Prop used in a composite in the figure itself, so take care how the figure bends so as not to expose the Prop.

FIGURE
7.13
The Zygote Mop Prop, from the Zygote Samples folder in the Props library, makes a fine head of hair on this Zygote Alien figure (from the Sampler Characters collection).

FIGURE
7.14
Another interesting Prop Composite uses the Zygote Pitchfork to add a quadruple antenna to the Alien's head.

MULTIPLE ELEMENT COMPOSITES

When we start to multiply the number of items, as well as the kind of items, that can be used to develop a Composited creation, the geometry of possibilities goes right through the roof. No more do we see Poser 4 as a simple application with a limited number of character sets, but instead are made to realize that the only limit to our capacities are the barriers we ourselves place on our creative intent, and our openness to possibility. This is what good creative software (and creativity in general) is supposed to do, to move us beyond the restrictions of our own limited belief systems, to push at the "rules."

Multiple Figure Composites

This section of the chapter introduces the use of Invisible Properties into the Composite mix. This is the most important of the Multiple Composite techniques, since you can use it to create some pretty spectacular beings without even using any Props. The general idea is simple: Combine the elements (or an element) of more than one Poser figure. To do this effectively, we'll have to introduce another option: Invisibility. Any selected element of a Poser 4 figure can be made invisible, simply by checking the Visibility box in its Properties dialog. See Figure 7.15.

A Vital Preparation

If it is your intention to combine multiple Poser 4 figures (models) into one, then you would do well to make some preparations beforehand. More than likely, you will be most interested in transposing the head, and possibly hands or feet, of one figure onto another, forming an interesting composite. To do this, the figure whose head you want to use should have all of its other elements made invisible (usually, you leave a neck in place as well). Instead of doing this

FIGURE   *By unchecking the Visibility box in any element's Properties dialog, that*
7.15   *element is made invisible in the Document window.*

rather tedious task each time you create a multiple figure composite, you can save a lot of effort by putting in some necessary preparatory work beforehand. Here's an approach that I took, because creating figure composites in Poser 4 is one of my favorite endeavors.

I looked at every head of every figure, People and Animal, that I found interesting. One at a time, I brought those figures into Poser 4, and proceeded to make Invisible (Properties dialog) all elements but those I wanted to work with. In the case of a figure's Head, I kept the Head, Eyes, and Neck parts. Everything else was marked as not visible. Then I created a separate directory in the Figures library called "Headz." After each figure was treated for visible/invisible elements, I saved out the Head and associated parts as a separate figure in my new Headz folder. This took about five hours, but in return, I now have a library collection of Heads that can be used to replace the head of any other figure. I did this with all of the internal models whose Heads I was interested in, and also with all of the Zygote extras. In my "Headz" folder are visible Heads for the following models: African American Casual Man and Woman, Alien, Asian Casual Man and Woman, Baby, Bass, Buck, Chimp, Dog, Dolphin, Frog, Heavy Man and Woman, Horse, Killer Whale, Lion, Old Man and Old Woman, Penguin, Raptor, Shark, Skull, Sumo, Wolf, and Zebra. This is quite a collection of heads!

When you have done the same thing with the models whose heads you want to use in composited figures, the steps to take for doing the actual compositing are simple to follow and remember.

1. With a selected figure already in your Document window (a figure whose body you will use in the composite), bring in the Head from your Headz folder that you want to use. Normally, this will be loaded as Figure 2.

2. Make the Head, Neck(s), and Eyes (if there are any Eyes listed separately) of Figure 1 invisible (Properties dialog).

3. Making sure that Figure 2 is highlighted in the Figures list, select Figure 2's "Body" element. This is because the Body must be selected (although it is invisible) for moving and rotation.

4. Move and Rotate the Head of Figure 2 (the figure whose Head you are using in the composite) until it is placed over the body of Figure 1 (the figure whose body will remain in the composite mix) in the correct orientation on its axis. Resize the new Head if necessary to suit the composited whole.

5. Select the lowest Neck of Figure 2, or select the Head if there is no Neck, and activate the Set Figure Parent command in the Figure menu. When

the dialog comes up, select Figure 1 for the figure and then whatever element is going to act as the Parent. For instance, if the Neck of the Head (Figure 2) needs a Parent, it is best to select the Neck of Figure 1 (the body). Note that a Parent does not have to be visible to still control the Child element. See Figure 7.16.

You can use the same technique to create a separate Figure library for Hands, Feet, and miscellaneous body parts such as Tails and Ears.

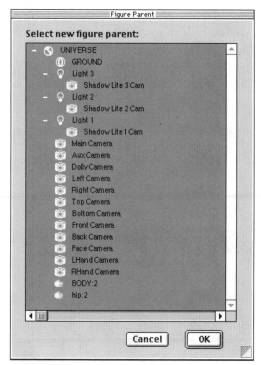

FIGURE   *To attach the figures together, you have to set the Parent hierarchy in the Set*
7.16   *Figure Parent dialog.*

Multiple Basic Prop Composites

We have already introduced the idea of Multiple Basic Prop Composites in Figure 7.8. Now let's push it a little farther. There are two ways to use Props in a composite relationship. The first is to simply Parent a prop to a hand, as if the hand were holding it. This is good for shields, weapons, and utensils of every kind. For instance, you could use this method to attach a broom to a figure's hands, and then pose the figure to sweep the floor. A sword could be parented to one hand and a shield to the other for a battle scene. The second way to utilize a Prop in a composite is to force it to substitute for a body part. One of the Heads from our Headz library could replace the head of a skeleton figure, creating a rather strange but definitely audience-attracting image (maybe just right for Halloween). See Figure 7.17.

If you want the Skeleton figure to show up more clearly on a white or light backdrop, color it a medium gray instead of its default cream-white.

TIP

If we take Figure 7.17 and add a Cane Parented to the Right Hand, a Ball Parented to the Left Hand, and a Cube parented to the Head, we have created a true multiple composite, using both the Head from an alternate source and three basic Prop sources. See Figure 7.18.

FIGURE *The Zygote Heavy Man Head replaces the Skeleton Head on a Skeleton body,*
7.17 *using the methods described previously.*

FIGURE *A more complex composited creation results when several different Props and*
7.18 *another Head are used.*

Two More Figure Choices

In the Additional Figures folder in the Figures library are two more figure types that we haven't covered yet: the Mannequin and the Male, Female, and Child Stick figures. You might think that these optional models are useful only for setting up poses, which they are, but they are also very useful when it comes to crafting composited models. Both the Mannequin and the Stick Figures are already composed of basic geometric elements, so modifying them by combining their geometries with more realistic elements, especially Heads, gives them a unique character. Use either the Mannequin or Stick Figures with a more realistic Head when you want to call attention to the Head, and also when you want to mystify your audience. Both of these options as bodies would also be great for crafting posed images for a children's storybook. See Figure 7.19.

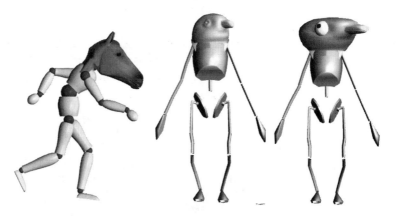

FIGURE *Left to right: The Mannequin with a Horse's Head attached; A Penguin Head*
7.19 *attached to a female Stick Figure; taper of –175 added to the Penguin's Head, with the Eyes resized to 700%.*

 *An advantage in working with the Mannequin and Stick Figures is that they render lightning fast. This makes them great for posing, and when your project is OK for it, also useful as body elements.*

Multiple Zygote Prop Composites

 Karuna! *The Zygote Animals, People, Props, and more are mentioned continuously throughout this book. If you don't have them, you can substitute other basic*
CAUTION *figure elements in their place. It is highly recommended, however, that you purchase the whole Zygote Extras collection at the earliest date possible, since it expands the uses that Poser 4 can be put to 10 times over.*

CROSS-SPECIES COMPOSITES

If you have been following along with the material on Composite Figure creation, then it's time for some visual learning. The next few pages display some of the myriad inventive creatures that are possible when you use these separated parts to build Multiple Figure Composites. By now, you should be able to look at these figures and understand how they are constructed. Most use the Zygote figures, so you will be somewhat at a creative loss if you don't have them yet. Look at the figures carefully for study, and also use them as a relaxing moment of eye candy. See Figures 7.20 through 7.22.

FIGURE **7.20** *There is no limit to the virtual genetic engineering that you can accomplish in Poser 4.*

FIGURE **7.21** *It's doubtful that your local zoo features any of these fine specimens.*

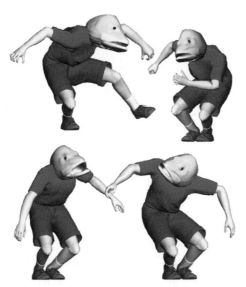

FIGURE *Poser 4 is an excellent resource when it comes to developing cross-species models.*
7.22

USING EXTRA HEADS AND HANDS

In the Additional Figures folder in the Figures library are four very important models that can play a large role in helping you create novel composite figures. There are two Heads, Male and Female, and two Hands, Left and Right. These are standalone elements, so no invisibility has to be applied. When you need to add a basic Hand or Head to another figure in the Document window, this is the place to shop for it.

What other types of scenarios might benefit from these elements? Well, there is no stopping you from adding as many Hands or Heads from this folder as your system memory will allow, remembering that each one can be posed separately. You can spread a number of posed Heads out on a table, stack them one on top of the other, or blend them together front to back. The same thing can be done with the Hands from this folder. Any multiple or configuration of these elements can be added quickly to your Document. See Figure 7.23.

INCORPORATING EXTERNAL FORMS

By "external forms," I mean any 3D element created in any non-Poser 4 application. Since Poser 4 can import 3D Studio, Wavefront, DXF, QuickDraw 3D, and RayDream formatted objects, you can use just about any 3D application to construct Poser 4 figure elements and/or Props. All 3D applications save out data in one or more of the formats that Poser 4 can import.

FIGURE **7.23** *This sculptured creation uses nothing but the generic Heads and Hands found in the Additional Figures folder in the Figures library.*

Karuna! *When possible, stay away from DXF content. It's a format every 3D application understands, but it's difficult to texture map correctly, and often it responds poorly to smoothing operations, leaving you with faceted object elements.*

It's obvious that you can use a 3D program outside of Poser 4 to create Props like chairs, pillars, and other environmental elements. We're confining our discussion here to composited figures, however, so that calls for some special attention in the 3D application you're using.

We are not spending time in this chapter talking about Poser 4's ability to handshake with RayDream Studio. That will be detailed in Chapter 17.

SEEING DOUBLE

With your Headz library folder filled with Head elements, you can easily assign multiple Heads, all separately controllable, to any figure in your Document. See Figure 7.24.

FIGURE **7.24** *Creating a Raptor with multiple Heads is easy, when you've saved out its Head-only element and read it back in, attaching the clone to the Raptor body.*

CREATING POSER 4 ELEMENT CONTENT

I am of the opinion that you will use Poser 4's native tools to create most of the bodies and heads you will need, and that any elements generated outside of Poser 3 will be mostly addendum Props and somewhat mechanical replacement parts for Poser figures. Added to this might be costuming elements, like suits of armor, headgear, and the like. This is not to say that you can't or shouldn't create organic elements outside of Poser; it's just that those elements will not be poseable like Poser's native body parts (at least not without a tremendous amount of hassle setting up complex Blend Zones). So let's focus our attention then on a project that you can handle in any 3D application for Poser 4 import.

RULES FOR BASIC ELEMENT DESIGN

There is no limit on the potential complexity of the elements that can be used to replace parts of a Poser 4 figure. Using an external 3D application, you can design as many customized parts for the Poser 4 figure as it has figure elements. In this way, you would import the parts into Poser 4, and then place them over the existing body elements. The original elements would be invisible, but they would act (and be assigned) as the Parents of the imported parts. Your beginning explorations in this area need not be this complex, however. All that you have to do is to minimize the number of elements used to replace the Poser figure's elements. How many unique parts, at a minimum, should you consider creating? Here's a simple solution:

- Create a unique "Head." The Head is always the focus of attention, so it should always stand out as a figure element. As a second, and sometimes better option, use a poseable Poser 4 Head as part of the new composite.
- Create one element to act as the Chest, Abdomen, Collars, Hands (but not the fingers), and Hip. This element can be resized so that it can be cloned and act as each of these three body parts.
- Create one element that will act as all of the Arm parts (including Hands and Fingers), and all of the Leg parts (excluding the Feet).
- Create another element that will serve as the Feet.

That's it! By creating five basic 3D forms in your favorite 3D application and porting them to Poser 4, you can create your own basic Poser 4D poseable figure.

A Total Figure Element Replacement Project

Here is one example of testing out the basic figure element design method we just discussed. Follow along, using your own favorite 3D application as the design environment.

1. Create a Head for your new model, or skip this step and add a Poser 4 Head once you're back in Poser 4.
2. Create one element that can be resized and cloned to use as the Chest, Abdomen, Collars, Hands (but not the fingers), and Hip. It can be as basic or as complex as your RAM will permit.
3. Create one element that can be resized and cloned for the Arm and Leg parts, including the fingers.
4. Create an object that can be used as the Feet. This same object can also be cloned to use as the Toes if need be.
5. Save out all of the elements in a format that Poser 4 can import (preferably as a Wavefront OBJ file, if your 3D application supports that format). See Figures 7.25 through 7.27.

I used Organica, a MetaBlock 3D design application from Impulse for this project. Organica is available for both the Mac and Wintel systems.

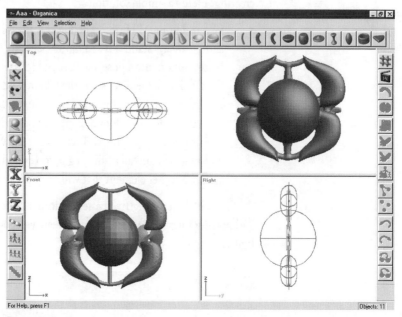

FIGURE *The main body element is created, and saved out as a 3D Studio format object.*

7.25

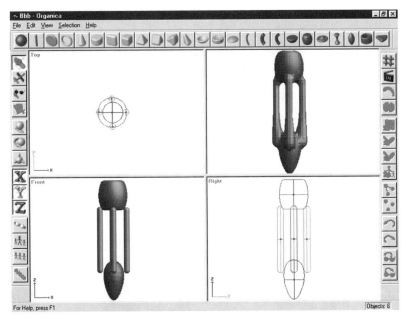

FIGURE   *The Arm and Leg element is created, and saved out as a 3D Studio format*
7.26   *object.*

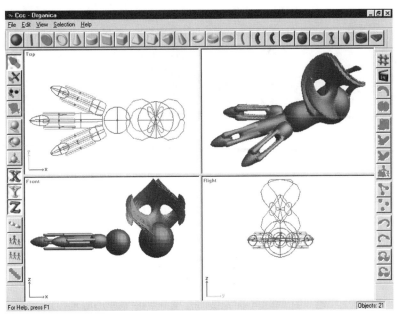

FIGURE   *The Foot element is created, and saved out as a 3D Studio format object.*
7.27

6. In Poser 4, import each of the elements you just created.

7. Import a figure whose Head you want to use, or import a previously saved Head from your Headz folder, or import a Head from the Additional Figures folder in the Figures library.

8. Import all of the other elements as many times as necessary to use as elements for all of the figures parts. Place each part in its proper orientation.

9. Parent each imported part with its control element on the Poser figure.

10. Make all of the original Poser elements invisible in their respective Properties dialogs.

That's it! If you have parented everything correctly, you can pose this new model to your heart's content, using the Parameter Dials. See Figure 7.28.

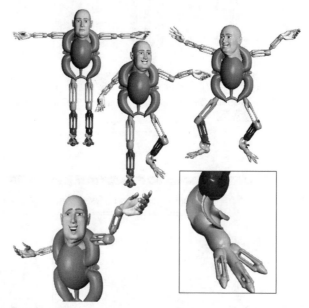

FIGURE **7.28** *Your new model with its imported elements can be posed by using the familiar Parameter Dials. Total weight of this file as a Poser 4 project is almost 18MB.*

CAUTION

Karuna! *Do not try this exercise unless you have at least 128MB of memory on your system. Even with that much memory and more, you may still run into trouble. Poser 4 is not optimized for large files, and it seems to make them much larger when importing objects. Multiple imported object files can severely tax your system, and it may crash. One way to conserve memory is to use only limited imported objects to do this exercise, so that one object might be used for the Chest, Abdomen, and Hip combined. Perhaps another might be used for the Shins, leaving the original figure's Thighs in place. Poser 4 will warn you when memory is low.*

RIDERS

Another type of Composite is any two or more figures that are connected to each other, but not blended together. A perfect example of this is a horse and rider, or any figure with another figure riding it (it could be a horse riding a person for variety). The most important consideration here is how the Parenting takes place, from what part to what part. This has important considerations for animation work, which we'll look at in Chapter 13, "Composite Character Animation."

As far as developing an interesting graphic composite that shows the Rider situation, there are a few cautions to observe:

1. Make sure the Rider is posed so that none of its parts are immersed inside of the transporting figure. This means posing legs more than anything else so that they are opened wide enough and at the correct angles. It's a good idea to place the Rider above the transpiration (Y axis) and to adjust the pose from there. That way, you can test the composite by dropping the Rider down until everything looks OK.

2. Think about using IK on both of the Rider's legs, and Parenting one or both feet to the body part of the Transporter that the feet are closest to. That way, you can make the Rider separate from the Transporter every once in a while to make it seem as if the Rider is bouncing. More on this in Chapter 13.

3. Give the Rider a little slouch, no matter if the transportation is an Animal or a Vehicle. Nobody sits up straight except robots, so a slouch looks more natural. See Figure 7.29.

FIGURE
7.29
Baby Sumo loves the Bear. Because the Bear has thick fur, it's OK to allow Baby Sumo to sink into it a bit.

TAIL TALES

Don't be restricted by what you think a standalone element is, and how it must or must not be used. Instead, try and look at all elements as having no defined purpose, and you'll be surprised what novel ideas come to mind. In Zen, this is called "Beginner's Mind," and to be creative in Poser, to push it to the edge, you have to approach your work with Beginner's Mind.

Let's assume that you have saved out an animal's Tail, making all of its other body parts invisible. You could apply the Tail to anything— another Animal, a Human model, or a Prop. But there is yet another use for a Tail object, many uses in fact, that have nothing to do with its being called a "Tail" at all. Instead of thinking of its name, think of its geometry, its shape. Of course, the Animal Tails you have saved out might be slightly different. The Raptor's Tail is very smooth and conical, while the Lion and Zebra Tails have tufts on the end. What do all of the Tails have in common? They are long elements that move from slightly wider at one end (in most cases) to thinner at the other, and they can be posed in a curve.

Can you think of any Animals that are long and shapely like the Tail, and have the ability to shape themselves in a curve? If you answered "Snakes," you have just seen the Tail with Beginner's Mind. Tales make very interesting Snake-like objects, and you can put any Head on the wider end that you prefer. See Figure 7.30.

FIGURE *Snake-like creations can be generated quite easily if you use a Tail as the*
7.30 *Snake's body.*

A Starfish of Tails

One unique model you can create quite easily from the Dog's Tail is a Starfish. Here's how:

1. Import the Dog, and make everything invisible except for its Tail parts. Save this as a figure called "Dogtail1" to a new folder in your Figure library called "Other."
2. Select New from the File menu, and import Dogtail1 five times.
3. Go to the Top View, and rotate four of the Starfish arms at increments of 72 degrees (72, 144, 216, and 288) on the Y axis. This forms a star shape made of Dog's Tails.
4. Place a Ball Prop in the center, and squash it on its Y axis, so that it flattens out. Make the Ball the Parent of all five Starfish arms. You can shape the arms by selecting any of the sections, but the first one, and rotating it. See Figure 7.31.

FIGURE *A Starfish created from Dog Tails is another example of a unique composite model in Poser 4.*
7.31

**Using the
Hierarchy**

When you need to Parent an object or make it invisible for compositing figures together, you will be presented with the Hierarchy list. It is very important that you are comfortable with using the Hierarchy list, for these and other reasons. Just as a reminder, to make anything invisible, just find it in the Hierarchy list and click on its visibility icon (the eye). It will disappear from sight in the Document window.

**Poseable
Clothes**

This is a brand new feature in Poser 4. You can find a selection of Poseable Clothes in the Figures/Clothing Male and Clothing Female libraries. Poseable Clothes are composed of articulated parts, just like a figure. First, after importing your Clothes selection to the scene, you position the Clothes over the figure, lining them up on all axis. Most times the clothes will pretty much snap into place over the figure, just like Hair. Next, with the clothes selected (you would select "Body" for the Clothes Figure), you select Conform To from the Figure menu. A window pops up that allows you to select the name of the Figure to conform the clothes to. See Figures 7.32 and 33.

You can always make a part of the underlying figure invisible if it protrudes where it shouldn't. Please note that Zygote and other developers are releasing more Poseable Clothes Libraries. See Figure 7.34.

You can also use the Conform To command when locking figure parts together to create composite figures. See Figure 7.35 as one example.

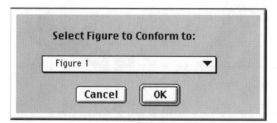

FIGURE *After selecting Conform To, you select the appropriate figure that will act as the*
7.32 *Parent to the Clothes from the pop-up window.*

FIGURE **7.33** *Select Poseable Clothes from the Figures/Clothing Male and Female libraries.*

FIGURE **7.34** *With an Overcoat added from the Male Poseable library and a Prop Hat, the personality of the Business Man model undergoes a change.*

FIGURE **7.35** *The Conform To command was used to lock the Mermaid bottom half to the Businessman top half. Unwanted parts of each figure were made invisible in the Hierarchy Editor.*

Prop Morphing

Unlike Poser 3, where Props were unalterable inside Poser, Poser 4 allows you to use Deformations on them just like you can on figure elements. Use the same Grouping and Morph Target Deformation Tools covered in previous chapters to augment the shape of any Prop. See Figures 7.36 and 7.37.

FIGURE **7.36** *This perfectly symmetrical three-legged stool has a Wave Deformer applied to it, giving it a very cartoony look.*

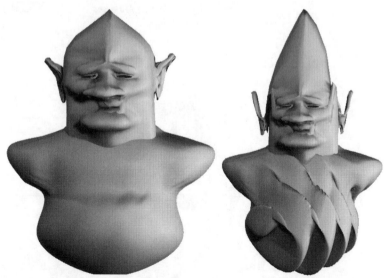

FIGURE **7.37** *On the left is a model sculpted in PLAY Inc's Amorphium, and exported to Poser as a DXF file. On the right is the same imported Prop with three Wave Deformers applied.*

Spawning Props   This is another exciting new feature in Poser 4. Simply described, this process allows you to create new Props by cutting away sections of any Props targeted. Here's how:

1. Load any figure or Prop you want to make a unique Prop from, and select the Grouping Tool.
2. Name the New Group whatever you like, and use the Grouping Marquee to select that part of the targeted figure or Prop the new Prop is to be generated from. If you are making a new Prop from the Head of a figure, it is best to consider making the new Prop from the entire Head. This is because stray polygons can cause some problems if you select only a part of the Head.
3. Select Create Prop, name it, and that's it. Your new Prop will be on the screen. See Figures 7.38 through 7.40.

FIGURE   *This Prop was created by selecting the entire Head of the Zygote Wolf.*
7.38

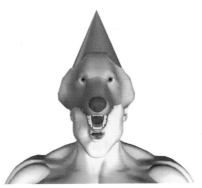

FIGURE   *The Wolf Head Prop can now be used as a headdress for any figure.*
7.39

FIGURE   *Exporting the Prop to Bryce as an OBJ file, it can be used to create an*
7.40   *interesting totem pole.*

Moving Along   In this chapter, you were invited to explore the creation and modification of
Composited figures. In the next chapter, we'll look at backgrounds and Props
in detail.

8

BACKGROUNDS, PROPS, AND RENDERING

When you create a Poser 4 animation or image, it looks rather incomplete if just placed against a single-color backdrop. Backgrounds and props add more than interest to your Poser 4 work, they add emotional and narrative context. Remember that if a picture is worth a thousand words, then a well-composed picture, one with other support elements placed in proximity to your main actors, is worth a million words. A story can be told in seconds by the visual relationships alone, so crafting multifaceted virtual worlds is always the artist's and animator's goal.

The Ground Plane

The Ground Plane is a rectangular plane that acts as the recipient for object shadows and also as the base upon which the actors stand or move. The Ground Plane is toggled on or off by selecting it from the Display menu under the Guides listing. If Ground Plane is checked, it's on, even though you may have selected a color that makes it seem invisible. One way to check for it is to move any figure or object in your scene in a negative Y-axis direction. If the Ground Plane is there, your selected item will start to dissolve as it travels beneath the Ground Plane.

QUESTIONS AND ANSWERS ABOUT THE GROUND PLANE

Here is a listing of general questions and answers that refer to the Ground Plane and its uses.

Can I see the Ground Plane from all Camera Views?

No. The Ground Plane remains hidden in the Front, Left, and Right Side Camera Views, but is visible in all other views.

Can the Ground Plane Be Rotated?

Yes. The Ground Plane can be rotated in all Camera Views in which it can be seen. Use the Turn Parameter Dial to rotate the Ground Plane on its Y (vertical) axis. When in the Dolly, Posing, Left/Right Hand, and Main Camera views, you can use the Trackball to rotate the whole scene, and the Ground Plane along with it. There are no independent controls for rotating the Ground Plane left or right, or back to front. For this reason, you can't use the Ground Plane as a wall, except if you reorient the whole scene after using the Trackball.

Can Items Emerge From Beneath the Ground Plane?

Yes! If you have a Ground Plane textured like water or colored blue, for example, you can place the Dolphin beneath it, and have it jump in and out of the virtual "water." To move something beneath the Ground Plane, move it on its negative Y axis. The only stipulation is that you must **Turn Shadows Off**, because objects below the Ground Plane cast shadows on the Ground Plane itself, leading to strange confusion for the viewer. When an object is placed below the Ground Plane, its shadow looks like a hole, colored in the shadow color, that sits on the Ground Plane.

Can the Ground Plane Accept Textures?

Yes. The Ground Plane will accept any single-picture textures in any of the formats that Poser 4 can read. In a future version of Poser 4, it would be nice to be able to assign movies to the Ground Plane. One of the best applications you can use to design Ground Plane textures is MetaCreations' Bryce, because of Bryce's texture realism. Usually, though, Poser content is ported to Bryce itself when realistic ground textures are required.

Can the Ground Plane Be Resized?

Yes. It can be resized on its X (Horizontal) and Z (in and out) dimensions. It has no thickness, so it can't be resized on its Y (vertical) axis. If you require a Ground that has discernible thickness (a dimension along the Y axis), then use a resized Box primitive or another imported object that has a flat surface upon which your actors can stand. The Ground Plane can also be resize-animated (see Section II).

CREATING PATTERNED GROUND PLANES

CAUTION

Karuna! The following information is not available in the documentation, but only in this book. Using this information will enable you to create stunning optical illusions.

You are not limited to the single Ground Plane Poser pretends to give you. With a simple trick, you can create an infinite array of multicolored or multitextured Ground Planes. Here's how:

1. Go to the Top Camera view. Check Ground Plane in the Guides listing in the Display menu.
2. With the Ground Plane selected, color and resize it until it covers about 1/4 of your Document window. Paste it to the Background.
3. Recolor, resize, and relocate it somewhere else. Paste it to the Background again.
4. Do this until you have created an interesting pattern of multicolored rec-

tangular shapes. Render the composition (making sure Background Picture is selected in the Render Options dialog), and save to disk. See Figure 8.1.

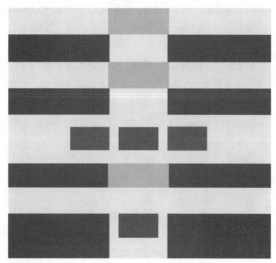

FIGURE *One example of a multiple Ground Plane pattern.*
8.1

Using "Paste to Background" techniques is one way you can use Poser 4 as a painting application to create bitmaps that can be applied to other Poser 4 elements.

OBLIQUE ABSTRACTED PATTERNS

The preceding method creates horizontal/vertical grid-like patterns. If you want to create oblique patterns using a version of the same method, do the following:

1. Make sure the Dolly Camera is selected. Turn on the Ground Plane from the Guides listing in the Display menu.
2. Use the Dolly XYZ, Yaw/Pitch/Roll, and Scaling Parameter Dials to adjust the view so that you create an oblique view of the Ground Plane. Paste it into the Background.
3. Do this as many times as needed to create a series of oblique trapezoids, as seen from the Dolly Camera view.
4. When you get something you like, render and save it to disk. Make sure Background Picture is selected in the Render Options dialog. See Figure 8.2.

FIGURE **8.2**   *Here's an example of oblique pattern development, using the technique described.*

One Step Farther

When you've finished creating your patterned backgrounds, you can use them as texture maps for the Ground Plane. See Figures 8.3 and 8.4.

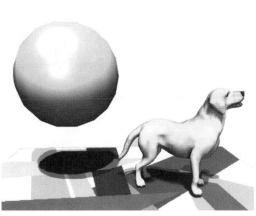

FIGURE **8.3**   *The oblique pattern is shown here mapped to the Ground Plane.*

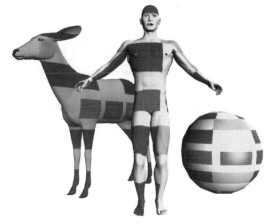

FIGURE **8.4**   *The rectangular pattern is shown mapped to a Deer, a Heroic figure, and a Ball Prop.*

Shadow Letters and Logos

Construct a letter Prop out of cube Props, or import a letter object in one of the formats that Poser 4 accepts. Make sure Shadows are on. Turn on Shadows in the Render dialog as well. Place the object out of view on the Y (vertical) axis, so all you can see in the Document is its shadow. Try rendering this image with a dark shadow on a light Ground Plane, and as a light shadow on a dark Ground Plane. If you explore the placement of the elements carefully, you'll be able to cast a shadow of a word or even a logo on the Ground Plane and anything else that's resting on it. See Figures 8.5 and 8.6.

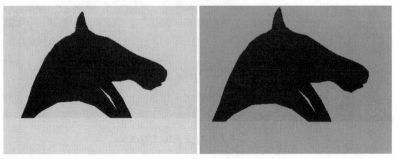

FIGURE **8.5**   *Figure 8.5 Here is the Zygote Bullhead Prop, casting a shadow on a Ground Plane. The view was Pasted to the Background and the Prop removed. Poser 4 can be used to develop logos using this same shadow method, and the saved images can then be mapped to figures or Props. On the right, the saved image is mapped to a Ball Prop.*

FIGURE **8.6**   *We can paste the new logo into the Background as many times as we like, using it to texture a Ground Plane or any other selected item later on. The image on the right shows a Zygote Lion figure, surrounded by elements mapped with the texture we developed in Figure 8.5.*

Rendering an object profile as a Silhouette, and pasting that to the background, does basically this same thing.

Shadow Spotlights

When does a Shadow suffice as a Spotlight? When it is much lighter than the Ground Plane and the other elements in a Poser 4 Document. There is a way that you can achieve this effect in Poser 4, remembering that the Displayed image does not show what light and shadows really look like when rendered, so a screen capture application is sometimes needed if you like what you see in the Document Display. Do the following:

1. Create a Ground Plane colored black.
2. Place a large Ball over it, so that the Ball is centered out of sight at the top.
3. Make sure Shadows are turned on in the Display menu, and that the Shadow Color is set to white.
4. Move the lights so that they shine down from above the scene. You should see a white oval on a black Ground Plane.
5. When you have the view you want, use your screen capture application to grab just the Document window, avoiding any outlines of the window itself.
6. From your capture application, save out the image in a format that Poser 4 can read.
7. Import the image into Poser 4 as a Background. Place any figure you want over it, and the figure will appear to be in a spotlight. See Figure 8.7.

FIGURE **8.7** *Using the technique described, we have forced a Ball object (out of view at the top) to cast a white shadow on a black Ground Plane, and then the Document window was captured and saved. The figure was rendered over the image after it was read back in.*

There are a number of screen capture applications that you can use to grab a portion of a screen. Flash comes to mind for the Mac, and PaintShop Pro for Windows systems. Search them out on the Web by looking up "Grab" or "Capture," or ask your friends what they use and recommend.

DEFORMATIONS AND THE GROUND PLANE

Using Deformers on the Ground Plane is another advantage Poser 4 has over Poser 3. Previously, the Ground Plane was a rather basic element, one that you had very little control over as far as its geometry. This is no longer the case. When you use a Deformer (Magnet of Wave) on the Ground Plane, you effectively give it Y-axis content and variability. Using a Magnet Deformer on the Ground Plane creates cone-like elevations. See Figure 8.8.

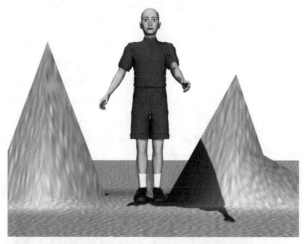

FIGURE *The Magnet Deformer was used on the Ground Plane to create these conic hills.*
8.8

The Magnet Deformer does respond to Groups that are configured on the Ground Plane.

The most interesting Ground Plane deformation effects, however, are reserved for the use of the Wave Deformer. Using this Deformer in conjunction with Grouped areas of the plane creates all manner of wave effects, depending on how you adjust the Wave's Parameters. See Figure 8.9.

When you deform the Ground Plane and have a figure standing on it, the Ground Plane may be lowered under the figure. There is no way to automatically compensate for this, so you'll have to lower the figure on its Y axis until it sits realistically on the now-contoured plane.

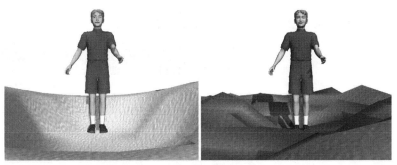

FIGURE   *Two Wave Deformers applied to the Ground Plane. Left to right: Crater from*
8.9   *Amplitude of 0.344 and a Wavelength of 1.8; Sand with an Amplitude of*
0.075 and a Wavelength of 0.060.

Karuna! *If you want to have more control over the Ground Plane as far as its placement and Deformation looks are concerned, do not use it at all. Instead, create a planar surface in another application that writes Wavefront (OBJ) files, and import it to Poser. The problem with the Ground Plane in Poser is that it doesn't have enough polygons to lead to effective deformations, and there is no way to increase its polygon count.*

REFLECTIVE AND TRANSPARENT GROUND PLANES

With Poser 4's capability to map reflective and transparent attributes as well as image maps' colors, Ground Planes can assume an entirely new character.

Ground Planes with Reflection Mapping

Reflection Mapping is only noticeable when the object or figure it is being mapped to is in motion. Otherwise, Texture Mapping is the best alternative. The only case where this varies is when you want to show that an object is metal, and that it is proven so by reflecting some measure of its virtual environment. In that case (and Ground Planes are not the best example for this), the object or figure should also have its own color or texture, and even Bump Map. This makes it more believable that the Reflection Map is just that, and not an applied texture. Apply the bitmap to be used as the Reflection Map and its reflective value in the Surface Materials window. See Figure 8.10.

If you plan on using a Reflection Map on the Ground Plane, then explore using the same map on a moving object in the scene. This will make it apparent that the mapping is indeed a reflection and not simply an applied surface texture. See Figure 8.11.

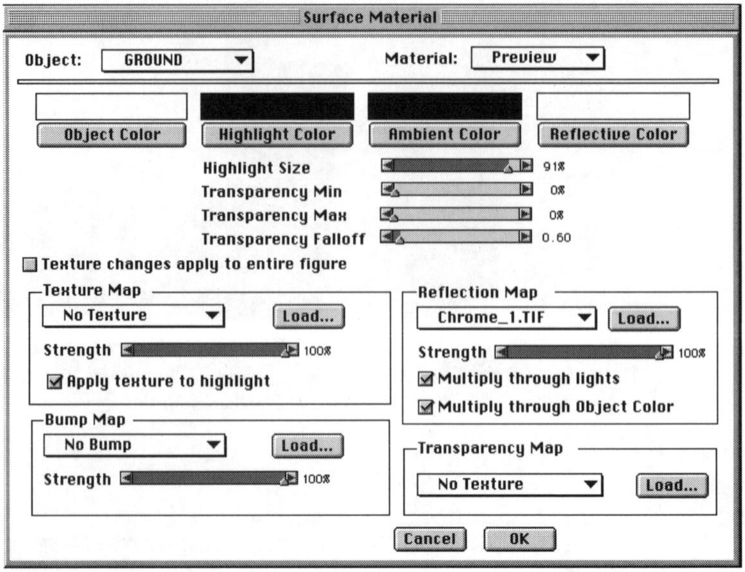

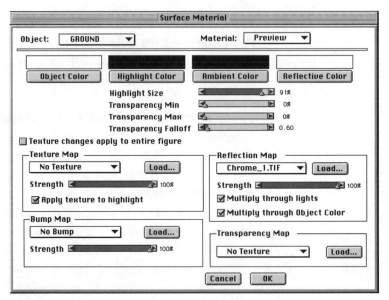

FIGURE **8.10** *Configure the Reflection Map location and the degree of reflection in the Surface Materials window. Using a color other than white, as a Reflection Map tints the targeted object or figure.*

FIGURE **8.11** *The Reflection Map used here on both the Ground Plane and the objects is a colorful Chrome gradient created in Photoshop. You can use any suitable bitmap application to create unique Reflection Maps. Because none of the objects reflect each other, you can see that Poser's Reflection Mapping option is not a real raytraced reflection alternative.*

Karuna! *Remember that you need light to see reflections on an object or figure. For that reason, you need to pay attention to the intensity of the light(s) and what direction it is shining from.*

There is a special trick that many computer artists use that emulates Reflection Mapping, and in some cases, it looks better. It is called Environmental Mapping, and you can do it in Poser. Simply render a scene devoid of the object(s) you want to show reflections on, and save the rendering to disk. Add the "reflective" object(s) or figures. Now, instead of using a Reflection Map on them, apply the saved rendering as a texture. You can achieve some startling pseudo-reflections in this manner.

Ground Planes with Transparency Mapping

Karuna! *This is the rule to remember at all times when using Transparency Maps in Poser: Solid Black is 100% Transparent, and Solid White is 100% Opaque.*

See Figures 8.12 through 8.14.

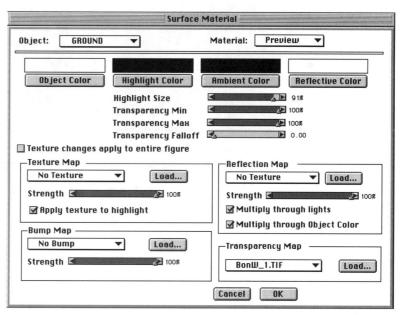

FIGURE *Configure the Transparency Map's parameters in the Surface Material Window.*
8.12 *Most of the time, the Max/Min settings are kept all the way if the Transparency Map is black and white with no grays.*

FIGURE   *Here is a simple Transparency Map that can be used on the Ground Plane. The*
8.13   *Black Circle will be the Transparent area.*

FIGURE   *The result of using the Transparency Map in Figure 8.13 on the Ground Plane*
8.14   *is a hole cut in the plane that shows the background. The castle sits partially*
         embedded in the hole.

Backgrounds

Imagine that you are standing in front of the painting of the Mona Lisa. There is a certain impression you take away when viewing this painting, caused by all of the elements in the image, including its background composition and coloring. Now imagine that the background is a scene of New York traffic. Her smile just doesn't seem the same, does it? Perhaps it has changed from an impression of satisfaction to a more sardonic look. But nothing in the smile has changed at all. It is the alteration of the background that has lent a whole new emotion to the image.

An image excites emotion because of the proximity and content of all of the elements contained within it. Backgrounds are not arbitrary, but play a large role in how we interpret the deeper meaning of the image as a whole. See Figure 8.15.

FIGURE   *Here, the same foreground Poser figure is superimposed over different backgrounds,*
8.15   *allowing you to experience how important a role background content can play.*

SINGLE-COLOR BACKGROUNDS

Just use the Eyedropper attached to the Background Color button to bring up a system palette, select a color, and that's it. A few things to remember about what color to choose will serve you well.

- Select white if you plan to print your work, since that saves on ink used for the background color.
- Select black for work to be transferred to tape, since it pops out the images better for video and multimedia, and also lends a better 3D look to the composition.
- Select a color NOT present in your Document elements if you plan to use Alpha compositing to drop the background out.
- If you want to emphasize the colors in the rest of your Document, select a background color that is the Complimentary of the dominant color in your work. For instance, if you have a lot of pink, red, or brown skin tones, use a green background color. If you have blue tones that dominate your composition, the Complimentary would be orange. The basic Complimentaries are red/green, blue/orange, and violet/yellow.

COLOR GRADIENT BACKGROUNDS

There is no way to create gradient backgrounds in Poser 4 directly, so it means developing them in an outside application. Use any bitmap painting application that offers gradations (Photoshop, PhotoPaint, Paint Shop Pro, Painter), and create a gradient with the size and resolution that fits your Poser 4 project. Then simply import it as a background Picture.

Karuna! NEVER use a gradient background if you plan to Alpha composite your Poser 4 output.

PHOTOGRAPHIC BACKGROUNDS

You can add an amazing amount of realism to your Poser 4 work if the background is photographic. Your audience may well wonder if the figures they are seeing are virtual or real. Select your photographic background imagery to enhance the mood you're trying to create. One of my favorite background themes is clouds, which seems to enhance almost any foreground pose or animation. There are hundreds of stock image CD collections that feature just about any theme you can imagine.

Karuna! When using images that come from a purchased CD collection, make sure they are not copyrighted, and that they say in clear bold type that you may use them on your own projects without paying a fee.

MOVIES AS BACKGROUNDS

Poser 4 allows you to select an AVI (Windows) or a QuickTime (Mac and Windows) movie file as the background for your compositions. Sometimes, the foreground doesn't have to move at all to create an interesting final composite using this alternative. If you face your figure so that its back is facing the camera, for instance, and it is rotated so that it seems to be flying into the screen, you can use animated footage in the background to give the scene a real sense of flying motion. This is, in fact, the exact way superheroes take flight in film work, by being composited against a background in motion.

It's very important to remember that any animation that you create in Poser 4 can itself become a background animation, for use with additional foreground figures and props. Doing this several times in a row results in very complex animations with several layers of interest. See Section II for more details on the animation process.

USING YOUR DIGITAL CAMERA, SCANNER, AND VIDEO CAMERA

You have at your disposal some awesome graphic power if you own a scanner and/or a digital still or video camera. Remember that the whole idea behind computer graphics and animation is to integrate it seamlessly with the video medium. Computer graphics and animation began as a way of initiating inter-active television.

If you plan to use your video sequences as a Poser 4 background, you'll need all of the devices that allow you to connect your camera to the computer. This usually consists of an interface that reads in the analog video signal on one end, and outputs digital video to the computer on the other. Check with you cam-era manufacturer to get the details and pricing.

Using your scanner to develop Poser 4 background footage is a simpler mat-ter, since it is already connected to your computer. Just make sure you resize the images captured so that they fit the Poser 4 Document size you're using.

CAUTION

Karuna! When using images that are scanned from printed copy, make sure they are not copyrighted. The best assurance you have of this is to scan in photos you have taken yourself.

Props

We've already looked at props in some detail in Chapter 7, "Composited Fig-ures," especially concerning their ability to modify a figure. In this chapter, we'll stretch your knowledge of ways to use and modify Props in your Poser 4 compositions.

HATS AND THEIR MODIFICATION

What is a hat? Instead of defining a hat as a Prop that is shaped like a com-monly accepted geometry of a hat, let's open it up a bit. For creative purposes, a hat is anything you can place on the head of a figure. Some Props, like a chair, will create a rather bizarre hat, so there is degree and extent. Other Props, like a Box or a Ball, may suffice as hats in certain circumstances. See Figure 8.16.

Composited Hats from Basic Props

You can use any number of Props to create your own composite hats; just make sure the parenting is in the correct order. The lowest member of the group should have the Head as its Parent, and the other members of the hat group can then be parented to each other. See Figure 8.17.

FIGURE   *Various basic Props, resized, and placed as hats (Ball, Torus, and Cone). The*
8.16   *Head is selected as the Parent of the Prop.*

FIGURE   *Left to right: Top hat created from two cylinders; Wizard's hat from a Cone*
8.17   *and squashed Torus; hat created from two Stairs Props, a Ball, and a Torus.*

CREATING STRANGE HAIR PROPS

In Chapter 7, we've already looked at how Hair Props, from the Hair library or
the Zygote Extras CD, can be resized and composited with other Hair Props.
There are yet other ways we can create Hair Props from non-Hair Props. In
Chapter 17, "Handshaking," when we look at exporting Poser 4 elements to
RayDream, we'll discover even more radical ways to develop Hair Props.

Internal Props for Hair

It's easy to create the famous Marge Simpson look in Poser 4. All you need to
do is to stack a series of balls on the head of a figure, making sure each is parented to the next, and that the bottom one has for its Parent the Head of the
figure. See Figure 8.18.

Hair from Zygote Not-Hair

In the Zygote Extras Props library, in the Sampler folder, is a Prop called House
Plant. It makes interesting, though radically contemporary, Hair. See Figure
8.19.

FIGURE   *Marge, eat your heart out! A single, double, and quadruple beehive hairdo.*
8.18

FIGURE   *The Zygote House Plant Prop presents a more radical hairpiece.*
8.19

If we can use a plant as a Hair substitute, can a tree be far behind? In the same Sampler folder is a Prop called Tree. It, too, can be used as a rather alien-looking Hair Prop. See Figure 8.20.

BUILDING PROP VEHICLES FROM INTERNAL ELEMENTS

You can import all manner of Props from external sources in any format that Poser 4 recognizes. But you can also challenge your creative potential by constructing Props from elements in the standard Poser Props libraries. The following are just a few examples.

FIGURE
8.20
The whole Zygote Tree Prop can be used as a strange hair element.

The Wagon

You can construct basic composite Props using the simplest of elements from the Prop Types folder in the Props library. This wagon uses three Boxes, four Cylinders, and two Canes. Look at Figures 8.21 and 8.22, and see if you can construct this wagon to closely match the illustrations. As a hint, the wheels are Cylinders whose X dimension has been resized to 15%.

    The wagon may be pretty basic, but once you add an animal pulling it and a rider, and include a background image, the whole scene looks almost photorealistic. The Zygote Zebra and Heavy Man have been added here, and the Zygote Cowboy Hat Prop sits on his head. See Figure 8.23.

FIGURE
8.21
All of the parts of the wagon use the main body as the Parent.

FIGURE
8.22
One last touch might be to add two elongated Cylinder Props as wheel axles.

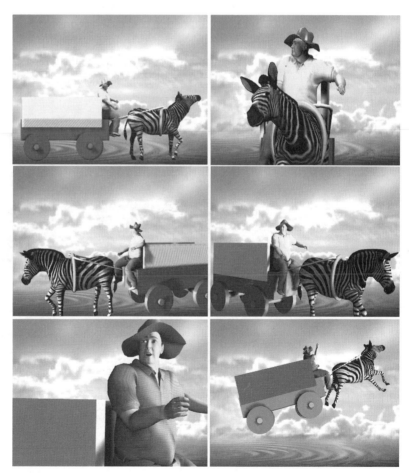

FIGURE
8.23
Adding a rider and a transport animal, the basic wagon Prop blends into the image quite well.

The Basic Biplane Composite Prop

Karuna! *When you are using multiple Props to build a composite model, the very first thing you should do, before altering any dimensions or rotating the Prop, is to attach it to its correct Parent. Otherwise, if you alter it first, it will warp out when Parented later.*

It's amazing what one Prop can provide. Resizing it on its various axes allows you to construct an infinite number of shapes. This is what was done to create the Biplane composite Prop. Only the Cylinder Prop was used. The main fuselage is the Parent of everything except the propeller. The Parent of the propeller is the hub on which it sits, so it can be animated to spin in space. Different views of the Cylinder constructed Biplane are provided in Figure 8.24. Study this illustration, and use it to construct your own version of the Biplane Prop.

After you've finished the Biplane Prop, place a Poser 4 Head (from the Additional Figures folder) in the cockpit, and render a few images. See Figure 8.25.

FIGURE *Study these illustrations carefully, and use them as a blueprint to construct the*
8.24 *Cylinder-based Biplane Prop.*

FIGURE *Adding a Head and a Background image completes the scenario.*
8.25

The Ear-Boat

You can even resize the Ear of a Doe so that you can place a meditating figure sitting inside of it. See Figure 8.26.

FIGURE *The Zygote Heavy Woman model sits in meditation inside of a Doe's Ear boat.*
8.26

INTERNAL REPLACEMENT PROPS

You can replace every body part of a figure with a Prop. All you have to do is place as many Props on the screen as there are parts of the figure and put them in position over the body element they are to substitute for. Next, with each body part selected in turn, go to Replace Body part With Prop in the Figure menu. When the dialog appears, simply select the Prop that will be replacing that body part. See Figure 8.27.

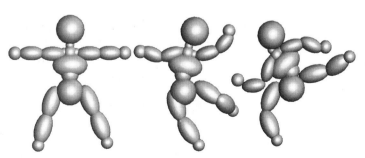

FIGURE *This Sphere being was created by replacing all of the body parts of a Stick*
8.27 *Figure with Ball Props. It can be posed like any other figure.*

If you plan to replace all of the body parts with Props, make sure to use the Stick Figure or Mannequin figure as a base. Neither has finger joints, so the replacements are simpler. Of course, if you plan to use Posed Hands, then you'll have to use an initial figure that has finger joint elements.

CAUTION

Karuna! *Under normal circumstances, when you bring a Prop into your Document, you cannot use the Taper operation on it. This is too bad, since it robs you of a way to create some interesting new shapes. However, when you use any Prop to replace a body part, it can now be tapered. This can lead to all sorts of new figure looks! See Figure 8.28.*

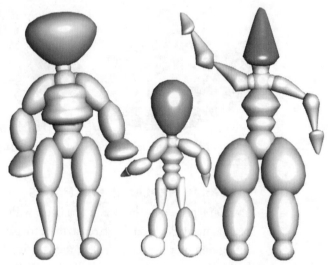

FIGURE **8.28**   *When a Prop is used to replace a body part, you can use the Taper operation on it. This is not something you can do on an ordinary Prop. All of the elements you see here are tapered Ball Props.*

How to Use Taper on Any Standalone Prop

Here's a way to do the impossible, to use the Taper operation on any Prop you import.

1. Place a Head in your Document window (from the Additional Figures folder in the Figures library).
2. Import any Prop you like from the Prop library. You can force this to work on any imported object as well, but the results are often erratic. Better to use a Prop already in the Props library.

3. Place the Prop directly over the Head, covering it. Click on the Head, and select Replace Body Part With Prop from the Figure menu. Replace the Head with the named Prop from the list.

4. Make both Eyes invisible. Select the Prop, which is now called Head, and use the Taper Parameter Dial to taper it as you like. See Figures 8.29 and 8.30.

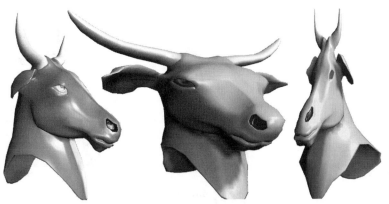

FIGURE
8.29 *Any Prop can be customized with a Taper by using the method described. The Zygote Bullhead Prop is on the left, and its Tapered versions on the right.*

FIGURE
8.30 *The Tapered Bullhead Prop used over a Nude Male model, replacing the Head. Different Tapers create different personalities.*

FIGURES (AND PARTIAL FIGURES) AS PROPS

Just as you can use Props to replace body parts, and give the Props movement and poses, so too you can perform the reverse action. Body parts can be used as interesting Props in your compositions. The following are a few ways to do it.

Statues

Take any figure, pose it, and put it on a Cylinder or a Box, and you have an instant statue. Remove the figure's texture map, and colorize all of its parts with the same color. See Figures 8.31 and 8.32.

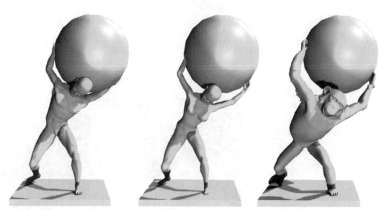

FIGURE *Any figure can be used as a posed Prop Statue.*
8.31

FIGURE *Imported into Bryce as a OBJ file, the statue can be cloned and textured.*
8.32

Hand Chairs

One of the most popular contemporary pieces of furniture in recent years has been the molded Hand Chair from Sweden. Poser 4 allows you to create your own. Simply import a Hand from the Additional Figures folder in the Figure library, pose it, and place a seated model on it. See Figure 8.33.

Table Legs

If the museum you visit has an Egyptian or a Medieval furniture collection, you're bound to see some tables with carved animal legs. Poser 4 allows you to create this furniture style as well. Just select the animal you want, and make everything invisible but its legs and feet. Save it to disk, and then import another pair. Place as needed, and attach a Prop table top (either a squashed Box or Cylinder). See Figure 8.34.

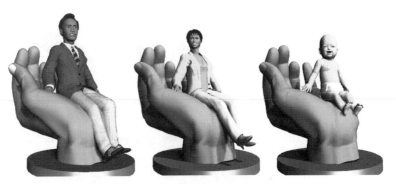

FIGURE *The Hand Chair is a comfortable place to rest.*
8.33

FIGURE *A table with carved animal legs.*
8.34

Doorway

In the same manner as used to develop the table in Figure 8.34, we can develop a doorway frame by using the arms of a Human or Animal model. See Figure 8.35.

The Oracle

One of the most evocative fables in mythology is that of the severed Head that lives to prophesy the future. Sometimes, the Head is embedded in a rock or a crystal, and sometimes it sits alone on a table. Poser 4 has all the tools you need to create this mythic object. Just import a Head from the Additional Figures folder in the Figures library. Decide whether you want to embed it into a Box or Sphere, or another Prop, and make that Prop the Parent of the Head. See Figure 8.36.

FIGURE **8.35** *The arms of a Zygote Chimpanzee model were used to create this doorway.*

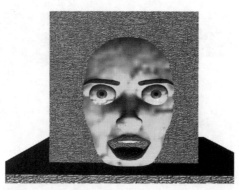

FIGURE **8.36** *The talking head is a marvel to behold. Everything uses the Ground Default texture. The Eyes are resized to 280%, and moved forward on the Z axis by .005.*

CD Content Collections

We have mentioned the Zygote collection of Props, available on separate CD-ROMs, but Zygote is not alone in offering the Poser 4 user a wealth of extra Prop and other content collections. The following are some other Poser CD developers to be aware of (be sure to look at the list in Appendix D as well for Web addresses of these and other additional content developers).

BAUMGARTEN ENTERPRISES

This developer has released two Poser-related CD collections as of this writing, with more on the way. The first volume (Meshes 1) contains all manner of Poser Props in a wide variety of categories, and it was released concurrently with Poser 4. The second volume (Meshes 2) is one that not only all Poser users should own, but it should be in the resource library of anyone who does computer graphics. This is especially true for anyone who uses Poser in combination with MetaCreations' Bryce. This volume is jam-packed with over 200 files of plant models in 3DS format with JPG textures. They can be imported directly into Poser for Morphing and rendering, or work just as well when included in a Poser-inhabited Bryce scene. What is impressive is the high quality and variety involved. See Figure 8.37.

FIGURE *Here is one beautiful example of a tree from the Baumgarten Enterprises' Mesh*
8.37 *2 CD. It's just the right touch for the Zygote Buck.*

PoseAmation

This CD set is from Chris Derochie, a professional animator with many films to his credit. The two-CD set comes in a beautiful leatherette pouch, with CD envelopes meant to store future releases in the series. In addition to the large collection of Poses, which are ready to be placed in your Poses library, these CDs are loaded with additional content. As for Props, there is a collection from different digital sculptors, and the list includes a set of armor, weapons, a wide array of clothes, hair pieces, furniture, accessories, and more. The Props are in 3DS and OBJ formats.

Chris is a professional animator, so as you might expect, there is a collection of QuickTime and AVI movies that show his poses in action. These are poses meant for professional use, and they address all of the areas you might require if using Poser for film work. The poses come both as animated sequences and as still frames. There are also geometry files for an ant and a spider, and more. There is a collection of over 20 new face expressions in both FC2 (Mac) and RSR (Windows) formats. Over 30 new hand poses are also included. See Figure 8.38.

FIGURE   *The glasses and the goatee are from the PoseAmation CD. Both are the work of*
8.38   *professional computer artist H. L. Arledge (www.sherlocksoftware.com/studio).*

WhiteCrow 3D

The CDs from this developer include the following Poser titles:

Household 1: A collection of furniture and household items.
Household 2: A collection of more furniture and household items.

Household 3: A collection of more furniture and household items.
Weapons 1: A collection of medieval and historical weaponry.
Computer 1: A collection of computer/technology related items.

Each CD contains 100 high-quality original models in PP2 format (Poser Prop files) and are easily installed using the CD's own auto executable file.

Online ordering of the CDs is available as well as individual Prop buying and downloading (see Appendix D for the Web address). As well as the Props, they also have several Texture CDs. Development continues on even more Poser-related CD collections. See Figure 8.39.

FIGURE   *The pictured earphones are just one of WhiteCrow 3D's objects.*
8.39

Creative Rendering

When rendering to disk, especially for multimedia sizes (320 × 240), your Display Renders will look just about as good as the Render Settings renders. The difference is, Display Renderings often render three to five times faster. Just make sure that the Display Render selection is on its highest option (). Keep this in mind when time is a consideration.

USING RENDER STYLES

Refer to Table 8.1 for ideas on where to use various Render Styles. Also see Figure 8.40.

Table 8.1 You can select from amongst Render Styles to create looks for different uses in Poser 4.

Rendering Style	Media Look	Uses
Silhouette	Filled-In Silhouette	Use this style when you want to see just the silhouette of the image or animation. This is the option to use when you want to create an Alpha matte of the Document, useful in After Effects and other media effects applications.
Outline	Quick Pencil Sketch	This style resembles what animators call a "pencil test." It's also useful for exporting to a paint application, and applying color or textures there.
Wireframe	Complex Ink Sketch	This style allows you to see all of the data on all of the layers of the Document. Use it when you want to create a structural blueprint of the image.
Hidden Line	3D Ink Sketch	This style drops out data hidden by the frontmost layers. Use it to create a more eye-friendly structural image than the Wireframe style.
Lit Wireframe	Colored Pencil	This style creates beautiful color pencil Rotoscopes of the data, for use in single images or animations.
Flat Shaded	Faceted 3D Look	When you want a faceted look, this is the style option to select.
Flat Lined	This selection adds the Hidden Line Wireframe lines to the Flat Shaded selection.	Use when you want a faceted look with the Hidden Line Wireframe lines added.
Cartoon (was called Sketch in Poser 3)	Very flat and cartoony-Looks like a Wash media	This is the style to target when you want to create a 2D Anime look.
Cartoon With Lines (new in Poser 4)	This option adds outlines to the Cartoon Shader.	The outlines added to this option pop the figures out more against complex backdrops.
Smooth Shaded	Default 3D	This is the default Display style.
Smooth Lined (new in Poser 4)	This adds Hidden Line Wireframe lines to the Smooth option.	Use this if you like the added lines.
Texture Shaded	Textured 3D	Click on this style to get a pretty authentic preview of the textures applied to your Document elements.

You can only render these styles in three ways: You can use the Make Movie operation with Display Settings selected, you can grab the image with a screen grab application, or you can Export the image from the File menu. No other rendering method will allow you to render in these styles.

FIGURE *Left top to right bottom: Silhouette, Outline, Wireframe, Hidden Line, Lit*
8.40 *Wireframe, Flat Shaded, Sketch, Smooth Shaded, and Texture Shaded Render Styles of the same image.*

FINISHED RENDERING

When you are ready to render final images to a file, you have four options, the Render dialog offers you a number of options. We present these options in Table 8.2, along with their uses.

THE SKETCH DESIGNER

If you have experience with and appreciation for MetaCreations' Painter, you will find this new Poser 4 rendering feature absolutely addictive. In fact, the rendering options presented here, and the way the interface is designed, give it a more intuitive approach for creating a diverse array of media looks than Painter itself. The Sketch Designer interface is activated when you select it from the Windows menu. See Figure 8.41.

Table 8.2 Finished Rendering options and uses.

Rendering Options	Uses
Main/New Window	Most of the time, you'll want to render in a New Window, because that allows you more options for size and resolution. You can do quick test renders by selecting Main Window.
Width/Height	The Width and height of your rendered output is based upon a proportional size related to your display size. Pixels is the standard measure, though you may also select Inches or Centimeters (only when New Window is selected).
Resolution	Select 72 DPI for video and multimedia, and at least 300 DPI for print purposes.
Antialias	As a rule, leave this checked. Jaggies are bad news, and Poser 4 renders fast enough to warrant Antialiasing even for previews.
Use Bump Maps	If you have Bump Mapped Textures in the Document, check this option.
Use Texture Maps	If you have Texture Maps in the Document, check this option.
Cast Shadows	This is the one option that can slow down your rendering dramatically. Check it for more realistic output that displays the shadows related to the three light sources and their blended colors.
Background Options	Your three choices are Background Color, Black, or Background Picture. If you have a background Picture (or animation) loaded, select this choice. Black makes video output look a lot more three dimensional. Printed images should have a light or white backdrop as a Background Color.

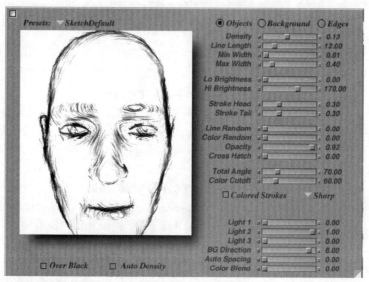

FIGURE *The Sketch Designer window.*
8.41

Karuna! The documentation does not point out the importance of the connection between selecting a Rendering Style and choosing a Sketch Designer option. You must remember that the Sketch Designer options and presets use your selected Rendering Style as a base, so select the appropriate Rendering Style you want first.

The Sketch Design is especially important to those of you interested in developing "Rotoscoping" animations. Rotoscoping is the look created when you transform film footage to natural media looks (pen, pencil, paint). One of the most important features of the Poser Sketch Designer options is that you need not have any Poser content on screen to use it. You can import a background animation and use Sketch Designer to transform the animation into natural media, then save out the animation to file. You could even read the animated Sketch Designed background back in as footage for the background, and superimpose Poser content (in any combination of Rendering Styles and Sketch Designed media) over it.

Understanding the Sketch Designer Options

Referring to Figure 8.41, let's take a brief look at what the commands and options in the Sketch designer do.

- **Presets.** By clicking on the Preset arrow at the top left of the screen, you can access the Sketch Presets that come with Poser. As you select any one of these, the preview image updates to show you exactly what the settings for that look will create if accepted as is. You can also use any of the Presets as a starting point to develop an infinite variety of your own looks. Presets can be deleted from this list, and new ones can be added. Eighteen Presets are included: Caterpillar, Colored Pencil, Colored, Dark Clouds, Inverts, JacksonP-BG, Loose Sketch, Pastel, Pencil and Ink, Psychedelica, Scratchboard, Scratchy, Silky, SketchDefault, Sketchy, Smoothy, Soft Charcoal, StrokedBG.

- **Over Black/Auto Density.** Checking either or both of these boxes at the bottom of the Preview area selects that option. Over Black creates a negative of the image. Auto Density allows the system to determine the density of the strokes (this can take a long time to compute, compared to setting the Density on your own).

- **Objects, Background, Edges.** You can select variations of the Sketch style for all three of these components. Edges settings determine how the edge of the object(s) is treated, so you can make this a thicker or thinner outline if you like.

- **Density, Line Length and Width**. Set the Density (0 to 1) to determine the strength of the lines. Line Length (0 to 300) sets the length of the rendered stroke. Line Width (0 to 40) is set separately for the start and end of the stroke.

- **Lo and High Brightness (0 to 256).** Altering these sliders determines what parts of the targeted Object, Background, or Edge gets a visible stroke. Setting the Lo to minimum and the High slider to about half gives normal results, but each change creates a new Sketch Style (any of which can be saved as a Preset in the list). Moving the High Brightness slider to maximum creates a very dense drawing, with too many strokes. Experiment to learn what you like best.

- **Stroke Head and Tail** (0 to 1). These sliders work in combination with the others to set stroke visibility.

- **Line and Color Randomness**(0 to 1), **Opacity** (0 to 1), and **Cross Hatch** (0 to 1). Randomness of either Line and Color attributes adds a looser look to the render. Opacity sets the intensity of the Color areas, while Cross hatching values determine the extent of the added cross-hatch pattern.

- **Total Angle** (0 to 256) and **Color Cutoff** (0 to 256). Total Angle helps to set the amount of color strokes applied. Color Cutoff sets a threshold for color strokes.

- **Light 1, 2, 3** (0 to 1). The higher the value for any of these three sliders, the more that light will influence the direction of the strokes.

- **Background Direction** (0 to 9). This value determines the direction of the strokes used to render the background.

- **Auto Spacing** (0 to 3). This slider determines the space between strokes when Auto Density is enabled.

- **Color Blend** (0 to 1). You can blend the original image content with the Sketch content by manipulating this slider. A "pure" Sketch-based color requires this be set to 0, while a value of 1 blends the original content with the Sketch content color at 100%.

Devote at least some sessions to nothing else but exploring different Sketch settings, saving the ones you like to the Presets list. See Figures 8.42 and 8.43.

Transparent Figure Textures

Any element in a Poser scene can accept a Transparency Map, simply by selecting the element and then selecting the Map in the Surface Material window. You can create Transparency Maps in any 2D bitmap application, saving them out in any format that Poser can import. Remember that all you really need for a basic Transparency Map is a two-color image: Black and White. The areas

FIGURE   *Here are examples of all of the Sketch Presets (left top to right bottom):*
8.42   *Original figure without Sketch applied, Caterpillar, Colored Pencil, Colored,
Dark Clouds, Inverts, JacksonP-BG, Loose Sketch, Pastel, Pencil and Ink,
Psychedelica, Scratchboard, Scratchy, Silky, SketchDefault, Sketchy, Smoothy,
Soft Charcoal, and StrokedBG.*

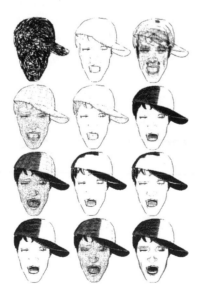

FIGURE   *In this figure, just to demonstrate the effect that different Render Styles have on
8.43   the same Sketch Preset. Pencil and Ink is used on the following Styles (left top to
right bottom): Silhouette, Outline, Wireframe, Hidden Line, Lit Wireframe,
Flat Shaded, Flat Lined, Cartoon, Cartoon w/Lines, Smooth, Smooth Lined,
and Texture Shaded.*

that are Black will be 100% transparent, and the areas that are White will be 100% opaque. Here's what to do.

1. Select any figure you like that has a Texture Map you can customize (in this example, I have used the Zygote Heavy Man). Pose the figure. In a separate bitmap application, import the figure's Texture Map from the Poser Textures folder.

2. Change the image to a Grayscale format from its original RGB format.

3. Paint the image in solid black with whatever pattern you like, realizing that all black areas will be 100% Transparent. Experiment with various patterns. When finished, paint all areas of the image that are not solid black, solid white. See Figure 8.44.

4. Do not alter the size of the image in any way. Save the altered image out to the same folder that the color image is located in, with a "G" in its name to indicate that this new image is a grayscale.

5 In Poser, with the Body of the figure selected, open the Surface Material window. Under Transparency Map, locate and load the grayscale image you just saved. Set the Min and Max Transparency sliders to 100%, with Falloff set to 0. Close the Surface Material window.

6. Render the results. In this example, the black of the grayscale image was painted on the figure's pants, making them transparent wherever the pattern appears. You can get extremely creative with this procedure and create all sorts of transparent drop-out areas over a figure. See Figure 8.45.

FIGURE *On the left is the original grayscale texture map for the Zygote Heavy Man. On*
8.44 *the right is the texture map with black used for transparent dropout areas and the rest of the texture map solid white.*

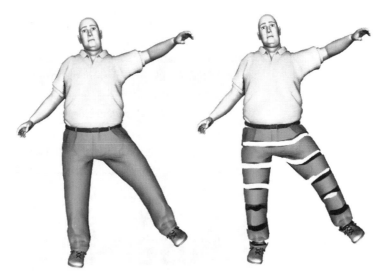

FIGURE *On the left is the original figure, and on the right the same figure with a*
8.45 *Transparency Map applied to his pant legs.*

POSER FLYING LOGOS

Flying Logos (sometimes called DVEs, or Digital Video Effects) represent one of the common uses of computer graphics and animation, and you can develop Flying Logo content within Poser 4. All it takes is the right imported bitmap, and a knowledge of how to use Transparency Maps.

FIGURE *Here is an example of the Logo bitmap we are using.*
8.46

1. Create the content for your Logo design in any bitmap application by using white lettering or symbols on a solid black backdrop. Save it in a format that Poser can read. See Figure 8.46.
2. In Poser, add a Square from the Props/Prop Types library.
3. With the square selected, open the Surface Materials library. Under the Transparency Map item, locate and load your Logo bitmap. Use no Falloff, and set both the Max and Min sliders to 100%. Bring in any background image or footage you like. See Figure 8.47.

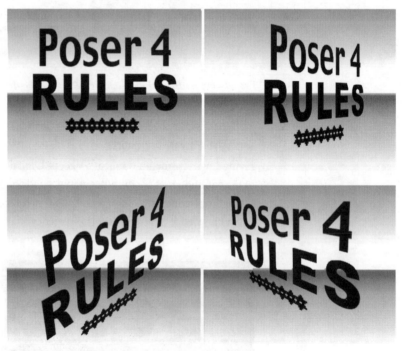

FIGURE
8.47   *The Logo image can be rendered and rotated in Poser to create interesting Flying Logo animation possibilities.*

Material Group Painting

Although you may use the new Poser 4 Grouping Tool to create your own target Morph areas on a Prop or figure, there is another way to utilize Grouping. Each separate Group can have its own Material assigned to it, and this includes the Transparency and Reflectivity options. You could, for instance, make the top of the Head of a Poser figure partially transparent, and place machinery inside. You could make just portions of a Prop reflective with an assigned Reflectivity Map, leaving the rest of it a default color. These new options make Poser 4 a unique 3D painting system. Creating a new Material area for painting is simple. Use the Group Tool just as you would if creating a Target Morph, and click on the Assign Material button. Name the new material as you like. After that, you'll find the area listed along with its new material name in the Surface Material window, just like everything else.

CAUTION

Karuna! It is extremely important to remember that the Grouping process allows you to select polygons in two ways: with the marquee, and by clicking on individual polygons. Because of the second method, it is important to consider working in Hidden Line mode when Grouping, no matter if your purpose is to create target Morphs or New Material areas, or both. This allows you to select only those exact polygons you want included.

GROUP PAINTING FACTOIDS

When you use the Grouping Tool to indicate areas for New materials, here are some important considerations to keep in mind:

- Work in Hidden Line mode so you can see only the polygons on the items' faces currently facing the Camera, in order to be able to select your areas clearly.
- Keep in mind that any Material area can be targeted for Transparency or Transparency Maps, allowing you to do such things as placing "windows" on an object.
- Configuring a New Material set of polygons that overlap older assigned material areas causes the New area(s) to overwrite the older ones.
- New Material areas can be addressed with their own textures and Bump Maps as well, giving you even more control over how each object and figure in your scene renders.
- When used on a human figure element (arms, legs, head, and other parts), you can use the Group Painting technique with specific textures designed in a bitmap application to assign and render tattoos, birthmarks, scars, or other targeted features. The only limitation is your patience in defining the exact area indicating the New Material.

See Figure 8.48.

FIGURE **8.48** *Face painting is easy with the new Grouping Tool. Left: Color used to differentiate between the Skin and Grouped areas. Right: Separate textures used to differentiate between the Skin and Grouped areas.*

Moving Along

In this chapter, we have explored Backgrounds and Props and how to customize and modify their parameters. We also looked at Rendering options, including the new Poser 4 Sketch Renderer, and the Transparency and Reflectivity options in the Render dialog. The next chapter of the book begins Section II, which is dedicated to creating animations in Poser 4.

POSER 4
ANIMATION

Poser has evolved from a 2D graphics utility in Poser 1, through a user-friendly animation toy in Poser 2, to a more professional set of features in Poser 3, to a fully customizable art and animation application in Poser 4. What began as software dedicated to supporting 2D painting (allowing you to import 3D posed figures into Photoshop and Painter so they could be painted on) has risen far from its original roots. Not that you can't use Poser 4 renders as a 2D painting utility, but Poser 4 boasts anatomical animation capabilities no other software at any price can compete with. All of this has been accomplished in an intuitive creative environment with a very easy learning curve, so that beginners and professionals alike can create startling animated figures in just a few minutes. Chapters 9 through 15 are dedicated to Poser's animation options and techniques.

9

ANIMATION
CONTROLS

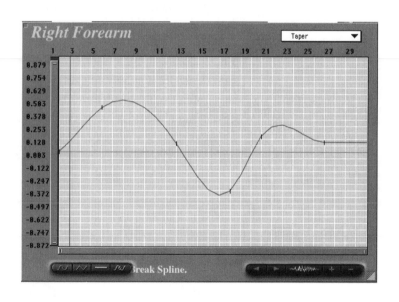

The Idea Behind Keyframing

The terms "keyframe" and "keyframing" are buzz words heard a lot around animation studios. Traditionally, there are two classes of animators: *Keyframers* and *Tweeners*. A Keyframer is an artist who draws the main poses in an animated sequence, while the Tweener fills in all of the frames, the "in-betweens," from one keyframe to the next. Both take a lot of work and a lot of thought. When the computer came on the animation scene, everyone began to realize that the manual labor of tweening was about to be replaced by a nonhuman approach. As a number cruncher and data analyzer, the computer rules. In a computer animation application, all that the computer needs is an indication of where the keyframes, the main poses, are at. From there, all of the in-betweens can be interpolated mathematically, so there is smooth motion from one keyframe to the next. The main job of the Poser 4 animator then is to set up the keyframe poses. This is not always as easy as it sounds.

A walk cycle is the most common example of this. In a walk cycle, several things are happening at the same time. Legs are in motion, joints are bending, arms are swinging, the torso may be bending or swaying from side to side, and the head may be bobbing around. The best way to handle keyframes is to get the gross movements under control first, and then move to the finer motion attributes. In a walk cycle, the simplest way to do this is to set keyframes that show the left leg at its forward most position, and the right arm at its backward most position at the first frame. Then set the middle keyframe with the right leg at its most forward position, and the left arm at its most backward position. The last keyframe would be a repeat of the first frame, so that the animation could loop and show the cycle repeating. See Figure 9.1.

FIGURE 9.1 *The standard keyframe poses in a walk cycling animation.*

We'll have more information on walk cycles in Chapter 14, "The Walk Designer," and when we explore the uses of IK (Inverse Kinematics) later in this chapter. For now, let's look at the modules that allow us to set keyframes, and associated animation menu commands in Poser 4.

CAUTION

Karuna! The trick behind good keyframing is to use only enough keyframes to accomplish the movement you want. Keyframing every frame makes it very difficult to edit a frame, because it can lead to jumpy movements in the surrounding frames.

Two Animation Control Environments

Poser 4 features two separate but linked control environments where animations can be composed and edited: the Animation Controller, and the Animation Palette.

THE ANIMATION CONTROLLER

The Animation Controller is located at the bottom of the Poser 4 screen, and is brought up by clicking on its control bar. See Figure 9.2.

Let's spend a little time looking at each element on the Animation Controller interface, describing what each of the components does.

At the top left are the VCR controls. These are used to locate any frame in an animation sequence, and to play/stop a Preview Animation. See Figure 9.3.

At the center are two input areas: a Frame Counter that tells you what frame you are at, and the total number of frames in the sequence. To set the number of total frames in a sequence, just click in this second area and type in the number of frames you want. By the way, if you attempt to enter a number in the frame field that is higher than the number of frames in the animation, you will get an error message that states that your number is out of range. The very first

FIGURE *The Animation Controller.*
9.2

FIGURE *The VCR controls, left to right, are First Frame, Last Frame, Stop, Play, Previous Frame, and Next Frame.*
9.3

thing you should do when starting to configure an animation is to set the total number of frames you want. Remember that the Frame Rate (frames per second) will determine how much time the animation will take to run once through. See Figure 9.4.

At the top-right of the Animation Controller are controls for setting and maneuvering keyframes. See Figure 9.5.

Previous and Next Keyframe will take you to the frame for the selected element. If that element has no keyframes, you will not move to another frame.

At the bottom left, the word "Loop" appears. There is a small light next to it. Clicking on this area turns the light on or off. When on, your preview animation will play over and over again until manually shut off. If the light is off, the preview will only play once. See Figure 9.6.

In the center is the Interactive Frame Slider. Moving the Frame Indicator arrow allows you to go to any frame on the timeline. The Frame Number Indicator above displays the frame number. See Figure 9.7.

FIGURE   *The Frame Counter and Number of Frames indicators.*
9.4

FIGURE   *These controls, from left to right, do the following: Previous Keyframe, Next*
9.5   *Keyframe, Edit Keyframes (brings up the Animation Palette), Add Keyframe, and Delete Keyframe.*

FIGURE   *The Loop Indicator.*
9.6

FIGURE   *The Interactive Frame Slider.*
9.7

Last, the Skip Frames Indicator is on the bottom right. This toggle allows the preview to play the keyframes, or every frame in the sequence.

Skip Frames ⦿

FIGURE   *The Skip Frames Indicator.*
9.8

Animation Controller Hints and Tips

When using the Animation Controller, here are some things to keep in mind:

- Always set the number of frames first, realizing that the number, when divided by the frames per second rate, gives you the runtime of the animation.
- As a default, keep looping on. When a preview runs a few times, you can see flaws more clearly, and then find the offending frame(s) and make necessary corrections.
- You seldom have to use the "+" key to create a keyframe, as every time you adjust an element in the Document window, a keyframe is created automatically. I sometimes use it as a "paranoid factor," just to make doubly sure that a keyframe has been made at a certain frame. Using the "-" key, however, is a different matter, since removing offending keyframes is often necessary to get the exact movements you want.
- Assign your gross movements first, and preview the results. Then add finer motions, previewing as you go. Set the Skip Frames to off so you can see the details in the preview.

THE ANIMATION PALETTE

Clicking on the Key Symbol in the Animation Controller brings up the Animation Palette, which has its own definitive controls for editing the animation. See Figure 9.9.

CAUTION

Karuna! This section on the Animation Palette is a refresher that points out some of the important elements. It is not a substitute for reading and working through the Poser 4 documentation and tutorials on this topic.

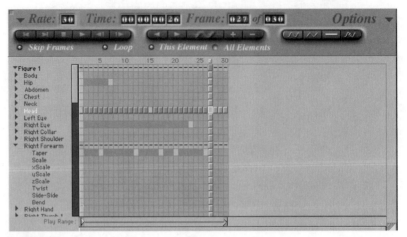

FIGURE   *The Animation Palette.*
9.9

Just as we did with the Animation Controller, let's walk through each of the elements that make up the Animation Palette.

Our first stop is at the bottom of the palette. You should see a green line with an arrow on each end. This represents the Play Range of the animation. You can move the right arrow to the right until it reaches the last frame in the sequence, and to the left to any frame before that. You can move the left arrow to the right to any frame before the right arrow, and to the left as far as the first frame. Limiting the play range allows you to preview a sequence of any length, which is very useful for catching and correcting unwanted glitches. See Figure 9.10.

Our next stop on the tour of the Animation Palette is the center area. You will notice a long list of items on the left, representing every element in your Document window, Highlighting any element by clicking on its name will also highlight all of its frames to the right of the name, which turn white. Green frames indicate that there are some keyframes already set for that element and that they are Spline Interpolated, and red frame indicators tell you exactly where the keyframes are located. Pinkish frames indicate that a Linear Interpolation is going on. You can click on any frame to highlight it, and the resulting vertical highlighted column tells you exactly what each element is doing at that

FIGURE   *The interactive Play Range indicator.*
9.10

particular frame. If any element in the vertical stack is red, it is a keyframed element. If it is green, it is an element in motion between keyframes (a tween). If it is white (or gray when not selected), it is stationary. See Figure 9.11.

Right above this frame area are four text-based controls: Skip Frames, Loop, This Element, and All Elements. The first two, Skip Frames and Loop, have already been adequately covered in our look at the Animation Controller. This Element and All Elements are two sides of one control, since selecting one inhibits the other. What are they used for? If you select any element frame in the frame area below, you will see a vertical highlighted stack, showing each element in your Document at that point in time. If you wanted to press the Plus key to make that frame a keyframe, or the Minus key to delete it as a keyframe, it would matter if either This Element or All Elements were chosen. Selecting This Element would act to add or delete a keyframe for just that element. Selecting All Elements would add or delete keyframes for every element in the highlighted vertical stack. See Figure 9.12.

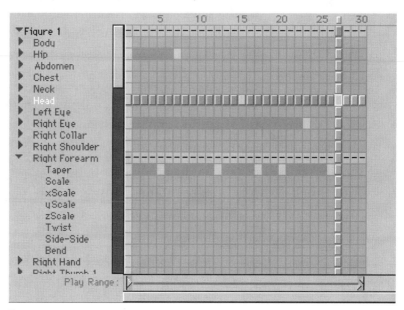

FIGURE *The element list on the left, and the frame indicators on the right.*
9.11

FIGURE *The most important commands here are the last two: This Element and All*
9.12 *Elements, and how they each address keyframe alterations.*

Above the text-based controls are three rows of buttons. The first is the familiar VCR controls already covered under the Animation Controller. The second row is also familiar, with the exception of the center button, which is unique to the Animation Palette. This center button, with the symbol of a squiggley line on top, is the Graph Display Toggle, which we'll detail in a few paragraphs. The third row contains three Interpolation buttons, and is better left untouched, because these same three Interpolation buttons also appear in the Graph Display. It make more sense to use them there. See Figure 9.13.

At the very top are the time and frame displays, and the Options menu. The displays address Frame Rate (frames per second), Timecode indicator (Hour/Minute/Second/Frame), present Frame, and total number of Frames. This is a display, not meant to be altered. The Options list includes the following items that can be selected or deselected, simply by accessing them: Display Frames or Timecode, Loop Interpolation, and Quaternion Interpolation. Selecting either Frame Display or Timecode Display will use that system as a rule of measurement over the frame selection area. Loop Interpolation and Quaternion Interpolation are separate items, and both can be selected or deselected individually (see the definitions of both later in this chapter). See Figure 9.14.

The Graph Display
Clicking on the Graph Display button brings up the Graph Display for whatever item is selected in the hierarchy list. Readjusting the display via a Splined or Linear curve allows the selected element to have whatever priority that is selected animated according to the shape of the curve. The properties include Taper, Scale, Xscale, Yscale, Zscale, Twist, Side-to-Side, and Bend. If the Head is selected, all of the animatable elements can be edited via a motion graph. It takes practice to configure animations with the Graph Display of specific ele-

FIGURE *The three control groups of buttons: the VCR controls, the Keyframe controls, and the Interpolation controls.*
9.13

FIGURE *The top row of display items and the Options menu.*
9.14

ments, so be prepared to spend some time learning the techniques. See Figure 9.15.

The best way to learn to configure animations with the Graph Display is to avoid setting any movement with the Animation Controller at first. Simply set the number of frames, and jump onto a selected element's Graph Display, and modify the graph. Preview the animation to see what you've accomplished.

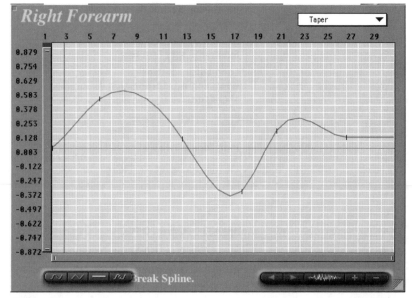

FIGURE   *The Graph Display modified to animate Lip Movements on a human model's*
9.15   *Head.*

Using the Graph Display and altering Mouth attributes and Eye Blinks leads to more realistic movements, and is 1000% faster than accomplishing the same animated poses via Parameter Dials.

Animating to Sound

If you will notice, the bottom-right row of buttons on the Graph Display shows what appears to be a sound wave. Clicking on this button will bring up a visual display of a sound file, if one is loaded into the Document. By following the amplitude shape of the wave (where it is higher and lower), you can edit the motion curve of any selected element to move accordingly. In this manner, you can accomplish lip synching and other choreography.

The Animation Menu

The Animation menu at the top of your screen contains essential items that you must be aware of in order to creatively interact with your Poser 4 animations. Let's look at each of the listings in some detail. See Figure 9.16.

FIGURE *The listings in the Animation menu.*
9.16

ANIMATION SETUP

This is where you configure the animation output settings, including Frame Rate, Output Size, Frame Count, and Duration. It's a lot easier to do this all in one place, rather than to address these parameters in a series of different locations. See Figure 9.17.

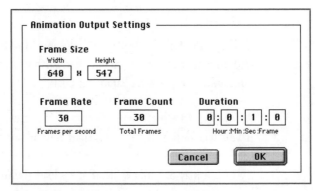

FIGURE *The Animation Output Settings dialog.*
9.17

MAKE MOVIE

When you are ready to record your masterpiece, this is the doorway to enter. You'll be taken through three separate steps, each with its own dialog: Movie Parameter Settings, Compression Settings, and the Save Path dialog. When using compression, I prefer Cinepak at full quality, but you can explore other options. See Figure 9.18.

RETIME ANIMATION

You may decide that the animation has to fit into a different time slot, and that you can't spare the time to reconfigure all of the keyframes. In that case, you can use this simple process to retime it from one length to another. See Figure 9.19.

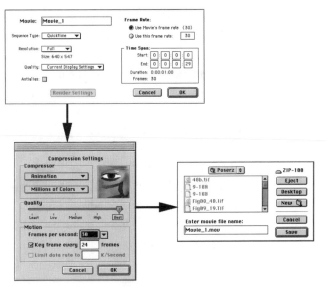

FIGURE
9.18
When you select Make Movie, these three dialogs allow you to adjust all of the parameters you need.

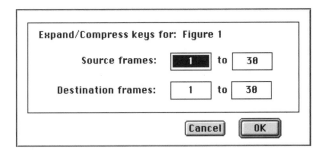

FIGURE *The Retime Animation dialog.*
9.19

RESAMPLE KEYFRAMES

When would you need to resample the keyframes? If you've done a lot of editing on separate elements in the animation, and you notice that there are places in the preview that look less smooth than you would have hoped, Resampling the Keyframes might help. You can either resample the animation by giving the computer the power to select where resampling should occur, or set resampling to force the addition of keyframes every nth frame. There's no guarantee that this will solve all of your concerns, but it may be worth a try. See Figure 9.20.

LOOP INTERPOLATION/QUATERNION INTERPOLATION

Here are definitions for both Loop and Quaternion Interpolations, written by Larry Weiner, the main programmer for Poser 4:

Quaternion Interpolation is a special mathematical interpolation technique that produces in-between motions that are more predictable between poses, but can cause strange-looking discontinuities when you look at the graphs of individual rotation parameters. The interpolation happens by using all three rotation channels at once, instead of simply interpolating each one individually (which is the default). It's only useful for animators who are really getting into the nitty-gritty of working out animations, and are having trouble with fine-tuning their animations. If you don't need it, it's probably easiest not to use it.

Loop Interpolation allows for easier creation of cycling animations. If you have a 30-frame sequence, and put keyframes only at frames 1 and 15 (introducing some change at 15), and turn on Loop Interpolation, you will see that the animation smoothly blends through frame 30 back to frame 1. Viewing the

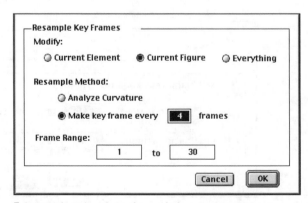

FIGURE *The Resample Keyframes dialog.*
9.20

graph will also show this. If you put keyframes near the end that are not similar to frame 1, you may get some very unexpected and strange in-betweens in the frames just before these because the last frame is essentially the frame before the first frame.. Viewing the graphs really helps make it clear what is going on.

SKIP FRAMES
This is a menu repeat of the same item shown in the Animation Controller.

MUTE SOUND/CLEAR SOUND
These commands work when you have an audio file loaded as part of the animation.

PLAY MOVIE FILE
Play AVI (Windows) or QuickTime (Windows and Mac) movies inside of Poser 4. Play Movie File is useful when previewing an animation you just rendered, and also for previewing an animation you are considering for use as a background.

IK

IK means Inverse Kinematics, and Poser 4 has a powerful IK engine. Kinematics itself refers to the movement of chained elements. The best example as far as the human body is concerned are the links between the Shoulder, Upper Arm, Lower Arm, and Hand, or that between the Thigh, Shin, and Foot. Many Human and Animal models come into Poser 4 with two or four limbs IK enabled by default. I usually disable it for most animations, but your work habits may incline you to leave it assigned.

I prefer to use IK when there is no looping of the animation involved. Using IK on a looped sequence can lead to some run-ins with chaos, because a lot of adjustments have to be made to make the last frame equal to the first as far as the modification of the elements. You can think of IK as glue. With IK enabled for a limb, the end element of that limb will remain glued to the spot if any elements higher in the chain are moved or rotated. This is great when a figure is to do push-ups, since the hands (if the arm is IK enabled) will remain on the floor. It's even OK if the figure is to throw a ball, as long as you maneuver the hand and not any other part of the arm. It is less useful if the throwing motion is to be repeated over and over in a continuous loop, because the position of all of the elements will have to be returned to their original orientation, by using either the Parameter Dials or the Motion Graph.

Preparatory Movements

Just a word or two about preparatory movements in an animation. Before an actor participates in an action, there is usually some hint about what is to occur. Think of a tiger about to leap on its prey. The tiger's body tenses, it goes into an anticipatory crouch, and the powerful spring of its muscles readies for the jump. A warrior is about to cast a spear. The spear hand is brought back slowly, and a concentrated look zeroes in on the target. The spear arm is brought back on a line to the target. The release is sudden, compared to the preparation. Preparatory motions create more realistic animations. Compared to actions, like leaping or throwing, preparatory motions take up to three or four times (and sometimes more) what the action will take. Actions are sudden, so that the keyframes set up for a quick action are very close together. Preparatory movements, on the other hand, take a lot longer. The keyframes are widely spaced apart, leading to slower and smoother motion overall. It is this preparatory movement that lends an air of anticipation and suspense to an animation.

Moving Along

This chapter opens the door to configuring animations in Poser 4. In the rest of the chapters in this animation section, we'll explore how various elements in a Document can be prepared for animated output.

10

ANIMATING ARTICULATED HANDS

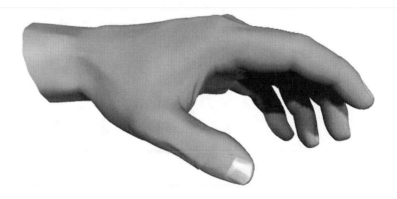

One of the most spectacular attributes in Poser 4 is both the sculpted excellence of the Hand elements, and the ability to animate all of the digits. The sculpted quality owes its existence to the modeling masters at the Zygote Media Group. In editions of Poser previous to version 3, hands viewed from close-up looked terrible, more like a childish attempt at drawing. Since Poser 3, all of that has changed for the better. The hands are of such high quality that they can appear absolutely photographic under the right lighting. Hands exist as two types of objects: connected to figures, and stand-alone constructs. Each type has its uses.

Pre-Attached Hands

In this chapter, when I use the word "Hands," I am speaking about the hands on Human models. Some of the Animal models have front paws or claws that are called "Hands," but we'll leave Animal model animation for Chapter 12, "Animal Animation." Pre-attached Hands, then, refers to the hands that come as part of a Human model when you import that model into your Poser 4 Document. As such, hands are animated whenever you move any body part that causes the Hand to tag along in some movement. The simplest and most common case would be any movement of the arm parts to which the hand is attached. To make a model wave hello, for instance, is to animate the forearm to which that hand is attached. See Figures 10.1 and 10.2.

FIGURE **10.1** *The Hand in this sequence can be seen waving, because the forearm to which it is attached is set to animate from side to side.*

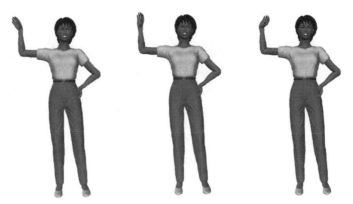

FIGURE *In this sequence, the Hand itself is seen waving side to side, while the forearm*
10.2 *remains stationary.*

Rule number one for animating a Hand is to use either the Left or Right Hand Cameras. See Figures 10.3 and 10.4.

FIGURE *The Hand Cameras zoom in on the hands.*
10.3

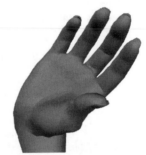

FIGURE *The Right Hand in Figure 10.2 is zoomed in on*
10.4 *using the Right Hand Camera.*

MANUALLY ANIMATING A HAND

Having zoomed in on a Hand with either the Left or Right Hand Camera, you are set to animate its separate parts.

1. Move any of the elements you desire to pose.
2. Now go to the Animation Controller, and move to another frame.
3. Pose the Hand elements again.
4. Repeat this process until you have posed the elements at the last frame.
5. Preview the results, edit where necessary, and save to disk.

See Figure 10.5.

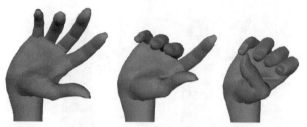

FIGURE *By selecting any of the movable elements of a Hand, while in the appropriate*
10.5 *Hand Camera mode, you can keyframe animate the Hand with the Rotation Tool.*

 *If you decide to animate the hands on a figure that is also to be animated in other ways, it is strongly suggested that you animate the rest of the figure first, saving the hands for last. That way, you can animate the Hand elements and also adjust whatever positions in space the hand is to be at the same time.*

A SIMPLER WAY OF ANIMATING HANDS

There is a far simpler method to use when it comes time to animate hands. Instead of starting from scratch, use one of the preset poses from the Hands library as a start, and tweak the elements as necessary. Go to the last keyframe in your sequence, and select another pose from the Hands library, and tweak that into position. This can be up to 10 times faster than trying to shape the poses manually. See Figure 10.6.

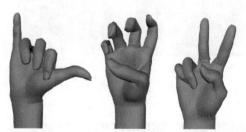

FIGURE *These three poses from the Hands library can be used as keyframes, so you can*
10.6 *animate from one to the other.*

Standalone Hands

There are two Standalone Hands, left and right, in the Additional Figures folder in the Figures library. These hands float in air, and can be used when you need just the hand in a scene, without the rendering or storage overhead of including other body elements. As we'll see in Chapter 13, "Composite Character Animation," they can also be used to create some unique animated effects. See Figure 10.7.

FIGURE   *The Standalone Hands float free of any body element connection.*
10.7

HAND POSING STANDALONE HANDS

You can use all of the techniques available to you for animating Pre-Attached Hands to animate the Standalone Hands. Just select the element you need to adjust, go to the keyframe you want, and use the Rotation Tool to reposition it.

ANIMATING STANDALONE HANDS WITH THE HANDS LIBRARY

You can use all of the techniques available to you for animating Pre-Attached Hands to animate the Standalone Hands, using the Hands library method. Just select the element you need to adjust, go to the keyframe you want, and select a new Hand pose from the Hands library. Tweak as needed.

Animated Hand Projects

There is an infinite variety of situations where you might focus upon animating the hands of a model, or other situations where using the Standalone Hands might suffice. Here are just a few ideas that challenge your Poser 4 interactions:

1. **The Balinese Dancer**. Balinese ritual dances are known throughout the world for the intricate and animated hand movements required of the practitioners. If you want this animation to be authentic, it will require a lot of research on your part, either from books or from detailed videos, or both. Make sure you are zoomed in close enough to allow the viewer to appreciate all of your detailed Hand posing if you take this project on.

2. **Pebble Pickup.** This is a project that can use either hands attached to a figure, in which case you'll also have to animate the figure stooping down, or with a Standalone Hand. Prepare for this animation by observing your hand, or a friend's hand, doing this task. Watch the way that the hand prepares to close on the object (which can be a Ball from the Props library), and observe how each finger plays a part in the action. You can do all the keyframing manually, and use the Grasp Parameter when the hand is over the ball, and use it again (negatively) when the Hand is to release the ball.

Karuna! *If you notice that your hand model is shaking in the animation, which makes you think the hand has the shivers, you can correct this in the Motion Graph. Just select the offending finger elements, and go to the Bend option in the list. If the motion curve jogs up and down, simply straighten it out in the frames where there is to be no bending. You will probably have to break the curve as well at those keyframe points. See Figure 10.8.*

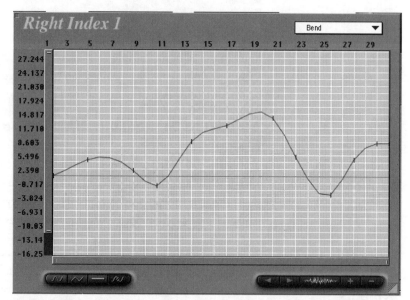

FIGURE *If there is shaking going on that you want to stabilize, open the offending*
10.8 *element's Motion Graph and straighten out the keyframes. The keyframes on the left have been straightened out.*

Karuna! *Be aware that the Grasp Parameter places a keyframe at every tween, so editing may take a while.*

Hand Jewelry

Using a few simple props creates hand jewelry, which can be animated itself.

STRANGE HAND

Resizing and elongating the elements of a Hand on various axes leads to some strange hands, like those used in a horror movie, as the actor transforms into a creature less than human. Using a resizing animation, you can also make a thumb throb, as if hit by a hammer. See Figure 10.9.

FIGURE *Hands may be animated to throb and morph.*
10.9

TALKING HEAD RING

Using a Torus for a ring, you can easily attach a free-standing Head to it. Once the Head is attached, it can be animated, providing the viewer with an eerie apparition. See Figures 10.10 and 10.11.

FIGURE *The Talking Head Ring sits on an animated hand.*
10.10

FIGURE *The Talking Head Ring close up, ready to slip on a finger.*
10.11

SHARP WARRIOR WRIST BANDS

In the movie *Ben Hur*, the chariots are outfitted with sharp blades. You can easily place a wristband around a hand that has retractable knives. Just use Cone Props, and elongate them in a keyframe animation to create this effect. See Figure 10.12.

FIGURE *A dangerous animated wristband.*
10.12

Study Your Body   When you need a special animated hand gesture, you have the best modeling tool at your disposal, your own hands. Open your hand and slowly make a fist. Watch how each finger and your thumb moves; some parts moving faster than others, and some at different angles. The animator has two friends, his or her own body, and a mirror. Using these two readily available study items, any body part can be animated realistically.

New in Poser 4   Brand new in Poser 4 are the Standalone Woman's hands, found in the Figures/Additional Figures library. See Figure 10.13.

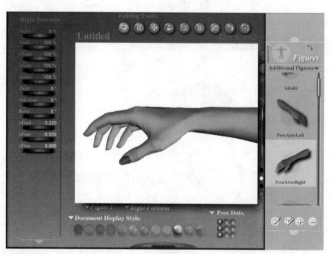

FIGURE *The new Woman's Hand model.*
10.13

Moving Along   OK. We've looked at animating Hands in this chapter. As we move to the next chapter in the animation section, we'll be studying facial and eye animation.

11

FACIAL, MOUTH, AND EYE MOVEMENTS

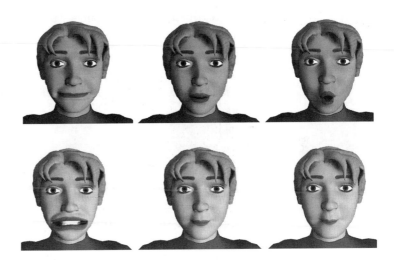

Compared to all of the other ways that computer animators have had to deal with when it comes to the difficult task of animating faces, Poser 4 is a miracle. Gone are the tedious manipulations of "bones," or the construction of countless individual morph targets. Instead, with just a few turns of a set of Parameter Dials, the targeted head of a model is reshaped into a new expression, or a whole new being. This opens up the craft of character development and animation to everyone, young to not so young, novices to professionals. Even if you have no interest in animating anything else in Poser 4, you're sure to spend hundreds of hours staring at the screen as your animated characters' faces come to life.

Animating the Mouth

The mouth of any person we meet, along with the eyes, tells an immediate story about that person's intentions and motives. Not a word need be spoken for this to occur. Think of the times that you have met someone new, and just the way that the pose of their lips suggested either an invitation to deeper communication, or a warning that you had best maintain your distance. This is obviously true in romantic encounters, but reaches far beyond that specific intent. The other night, while watching a news program on television, I was struck by the downward turn of the mouth of a high government official. It turned out that his views matched the message his mouth transmitted before he even uttered a word. Animation is about observation, because you can't shape a story for anyone else until you are well aware of all of the ways that stories can be told.

ANIMATING WITH MOUTH CONTROLS

Poser 4 offers you three main ways to shape the mouth with Parameter controls for keyframe animation purposes: Open Lips, Smile, and Frown. The Parameter Dials that control these feature-warping options can be adjusted in either a positive (right) or negative (left) direction, resulting in some very different looks. In addition to this, a nearly infinite variety of mouth shapes can be created by combining two or all of these Parameter settings. Expanding upon the Mouth parameters even farther, there are also Parameter Dials that control the shaping of the lips for the sounds "O," "F," and "M," and Tongue controls for "T" and "L."

CAUTION

Karuna! Be aware that the following parameter settings may differ slightly, depending upon the model you are working on. This is because different models deform according to their own unique structures.

Open Lips

As a standalone parameter, the effective range of Open Mouth lies between –.9 to +2.5. Higher or lower values begin to cause severe distortion of the face, from poking the teeth through the lips (values lower than –.9) to poking the lips through the upper head and chin (values higher than 2.5). For all but the strangest types of animated figures, stay within these suggested limits. When combined with the other Mouth Parameters, however, you will find that you can stretch these limits a bit. See Figure 11.1.

FIGURE *From left to right, Open Mouth settings of –.9, .5, and 2.5.*
11.1

Practice Session

Create an animation, keyframing nothing but the Open Mouth Parameter at different settings. Use the Face Camera. Using just the Mouth Open Parameters, you can simulate a chewing action.

Smile

The textbooks say that the act of smiling is actually based on an archaic aggressive display, a baring of the teeth. This explains why some smiles look absolutely frightening, while others seem sanguine. Use a range from –1.5 to +2.2 for the most common parameter values. Ranges lower or higher create facial distortions, because Smile also pulls and pushes on the skin below the eyes. Negative settings create a pouty, sad look (the lower lip actually starts to tuck under the upper lip), while higher settings light up a face with a smile. See Figure 11.2.

FIGURE *From left to right, Smile values of –1.5, 1, and 2.2.*
11.2

Adding Mouth Opens to a Smile makes it a laugh, and adding negative Mouth Opens to a negative smile emphasizes the sadness.

Practice Session

Create an animation, keyframing nothing but the Smile Parameter at different settings. Use the Face Camera. Using just the Smile Parameters, you can simulate an emotional roller-coaster.

Frown

At first glance, you might think that a Frown Parameter is just the opposite of a Smile, and since a sad countenance can be generated with a negative Smile, why bother to have a Frown Parameter. This is not the case, however. A Frown pulls on different areas of the face, so using a Frown negative alone creates a different quality of smile, and using a positive Frown creates an alternate sadness component. A standard range is from –2 to +1.5. A –2 value creates the smile of a naive simpleton, complete with dimples. A +1.5 value creates a caricature Frown, like that of a sad clown. See Figure 11.3.

The Smile and Open Mouth Parameters can either moderate or accentuate the Frown Parameter, depending if its value is set negatively or positively. See Figure 11.4.

FIGURE
11.3   *From left to right, Frown values of –2, .9, and 1.5.*

FIGURE   *Left: Frown of 1, Open Mouth of –.5, and Smile of 1.8. Right: Frown of 1,*
11.4   *Open Mouth of 1, and Smile of –1.5.*

Practice Session

Create an animation, keyframing nothing but the Frown Parameter at different settings. Use the Face Camera. Using just the Mouth Open Parameters, you can give your figure a dimpled smile at negative values, or a clown-like frown at positive values.

Combining the Three Basic Mouth Parameters

By using different parameter combinations of Open Mouth, Smile, and Frown, you can create some startling keyframes that morph from one emotional expression to another. See Figure 11.5.

FIGURE   *Left: Chagrin—Open Mouth of 1, Smile of –.8, and Frown of .8. Center: Uh-*
11.5   *Oh—Open Mouth of .325, Smile of .09, and Frown of 1.116. Right: Guilty—*
Open Mouth of –.130, Smile of –1.027, and Frown of .8.

Mouth Shapes for Phonemes

To shape a mouth as if it is pronouncing a word, you'll have to take the syllables of the word and shape the word from those mouth structures. You can explore phonemes in Poser 4 in two ways. One is to experiment with the Mouth Letter Structures (O, F, and M), and one by one, with nothing else animated, see what happens when you alter their parameters, and see if you can hear the imaginary sound being made. Write down your observations. See Figures 11.6 through 11.8.

FIGURE   *Parameter Values for "O" from left to right: –.9, .5, and 1.5.*
11.6

Karuna! *Shape the mouth into a kiss-ready pucker by a Mouth Open setting of –1.2 and a "O" setting of 2.3.*

FIGURE   *Parameter Values for "F" from left to right: –2 (puffs out lower lip), 1, and 3*
11.7   *(best for "F" look). Values higher than 3 push the teeth through the chin.*

FIGURE   *Parameter Values for "M" from left to right: –5 (open lips and clenched teeth,*
11.8   *great for that "G-forces look," or letter "I" if mouth is opened), 2, and 2.7*
             (maximum without facial distortion).

Practice Session

Create three animations, keyframing nothing but each of these three Mouth shapes separately, adjusting the Parameter to different settings. Use the Face Camera. Using just these three Mouth Parameters. See what words or sounds you can hear as the mouth moves.

Karuna! *Don't forget that you can apply phoneme mouth shapes very quickly by simply assigning them from the ready-made poses in the Phonemes folder in the Faces library.*

The Tongue

The placement of the tongue plays a large role in producing sounds, and the Tongue Parameter Dial settings in Poser 4 help you create the look of certain letters. The present Tongue settings are for "T" and "L." See Figures 11.9 and 11.10.

FIGURE **11.9**   *Parameter Values for Tongue "T" from left to right (all with Mouth Open of 1.5): .5, 1.1, 1.8. You can see the effect of the T Tongue best when the mouth is open, except when it is used to modify and deform other Mouth settings.*

FIGURE **11.10**   *Parameter Values for Tongue "L" from left to right (all with Mouth Open of 1.5): .5, 1.1, 1.8. You can see the effect of the T Tongue best when the mouth is open, except when it is used to modify and deform other Mouth settings.*

Practice Session

Create animations, keyframing nothing but each of these two Tongue shapes separately, adjusting the Parameter to different settings. Use the Face Camera. Using just these two Tongue Parameters, see what words or sounds you can hear as the mouth moves. The Tongue Parameters act as interesting modifiers to other Mouth Letter Parameters. Using a series of alternate Parameter settings for the Tongue "L" shape, with the mouth open at 1.5, you can create a character that is singing "La" sounds, just right for caroling during the holidays.

Animating the Eyes

An ancient proverb says that the eyes are windows to the soul. When we want to know if someone is lying, or what their real intentions are, we look deep into their eyes. The way that eyes dart around or remain focused and steady indicates a lot about the personality whose eyes they are. Everything that the eyes do has a powerful effect on the total personality.

SIZE MATTERS

Small beady eyes, like those of the rat, are interpreted by us as denoting a sneaky or conniving character. Large, wide eyes, like those of the doe, are interpreted by us as a sign of docility or child-like consciousness. You can alter the size of a model's eyes in Poser 4. See Figure 11.11.

FIGURE *The same model with small, beady eyes (40%), large-sized eyes (122%), and*
11.11 *large bulging eyes (122%, with a Z Trans of .002).*

Vampires, villains, and addicts are usually depicted with small, beady eyes. Heroes and lovable characters are many times depicted with large eyes, although when they bulge out excessively, the personality types become more bothersome.

The difference between large eyes and bulging eyes is their placement on the Z (in and out) axis. To keep large eyes without making them bulge, move them on the Z Axis a distance of from –.002 to –.004.

BLINKS AND WINKS

A Blink works on both eyes at the same time, while a wink works on only one eye. Use the Left and Right Blink Parameter Dials to animate either. Using a negative value opens the eye very wide, and can be useful for emotional responses like surprise or shock. See Figure 11.12.

FIGURE *Blink Parameters set to create the following, left to right: Sleepy Eyes (values of*
11.12 *.6 for each Blink, with opposite eyebrows raised and lowered); Blink Right; Negative Blink value of –1.25 for each eye (eyebrows also raised up).*

If your character's eyes are to blink during an animated sequence, do not time them too symmetrically. Instead, add some randomness to the timing of the keyframes for a more natural look.

SPROING!

By using the Z Trans Parameter Dial with higher values, you can move the eyeballs right out of the head, for a pretty startling animated effect. See Figure 11.13.

FIGURE **11.13**   *Using higher and higher Z Trans values, you can pop the eyes out of and away from the head.*

An interesting variation on this effect is to make the eyes smaller (40%) in the first frame, and larger as they leave the eye socket (200% for the last frame).

ATTENTION TO EYEBROWS

You should always think about adding animation to the eyebrows to enhance whatever animated expressions your model is invoking. The Eyebrow movements in Poser 4 also pull at the skin around the eyes, further enhancing any animated eye movements. Eyebrow Parameter Dials exist for three separate movements: Up, Down, and Worry.

Left/Right Eyebrow Down

Positive settings move the eyebrows down, and negative settings move them up. Do not conclude, however, that the negative settings are the same as using the Eyebrow Down Parameters, since different areas of the face are stretched. See Figure 11.14.

FIGURE *Left to right, Eyebrow Down Parameters: –3.1 (surprise or awe); 2 (concern);*
11.14 *separate settings (Left –2.8, and Right 2.5, an investigative look).*

*Explore animating each eyebrow with its own unique parameters to create some
very subtle emotional variations.*

Left/Right Eyebrow Up

Positive settings move the eyebrows up, and negative settings move them down.
Do not conclude, however, that the negative settings are the same as using the
positive Eyebrow Down Parameters, since different areas of the face are
stretched. See Figure 11.15.

FIGURE *Left to right, Eyebrow Up Parameters: –1.3 (sad concern); 1.5 (mild surprise);*
11.15 *(Left –2, and Right 2.5, probably physically impossible).*

Left/Right Eyebrow Worry

Negative settings create an angry countenance, while positive values create
worry and guilt. See Figure 11.16.

FIGURE *Left to right, Parameter settings for Worry: –2 (Anger); 1.6 (Worry); Verge of*
11.16 *Tears (Worry of 2.2, Smile of 1, and Frown of 1.3).*

Practice Sessions

Create animations, keyframing nothing but each of these three Eyebrow Parameters separately, adjusting the values to different settings. Use the Face Camera. Using just these three Eyebrow Parameters in conjunction with animated eyes, a wide range of emotions can be indicated.

Two Approaches to Animating Facial Characteristics

There are two main approaches to animating faces. One is to animate the distortions of the face caused by altering tapers and sizes. The second is to animate the mouth, eye, and eyebrow features. A third option, morphing, will be reserved for Chapter 15, "Morphing Madness." Actually, you can consider all of the options to be morphing based. Using tapers and resizing, as well as animating features (because distortions are involved) can be considered internal morphing. All of these methods can be used singularly or in combination, depending on your needs and goals.

FACIAL DISTORTION ANIMATIONS

You can alter the tapering of the head, positively or negatively, to create interesting facial animations. The eyes are not included in tapering the head, so they will have to be treated separately, unless you want to leave them as they are. The eyes are included when you alter the head's size. Any Prop attached, like hair, has to be treated separately in these modifications.

Size-Wise

You can use any of the Axis Parameter Dials to resize the head, which will also distort the face. Shortening the Y axis and widening the X axis creates a character that can be used as a bully. Other axis modifications create different characters. Animating size modifications creates a head that bulges in and out, useful for cartoon or science fiction projects. See Figure 11.17.

You will have to resize the neck when modifying the size of the head on any axis.

FIGURE *A collection of head resizes, left to right: Y of 82, and X of 227; Y of 137, and*
11.17 *X of 110; Pinhead displays a head resized to 25%.*

Practice Session

Create an animation that starts with a Head Y axis and globally sized to 0%, and ends with its Y axis and globally sized to 125%. Watch the head grow on the neck like a melon.

Tapering Reality

A positive Taper on a Head creates a conehead figure, while a negative Taper creates a figure wider at the bottom of the face. Alter between the two for a bizarre face-warping animation. See Figure 11.18.

FACE LIBRARY KEYFRAMING

Every time you create a face that displays an interesting emotion, or a distortion that you appreciate, save it to the Faces library in your own Custom folder. Faces can be applied as instant keyframes later on, to any figure, saving you a lot of time and energy.

Karuna! *If you are serious about creating characters that can be animated in Poser, with all of the facial subtleties that represent living beings, then you must investigate the purchase of two excellent resource volumes from Charles River Media: Animating Facial Features and Expressions by Bill Fleming and Darris Dobbs (ISBN 1-886801-81-9), and 3D Creature Workshop by Bill Fleming (ISBN 1-886801-78-9). These are absolutely vital resources for your library. See Figure 11.19.*

FIGURE *A Taper of 160 and −100 used on the same figure.*
11.18

 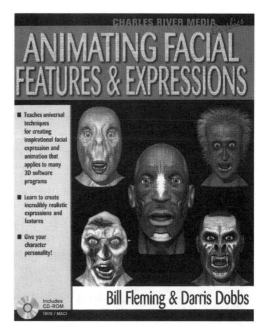

FIGURE   *Get these two Charles River Media volumes if you want to learn the secrets that professionals use in designing*
11.19   *and animating facial features.*

Moving Along   In this chapter, we have explored how Poser 4 faces can be customized using
controls for the mouth, eyes, and eyebrows. We also looked at the application
of phonemes and the tapering and resizing of heads, all as animation techniques. In the next chapter, we'll explore the animation of animals.

12 ANIMAL ANIMATION

We share the world we live in with myriad other creatures, creatures with personalities and lives very different from ours. For the animator, animals represent a unique opportunity to tell stories. Disney Studios keeps the animal mythic tradition alive, by introducing films every year that allow animals to speak as stand-ins for human characters and personality types. This tradition is worldwide, since animals have always played a major role in children's fables and teaching stories. Every culture has its favorite animal myths, from the Trickster Raccoons of native America to the Tigers of India. The Animal models included with Poser 3 and 4, and the addition models offered on the Zygote Extras and other CDs, provide new resources for the computer animator to retell the old myths, as well as to create new integrated Human and Animal model productions.

Where Are the Poser Animals?

The Poser Animals can be found in your Figures directory, in the Animals folder. If you have purchased the Zygote Animals collection, then they can be found in the same directory in a folder called Zygote Animals. The standard animals included with Poser are the Cat, Dog, Dolphin, Horse, and Raptor. The Zygote Animals include the Doe, Bass, Bear, Buck, Chimpanzee, Cow, Frog, Killer Whale, Lion, Penguin, Shark, Wolf, and Zebra. See Figure 12.1.

There is no way this book can walk you through definitive animation controls for all of the animals involved. Learning how animals move requires a lifetime of study and attention to detail. At the end of the chapter, we will suggest a unique way that you can tap into one resource for studying animal movements. In addition to that, if you are interested in creating realistic animations for your Poser 4 animals, it is highly recommended that you observe animals in motion every chance you get. Many of you probably have house pets, which is a good place to start. Cats and Dogs are always on the move. Carry a sketch book with you, and jot down the major points that determine their movement, where their feet are, what their heads are doing, and what bends first and in what order when they walk or run or recline. After that, the next best thing to do is to take a trip to a local zoo, carrying along the same sketch book. Look at the animals that match those offered in Poser 4, or included on the Zygote CD. Spend a day sketching their movements, and how their movements reflect their attitudes. If you do this five or six times, you'll be amazed how much your observations will be translated into your digital animation skills. Another way to study animal movement is to watch, and even purchase, a collection of the nature shows offered on public television, or other suitable TV channels. Those of you who have the appropriate hardware can even digitally capture frames of an

FIGURE *The full complement of Animals added in Poser 3, from the standard shipping*
12.1 *models to those contained on the Zygote Extras CD. A separate image at the end*
of this chapter shows some additional Poser 4 animals.

animal's movements, so you can study them more closely. And then there is one of my favorite ways of studying animal movements, by accessing the *Muybridge Complete Animal and Human Locomotion* volumes.

Eadweard Muybridge

If you've never heard or seen the name Eadweard Muybridge before ("Eadweard" is pronounced "Edward," by the way), then you haven't explored the history of animation. Muybridge was one of the founders of the principles of animation, and his work still holds a sacred place amongst the texts that beginning animators are required to study.

The story of how Muybridge got into animation in the first place is fascinating. Reportedly, someone made a bet with him that a running horse always has its feet on the ground. This was in the late 1800s, and photography was just in its infancy. Muybridge set up an ingenious experiment to prove once and for all if the running horse ever had all of its feet off of the ground at any point. He set up a series of cameras at a race track, with each one connected to a trip wire. The rest is history. When the photos were developed, they showed clearly that at one point in the horse's stride, all of its feet leave the ground. After this experiment, Muybridge spent the rest of his life filming motion studies of humans and animals.

Since the last copyright on Muybridge's work was filed at the turn of the century, his books and photos are totally copyright free. This means that you can use his extensive single-frame animation studies any way you want to, even republishing them on your own. I have checked this out thoroughly. He has three volumes published, and lately republished. They aren't cheap ($75.00 a volume), but for any animator, they are a must-have. The three-volume set ($225.00) is sold by Dover Press: order numbers 23792, 23793, and 23794. See Figure 12.2.

Dover Publications, Inc.
31 East 2nd Street
Mineola, NY 11501
(516) 294-7000
(no email address)

FIGURE
12.2
The Muybridge volumes published by Dover Press are all called Human and Animal Locomotion. The two-volume set pictured here is an older release from my private collection, separately configured for Humans and Animals.

USING THE MUYBRIDGE BOOKS

The Muybridge books are packed with single-frame sequences taken from Muybridge's movies. The sequences depict various animals and humans in different kinds of motion. Many of the animals are ones not yet addressed as Poser models, though the list of available animal models is sure to expand in the future. Because they are copyright free, you can scan in the pages and put the animations back together as a movie if you like. Their real value for Poser studies, however, comes after you scan them in and use the separated animation frames. Here's how:

1. Scan in a page from a Muybridge volume that depicts an animal in motion that resembles one of the Poser 4 models you have. The horse might be a good example.

2. In a suitable paint application, cut out and save each frame separately. Make sure that each frame is saved in the same size.

3. Open Poser 4, and load in the Animal figure that is represented in the Muybridge files you saved out. Import the first frame of those files as a Poser 4 background, and place the animal in the same position and size as that indicated by the imported frame.

4. Turn off Inverse Kinetics (IK). Rotate the animal's limbs until they match the background pose as closely as possible. Save out this Pose in a separate folder in your Poses library.

5. Load in the second frame, and go through the same process. Repeat this process for every frame you have to pose.

6. Delete the Figure, and start a new Poser Document. Configure an animation with a length equal to the movie you will create. To determine the length, multiply the motion frames you will be importing by 15. For example, if the Muybridge motion frames number 8, then the length of your movie will be 8 x 15 = 120. At 30 frames a second, this works out to a 4-second animation.

7. Load in your figure again. At every 15th frame, starting with frame #1, load in the poses you saved out. These will be the keyframes in the animation, and your computer will create the Tweens. When you are finished, you will have a real-world animal animation study.

See Figures 12.3 through 12.12 for some examples of the Muybridge Animals in Motion sequences.

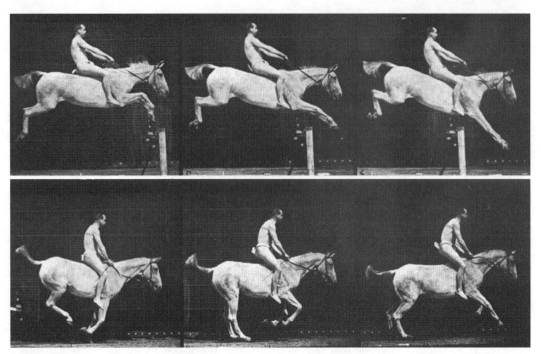

FIGURE *Horse jumping an obstacle. Start with the gallop, then keyframe the jump, and keyframe the gallop again.*
12.3 *You'll have to tweak some of the Tweens.*

FIGURE *Mule kicking. This could also be a Horse kicking, or any other suitable animal.*
12.4

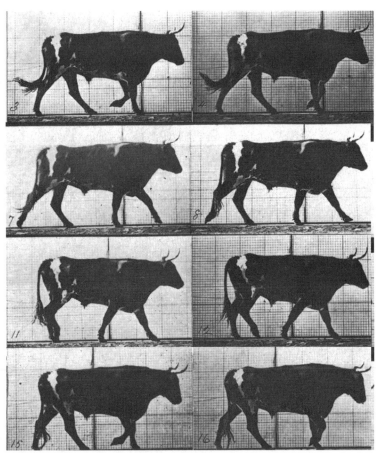

FIGURE   *Cow walking. This could also be a Bear, or other suitable animal.*
12.5

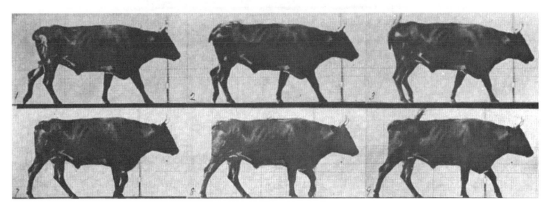

FIGURE   *Another Cow walk.*
12.6

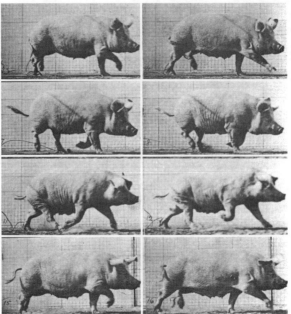

FIGURE *Pig running. These poses work great for the Bear, or any other lumbering*
12.7 *animal.*

FIGURE *Horse trotting. Use this with a rider atop your steed, and pose the rider's bounce*
12.8 *as well.*

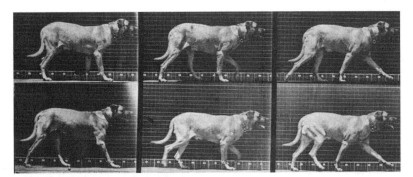

FIGURE *Dog running.*
12.9

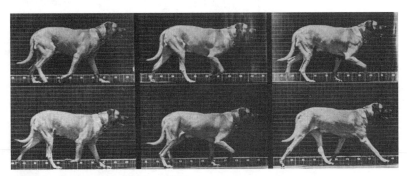

FIGURE *Dog running faster.*
12.10

FIGURE   *Cat run and pounce.*
12.11

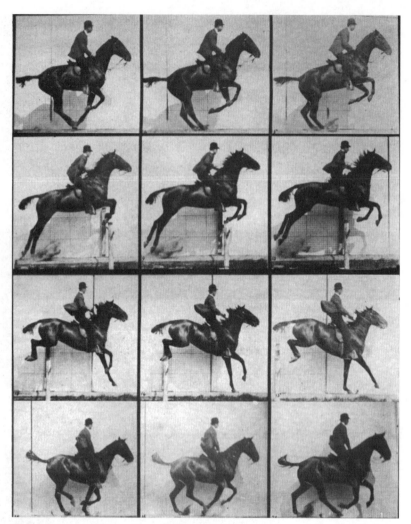

FIGURE *Horse jump.*
12.12

CAUTION

Karuna! *All of the Muybridge studies are in various stages of completion, so to use the poses in a finished animation, you'll have to adjust and add keyframes. You can apply the poses to any model; when animal poses are applied to a human model, be ready for comical surprises.*

The following figures display a few of the human motions in the Muybridge volumes. You can go through the same process described, and apply the animated poses to the Chimpanzee and the Raptor, because their body parts have some similarity to the human body. See Figures 12.13 through 12.17.

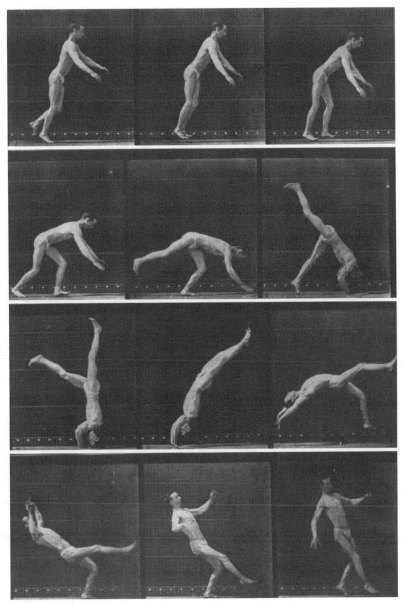

FIGURE   *Somersaulting. This is interesting applied to the Chimpanzee.*
12.13

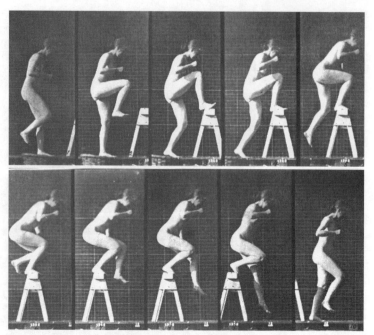

FIGURE *Climbing over an obstacle. This could be used to depict the Raptor climbing*
12.14 *over a rock, on its way to the prey.*

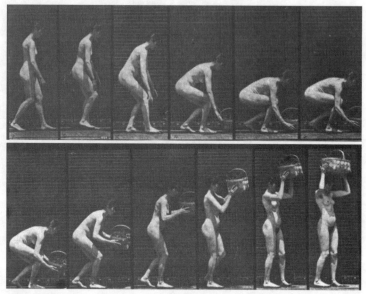

FIGURE *Bending and lifting a rock. Another Chimp possibility.*
12.15

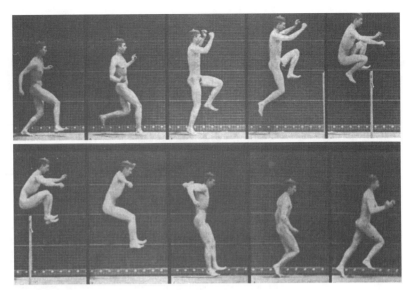

FIGURE 12.16 *Run and jump. Very funny when applied to the Raptor.*

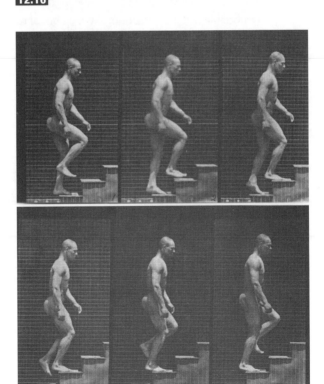

FIGURE 12.17 *Walking up stairs. This would make the Chimp look part human.*

Tips on the Poser Animals

There are some things to be aware of when animating the Poser and Zygote animals.

THE CAT

Aside from animated whole figure poses, like running, stalking, and leaping, the cat's personality is best defined by close-ups of the head. The best stories cats can tell is with their ears and eyes. The ears especially determine emotion on the cat. Try and observe a cat, and watch as its ears tell you how it feels. When the ears are back and straight up, the cat is usually saying, "I am not comfortable with this situation." When both of the cat's eyes blink, it is often a sign of love and appreciation.

THE DOG

The Dog's personality is often determined by the position of its tail, whether up in friendliness or tucked between the legs in anger. The most telling sign of aggression is when the head is down and the shoulders higher than the neck. To set the Dog on a walk with this pose is very effective for stalking. The Poser Dog model can be posed on two legs like a human, so various human poses can create animated dog cartoons.

THE DOLPHIN

When you animate the Dolphin's tail moving from side to side, as if swimming, move the head in the opposite directions. This provides interesting animated contrast. Animate the Dolphin's tongue moving up and down when you want to create the impression that it is speaking.

THE HORSE

The Muybridge volumes are especially useful when it comes to configuring animated poses for the Horse, since there are so many plates devoted to the Horse in different motion studies. When the Horse is simply standing in the background in your animations, make its tail flick from side to side. This simple technique is very effective, and lets the viewer know that the Horse is alive.

THE RAPTOR

The most interesting parts of the Raptor are its teeth and claws, the very same body parts that are frightening. No matter what the Raptor is doing, whether standing or in motion, keep these parts in motion. Even a slight opening and closing of the jaw, coupled with a twitching movement of the claws, is enough to give your viewers a chill. Try applying various human poses to the Raptor for more comedic effects. Don't forget to animate the claws on the feet. When the Raptor starts to run, its tail should be straight out, or even up a little.

THE DOE

As the gentlest of creatures, animate the Doe's movements to be subtle and slow. The Doe tends to move its head side to side frequently to search for possible predators when they're in the area. When the Doe runs, it should leap every once in a while.

THE BASS

All that needs to be animated on the Bass when it is swimming peacefully in the river are the belly fins and the mouth, and both very little. Of course, when it's caught on a hook, the whole body thrashes wildly.

THE BEAR

The Bear lumbers as it walks. When it runs, it tends to leap a little, with its front half leaving the ground, followed by its back half doing the same. Poser provides the necessary parameters for you to give the Bear a great animated snarl, especially effective for close-up head shots.

THE BUCK

You can use many of the Horse sequences from the Muybridge volumes to animate the Buck. Animate it running with head down for a dramatic effect. Try your hand at animating two Bucks in combat, locking their horns.

THE CHIMPANZEE

More than any other animal, the Chimp responds very effectively to any human pose, though sometimes comically. Use standard human poses as keyframes to animate the Chimp, especially the dramatic poses like the karate kick. When we explore the Walk Designer in Chapter 14, we'll see that the Chimp also can be animated through this alternate method.

THE COW

Cows usually move with their heads down, and they seldom run. Consequently, to show a complete cycle of a Cow's walk, you have to have a larger animation (10 seconds is adequate). If you want to add horns and show the Cow as a Bull, animate the head up and down and side to side to show the aggressive horn movements.

THE FROG

When leaping, the Frog's back legs go from a folded position to straight out. To emphasize the animated explosiveness of a leap, make the legs longer when stretched out, and shorten their length when folded. When the Frog opens its mouth, bulge the eyes out.

THE KILLER WHALE

Except for a slight movement from side to side of the tail sections, all you have to do to animate the Killer Whale is to set it on a path that takes it in and out of the water. Curve its body to make the motion look more fluid.

THE LION

The Lion should always raise its head skyward when it roars. Except when chasing prey, the Lion walks rather leisurely. Its tail flicks regularly to keep flies away.

THE PENGUIN

Make sure that the Penguin rocks from side to side as it waddles along. Its wings should also flap while this is happening.

THE SHARK

The most frightening aspect of the Shark is that it shows little movement while gliding along, so animating it is rather simple. When it bites prey, however, it tends to spin wildly to tear away what it wants.

THE WOLF

Animate the Wolf much as you would the Dog. The most effective animated pose for the Wolf is to show it in silhouette, baying at the moon.

THE ZEBRA

Animate the Zebra much as you would the horse, making the Muybridge volumes a good resource. When standing around, animate the tail flicking a lot, along with the ears.

More Animals

More Animal models ship with Poser 4, and even more will be available on future CDs from Zygote and other developers. In addition to that, the Poser community itself is a rich online resource for models and everything else. See Figure 12.36.

FIGURE *The collection of Poser models keeps growing with each edition, and also*
12.36 *through the efforts of Zygote and other developers.*

Moving Along

In this chapter, we've explored some of the aspects of animating Animal models in Poser. The next chapter looks at Composite models, and how they can be animated.

13

COMPOSITE
CHARACTER
ANIMATION

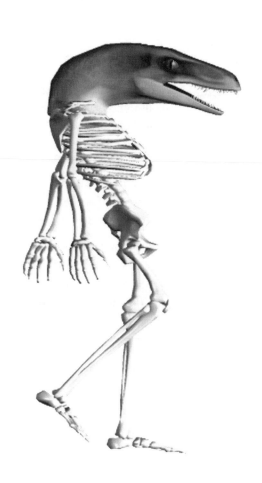

Having already covered the development of composite characters in Chapter 7, "Composited Figures," it is important to spend some time exploring how to animate your composited creations. Depending upon the type of composited model you are working with, there are some problem areas that may arise when you try to animate it. In this chapter, we'll look at how to animate three different types of composites: Multiple Composite Poser Models, Prop Composites, and Composites that combine models and props.

Karuna! *Note that some of the tutorials that follow mention that you should turn off visibility of some elements in the Properties window. This information is correct, but when it comes to making a large number of figure elements invisible, it is simpler to do this by clicking on the Eye icon for that element in the Hierarchy Editor.*

Multiple Composite Poser Models

As you saw in Chapter 7, it is very possible to combine two or more Poser models into one character, making unwanted parts invisible. So that's what we are about to do again, but this time, animating the composited character. So to begin, we'll use two models from the standard sets that ship with Poser 4, just to make sure everyone has them and can follow along.

THE RAPSKELION

For this exercise, we'll use the Male Skeleton from the Additional Figures folder, and the Raptor from the Animals folder. Do the following:

1. Open Poser, and load in the Male Skeleton and Raptor models. make the Neck, Jaw, and Head of the Skeleton invisible in the Male Skeleton's Properties dialog. Make everything on the Raptor model invisible except for the Neck sections, and the Raptor's Head. See Figure 13.1.

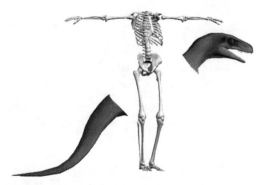

FIGURE *The composited figure starts with these components.*
13.1

Karuna! Always remove all Inverse Kinematics (IK) from all models used to construct a composited figure.

2. Turn both models so they are facing in the same direction. You will have to adjust the Skeleton so it is larger, and the Raptor so it is smaller as we go along, so the parts look like a natural fit. Select the Raptor Body from the list, and carefully move the Raptor Body until the Head sits on the Male Skeleton's upper Chest. See Figure 13.2.

3. As shown in Figure 13.2, you can see the way that I bent the body as a standing pose. I did this because the head is large, and I wanted to adjust the spine so it looked like it was accommodating the weight of the head. You should look at the figure and make the same adjustments.

4. In the list, if the Skeleton was added first, it shows up as Figure 1, and the Raptor as Figure 2. When you want to move body parts of the Skeleton, make sure Figure 1 is selected. Select Figure 2 when you want to animate the Raptor's Head parts.

Karuna! Make sure that you save this figure as a Poser 4 Document file, and not as a library figure. The reason is that if saved as a figure, only the selected half of the model will be saved.

5. Go to the Animation Sets folder in the Poses library, and double-click on any of the walking or running sets. You'll see how many frames it takes

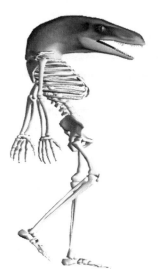

FIGURE *The Raptor Body is moved so the Raptor Head sits on the Skeleton Body.*
13.2

below its name. Change the number of frames in your animation to 120 at 30 FPS (that's four seconds).

6. The animated pose has been added starting at frame 1 of your animation, but the whole animated pose only covers part of your 120 frames, so you have to expand the animation to address all of your frames. Open the Retime Animation dialog in the Animation menu on the top toolbar. See Figure 13.3.

7. The first row asks you for the number of frames you want to expand, and the second row asks what you want to expand the animated frames to. In the first row, input the number of frames in the animated poses you loaded in. If that number was 24, for instance, the first row should read 1 to 24. You shouldn't have to do anything in the second row, as that lists the total number of animated frames; in this case, 1 to 120. Press OK. The animation is now retimed. You can also compress animated frames in the same manner.

8. Preview the animation. Tweak where necessary, and when satisfied, render to disk.

CAUTION

Karuna! *Make sure you check out the animation from different angles before rendering. You may even want to render more than one angle for later editing together.*

SHARKBOY

Those of you who have the Zygote Sampler and Animals libraries can try this one. It's called Sharkboy for obvious reasons. Load in Baby Sumo from the Sampler set, and the Shark from Zygote Animals. Make everything but the Shark's Head invisible, and make Baby Sumo's Head invisible. Carefully place the Shark's Head on top of Baby Sumo's neck in a vertical position (select the Shark's Body to move it, and rotate it on the X axis). Make Baby Sumo's Neck the Parent of the Shark Head. Rotate Baby Sumo's body so that it is horizontal.

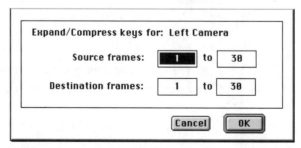

FIGURE   *The Retime Animation dialog.*
13.3

This is important. Many times, when you create a composite out of two or more models, it is important not to use either model's texture. Instead, use the Paint Tool to color both models so the parts match hues. This makes the finished composite look less like two separate models. It's also effective to use colored lights to blend the seam where the models meet.

See if you can animate the arms and legs of Baby Sumo so they look like they are flapping in water. Set the first and last keyframe of your animation first, making them the same. This allows you to loop the animation as many times as you like. See Figure 13.4.

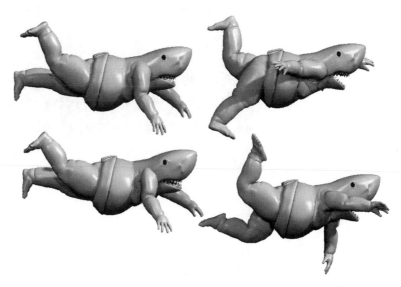

FIGURE *Sharkboy is a combination of Zygote's Baby Sumo and the Zygote Shark.*
13.4

Prop Composites

There may be times when you want to create an animation in Poser that has no human or animal models in it. It may be that you need a background animation, or perhaps an animation for a non-Poser project. You can use Poser to animate any Props in the Props library, or any 3D objects whose file format Poser can import. Poser's keyframe animation capability is far more variable than addressing human and animal models alone. See Figure 13.5.

Take a close look at the objects being animated as displayed in Figure 13.5. They are all very simple objects. The best way to learn how to animate complex scenes is to start with simple objects. That way, your interest is centered upon the animation, not the allure of the objects. The same principle is applied to

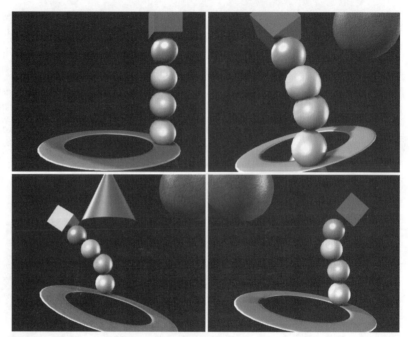

FIGURE *Here is a selection of frames from an animation, all of whose elements are basic*
13.5 *3D models from the Props library.*

movie-making in general. If you can tell a story with basic objects, think how much more you can do when it comes to developing themes with more complex objects. Basic objects are seen as symbols anyway, and can sometimes force the viewer to create his or her own imagined dialog.

Objects can easily be linked or parented to each other in Poser. The stack of spheres and the top cube shown in Figure 13.5 are all hierarchically connected, with the bottom-most object set as the Parent of the object above it. The bottom sphere has the flattened Torus as its Parent, so as the Torus tilts, the moving stack of objects tilts with it. The background sphere and the rising cone were added to add viewer interest, but they are dispensable to the main action. The stack rotates around the flattened Torus, and is also affected by the motions of the Torus itself. Take a look at this animation on the CD-ROM. It's called Props1.mov.

EXTERNAL PROP CREATIONS

You can create a Poser 4 life form completely out of Props. It can take any form you like, from an emulation of a dog or cat to a more other-worldly creature. No Human or Animal models are involved, but you can use the Props Parameter Dials for rotational and positional movement. In a composited Prop character, each of the Props is linked in a series of parental chains. See Figures 13.6 and 13.7.

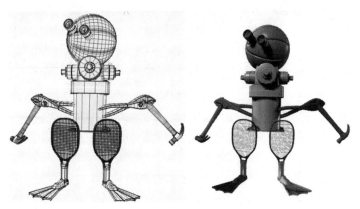

FIGURE **13.6** *Each of the elements of this figure consists of a Tool or Sports prop from the Zygote Prop libraries. Here, the Fire Hydrant is the central Parent figure.*

FIGURE **13.7** *Hammers for legs, Spears for arms, a Shield for a body. All this topped by a Basketball for a head, wearing Sunglasses and covered by a Cowboy Hat. This figure can be animated by rotating any of its Zygote Props parts.*

Mixed Composite Combination Animations

In addition to replacing a figure element with a Prop, you also have the option of Parenting the Prop and any selected element of the model. Using a sword prop, for instance, you can move it into position over one of the hands of the model, and use that same hand as the Prop's Parent. The Prop still has independent movement on its own when it is selected, but any additional movement of its parental model element will also animate the parented Prop.

Karuna! Here is an invaluable tip for working with the Zygote Props in the Props library. The Zygote Props are written to the Document in a tilted orientation, with their Origin Points messed up, and their icons missing from the library. If you have the time and patience, here's what to do to fix them. First, set their Rotation to 0 after importing. Then, move their Origin Point so that it centers on the object. Use the Outline Display Mode when moving the Origin Point so you can see it more clearly, and jump between views to center it. Last, delete the object from the library (but not from the Document). Now add it to the library again, making sure to press the OK button on the dialog, and not the Return key on your keyboard. You will now have a color icon in the library. That fixes everything. Now, when you make a composited model using the Zygote Props, they will come in perfectly, and rotating them will do what you expect.

RULES FOR USING PROPS WITH HUMAN AND ANIMAL MODELS

Whether attaching a sword to an animated musketeer, or a hat to a horse, here are some suggested rules to attend to:

- Always move the Prop into position before posing the model. Use the orthographic views to make sure the Prop is positioned exactly where you want it.
- Turn off IK, so that necessary editing later avoids having keyframes assigned to every frame.
- Turn on Full Tracking in the Display menu when positioning Props, so you are aware of the exact position of the Prop as related to the body of the model when moving it.
- When placing a Prop in the model's hand, leave the hand open. After it is placed, close the hand on the Prop by using the hand's Grasp Parameter.
- If you are creating an animation with more than one Human or Animal model in it, you might explore (when possible) fully animating the first figure before loading the next one in. Otherwise, the Edits can get very tricky, and you will definitely have to adjust the motion curves.

See Figures 13.8 through 13.10.

Once the Props have been positioned and parented, you can use the model's Rotational Parameters to animate the character. See Figure 13.11.

FIGURE **13.8** *The unaltered Zygote Heavy Man model, surrounded by the Props before their placement. While placing the Props, leave the model in its defaulted position.*

FIGURE **13.9** *The Props are placed in position, related to the model. The Hat is Parent to the Knife, and the Head is Parent to the Hat. The Saw and Shovel are parented by their respective hands.*

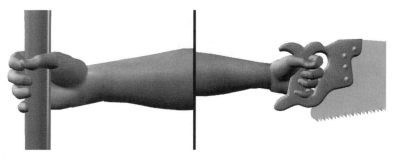

FIGURE **13.10** *Close-up cameras of the hands display the use of the Grasp Parameter Dial to "hold" the Props.*

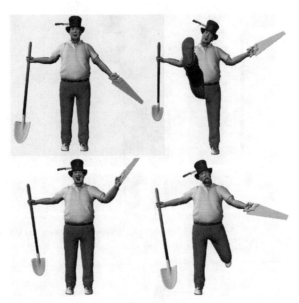

FIGURE   *Selected frames from the animation of the PropGuy model.*
13.11

COMPLEX COMPOSITES TO ANIMATE

Just how complex a scene can be animated in Poser 4? Look at Figure 13.12 for just one example. The head and hands of the large figure were replaced by spheres. A Zygote Police Hat is parented to the large head sphere, and a sword to the left hand sphere. A Zygote Alien model, with an enlarged head, sits on the right hand (sphere) of the large model. On the Alien's head is a parented Zygote Female Hair Prop. There are thousands of possible animations that can be created from just this one composited composition.

FIGURE   *One example of a fairly complex composite that can be keyframe animated.*
13.12

Shooting a Cannonball

One of the Props in the Zygote Tools and Weapons folder is a wonderful cannon, ready to play a part in your movies. To do this exercise, you will need to have the Zygote Props folder installed in your Props library. Use the frames in Figure 13.13 as a reference.

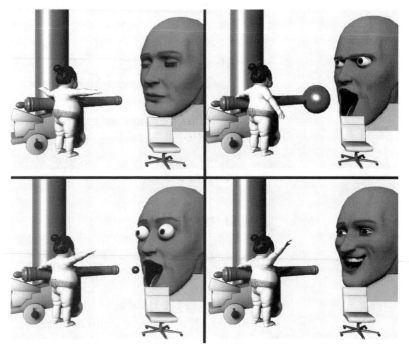

FIGURE   *Selected frames from the Cannonball animation, displaying the items described*
13.13   *in the tutorial.*

1. Load the Zygote Baby Sumo, or any other model you would like to use as the cannoneer. Load the Zygote Cannon Prop. Face them both away from the camera.
2. Make this a 150-frame animation. Move the cannoneer's arms at frame 1 so they are up in the air, and down at the side in frame 100. This is the "Fire" command.
3. You will be adding two Ball Props. One is for the cannon explosion, and the other for the cannonball. Place the Ball Prop to act as the explosion around the front of the cannon, and set its size to 0 at frame 1. Set its size to .001 at frame 99, and to 400% at frame 101. Set its size to 0 again at frame 106. Color it red.
4. For the cannonball, resize the Ball so that it fits comfortably in the barrel of the cannon, and color it dark blue. Place it just inside of the cannon

barrel at frame 1, and set its protrusion to .001 from the barrel in frame107. In frame 150, set its distance from the cannon on a straight trajectory off the screen. If you've done this right, the preview will show an explosion followed by the cannonball flying straight out of the barrel of the cannon.

5. Within plain view in your Document window, load one of the heads from the Additional Figures folder. Set it up so the mouth is in a direct line in front of the cannon. Set frame 1 and 80 to keyframe the mouth closed. Keyframe 105 to a wide-open mouth. Add some expression to the eyes and eyebrows at this same point.

6. The cannonball should head right into the wide-open mouth. At frame 125, close the mouth and give it a smile. Return the mouth to no smile and closed at the last frame, so the animation can loop.

7. If you like, you can add some other Props in the scene just for interest. Save the animation to disk after you render it.

Hand 'O Heads

In this final animation walk-through in this chapter, we will create an animation that would be nearly impossible to design with anything else but Poser 4. I call it "Head 'O Hands," and you'll see why.

1. Load the Left Hand from the Additional Figures folder. This is a Standalone Hand. Open it so that all of the fingers are pretty straight, and rotate it so that it is vertical with fingers upward as seen by the camera. Create a little space between the fingers. See Figure 13.14.

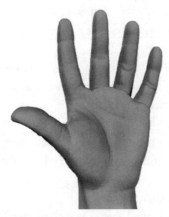

FIGURE *The Left Hand is loaded to the Document window.*
13.14

2. Now load five Standalone Heads from the Additional Figures folder. They can be any mix of the Male and Female Heads.

3. Resize each Head so it looks natural on top of a finger of the hand, and place each Head on the four fingers and the thumb. Each Head should be parented to the third finger or thumb part that it sits on. See Figure 13.15.

4. Place some Props, Hair and/or Hats, on each of the Heads. Parent the Hats and Hair to the same finger part that each respective Head is parented to. Give each of the faces a different expression. See Figure 13.16.

5. Keyframe animate each of the Heads, altering their expressions and rotations, and animate a slight movement into the fingers each sits on. Make this a 180-frame animation. Render, save to disk, and amaze your friends and family. See Figure 13.17.

FIGURE   *The Heads are in position on each of the fingers of the hand.*
13.15

FIGURE   *Each of the Heads now has a Hair or Hat Prop, and a unique expression.*
13.16

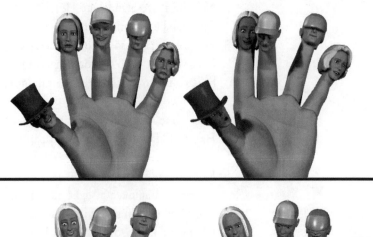

FIGURE   *Frames from the Hand 'O Heads animation.*
13.17

Moving Along   In this chapter, we have explored creating composited animations of different
types. In the next chapter, we'll look at the miraculous Poser 4 Walk Designer.

14

THE WALK
DESIGNER

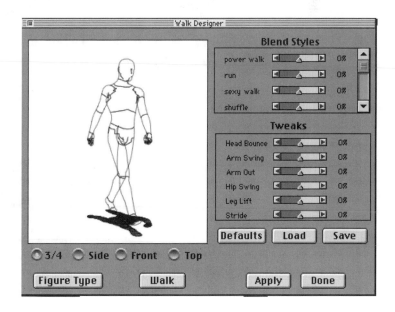

oser 4 addresses one of the most complex, and often supremely annoy-
ing, tasks that an animator faces: how to create a realistic walk pattern for
a targeted character. In Poser 4, the targeted character has to be bipedal,
but future versions of Poser may address quadrupeds as well. The Walk Designer is one of the most powerful features of Poser 4, though it is quite simple
to use and master.

The Walk Designer Control Dialog

The Walk Designer Control dialog is an interactive display that shows you exactly what the various Parameter Dials do as you adjust them. See Figure 14.1.

Let's take a quick tour of this dialog (refer to Figure 14.1). On the left is an
animated display that shows you exactly what your walk looks like as you adjust the dials on the right. You can watch the walk from a 3/4, top, side, or
front view. It is highly recommended that you switch amongst all of these view
options before designing a walk, since that enables you to catch any anomalies
in your walk design that might be hidden from one view alone.

CAUTION

*Karuna! Make sure the Foreground color is very dark in order to see the animated
preview in the Walk Designer.*

On the right are two groups of walk design Parameter Dials: Blend Styles and
Tweaks. Think of Blend Styles as the major parameters, and Tweaks as adjust-

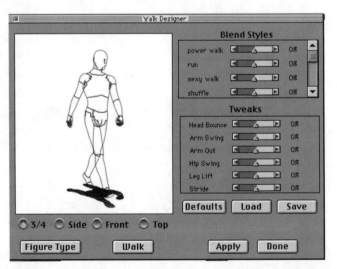

FIGURE *The Walk Designer Control window, accessed from the Window menu.*
14.1

ments within those parameters. In Table 14.1, we will look at each of the Blend Styles and Tweaks in detail, describing what various parameter settings do.

Below the Tweaks Parameter Dials are three buttons: Default, Load, and Save. Pressing Default zeroes out all of the parameters. Anytime you design a walk that you like, you can Save it to disk by first clicking on the Save button, and then selecting a name and target drive path. Click on Load to import previously saved walk designs.

The bottom row of buttons includes Walk, Apply, and Done. Click on Walk (which then becomes Stop) to activate the Mannequin walking with your adjusted walk style, and Stop to cease its motion. Apply brings up the Apply dialog, with another list of specific parameters to decide upon before committing the walk to the target model. After modifying all of the Apply parameters as you want them, you are returned to the Walk Designer Control dialog to click on Done.

THE APPLY DIALOG

After the walk has been designed to your liking, clicking on Apply is the next step. This brings up the Apply dialog. See Figure 14.2.

Refer to Figure 14.2 as we explore each option in the Apply dialog. At the very top of the dialog are two input areas, one for Start Frame and one for End Frame. The simplest way to configure the frames being addressed is to leave these settings at their defaulted indications, as this represents the total length of your frame settings, beginning to end. But as we'll see a little later in this chapter (under Non-Sequential Walks), there are reasons for selecting other than the

FIGURE *The Apply Dialog.*
14.2

defaulted frame number references here. Leaving this at the defaulted numbers results in the walk being applied to every frame in your present sequence.

Under the frame settings is a list of the Figures (models) in your Document window. Select the model from this list that you want to apply the present walk to. The walk remains resident in the Walk Designer, so you can apply the same walk to another model after applying it to the one selected, though it's always safer to Save your customized walks before applying them to the model.

The next setting down consists of a checkbox for Walk in Place. Walk in Place is most useful when you are going to export the animated sequence to RayDream, and set the figure on a path in that environment. Walk in Place is also useful when it's enough to show the figure walking in place for the project you're creating (perhaps a project that doesn't even require showing all of the foot movements). Walking and running in place over a moving backdrop is an old movie trick, and this can be duplicated in Poser 4. Another Walk in Place use comes about when you are going to map the animation file to a moving plane in another 3D application, and set the plane in motion. Most professional 3D applications allow you to do this, dropping out the background color. This is a way to export Poser 4 animation files to most every 3D application around, making no difference if Poser directly supports that application. On the right is another input area that remains ghosted out unless Walk in Place is checked, called Cycle Repeat. If a model is walking in place, without moving on a path, you can set the Cycle Repeat to any whole number. The higher this value, the faster the walk will seem, since the walk has to be stuffed in a finite number of frames. The number placed here is in direct proportion to speed, so 2 will create a walk speed 2X as fast as 1, and 3 would be 3X, and so on.

If you have designed a path in your Document window, it will appear in the Path selections, and can be chosen from there. Obviously, you cannot set the model on a path and have it walk in place at the same time. There is an interesting optical illusion possible, however, as follows:

Out of Body Experience

1. Create two figures exactly the same, and have them occupy the same exact space in your Document. Create a Path for one (covered later under Paths if you need a refresher), and not for the other.
2. Apply the same Walk Design to both, except make the one with no path Walk in Place. The path for the other should be Circular.

Can you guess the result? The figure will walk out itself like a ghost, and return to itself in perfect harmony. Use this to create an "out of body experience" animation.

THE APPLY DIALOG (CONTINUED)

At the bottom half of the Assign Dialog is a series of checkboxes.

Always Complete Last Step

If the animation is to loop, then this should be checked. If it is to be part of a patched sequence, then it need not be.

Transition From Pose/To Pose

Your model may be sitting at the start of an animation, and then get up, assume a pose, and walk away. In this case, the model will need some number of frames to complete its initial movements. Checking Transition From Pose, and inputting a number in the associated area (a path has to be assigned for this to make any sense) allows you to reserve frames for the initial pre-walking movements. In the same manner, Transition To Pose allows a model to end a walk by assuming another pose not associated with that walk. You have to carefully explore each of these options. Do not expect to get what you want on the first try. The main caution is to allow enough frames at the start and/or end of the walk sequence for the changes in action. The more radical the poses are from each other, the more transitional frames you will need.

Align Head To

If you have set the walk on a path, then you may command the model to look in specific directions while it is moving on the path. There are three options: One Step Ahead, End of Path, and Next Sharp Turn. The model's head will then move according to your selection.

CAUTION

Karuna! Do not assign any Head Bounce to the walking model when using the Align Head To options, or at most, very small values. It is disconcerting to see the model looking in a direction while its head is also bobbing up and down, unless you are trying to emulate a serious nervous condition.

Walk Design Parameters

Table 14.1 details what each of the Blend Styles and Tweaks accomplish when set to five different values: All the way down, half way down, defaulted, half way up, and all the way up. Note that the Blend Styles range from –200 to +200, while the Tweaks range from –100 to +100. Settings in between those indicated moderate the detailed results.

Table 14.1 Parameter setting conditions for Blend Styles and Tweaks. Note that these are examined here as unitary options, with all other settings defaulted to zero.

The Walk Designer

Parameter Setting	All the Way Down	1/2 Down	Defaulted at Zero	1/2 Up	All the Way Up
			Blend Style		
Power Walk Used at positive values to give the targeted figure a more purposeful walk style.	Creates a jumbled chaotic walk style, so the figure looks out of appendage control.	Makes the movements look slightly out of control, as if the figure can't keep its mind on what it is doing	No Power Walk effect. Devoid of seductive content.	Lends a march-like quality to the walk, determined and precise movements.	Gives an excessive power stride, as that of a robot or giant who won't allow anything to stand in its way.
Run This setting differentiates between walks and runs	Creates a wacky bouncing motion that can seriously jumble appendages like arms and hand positions.	Creates a skipping motion.	Creates a normalized walk.	Creates a bounding run, good for a fast race.	Creates a chaotic bouncy run, and can cause overlaps in arm swings and positions.
Sexy Walk This lends a seductive appearance to the figure's movements.	Creates a "gimpy" walk, as if the figure has some problems controlling the sureness of its movements.	Creates a lazy walk, likened to someone walking down a country road in a very relaxed fashion.	Devoid of seductive content.	Creates a very natural sexy walk with a noticeable hip swing.	Creates a radical and almost cartoon-like sexy walk, with more hip swing than the body can almost handle.
Shuffle A Shuffle is defined as a walk with a relaxed attitude.	Creates a jumble disorganized skip.	Creates an arrogant walk, as if the model were self-satisfied beyond criticism.	No effect on the walk.	Creates a plodding shuffle, as if the figure were looking at the sidewalk and just ambling along.	Creates an erratic shuffle, making the figure look like something is physically wrong with the legs.
Sneak Defined as a walk that remains unexpected when practiced.	Jumbles the entire upper body in a tangle.	Still pretty radical since it distorts other body parts.	No effect.	A caricature of a sneak, more like a New Orleans strut.	A cartoony strut, with the body bending back and forth radically at the Hip.

			Tweaks		
Strut a Strut is a display of pride sometimes used to attract the opposite sex to one's importance.	Creates a movement in the arms reminiscent of dancing or what some communities call the "Hand Jive."		No effect.	A real determined Strut.	A Strut that makes the arms look like they're shadow boxing.
Head Bounce The head bounces naturally to compensate for rhythmic impacts suffered by the lower body.	Makes the head shake violently, which would break the neck.	Creates a head bounce that makes the head shake as in signifying "yes."	No effect.	Reverse of −50%	Reverse of −100%
Arm Swing There is always arm swing in a walk, so this parameter setting just emphsizes it to various degrees.	Arms swing rather limply.	Arm swing a little less limp.	No effect, normal arm swing	Arms swing a little more purposefully.	Arm swing is very purposeful, as in a march.
Arm Out This parameter forces the arms away from or closer to the torso (definitely move the arms away from the torso in a walk if the model is heavy).	Arms crossed in front of chest for the whole walk.	Arms crossed in front of pelvis for the whole walk.	No effort	Arms pushed away from body, as if the model had very musclar arms.	Arms radically pushed away, forming a cross with the torso.
Hip Swing Used to emulate a seductive feminine walk.	Hips sway radically.	Moderate hip sway.	No Movement	Hip sway opposite of −50%	Hip sway opposite of −100%.
Leg Lift This parameter sets the height of the legs at their maximum.	Legs sort of slide along the ground.	Legs off the ground a little.	Normal height above ground during walk.	Legs lifted up noticeably.	Legs lifted off ground as in a march.
Stride This represents the distance covered with each step.	Walk in place.	Short stride.	Normal stride.	Above normal stride.	Very long stride, like Groucho Marx.

Walk Design Parameter Combinations

The real magic of the Walk Designer comes when you combine more than one Blend Style and Tweak. These combined parameters lead to all sorts of unique walk looks. We have detailed some of them in Table 14.2

Table 14.2 Unlike Table 14.1 (which shows the effects of just single parameter settings), this table shows how various combined parameter values create six unique walk styles. Imput these values, and see if you would name them the same as the author did, then explore your own settings. Save the Walk Designs you like.

Settings	Leaping Run	Max Pronging	Creepy Monster	Oh Yeah!	Tromp Romp	March
Run	83	−120	−3	0	3	0
Shuffle	0	0	0	0	−18	0
Sneak	0	18	25	0	25	0
Strut	0	0	0	0	0	0
Head Bounce	23	0	0	49	0	0
Arm Swing	20	−74	−100	0	−100	100
Arm Out	−38	100	100	0	38	0
Hip Swing	0	100	0	−100	0	0
Leg Lift	0	0	0	0	56	100
Stride	100	100	−70	0	−52	30

Paths

Poser 4 is not as enabled a 3D Path animation environment as are other more robust applications, but it does offer you the chance to set objects and models in motion on a path. To draw a animation path in Poser, do the following:

1. Click on the model to be animated, and go to the top camera view.
2. Under the Figure menu, activate the Create Path mode by selecting it.
3. You will see a path line extending out from the figure in the top view. Clicking on the line activates the path creation options. The Nodes that are displayed can be moved. Clicking on the path where no node is present places a node at that point. Explore these options. When you are finished, simply stop customizing the path. See Figure 14.3.
4. Human and animal figures can be assigned a path in the Walk Designer, but Props cannot. Props have to be keyframe animated. Whenever you design a path, it is given a sequential numerical name (Path 1, Path 2, and so on).

A Path cannot be moved in the Y axis (up or down), and it always rests upon the Ground Plane.

FIGURE   *use the mouse to place and move path nodes in the top view.*
14.3

5. Clicking on a Path activates it, and brings up its Parameter Dials, where it can be scaled and/or translated along its X or Z axis, and rotated on the Y axis.

Transitional Walks

By "transitional walk," I refer to a walk assigned from the Walk Designer that targets less frames than the total number in your sequence. The extra frames can be at the start, end, or both the start and end of your animation. This necessitates checking the Transition From at Path Start and/or Transition To at Path End. Be aware that transitional walk may require some tweaking of your poses, since movement from one pose to another in a set number of frames may jostle elements you want to remain stable. In that case, simply go into the Motion Graph and delete the keyframes that are causing the problem. Applying a Walk to a figure sets up keyframes for every frame, which often have to be deleted and re-posed when anomalies occur.

Animals and The Walk Designer

The only two animals in the present collections that work very well with the Walk Designer are the Zygote Chimpanzee (best) and the Raptor (second best). To some extent, you can also use the Zygote Penguin, but some frames may render with severe polygonal distortion, and the poses will have to be tweaked. The Chimp and Raptor have to be positioned first to mimic the standing position of a human model, before applying Walk Designer parameters. The Zygote Alien, Baby, and Baby Sumo can also be considered standard human models for purposes of the Walk Designer.

USING OTHER ANIMALS WITH THE WALK DESIGNER

Here is a technique that I discovered that allows you to have varying degrees of success using the Walk Designer to animate other Poser animals (except for fish, of course). Do the following:

1. After importing the selected animal from the Figure library folder, go to the Right Side View Camera.
2. Turn off all IK settings. Bend the animal as shown in Figure 14.4.

FIGURE *Note how the Animal model is bent, so that a Walk Design can be applied.*
14.4

3. In the Front Camera View, use the Side-to-Side parameter to rotate each shoulder 90 degrees as shown in Figure 14.5.
4. Go to the Walk Designer, and apply a walk to the animal. You will notice that most of the time, the animal's arms will be crossed when you preview the walk pose. See Figure 14.6.
5. To fix the arms, go to the Keyframe Editor. Place a marquee around the left and right shoulders, and all of their children (upper arms, forearms, and hands). Delete all of these keyframes. See Figure 14.7.
6. Back on your Document window, you can now keyframe animate the arms again, having deleted all of the Walk Designer keyframes. Exploring these options further, and perfecting their technique, you can de-

FIGURE *The Shoulders of the animal are rotated Side-to-Side as shown here.*
14.5

FIGURE *After applying the walk, the animal's arms will probably be crossed.*
14.6

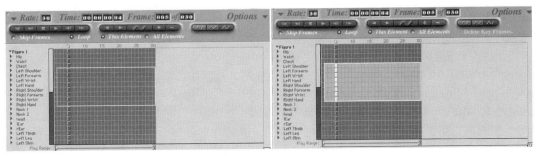

FIGURE *The selected keyframes are deleted from the animation.*
14.7

velop a whole library of animals perfect for fables and fairy stories. See Figure 14.8.

FIGURE *The finished animated animal is ready for your own Mother Goose production.*
14.8

**Using BVH
Motion Files**

Import a BVH Motion File, and it is instantly associated with your selected figure. I've found that the Z-axis option works best, when the question comes up on import. I've also found that the standard Poser figures work with BVH files better than many of the Zygote Extras models. This is especially true when it comes to hand and arm twists, which if they're pushed too far, distort the model. You'll have to explore BVH files on a case-by-case basis. If you find them useful for your work, you can contact BioVision or House of Moves via their Web sites. They often post freebies, which you can download and explore within Poser 4. BVH data works well when you expand the animation to a larger sequence. The motions still appear realistic when the sequence is expanded. See Figure 14.9.

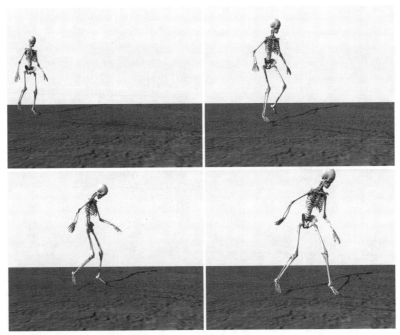

FIGURE
14.9
This series of frames is from an animated sequence that uses the Poser Female Skeleton as a target for the Drunk.BVH file in the Men's Motions folder, located in the Motion capture directory on the Poser 4 CD.

CAUTION

Karuna! If you have any uses for BVH motion files in your Poser productions, DO NOT miss the opportunity to avail yourself of the awesome collection of BVH animated content on the PoseAmation CD(s) by world class animator Chris Derochie. Each of the BVH files contained in this collection were painstakingly crafted to represent many of the movements requested and required for film and multimedia story lines. Find contact data for this collection in Appendix C, "Vendor Contact Data."

Moving Along

In this chapter, our focus has been to explore the intricacies of the Walk Designer, as well as to take a look at the application of BVH motion data files. In the next chapter, we'll detail how morphing works in Poser, and what it can be used for.

15

MORPHING MADNESS

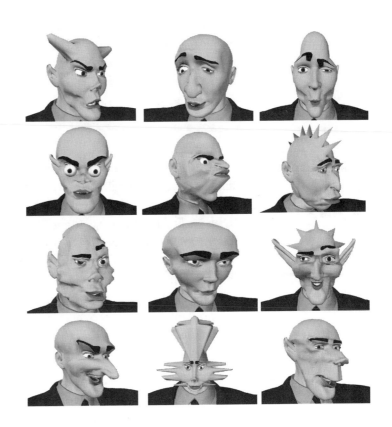

Everywhere you look in Poser 4, you will find tools and modules that are at the very edge of revolutionizing computer graphics and animation. The Morph capacity is another shining example. Actually, every time you tweak a Parameter Dial, you are engaging in 3D morphing. A Morphing Target can be thought of as a target point on an object, and in adjusting a Parameter Dial, you are moving toward (or away from) that 3D target point. It is also possible to move beyond a target point, which is where distortions are more likely to occur. Let's take an example to demonstrate.

Let's say that the optimum target point for the Smile Parameter is 2. If you move the Smile Parameter Dial so that it reads 1, you have moved 50% of the way toward the Smile Morph target point. Moving the value to 2 will place you at that target point. Increasing the value to 4 will give you a very wide smile, but because you've moved beyond the optimum target value of 2, you will also severely distort surrounding areas of the face. Sometimes this can be quite beneficial, since it can be controlled to create extreme caricatures. Most times, however, you will want to avoid it altogether. This is an example of internal morphing in Poser 4, but you also have the option of adding externally created Morph Targets.

Creating Your Own Morph Targets

Let's first talk about what external Morph Targets are, and why they are so useful. After that, we'll detail what you need to have and know to create them.

As you have by now discovered in your explorations of Poser 4, Parameter Dials are limited in number, so their potentials for transforming a targeted body part are also limited by what they address. There are no parameters, for instance, that deal with puffing out the cheeks, or for enlarging the forehead. Wouldn't it be useful to have Parameter Dials for these actions when you needed them? Of course it would, and that's exactly what developing Morph Targets is for, to accommodate the further customization of selected parameters.

CAUTION

Karuna! Since we have already covered the ways to create Morph Targets by using the Magnet and Wave Deformers in previous chapters, this chapter dwells upon the use of an outside 3D application to create the Morph Targets, so that you can import them back into Poser for the appropriate figure. We use RayDream Studio as the example 3D application, but you can use whatever application reads and writes OBJ file formats (like MetaCreations' Carrara), as long as it doesn't alter the number of polygons in the process.

WHAT YOU NEED TO PROCEED

At this time, in order to proceed with the development and customization of morph targets, you need an external 3D application. Poser 4 supports any external 3D application that can save in the WaveFront (OBJ) format when it comes to the development of morph targets, but its central focus is on MetaCreations' RayDream Studio version 5 or higher. At the time of this writing, version 5.02 of RayDream Studio is available as an upgrade to version 5.0. It can be downloaded from the MetaCreations' Web site (http://www.metacreations.com). You must already have RayDream Studio version 5 already installed to be able to upgrade to the latest version. The upgrade will automatically install what is needed over either the Mac or Windows versions of RayDream Studio 5.0.

The next step, if you haven't done this at the time Poser 4 was initially installed, is to install the specific Poser 4 RayDream plugins into RayDream Studio. If you are doing this after installing Poser 4, then open the Poser 4 installer, and select Custom. You will see the needed Poser 4 filters listed in your options. Simply check them and nothing else, and the Poser 4 installer will find the proper RayDream Studio plugins folder, and install the plugins.

Karuna! It is vital that when updating your RayDream application, that you should first remove it entirely. Copy any needed files to a separate storage space. Then reinstall version 5, and only after that, install the updater. This is because the updater is extremely finicky about finding anything extra other than the original RayDream Studio 5 application to update. You can replace any extra extensions or other files later, from the stored data you saved. Install the Poser files contained on the CD-ROM by selecting a Custom install of Poser 4.

Install the Poser Browser Files from the Poser 4 CD-ROM as follows:

1. Open RayDream 5.02, and go to the Browser. In the Browser menu, select Add Folder.
2. When your path dialog appears, find the Poser Browser Files folder on the Poser 4 CD-ROM, and open it.
3. You won't see any files, but that's OK. Click Open Document while the Poser Browser Files folder is open.

Now you will see a collection of Poser 4 models in the new Poser Browser File, ready for use in RayDream Studio.

Another alternative is to drop the Poser Browser Files in the 3D Clips folder in the Presets directory of RayDream Studio.

DEVELOPING POSER 4 MORPH TARGETS

If you have done everything detailed here so far, you have enabled Poser 4 and RayDream Studio 5.02 to talk to each other, or to put it more technically, to pass files back and forth. Now you're ready to explore another realm of Poser magic, developing your own Poser Morph targets.

Karuna! *If you are using Poser 4 to develop unique characters for animated sequences, then you absolutely must master the Morphing process. Morphing gives you the capability to create thousands of customized characters from the basic figures shipped with Poser 4.*

For your first Morph Target exploration using RayDream Studio, after you have successfully upgraded it and transferred the Poser filters over, proceed as follows:

1. Open RayDream. Go to the Import selection in the File menu, and find a figure you would like to work on in the Poser/Runtime/Geometries library. Import it as a WaveFront (OBJ) file.

2. Double click on the figure once it is viewable in the RayDream Perspective View window. This sends it into the Mesh Form Modeler.

Karuna! *Do not move or rotate the figure in any manner, or all will turn to chaos!*

3. In the Mesh Form Modeler, double-click on the body part you want to alter. Since the Figure is a grouped creation, that part will be highlighted.

4. Go to the Selection menu and choose Invert. Everything but your selected element will be highlighted. Delete the highlighted elements. Now all that is left is your targeted element.

5. Go to the Left View, or another orthogonal view that allows you to clearly see your selected element. You may want to zoom in (again, **DO NOT** rotate or move the element in any way!). Use the marquee or selection arrow to highlight that part of the model you want to alter.

6. Click on the Sphere of Influence (Magnet icon) in the toolbar. Select one of the four modification options in the dialog (Cubic Spline, Linear, Spiky, or Bumpy). Set the dimensions to 1 mm.

7. With the left mouse button held down, move the circular area that appears on screen over your selected points and vertices, so that you pull them away from their present position.

8. Click Done (lower-left corner of the display), which returns you to the preview screen. With the selected element still highlighted, choose Save As from the File menu.

9. Save your altered figure element in the same folder as its parent figure. Call it by a descriptive name, and make sure it is saved as a WaveFront (OBJ) file.

10. Open Poser 4. Select the same figure you added Morph Targets to, and load it to the Document window.

11. Activate the body part that has Morph Targets, and go to its Properties dialog. Click on Add Morph Target, and then on Locate, to locate the folder where the figure and its Morph Targets reside. Select one of the Morph Targets you created in RayDream Studio. Click OK. Name the Parameter Dial, and click OK again.

12. The Parameter Dial that controls how much of the Morph Target is activated is now resident in the Parameter Dials stack, and ready for keyframe animating and posing.

See Figure 15.1 for a visual map that shows you the route to take to develop a Morph Target.

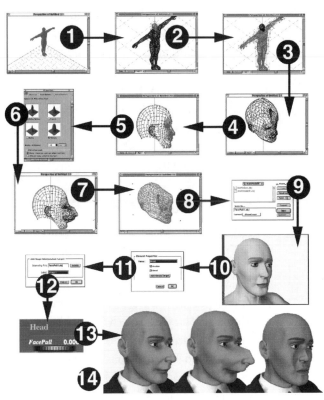

FIGURE *A visual depiction of the process of creating Morph Targets with RayDream*
15.1 *Studio for use in Poser 4.*

The following steps are displayed in Figure 15.1:

1. Poser Figure is imported into the Perspective View in RayDream Studio. Double-clicking on it transports you to the Mesh Form Modeler.
2. In the Mesh Form Modeler, double-click on the element you want to work on (in this case, the Head).
3. Select Invert from the Selection menu. Your selection is inverted. Delete everything selected, and only the Head will be left.
4. Zoom in so you can see the mesh.
5. Go to a view that allows you to choose points and vertices. Select the points you want to modify with the marquee or the Selection Arrow.
6. Click on the Sphere of Attraction Tool, and choose an attraction type.
7. Hold the mouse over the selected points, and drag out the modification.
8. Click Done, and you are returned to the Perspective Preview window.
9. Select Save As from the File menu, and save the object as an OBJ (Wave-Front) file in the same folder as the original figure.
10. Open Poser and load in the original figure.
11. Select the element on the figure (in this case, the Head). Go to the element's Properties dialog, and click on "Add Morph Target."
12. When the next dialog pops up, click on Locate to find the Morph Target file you created in RayDream Studio. Name the Morph Target. Click on OK, then on OK again.
13. You will now see a new Parameter Dial in the stack of dials, named accordingly.
14. Turn the Parameter Dial to preview the effect on your selected element on the figure.

TARGET MORPH TYPES

There are as many Target Morph Types as you have the patience to create. Every unique group of points on a targeted element of a figure can be modified in many different ways, and each one saved out as a unique OBJ file for that element. As long as no polygons are added or removed, and no rotation or repositioning of the element takes place, you can create dozens of original Target Morph dials for the intended figure element. This opens up Poser 4 as the most variable character creation tool around. Following are some examples of customized head Target Morphs you might like to investigate. All of the graphics examples are based on the Male Business Suit model, though you may apply variations like these to any model you like.

Earoidz

In this example, the ears are pulled outward and upward to create the Target Morph. The result ranges from Spok to head wings. See Figure 15.2.

Uplift

With this Target Morph, the whole front of the face from brow to lips can slide up or down. This, of course, pulls at the attached skin in either direction. Eye openings and placement may have to be adjusted with a negative Blink Parameter. See Figure 15.3.

Talouse

This Target Morph is named after Talouse laTrec, because by elongating the nose and chin of the head, the resulting look resembles a figure in one of his paintings. See Figure 15.4.

Spikes

This simple Target Morph was created by polling five spikes out of the head. You might even equate it with a Statue of Liberty look. Using negative values pokes the spikes through the face. See Figure 15.5.

FIGURE   *A series of alternate parameters using the Earoidz Target Morph.*
15.2

FIGURE   *A series of alternate parameters using the Uplift Target Morph.*
15.3

FIGURE *A series of alternate parameters using the Talouse Target Morph.*
15.4

FIGURE *A series of alternate parameters using the Spikes Target Morph.*
15.5

Nostril

This Target Morph moves just the tip of the nose, up with positive values and down with negative values. See Figure 15.6.

Wide Nose

This simple Target Morph adjusts the nose width within a narrow range before distortions set in. See Figure 15.7.

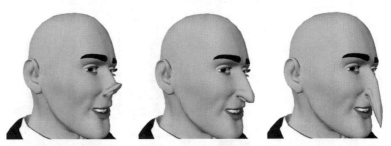

FIGURE *A series of alternate parameters using the Nostril Target Morph.*
15.6

FIGURE 15.7 *A series of alternate parameters using the Wide Nose Target Morph.*

Lowface

It's a good idea to develop two Lowface Target Morphs; one that stretches the lower half of the face vertically, and the other one that stretches it horizontally. Used together, you can create a large number of diverse characters. See Figure 15.8.

Long Chin

This Target Morph lengthens or shortens the chin. See Figure 15.9.

Lips Out

Lips Out was created so that only the lips move, and negative values are discouraged since they expose the teeth (maybe good for a monster). Pushed to extreme values, and you have a duck bill. See Figure 15.10.

FIGURE 15.8 *A series of alternate parameters using the two Lowface Target Morphs.*

FIGURE 15.9 *A series of alternate parameters using the Long Chin Target Morph.*

FIGURE *A series of alternate parameters using the Lips Out Target Morph.*
15.10

Two Horns

Growing horns is easy with a Target Morph that does nothing but size two horns on the side of the head. See Figure 15.11.

Eye Stretch

This target Morph stretches the eyes very subtly, addressing just a few polygons. The results can be just what's need for oriental looks, or for more radical deformations. See Figure 15.12.

Droop

This Target Morph selects points on the front of the face from the nose to just below the lips, so the face can move up or down, stretching other skin along with it. See Figure 15.13.

FIGURE *A series of alternate parameters using the Two Horns Target Morph.*
15.11

FIGURE *A series of alternate parameters using the Eye Stretch Target Morph.*
15.12

FIGURE   *A series of alternate parameters using the Droop Target Morph.*
15.13

Dome

The Dome Target Morphs address just the top of the head, making it stretch. So if you plan to use a wig they're not that useful. With a bald head however, you can create some neat effects. See Figure 15.14.

ChinJut

There is a lot of character defined by the shape of the chin. In this Target Morph, the chin can either jut out or in. See Figure 15.15.

Cheek Puff

Puffing the cheeks is easy. Simply select a cheek section from the left view in RayDream Studio's Mesh Form Designer, and resize it to 200% on the X axis. Save as an OBJ file as usual. See Figure 15.16.

FIGURE   *A series of alternate parameters using the Dome Target Morph.*
15.14

FIGURE   *A series of alternate parameters using the ChinJut Target Morph.*
15.15

FIGURE *A series of alternate parameters using the Cheek Puff Target Morph.*
15.16

Face Pull

This Target Morph pushes the face backward or pulls it forward, for interesting animation keyframes or character development. See Figure 15.17.

MORPHING MADNESS IN ACTION

The real fun comes about when you combine all of the Morph Targets you have, developing either unique characters and/or keyframe poses. Remember that added to all of the Morph Targets you create, you can add the variations offered by tweaking the standard Parameter Dials. All of this together gives you an unbelievable amount of customizing opportunities for altering your figures. As an example, see Figure 15.18, which starts with the Male Business Suit figure as a base, and through applying all of the Parameters developed in this chapter (as well as tweaking the standard Parameters), results in a myriad of unique characters. See Figure 15.18.

CAUTION

Karuna! We have used heads as a focus for our Morph Target descriptions, because that is the main way most of you will assign Morph Targets. However, you can assign a Morph Target to any figure element you like using the same techniques. Also remember that you can create a figure from as many Morph Targets as you like, and then save out the entire figure as a Full Body Morph. That way, by using just one Parameter Dial, the figure will be transformed into its target shape.

FIGURE *A series of alternate parameters using the Face Pull Target Morph.*
15.17

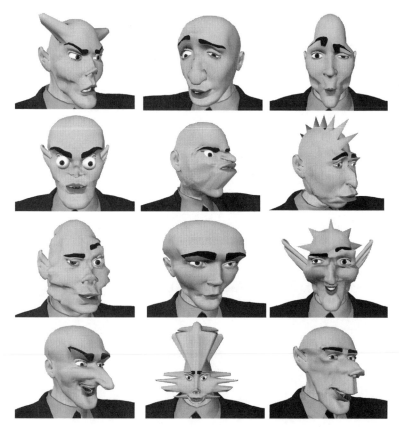

FIGURE *This display of diverse characters was generated from the same figure, by*
15.18 *altering the polygonal mesh with Morph Targets created in RayDream Studio.*

Moving Along

In this chapter, we have investigated the creation of Morph Targets, and detailed how they are used to modify and customize figure elements. In the next chapter we begin the Advanced Topics section with a look at hierarchical scripting.

S E C T I O N

ADVANCED
TOPICS

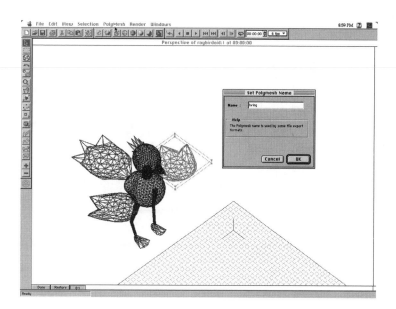

CHAPTER 16

HIERARCHIES

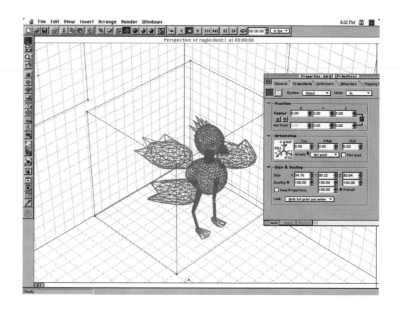

O ne of the most complex topics in Poser 4 concerns the creation and implementation of hierarchical structures, making it possible for you to create your own models in a 3D application for use in Poser. A Hierarchy is simply a list of the way that a figure's elements connect ("the head bone is connected to the neck bone, the neck bone is connected to the chest bone, etc.," as the old song goes). If the hierarchical procedure is correctly implemented, the models you import into Poser will have their own Parameter Dials, so they can be animated just like any internal Poser model.

CAUTION

Karuna! It is vital that you download and work through the Advanced Poser User's Guide from the MetaCreations Web site before working through this chapter.

This chapter includes a number of detailed approaches for developing figures outside of Poser, developing their hierarchies, and using them as animated elements in Poser 4. Each tutorial was written by Poser 4 master users, and coupled with the Advanced User Guide information and tutorials, should make it possible for you to incorporate your own models into Poser 4. The following four segments are included in this chapter:

- **Basic Hierarchy Development** by Jeffrey J. Howarth. The basics of Poser Hierarchy theory. This is useful for users who want to create a Poser model without resorting to the automated Hierarchy process.
- **A Primitive Toy Birdoid** by Cecilia Ziemer. A look at a Poser model created from the ground up, using RayDream and PHI Builder. This also avoids the newer automated Hierarchy process.
- **Automated Hierarchies** Poser 4's new capacity to automate the Hierarchy process.
- **Editing a Hierarchy** The ways to use the new Hierarchy Editor to your best advantage.

Basic Hierarchy Development

by Jeffrey J. Howarth

OVERVIEW

Your model starts as a group of separate parts (head, chest, abdomen...) created in a suitable 3D application that can save out WaveFront (obj) files. Then is exported in WaveFront Object format (.obj). That file can then be imported into RayDream Studio (or another suitable application like Carrara) for the naming of each part. After the various parts are named, the file is exported from the 3D application in WaveFront obj format and reopened in a text editor (BBEdit is a good choice). Using the text editor, the various parts of the model are given separate color assignments by typing in material statements for the object groups (see the details that follow).

Materials editing complete, the Object file is named "XXX.obj" (where XXX is any name you wish to use for the model) and saved in a new Poser 4 directory: " Poser4\runtime\geometries\ XXX." A hierarchy file is then created and converted in Poser 4. The newly created "XXX" figure is then opened in Poser 4 and given color assignments in the Surface Materials window. The Joint parameters are then edited and the XXX figure is added to the Figure library.

THE DETAILS

The following text details the exact methods used to develop any Poser figure.

RayDream STUDIO

To create custom figures for Poser 4, you will need a 3D modeling program that can successfully be used to create and edit models in Alias WaveFront Object format. WaveFront is the base format of Poser figures. For this example, MetaCreations' RayDream Studio 5.02 with the Poser plugin was used.

Setting Up RDS5 and Poser

First, make sure RDS5 is updated to at least RDS 5.02 (the patch can be downloaded from www.metacreations.com/downloads) and have the new Poser plugin installed. The plugin is installed from the Poser3 CD-ROM during CUSTOM installation, or it can be downloaded from the MetaCreations Web site.

The plugin includes updates for the MFM (RayDream Mesh Form Modeler), a new WaveFront import/export filter, and a New Poser Modeler addition (the latest update for the Poser Modeler can be downloaded from the Meta-Creations Web site). A necessary primer for the next steps would be to read the Poser Advanced Techniques Manual, which can be found on the Meta-Creations Web site in Adobe PDF format.

(http://www.metacreations.com/products/poser/resources2.html)

Importing the Model

The separate parts of your XXX figure should be exported as an assembled whole in WaveFront .obj format. In RDS it is imported with mesh form "object for each group" selected in the WaveFront Import Filter dialog when that appears. This makes it easier to manage in the MFM (Mesh Form Modeler).

Naming the Parts

Each part of the model is brought separately into the MFM and named using the "Name Polymesh" command from the MENU>POLYMESH. obj files that are native to the updated MFM. The head of your figure is named "head," the chest "chest," and so on. All segmented parts (legs, arms, hand and fingers) are named separately. Read the Poser 4 documentation and follow the naming conventions.

Exporting the Model from RDS

The various parts of the model are then grouped and exported in WaveFront format. In the Filter Options dialog, all options are checked, including the "Export Textures" option. When this option is checked, each group object of the model will be given surface material statements within the .obj file, so everything can be colorized separately once it is in Poser.

OBJ Text Editing

Next, the obj file has to be edited.

Editing the OBJ File

.obj model files are basically in plain text format; the materials statements are easily edited in a word processing program (BBEdit is a good choice on the Mac, and a similar text editor can be selected for Windows users). In this case, I used MS Works 4.0.

Open the file as a plain text (Windows format) in the word processor that has a word search function; this will be needed to easily find the group statements, which are headed by a "g." Search for all occurrences of the letter "g" to find the groups. They will look like this: "g head," "g lEye," "g lfLeg1," etc. Above each group you will see a materials statement.

```
usemtl head
g head
```

By "exporting textures" from RDS the "usemtl" statements were placed above each separate group, and now this has to be edited further. These statements are placed between the data sections of text and are the only parts of the OBJ file that can be edited in this manner. There will be too many for convenience for use in Poser, so we will reduce the material used for the legs to one "Legs." Here is an example of what to do:

```
usemtl rfLeg1
g rfLeg1
```

should be changed to:

```
usemtl Legs
g rfLeg1
```

Specify the material as "Legs" for each one of the leg parts.

Editing the Groups

Some parts of the model are separate, but you may want them to be part of the same group yet still retain the individual colors. The head is one example here. The eyes should be part of the head and need to be edited. The group and materials statements appear this way:

```
usemtl rEye
g rEye
usemtl lEye
g lEye
```

These statements should be changed to:

```
usemtl Eyes
g head
usemtl Eyes
g head
```

In this form, the eyes will be part of the head, yet retain their individual colors.

Save this in plain text to the "runtime\geometries\XXX" directory in Poser. The file may save as XXX.obj.txt and must be renamed to XXX.obj.

Setting Up the Hierarchy

Now the Hierarchy file, or .phi, must be created. This must also be in plain text form. The first line of the .phi points to the directory where the "XXX.obj" is located.

```
objFile :Runtime:Geometries:XXX:XXX.obj
```

The rest are statements that show the linkage of all the parts, including their rotation order and Inverse Kinematics (IK) chains. This will depend on what the object is. For instance, here is the file for a six-legged Ant figure:

```
1 thorax yzx
  2 abdomen yzx
2 head yzx
    3 lMand yxz
        3 rMand yxz
2 lfLeg1 xyz
```

```
   3 lfLeg2 xyz
      4 lfLeg3 xyz
 2 rfLeg1 xyz
   3 rfLeg2 xyz
      4 rfLeg3 xyz
 2 lmLeg1 xyz
   3 lmLeg2 xyz
      4 lmLeg3 xyz
 2 rmLeg1 xyz
   3 rmLeg2 xyz
      4 rmLeg3 xyz
 2 lrLeg1 xyz
   3 lrLeg2 xyz
      4 lrLeg3 xyz
 2 rrLeg1 xyz
   3 rrLeg2 xyz
      4 rrLeg3 xyz
ikChain LeftFrontLeg lfLeg1 lfLeg2 lfLeg3
ikChain RightFrontLeg rfLeg1 rfLeg2 rfLeg3
ikChain LeftMidLeg lmLeg1 lmLeg2 lmLeg3
ikChain RightMidLeg rmLeg1 rmLeg2 rmLeg3
ikChain LeftRearLeg lrLeg1 lrLeg2 lrLeg3
ikChain RightRearLeg rrLeg1 rrLeg2 rrLeg3
```

Save this file in plain text format as a .phi. It may save like XXX.phi.txt and must be renamed XXX.phi.

Converting the Hierarchy in Poser

By now, the OBJ file should be in the proper directory and the .phi should be ready for conversion. Open Poser and select "Convert Hier" from the File menu. Locate your newly created ant.phi and choose OK. If everything is as it should be, the file should process within a very short time, and the New Set dialog should open up. Specify a name for the new figure and choose OK. The figure should be added to the Figure library under "New Figures."

Colors and Joint Parameters

Go into the New Figures library and open the XXX figure. Center it in the Main Camera view. You will notice that the various parts of the model are colored differently. New colors can be chosen from the Surface Materials window. Once the colors are chosen, it's time to set the Joint parameters.

1. Disable IK for the legs, and then change the Camera view to TOP and the Figure Style to OUTLINE. Select the head, then open the Properties dialog and disable Bending. Do this for the Chest and Abdomen as well.

2. Select the Head and open the Joint Parameters dialog from MENU>WINDOW. You will see a Green Cross and a Red Cross appear

at the center of the head. Use the mouse to drag the Green Cross to the base of the neck. This will be its rotation origin. Next, drag the Red Cross to the tip of the nose. This will be the Limit point. Choose a side view from the Camera menu and continue making adjustments.

3. Select each part of the model and set the center and limits for each element segment. Save your new model to the library.

The joint parameters can be adjusted at anytime, but the changes must be saved as a new figure. The knowledge concerning the joint parameters is sparse, and experimentation may be necessary. For more information about Poser and Poser creation, please visit the Poser Forum Online and discussion board.

(http://www.iguanasoft.com/poser/ and http://www.paradise-web.com/ plus_le/plus.mirage?who=poser)

A Primitive Toy Birdoid

Written and Illustrated by Cecilia Ziemer

Don't panic. Hierarchies aren't as intimidating as they first seem. The overall view is: Make a model comprised of separate meshes, name the meshes, export the model in .OBJ format (the .OBJ file), list the meshes hierarchically in a text file (the .phi), put this in your Runtime/Geometries folder, then let Poser 3 convert it all to a model you can position for use in another 3D scene, or use as a reference object in painting 2D images, or animate in Poser. The number of things you can do with a Poser model grows with every new version of Poser.

Poser is adamant about a few issues: You must place the folder containing your hierarchy in the Runtime/Geometries folder, and before the files are converted there must be nothing in your folder but the .OBJ and .phi files. (After the conversion, Windows users will see an additional file, which is hidden on the Macintosh.)

My initial experience with hierarchies consisted of one successfully converted string of cubes, and then nothing. Nothing but crashes, errors, and the dreaded message, "no geometry to match nodes." I had begun piling new .OBJ and .phi files into the same folder and leaving it to Poser to sort it out. Poser, in no uncertain terms, declined to do this. After MetaCreations' tech support showed me the error of my ways, all went smoothly, and now I'm sure you can make an animatable object out of anything.

So, to begin with, you need a model to work on. You can grab something from the Hierarchies folder on the Poser CD, but sooner or later you'll want to make your own from scratch. The Toy Birdoid is a basic introduction to hierarchy objects for those fairly new to modeling (but have read the manuals thoroughly), and an exercise small enough to deal with when the inevitable boo-boo crops up (Poser is worse than your third-grade teacher about spelling). Birdoid is also an example of a model made using MetaCreations' RayDream Studio 5.0.2, a natural modeling companion to Poser. Since the model is all primitives with a minimum of tweaking, it goes fast—the quicker to get it into Poser.

TOY BIRDOID

These are the steps to making the model and exporting it from RayDream Studio.

Making the Body in Ray Dream Studio or Carrara

1. Drop the Magnet icon into the Perspective window to open the Mesh Modeler.
2. Create a sphere for the body and subdivide it twice (Menu> Selection>Subdivide).
3. Set the Camera to Top View (Cmd/Ctrl-8), and select a vertex at the back of the sphere.
4. Use the Magnet tool to drag vertices from right to left. This will be the Birdoid's tail end. See Figure 16.1.

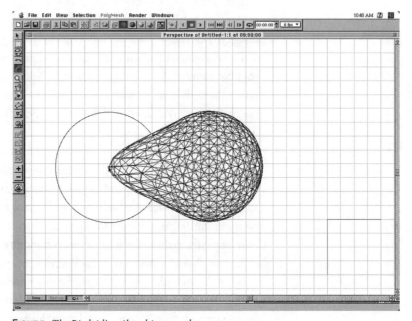

FIGURE   *The Birdoid's tail end is created.*
16.1

5. Switch to the left view (Cmd/Ctrl-4) and drag the vertices downward, then a little toward the head end. This is as much shaping of the body that needs to be done right now. See Figure 16.2.

6. Set the Camera back to default position (Cmd/Ctrl-0). Select the Body object (Menu: Polymesh/Name Polymesh) and name it "bod" (to prevent confusion with "Body" once it's in Poser).

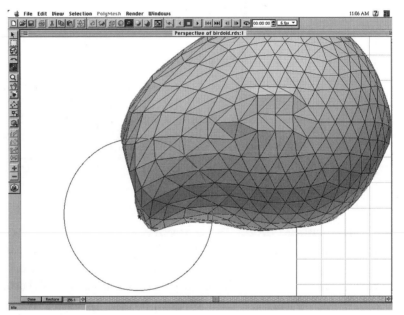

FIGURE   *The initial body shape is created.*
16.2

The Birdoid Neck

7. Create a cylinder for the neck, and resize it smaller—exact proportions don't matter here, you know what a toy bird looks like. You can subdivide the Neck object if you wish to give it more shape. See Figure 16.3.

8. With the Front View Camera (Cmd/Ctrl-1), select the cylinder (double-click to select one vertex, then hold down the Shift key to select entire objects) and drag it up above the top center of the Body object.

9. Switch to Left View and drag the cylinder above the head end of the bird bod, but not yet touching—just move it close for reference.

10. Flatten the area of the sphere on which you wish to place the neck by selecting a thin line of vertices at the top head-end of the body and dragging downward.

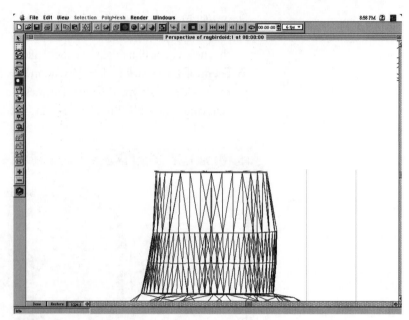

FIGURE *The Birdoid's neck is created from a cylinder.*
16.3

11. Use the Magnification tool to enlarge the view of this as much as you need. Objects comprising the model should barely touch, but not overlap. Exporting in the .OBJ format can cause overlapping vertices to weld together, thus creating a new object which, having no name, isn't listed in the .phi file and is therefore unrecognizable to Poser.

12. Move the neck down until it touches the flat space on the body. Select the Neck object and name it "neck."

The Birdoid Head

13. Create and subdivide (Menu> Selection>Subdivide) a sphere for the head and, switching among Front, Top and Left Camera Views, position the head very close to the top of the neck.

14. Tweak the top vertices of the neck into position to touch the bottom of the head sphere. Select the Head object, and name it "head." See Figure 16.4.

15. Select the Head object, and the vertices at the extreme head and tail ends of the body object, and hide them (Menu>Selection>Hide Selection: this makes the next step easier to see).

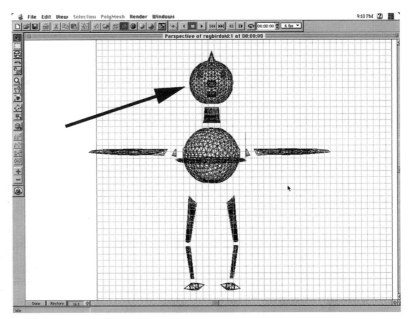

FIGURE *The Birdoid's head is created from a sphere.*

16.4

Creating the Birdoid's Shoulders

16. Using Front and Top Views, select some vertices on each side of the body where you wish the wings to go (I put mine bang in the center for this) and drag them one by one to flatten the area as you did for the neck.

17. Create a cylinder, then resize it (Menu>Selection>Resize>) in all dimensions for a Shoulder object. See Figure 16.5.

18. With the Camera in Front View, rotate the cylinder 90 degrees.

19. Use the Top and Front Views to position the cylinder to fit against the flattened area on one side of the body.

20. In the Front View, select the vertices on the end of the cylinder not touching the body and rotate them a little clockwise.

21. Return the Camera to Default View (Cmd/Ctrl-0) and make the left drawing plane active (Opt/Alt-click on the left side of the icon at the bottom of the toolbar). Select the shoulder cylinder and duplicate with symmetry (Cmd/Ctrl-D). Decrease magnification to find the duplicate object—it will be on the far side of the active plane.

22. Drag the duplicate to the other side of the body, and in Top and Left Views, check its Y and Z alignment to the first Shoulder object.

23. Select the shoulders and name them, respectively, "rshld" and "lshld."

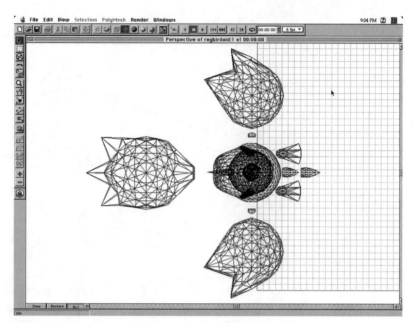

FIGURE *An exploded view from the Top Camera shows some relative proportions.*
16.5

24. Make the rest of the model visible (Menu>View>Reveal Hidden Vertices).

Creating the Birdoid's Legs

25. For the Thigh object, create a cylinder and resize its X and Y dimensions. In the Properties box, this should be the default 8 units in the Z field, and around 2 in the X and Y fields.

26. With the Camera in Left View (Cmd/Ctrl-4), select the bottom vertices and drag them to the left.

27. Then, with the Camera in Default View and the bottom drawing plane active, select the thigh cylinder and duplicate with symmetry. (Again, you will have to decrease magnification to find the duplicate.) This gives you the start of the Shin object (which you can temporarily hide).

28. In Front View, select the top vertices of the thigh cylinder and position them against the body, touching, but not overlapping. See Figure 16.6.

29. Next, select the entire thigh, make the left drawing plane active and duplicate with symmetry. Drag it to the opposite side of the body.

30. Make the shin visible, select it, and drag it underneath the thigh, positioning it to touch but not overlap the thigh. Select the bottom vertices

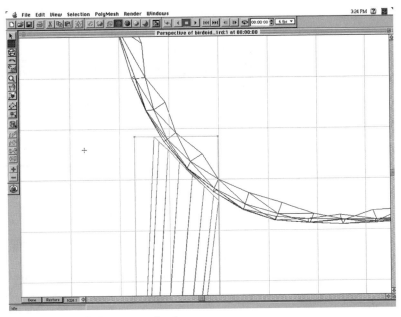

FIGURE   *The Birdoid's Legs are placed.*
16.6

and resize them down just enough to produce a little tapering at the bottom.

31. Select the shin and duplicate with symmetry for the other shin.

32. Create a cube and resize it for a foot. You can subdivide it and reshape it if you like.

33. Duplicate with symmetry and position each under its respective shin.

34. One by one, select and name the Leg objects: "rthigh," "lthigh," "rshin," and "lshin." Name the feet "rfoot" and "lfoot," keeping all consistent with the right and left shoulders.

Now for the wings and tail. (Refer back to Figure 16.2, which shows a top view of the entire Birdoid, exploded, you can use this as a guide to wing and tail shapes.)

Creating the Birdoid's Wings

35. Create a sphere and squash it (Menu>Selection>Resize) to about 30 in the Z direction (the X dimension in RDS is the Y in Poser).

36. Change the Camera to Front View (Cmd/Ctrl-1) Position the squished sphere at the same height as the shoulders, then select and drag it so that it's on the side of the bird closest to the toolbar.

37. Switch to the Top View, select a few vertices, and shift-drag them out toward the shoulder. You should be dragging toward the top of the screen. See Figure 16.7.

38. In the Front View, tweak the dragged-out vertices into a line, then select and rotate them using the Rotation tool to match the angle of the shoulder. See Figure 16.8.

39. Go back to the Top View and shape the wing such that it's not a disk—the shape it up to you.

40. When you've finished this wing, go to Default View Com-0, make the Y plane active, select the wing, and duplicate w/symmetry. Decrease the Camera magnification if the wing isn't visible.

41. Shift-drag the wing to the second shoulder. Leave the wings sticking straight out from the body and looking goofy—you'll do the rotations in Poser.

42. Name the wings " rwing "and" lwing." See Figure 16.9.

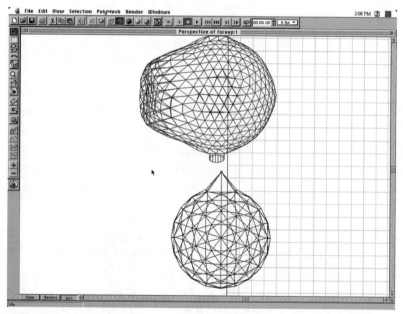

FIGURE *The Wings are shaped.*
16.7

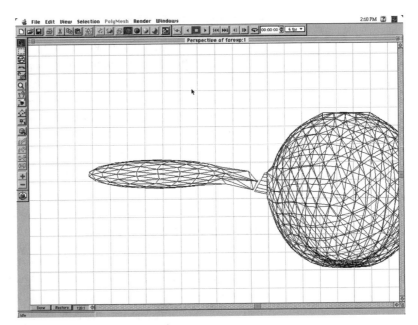

FIGURE   *The Wings are positioned.*
16.8

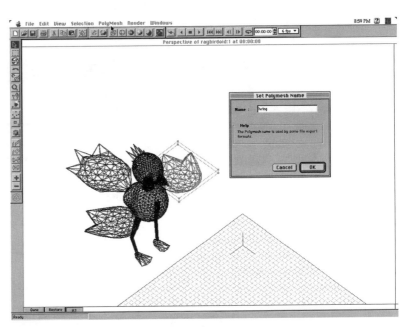

FIGURE   *The Wings are finished and named.*
16.9

Creating the Birdoid's Tail

43. Create a sphere, subdivide it, and resize its Z dimension to 30.

44. In the Left View, position the tail sphere directly behind the tail-end of the bird, then do the same in the Top View, centering it behind the body.

45. Select and shift-drag some vertices toward the body and do any shaping you wish to do from the Top View.

46. From the Left Camera View, position the tail with respect to the body, touching but not overlapping. As with the wings, leave the tail sticking straight out behind.

47. Name the tail "tail1."

Shaping the Birdoid's Beak

48. For the top of the beak, create a cube, resize and subdivide. (The size of the beak isn't critical, but it should be longer in the Y dimension than in the Z.)

49. With the Camera in Left position, select the vertices at the cube edge away from the head and weld them (Menu> Selection> Weld). See Figure 16.10.

50. Make the bottom plane active, select the beak, and Duplicate with Symmetry. Resize the duplicate (Menu>Selection>Resize) from 100 to around 90 in Y and Z dimensions.

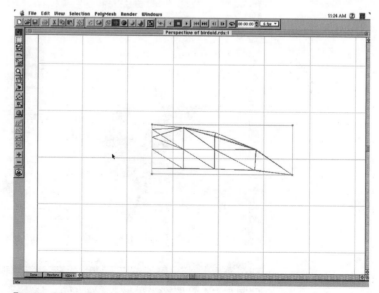

FIGURE *The Birdoid's Beak is created.*
16.10

51. Tweak both sections of the beak to fit the head. For speed, I just dragged some of the head's front vertices to make a flat area, then moved the beak parts to barely touch this.

The joints are awkward-looking here, but very informative once the model is in Poser and you're setting joint parameters.

52. Name the top beak object "tbeak," and the bottom, "bbeak,"

Recheck the Object Names

53. One by one, select the objects one last time to be certain each object has its name and its integrity as a separate object—just a good habit to get into. While this isn't a problem for models with simple joins, polymeshes made from single object models being prepared for a Poser hierarchy by Detaching Polymesh sometimes don't detach completely, or reattach. You know this has happened if you can't select individual objects, or if the objects have lost the names you have given to them. When you're satisfied that all the meshes are indeed separate and named, click Done to leave the mesh modeler. Save your work.

Exporting Your Model from RDS

1. Orient your model as you prefer it if that has not yet been done. Cmd/Ctrl-t to open Object Properties, then enter a value of 0 into all Translation and Rotation fields. See Figure 16.11.

CAUTION

Karuna! Do not change the model's size at this stage.

2. Select the Birdoid, and from the Menu bar at the top of the screen, choose File:Export.
3. Create a new folder in the Poser Runtime Geometries folder; name it "goonybird."
4. Choose Obj from the Format pull-down and export the Birdoid as "Birdoid.obj" to the goonybird folder.
5. Close RDS. If you've been staring at the screen all this time, go run around the block!

Making the Text (.PHI) File

1. You can write the hierarchy, (.PHI) in any plain text editor—Simple Text, Notepad, any plain text editor. Refer to the Poser Advanced Users Guide.

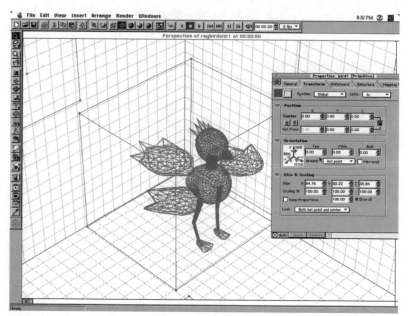

FIGURE *Enter values in Object Properties in RayDream.*
16.11

2. This is the .phi file for the Birdoid example:

```
objFile :Runtime:Geometries:goonybird:Birdoid.obj

1 bod yzx
   2 neck yzx
      3 head yzx
         4 tbeak zyx
         4 bbeak zyx
   2 tail1 zyx
   2 rshld yxz
      3 rwing xyz
   2 lshld yxz
      3 lwing xyz
   2 rthigh zxy
      3 rshin zxy
         4 rfoot zxy
   2 lthigh zxy
      3 lshin zxy
         4 lfoot zxy
ikChain rthigh rshin rfoot
ikChain lthigh lshin lfoot
```

The first line tells Poser what its looking for and where to find it; this line must be present at the beginning of the text file. The .OBJ file must be in the folder, and both .OBJ and folder names must be listed **exactly as they are named**.

The numbered lines are the segments of the model and must be listed exactly as you named them in RDS. The rotation order must be listed for each object. The direction in which the object twists should be listed first.

1 bod is the Parent object for the entire model, the objects numbered 2 are the first children, the objects numbered 3 are the children of number 2. Think of it as a tree, where object 1 is the trunk with everything, ultimately, branching from it. The Parent object (1) moves everything, object (2) moves only its dependents, object (3) moves only its dependents, and so on to the end of the hierarchy.

If you, say, wanted later to attach spurs to the feet, these would both be numbered 5 and you would enter them as: 5 spur under 4 rfoot, 5 spur under 4 lfoot.

IK Chain lines should be present even if you don't plan to use IK.

When you've made your text file (or copied and pasted this one), save it in the goonybird folder as Birdoid.phi. Make sure there's nothing in the goonybird folder but the Birdoid.obj and Birdoid.phi files.

Exit your text editor and open Poser 4.

Converting

These are the steps for converting the object and a text file to a bendable model.

1. Delete the current figure (Menu>Figure>Delete Figure).
2. Under menu: File select Convert Hier File and select Birdoid.phi from the goonybird folder.
3. If everything is working correctly, a box should appear midscreen prompting you to name the new object. (You can save something as New Set only once per library, so name the object Birdoid.)
4. Do not fear! The object doesn't automatically appear onscreen. You'll find it under Figures: New Figures in the libraries pull-down menu.
5. Select Birdoid, (the name appears in the New Figures library under a Poser Shrug icon), click on the double arrow to add it to the screen, or click the single arrow to replace the default figure if you haven't deleted it—and if you haven't, do it now.
6. You still may not see the new figure—it comes in huge. From the pull-down list at the bottom of the screen, select Body.
7. Use the Scale Dial to resize Body to 8 or 9, at which point you should see a naked and eyeless toy bird to which you can apply joint parameters, as described in the Advanced Users Manual. Save the Poser scene.

8. In general, joint parameters speak for themselves. Green starts, Red stops, and the blend zones are in between. Set the screen display to line, and it may all be easier to see with the background set to white, the foreground set to black.

9. The first thing to do after opening the Joint Parameter window, is to find the center of each object, and drag it to the point on the body part you want to pivot from. Usually, the default center settings are correct for objects, but bird toys with knees on backward (unless you're a bird) aren't normal objects. You will need to set the tail center close to the body and readjust the leg centers.

10. When centers are centered, set the Rotation parameters. If you tie the model in knots, Zero Figure will untie them, or you can Opt/Alt-click on the dials. See Figures 16.12 through 16.14.

11. Add a couple of spheres for eyes, scaling them down and sticking them onto the head, then making them the Child objects of the head.

Then you can add textures, by either importing a bitmap or by painting on the creature in a 3D paint program such as MetaCreations' Painter 3D. When the Birdoid is finished, click the + to add it to the library.

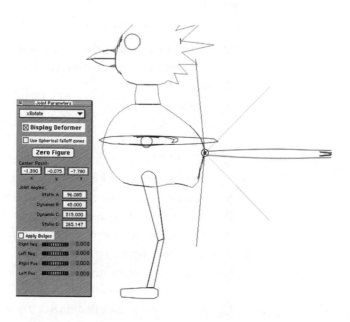

FIGURE *The tail's X Rotation.*
16.12

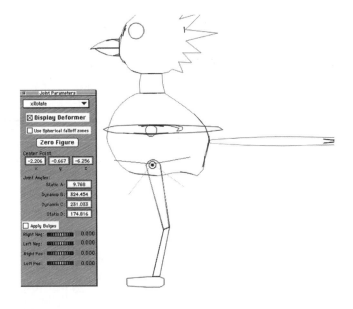

FIGURE   *The X Rotation of the Thigh.*
16.13

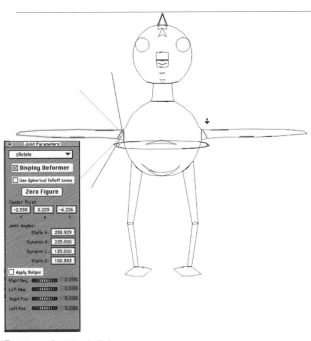

FIGURE   *The Wing's Z Rotation.*
16.14

NEED THE BOMB SQUAD?

Check the following if your hierarchy doesn't come booming into Poser 4 with a New Set Name prompt.

- If you get an error message instead of a New Set Name prompt, first check your folder to be sure everything is where it's supposed to be. If you're using a Mac, also check that the .OBJ file you exported from RDS does, indeed have the ".OBJ" after the model's name. This is automatic in Windows, but on the Mac you need to add it; if it's missing, you will get the "no actr..." message. If it looks right, then open the .PHI file and check the spelling—Poser is inflexible about spelling and typos. Also see that the names in the top line are the same, letter for letter, as the model's and the folder's names.

- If you've copied and pasted parts of your hierarchy list that duplicate (arms, hands, legs, etc.), make sure that you didn't overlook changing the handedness of the duplicates (although in some instances, Poser will convert the hierarchy anyway and what appears on the screen is a partial model).

- Check to see that you have only one Parent object (object 1) in the model.

- If none of this works, open your modeling application and import the model. Then open the .phi file and check polymesh names against the list. If you're unable to select a polymesh, one or more vertices may be shared with another mesh. This can happen even with a model as simple as the Birdoid if you deformed or resized the model before exporting it as an .OBJ. To correct this, select all the vertices of the offending polymesh, then detaching them as a new object. Name the new mesh, and select and rename the mesh from which it was detached, then make the corrections to the .phi file and save it.

Now try the conversion in Poser 4 again.

If you've converted an object, saved it to a library, and have then removed the Hierarchy folder from Runtime/Geometries, Poser will be unable to recreate it from your selection from the Libraries palette, and may even crash. When you remove a converted Hierarchy object folder from Runtime/Geometries folder, also delete the library entry.

CAUTION

Karuna! *You will find the birdoid.phi file and the Birdoid.OBJ file on this book's CD-ROM, in the Extras folder.*

If you intend to craft your .phi files as the previous two tutorials detail, then you will want to get Roy Riggs PHI Builder (as long as you are a Windows user). PHI Builder is a 32-Bit application for Windows 95, 98, or NT. What it does is to check your .phi text files for errors so they can be corrected prior to a Poser import. fur@edge.net (Roy Riggs)

Karuna! *Be absolutely sure you read and work through Chapters 14 and 15 of the Poser documentation.*

CAUTION

Automated Hierarchies

OK. You've read the first two pieces in this chapter on building a Poser .phi file, and you're still frightened out of your wits about doing it. Perhaps you just dislike working with text files. Well, have we got a surprise for you. If you dislike the text-file phi route for whatever reason, Poser 4 offers you the opportunity to import your hierarchical figures without all the text-file hassle.

Pages 306 to 312 of the Poser documentation are especially important for you to read and understand. These pages list the naming conventions that must be used in order for Poser to apply an automatic hierarchy to imported elements of a figure. If you call the elements by other names, you can still use the Import Hierarchy feature in Poser 4 to structure an animatable model. The difference is that then you will have to manually set up the hierarchical links. This is, of course, necessary when dealing with Alien or Animal models whose body parts differ in quantity, placement, and function from the human anatomy.

As long as you have used the exact naming conventions demanded by Poser for a Human or Human-like figure, it will import with its Hierarchy automatically configured. You may have to tweak the Joint parameters a bit to get the bends right, but other than that, you won't have to deal with the actual text file at all.

CREATING A NEW PROP FIGURE

Creating a new figure within Poser is also possible by using any Prop as a figure element. Here's an example:

1. Place three Cylinder Props in the scene (from the Props/Prop Types library), making sure their origins are at the center-top of each Cylinder. Line them up vertically to form a stack, moving each one as close as possible to the one on top without overlapping it.
2. Double-click on each one to bring up its Properties window. Name the top one "1," the center one "2," and the bottom one "3."

3. Open the Hierarchy Editor. Move Cylinder 2 so it is a subset of Cylinder 1 by dragging its name over Cylinder 1. Move Cylinder 3 so it is a subset of Cylinder 2 by dragging it over Cylinder 2.

4. Highlight the Universe item. Click on Apply Standard Rotation Order by clicking on it at the bottom of the window. Highlight Cylinder 1. Click on Create New Figure at the bottom of the window. Name the figure when the dialog pops up. The new figure will be written to the Figures/New Figures library.

5. Erase the scene, and load the new figure you just created into the new scene. Rotate the bottom and center cylinders. You will seer a skin connecting each of them as you do. You will want to tweak the new figure's Joint parameters to make sure it bends correctly.

Joint Editing

Joint Editing in the Joint Parameters Palette is the most difficult process to master in Poser, and it can only be done with a lot of trial and error along the way. Each model you work with presents different problems when Joints are edited. Basically, you are working to minimize the stretching and warping that can occur when bends take place. A Joint is a Deformation that takes place between two figure elements. Although exploration is the key to success every time, here are some basic rules to attend to when tweaking the Joint Parameters:

- Select "OuterMatSphere" and "InnerMatSphere" from the Body Parts list, and use a Wireframe display element style on them. This allows you to see them more clearly to adjust their size and position.
- Work with Apply Bulges on so that you can see how elements deform when they are rotated, and can then be adjusted with the Parameter Dials.
- Investigate the figures that come with Poser by looking at how their Joint Parameters are set up, applying your learning to your own imported figures. Tweak the dials and controls on a standard Poser figure, and in no time, you will have an intuitive grasp of how Joint Parameters function.

HIERARCHY EDITING TIPS

Using the new Poser 4 Hierarchy Editor, you can vastly speed up many of the editing operations you will need to perform.

- Collapse items in the Hierarchy list that you don't need to see or work on. It's easier to work in the Hierarchy Editor when there aren't so many items represented.

- Practice Parenting Props to different elements in the Hierarchy Editor by dragging their names to different places. Remember that anything highlighted here is selected in the Document.
- Take the time to build simple Prop-based figures, using the Hierarchy Editor to link the parts, before you attempt to bring in your own more complex 3D figures.

Moving Along

In this chapter, two very detailed tutorials were presented that should help you to create your own models and their associated Hierarchy files for import into Poser 4. In the next chapter, we'll explore some important ways that you can enhance your Poser 4 projects by handshaking with other applications.

CHAPTER
17
HANDSHAKING

Poser is capable of communicating with many other applications, handshaking, in a number of interesting ways. The closest association it has is with RayDream Studio, Carrara (MetaCreations' new flagship 3D environment), Canoma, and Bryce 5 (which will be able to import Poser animation files, among other niceties). In all of these MetaCreations' handshaking applications, WaveFront OBJ files can be passed back and forth. Since Poser can read in DXF, 3DMF, and 3DS file formats, as well as OBJ files, Poser can also communicate with 3D Studio/3D Studio Max output, and with any other application that outputs 3DMF or DXF files (all used for developing props and figure elements for Poser). Poser can read a number of bitmap file formats, which it uses for texture mapping and background imagery. This allows it to handshake with Painter, Photoshop, and many other bitmap painting and f/x applications. Poser outputs QuickTime and AVI animations, in addition to single-frame sequenced animations, so its output can be tweaked and customized in many post-production packages. Poser 4 can utilize audio files, so handshaking with various audio applications is possible. Some applications allow you to paint on objects in a virtual 3D environment, to create more intuitive texture maps, so suitable 3D Painting applications should be mentioned. Then there are the Motion Capture data files that Poser 4 can utilize, making it open for transferring Motion Capture data from a number of other applications. In this chapter, we'll take a brief look at each of these handshaking capabilities.

RayDream Studio

If you are doing professional work with Poser 4, or plan to, you will benefit if you also have RayDream Studio. Version 5.5 is the latest version. RayDream and Poser are part of a suite of animation solutions, surpassed only by the Carrara-Poser relationship. The following are RayDream Studio's Poser-related attributes.

READ-WRITE OBJ FILES

RayDream Studio reads and writes the WaveFront OBJ file format, which is a 3D format that Poser expects for importing Hierarchies. If you have enough RAM (100MB or more), you can run RayDream Studio and Poser 4 simultaneously, making the transfer and modification of 3D object data all the quicker.

MESH FORM MODELER

When it comes to creating Morph Targets for Poser 4 props or figure elements, use RayDream's Mesh Form Modeler. See Figure 17.1.

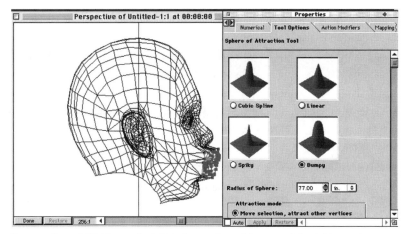

FIGURE *Poser OBJ files can be infinitely transformed for use as Morph Targets in*
17.1 *RayDream's Mesh Form Modeler.*

Using the ***Sphere of Attraction*** and other tools and deform processes in the
Mesh Form Modeler, you can create Morph Targets very quickly that are then
saved out as alternate OBJ files for Poser Parameter Dial deformations. See
Chapter 15, "Morphing Madness," for a very detailed look at this process.

FREE FORM MODELER

RayDream's Free Form Modeler can be used to create all manner of original
props for Poser, once you get the hang of its use. There is no other modeling
environment as variable as the Free Form Modeler, though it is also complex
enough to demand dedicated study and exploration time. See Figure 17.2.

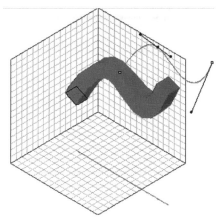

FIGURE *RayDream's Free Form Modeler can aid you in the creation of any prop you*
17.2 *might need for your Poser scenes.*

Once elements of a new Poser Prop are created in the Free Form Modeler, you can use other tools in RayDream to clone them, or to glue them together with other Prop elements. Then, export them as WaveFront OBJ files, or as 3DS or DXF objects.

POSER ANIMATING IN RAYDREAM

On the Poser CD and also on the MetaCreations' Web site is a plugin that allows you to place Poser elements in RayDream directly, modifying and animating them without opening Poser. This is the new Poser Modeler for RayDream. There are advantages and disadvantages to this. The advantage is that you have access to all of RayDreams' tools and Deformers. The disadvantage is that Poser itself is faster than RayDream when it come to animating these models. To activate the new RayDream Poser modeling environment, you simply drag and drop the Poser icon in the RayDream toolbar into the RayDream scene. See Figure 17.3.

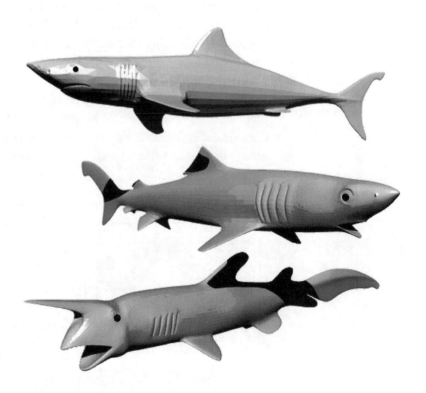

FIGURE **17.3** *Using the Poser Modeler in RayDream allows you to customize the figure's elements with the familiar Poser Parameter Dials.*

RAYDREAM DEFORMATIONS

RayDream Deformations are f/x that alter the geometry of selected objects. Most of these f/x also alter the polygon count of targeted objects, so they are of no value as Morph Target development for Poser. There are a few, however, that do not alter the polygon count, and these are very valuable as Morph Target modifiers.

Morph Target Deformations

The most valuable Morph Target Deformation in RayDream Studio is the Spike Deformer. Spike creates extruded polygons from the targeted mesh that end in sharp points, making Spike great for hair creation and other more bizarre cactus effects. Spikes can also be influenced by gravity and can evidence variable thicknesses. See Figure 17.4.

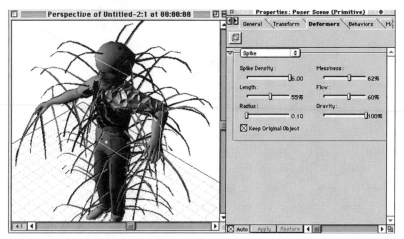

FIGURE **17.4** *Using the Spikes Deformer in RayDream, you can use a Poser Parameter Dial to grow instant spikey hair or other more radical deformations on a Poser figure, by altering a Morph Target with a Poser Parameter Dial.*

Other Deformations that can be used to create Morph Targets in RayDream Studio include Bend and Twist, Non-Uniform Scaling, and Stretch.

RayDream Studio's Internal Deformations

As long as you use the Poser plugin modeler native to RayDream, and don't plan to develop Morph Targets inside of Poser itself, all RayDream Studio's deformation capabilities are open for your exploration and use. Many of these create animated effects that can't be generated anywhere else without extreme effort. See Figures 17.5 and 17.6.

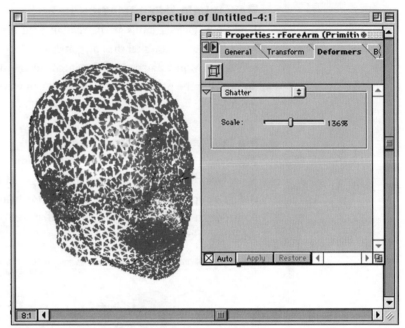

FIGURE   *The Shatter Deformer applied to a Poser Head in RayDream explodes the target*
17.5   *into separate polygons. It is not suitable for creating Morph Targets in Poser*
          because it alters the polygon count. Any Deformer can be used to create Poser
          Props, however.

FIGURE   *The exploded head, saved as a DXF prop, is used here to replace the Sumo*
17.6   *Baby's head in Poser.*

When importing a Prop, there are times when Poser will not accept it. If that happens, try closing and opening the program again, flushing out any remaining problems. This can happen when the Prop is large, like the exploded head displayed in Figures 17.5 and 17.6. Also note that the same Prop, when saved as a DXF and a OBJ from RayDream Studio, is oriented differently. OBJ props come in at the correct orientation, while DXFs come in with the Z and Y axes transposed. DXF files are notoriously larger than other file types.

http://www.metacreations.com

CARRARA

MetaCreations' Carrara was released after this book went to press. Carrara supersedes both RayDream Studio and Infini-D from MetaCreations, so version 5.5 of RayDream Studio is the last version. Carrara also folds in most of Ray-Dream's capabilities and tools, though conspicuously absent from version 1 is the Poser animation plugin. You can use Carrara to develop modeled figures for Poser, and also to craft Morph Target data, since it does read and write Wave-Front files. Carrara will have a closer connection to Poser's animation capabilities as it goes through future revisions.

Other 3D Applications

There are many more 3D applications whose output Poser can utilize than those we are mentioning here. Those mentioned, however, were selected because they are the author's favorites, and also because each has its own special attributes for doing Poser-associated tasks.

BRYCE

Bryce is another part of the 3D suite of products from MetaCreations, the third member of the triad that includes Poser and RayDream Studio/Carrara. As evidenced by comments from members of the Poser List (a MetaCreations Internet site at poser@onelist.com), Bryce is the application of choice when it comes to placing Poser figures in a rendering and animation environment. As of the 3.1 version of Bryce, Poser figures can only be brought in as models, and not as animated figures. The coming release of version 5 will add Poser-animated files to Bryce attributes. Bryce already has the capacity to read in WaveFront OBJ files and other 3D object formats, as well as to map objects with Parametric (UV) textures, so applying the Poser texture maps is no problem.

Bryce renders far slower than Poser, but does include infinite planes and extremely interesting terrains, creating a very realistic 3D world in which Poser figures can move. See Figure 17.7.

FIGURE *Bryce has the most votes for the final rendering of Poser figures. These Poser*
17.7 *Chimps were ported to Bryce as OBJ files, textured, and linked together so they could be animated within Bryce.*

If your rendering camera is not going to move in Bryce, and you need to incorporate animated Poser figures, you might select to animate the figures in Poser. Then, in a post-production application, like Adobe After Effects, you could overlay the Poser animations on a Bryce background. The only liability in doing this is that the figures will not cast a true shadow in the 3D world unless you use a shadow post-rendering plugin.

http://www.metacreations.com

CANOMA

Canoma is an example of the latest technical wizardry from MetaCreations. Using Canoma, you can translate a wide range of 2D photographic content into full-blown textured 3D objects for placement in Poser. In a few easy steps, Canoma creates true photorealistic object content.

How Canoma Works

Canoma makes ingenious use of translating and applying 2D information to perspective 3D structures, using a new "intelligent" technology that guesses how and where textures should be applied to a 3D object from a 2D source. Using Canoma's object primitives and altering their control points, 2D bitmap texturing data fills in the planes of selected 3D constructs. All of this takes place with the aid of an interface that is Bryce and Poser related. If you know Poser and/or Bryce, you already have a good working knowledge of how to master Canoma. See Figure 17.8.

As you can see at the bottom of Figure 17.8, Canoma offers a number of primitive shapes. These are wireframe constructs that are placed over areas of the 2D image that have a similar shape. The wireframe is then altered by moving control points until they match the bitmap area underneath, and texturing is set in motion. Once completed, you have a real 3D textured object that can be manipulated in XYZ space. Canoma also features "texture stealing," so that the invisible faces of an object can borrow textures from the visible areas. Multiple images can also be used to texture an object. You can also create animations in Canoma that can be saved out as QuickTime movie files, and then imported into Poser for use as animated backdrops. Poser users will want to export Canoma objects as WaveFront OBJs for use in Poser or Bryce worlds. The 3D Canoma models enter Poser or Bryce as Grouped objects. Ungrouping them allows you to use separate Poser or Bryce textures on any or all of the parts. See Figure 17.9.

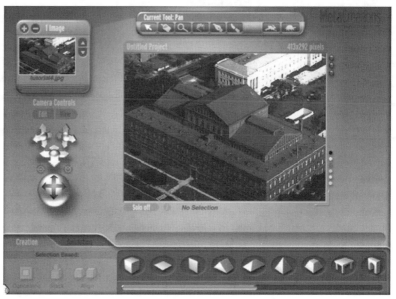

FIGURE *The Canoma interface is very similar to that of Bryce.*
17.8

FIGURE
17.9 *Figure 17.9 The same building depicted in Figure 17.8 was outlined in Canoma and saved out as a WaveFront OBJ 3D object file. Imported into Bryce and duplicated and resized, it becomes the archetype for a village by the sea, with roofs retextured with Bryce materials. It is now ready for Poser figure placement.*

FORM-Z

AutoDesSys' form•Z is available for both Mac and Windows, and is one of the most full-featured modeling applications on the market. It is much better suited to object creation than it is to the type of specific deformation needed to create Morph Targets for Poser. form•Z demands a rather extensive learning curve compared to less full-featured modeling systems, due in large part to its prioritized interface and tools. If you intend using it for Poser projects, use it for the creation of props or figure replacement elements. If you are brave and experienced enough, you can also take a model developed in form•Z and create a Poser hierarchy for it. As far as file formats that Poser can digest, form•Z objects can be saved as DXF, 3DMF, or OBJ. You may also want to explore using form•Z as a rendering environment. The quality of its textures is superlative, and its RenderZone speeds are almost instantaneous. See Figure 17.10.

http://www.autodessys.com

AMAPI

Amapi is available for both the Mac and Windows. It reads and writes a number of 3D object formats, but OBJ is not one of them. It has some unique ob-

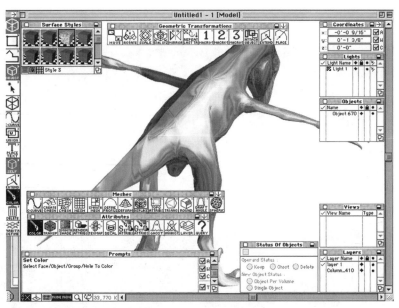

FIGURE
17.10 *Since form•Z can read and write WaveFront OBJ object formats, you can import the figures in the Geometries library and deform them, or create props for Poser.*

ject modeling tools, but be prepared for a challenging interface experience. It reads. It writes. Amapi is a solid environment for creating and customizing props for Poser. See Figure 17.11.

http://www.amapi.com

INSPIRE 3D (LIGHTWAVE JR.)

Inspire3D is the light version of NewTek's LightWave, and has features that are just right for deforming Poser figures and creating figures and props. It is both Mac and Windows enabled, and reads/writes WaveFront OBJ files, in addition to DXF and 3DS. Inspire 3D is your gateway to incorporating hundreds of detailed LightWave Objects (LWO) files into Poser, because it writes out OBJ files. Most times, however, the OBJ files cannot be read directly into Poser. In fact, Poser can't even see them. The solution is to load them into RayDream Studio or Carrara, and from there save them out again as WaveFront OBJ models. Inspire 3D also writes 3DS and DXF models.

The other great feature of Inspire 3D as far as Poser is concerned is that it has a number of deformation tools not found in RayDream or anywhere else. This means that you can warp your models and figures in new and exciting ways in Inspire 3D for Target Morphing. See Figures 17.12 and 17.13.

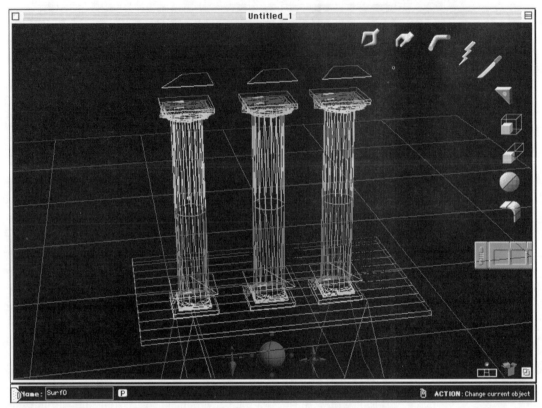

FIGURE
17.11
Amapi has an interface different from any you will ever experience, and can be used to create and customize props for Poser.

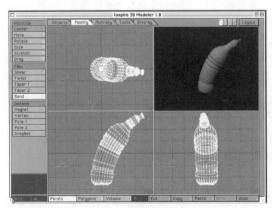

FIGURE
17.12
On the left is a LightWave object (LWO) bottle, warped in Inspire 3D. On the right is the same object, saved out from Inspire 3D as an OBJ, imported and resaved in RayDream, and then read into Poser.

FIGURE *The same warped bottle can be used as a strange helmet for a Poser figure,*
17.13 *parented to the Head.*

Karuna! *If you find that Poser looks like it is loading a prop in any format, and*
then nothing appears, quit and restart the application again. This usually fixes the
problem, which is more times than not associated with not having enough RAM.

http://www.newtek.com

STRATA STUDIO PRO 2.5

Available for Mac and Windows NT platforms, Strata Studio has a large collection of Modeling and Deformation tools, and is extremely intuitive to use. It
does not address OBJ files, but does read in DXF, 3DS, and 3DMF formats.
Strata Studio Pro has excellent modeling features, and they are extremely easy
to learn and use. Creating Props or figure elements for Poser with Studio Pro is
a simple task. Studio Pro has one more feature that allows you to animate polygon mesh objects with ease: Bones. See Figure 17.14.

Animating a Boned Poser Figure in Strata Studio Pro

1. Import a Poser figure from the Runtime/Geometries folder into Ray-
   Dream, and save it out as a DXF object file.
2. Open Strata Studio Pro, and import the Poser DXF figure.
3. Change the figure to a Polygon Mesh from the Convert dialog.
4. Create a Boned skeleton, and attach it to the Poser polygon mesh.
5. Animate the mesh by rotating the boned skeleton.

Animating facial features using Strata Studio's Bones would be far too complex, but
you could animate the rest of the figure. You might have to increase the polygons
with a smoothing operation so the mesh doesn't fold in the wrong places.

http://www.strata3d.com

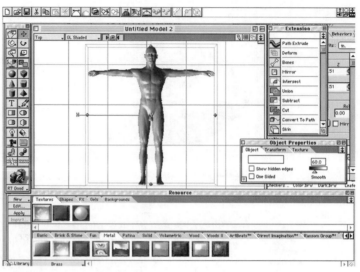

FIGURE *You can import Poser figures as DXF models into Strata Studio Pro, transform*
17.14 *them into polygon meshes, and animate them with Studio Pro's Bones IK Chains.*

3D STUDIO MAX 2+

3D Studio Max (Windows only) has a worldwide reputation as a superlative modeling and animation environment. It can handshake with Poser both ways, since Poser can read and write 3DS object formats. Working in 3DS Max, there are several ways to create projects that can incorporate or enhance Poser elements (see Figure 17.15).

- You can import 3DS Poser figures, and animate them with the Bones Pro plugin from Digimation. This is a full-featured Bones utility. It's wiser to use 3DS Max Bones to animate global body movements, but facial boning can be a frustrating experience, so should be accomplished in Poser itself.

- You can develop props and body replacement elements in 3DS Max, and then export them to Poser for developing your figures. Max plugins offer modeling processes found in no other software.

- Character Studio, a Max accessory, reads and writes BVH Motion Data, and Character Studio also has its own walk-generating system. Since both Poser and Character Studio can handshake with Motion data, that makes each one a possible help to the other when developing animated movements.

http://www.kinetics.com

FIGURE *3D Studio Max offers an array of possibilities for handshaking with Poser.*
17.15

TRUESPACE 4+

Caligari's trueSpace is a Windows-only application, and offers many options useful for Poser figure, animation, and prop development. Poser can write out both 3DS and DXF object file formats for use in trueSpace. Although true-Space can read in OBJ files, it does not write them out. trueSpace has a very intuitive Bone utility, so imported Poser figures can be animated in trueSpace. trueSpace has a number of prioritized object creation and modification tools, so it is a very valuable environment for creating Poser props and figure elements for Poser scenes. See Figure 17.16.

http://www.caligari.com

AMORPHIUM

Amorphium, from PLAY, Inc., is one of the best and most intuitive figure creation modelers you will find. Although it does read and write Wavefront OBJ files, you cannot use it to develop Morph Targets for Poser figures. This is because it translates all input data with its own selected set of polygon counts. It is just right for creating figure elements that can be interpreted as Poser Hierarchies, however, since it is the only available modeler that truly lives up to the "clay modeling" name. Working with Amorphium is truly like working with clay, and it even features an interactive Potter's Wheel mode to prove it. You

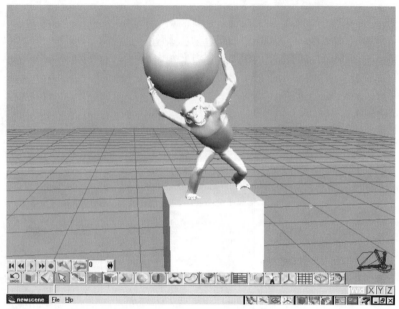

FIGURE *trueSpace can read in Poser figures exported as OBJ, 3DS, or DXF formats, but*
17.16 *does not write OBJ files.*

will be hard-pressed to find a tool that is more enjoyable or intuitive to use for
developing Poser Props and original figure elements than Amorphium. See Figure 17.17.

ORGANICA

As far as Metaball modeling, Impulse's Organica is tastier than sliced bread.
Metaballs are modeling elements that stretch out to each other when brought
into proximity, so creating very organic-looking components is extremely intuitive. You can use Organica to create entire figures for hierarchical interpretation or Poser Props. You can also create singular or multiple body elements
that can replace any selected Poser body element. In terms of 3D object file formats, Organica (available for both the Mac and Windows) can write out 3DS
and DXF files, both of which Poser can read. The main item that differentiates
Organica from other Metaball modeling utilities is that it includes a large library of primitive shapes in addition to spheres. Organica is not a good choice
for developing Morph Targets, because it adds and subtracts polygons as you
work and save. See Figure 17.18.

http://www.impulse.com

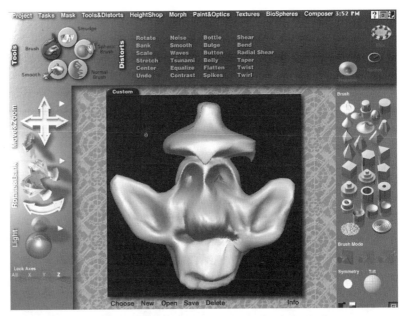

FIGURE
17.17   *Using Amorphium (which has a curious Poser-related interface), you can develop very organic figure elements for Poser hierarchy applications.*

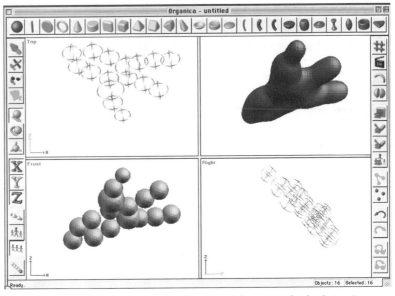

FIGURE
17.18   *Impulse's Organica is a perfect organic modeling system for developing Poser figures or figure parts, like this foot.*

NENDO

Nendo is Nichimen Graphics' polymesh modeler. It can import both 3DS and OBJ files, and can output 3DS and OBJ files. Nendo is mainly a polygon mesh modeler, using its own primitives as a start, and is less intended as a 3DS or OBJ customization application. Although you can import OBJ and 3DS models into Nendo, it does this extremely slowly, and overloads easily. Its best use as a Poser helper is as a Prop modeler, a task it performs extremely well. With time and patience, you could also develop entire Hierarchical figures with it, but only one element at a time. Nendo is one of the easiest polygonal modelers around, and it also features a full 3D painting module. The 3DS models it creates load very quickly into Poser and Bryce. See Figure 17.19.

http://www.nichimen.com

CYBERMESH IS A MUST!

Knoll Software's CyberMesh is a 3D application that lives as a plugin in Adobe Photoshop, a 2D bitmap graphics application (for Mac and Windows users). Although it exists in a 2D world, it creates DXF, 3DS, and OBJ object formats that can be used in Poser as replacement body parts or as Props. CyberMesh transforms grayscale art into height data, so that a flat bitmap painting becomes a 3D object. The lighter the bitmap, the "higher" the object is at that point. You can use CyberMesh to wrap your 3D data around a sphere or cylinder, and then save it out as a true 3D object.

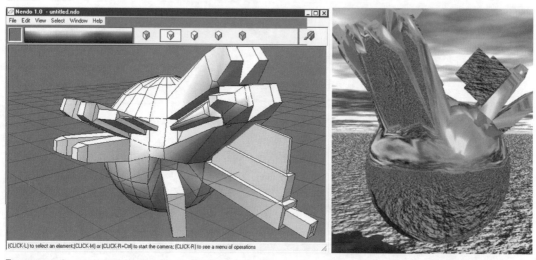

FIGURE **17.19** *Nichimen's Nendo makes prop modeling easy, though you can generate very complex volumes from a single primitive. This complex object started as a basic sphere. A Bryce rendering is on the right.*

The most important use for CyberMesh for Poser users is that facial portraits can be translated into 3D objects, making all sorts of new heads or facial masks for Poser figures. Here's how to do it (obviously, you'll need CyberMesh installed as a Photoshop plugin).

Creating a CyberMesh Head for Poser

To create a CyberMesh head for a Poser figure, do the following (this tutorial requires that you have placed a copy of CyberMesh in the Plugins/Exports folder in Photoshop).

1. Take a picture of a head with a digital camera, or use a copyright-free picture of a head found on a CD-ROM collection.
2. Bring the image into Photoshop. Make the resolution 72 DPI, and shrink the image to no more than 256 pixels wide.
3. Translate the image into Grayscale from RGB.
4. CyberMesh creates the best 3D objects when the image it references is vertically symmetrical, so do the following. Select the left or right half of the image, whichever looks better, and copy-paste it, creating a new image layer. Move the half that you pasted over the other half, creating a perfectly symmetrical image left and right. This balances out the lights and darks, which is what CyberMesh uses as a reference to create height data.
5. Blur the image several times. Make the nose slightly lighter than the rest of the head, so that it is a little higher.
6. Go to File/Export/CyberMesh. Play with the controls in CyberMesh until you can see a 3D mapping that you like. In general, start with the Rectangle map, with a height of about 20, and Full Resolution. When you have created a 3D map that looks OK, Save out the DXF.
7. Bring the DXF head into Poser, and use it to replace the head of a Poser figure. See Figures 17.20 and 17.21.

 *CyberMesh heads work best when your Poser animation views the head from a fairly straight-on position, and looks less suitable when the head is seen in profile. CyberMesh heads are really 3D masks. The best way to make them serve as 360-degree 3D heads is to place them inside of a hood or another prop that hides their somewhat flat nature.*

http://www.puffindesigns.com

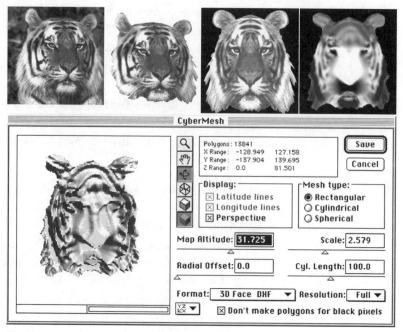

FIGURE
17.20 *A progression of images, showing the transition of a CyberMesh operation from original bitmap (upper left) to Poser 4D Head.*

FIGURE
17.21 *The finished CyberMesh Head is used to replace the head of a Zygote Baby figure, keeping the eyes intact. The Ground Texture was used as a Bump Map on the baby's body for effect.*

The Greatest Accessory Available for CyberMesh-Poser Operations!

Faces from InterQuest, Inc. (for both Windows and Mac users) is real police face-identification 2D software, and it's one of the most fun-packed utilities I have ever seen. The idea is simple, and it's based on the Mr. Potato Head toy design popularized years ago. Just give users a library of thousands of face parts, all based upon photographic data, and let them loose to create an array of different faces. The software is both Mac and Windows compatible, and the results will flip your flippers, guaranteed.

Using the photographic facial elements in the Faces libraries by simply clicking on them, you can create a whole population of diverse faces and ethnic types. There is absolutely no limit to the variety of faces possible. Pict/BMP bitmapped images of any face can be saved, and you can also store the formula of elements used to construct it. Elements can also be resized and moved. You can use the random access function and allow the software to generate a myriad of alternative face designs, which you can then customize. The images are grayscale, so they make great displacement maps in your 3D application. This output is perfect for CyberMesh use, allowing you to develop all manner of face Props and face figure elements based upon photorealistic composites for Poser use. With about a gig of storage space, you can install this software to hard disk. It's a lot wiser, however, to run it right off of the CD. See Figure 17.22.

http://www.facesinterquest.com

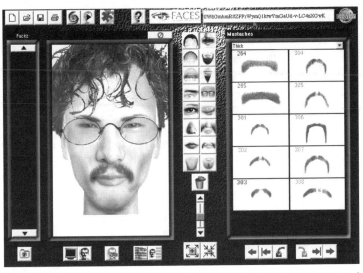

FIGURE *With Faces, you can create any of thousands of unique facial types. Use them as*
17.22 *models for 3D work, or as displacement maps in CyberMesh.*

PLANT STUDIO

If you have any need whatsoever to place 3D plants in a scene, from common varieties to your own esoteric designs, do not pass Go until you collect Plant Studio (Windows). This is the best botany investment you can make. See Figure 17.23.

http://www.kurtz-fernhout.com.

FIGURE   *Plant Studio renderings in Poser.*
17.23

2D Painting Applications

Our discussion of 2D Bitmap Painting applications in this chapter is fairly brief. That's because Chapter 18, "Customizing Templates," deals with a more important and direct 2D handshaking Poser-related option, template painting, in a very detailed manner.

Use bitmap painting applications to create textures and backgrounds for your Poser figures and scenes. There is a wide array of choices available, but here are some of the most accessible.

METACREATIONS' PAINTER

MetaCreations' Painter is an awesome bitmap painting application with loads of brushes and other image-enhancing options. It is extremely complex to master, but easy to get a basic understanding of. For textures, my favorite tool is its Image Hose, a utility that allows you to spray sizable images. The

Image Hose has a large collection of Nozzle libraries to select from. See Chapter 18.

http://www.metacreations.com

ARTMATIC

ArtMatic (Mac only) is a fractal graphics and animation creation utility by Eric Wenger (U&I Software), the original creator of Bryce. ArtMatic also translates images into sound, and saves out audio data graphic files for U&I's MetaSynth (described later in this chapter). ArtMatic features a long list of control variables, making it possible to create a myriad of images and animated sequences that can be used as Poser backdrops or as textures for figures and Props. See Figure 17.24.

PHOTOSHOP

Photoshop is the most common and widely used bitmap painting application. Besides being the repository for a huge library of plugin effects, it has an excellent (and industry standard) layering capability. This makes it a gem for creating Poser-associated textures and backgrounds. See Chapter 18.

http://www.adobe.com

FIGURE   *The ArtMatic interface is designed to invite your creative explorations.*
17.24

COREL PHOTOPAINT

Corel's PhotoPaint has effects and tools that Photoshop lacks, and also has the capacity to load animation files, so you can add painted effects to every frame, before saving the animation out again. PhotoPaint is useful for Poser texture and background creation because it contains effects normally sold separately as plugins.

http://www.corel.com

Great 2D f/x Plugins

This single topic could be five books in itself. There are literally hundreds of plugins that create a wide variety of effects in Photoshop and Photoshop-compatible applications. So I asked myself, if I was marooned on a desert island with my graphics systems, Poser, and Photoshop, which six 2D plugin effects would I want along to develop textures for Poser figures? Here are my top six Poser-related choices (though I use a lot more), and why I would choose them.

Kai's PowerTools 3

What computer graphics artist could live without Kai's PowerTools from MetaCreations? It is the most popular effects plugin collection ever developed, setting a high standard for others to follow. Kai Krauss's interface design rocked the industry, and gave ideas to a whole generation of designers on how interfaces could be both effective and interesting. This is a large collection of tools, with my favorites for Poser textures being the Texture Explorer, Vortex Tiling, and the Spheroid Designer.

http://www.metacreations.com

Alien Skin's Eye Candy

Eye Candy was developed by Alien Skin Software as a successor to their Black Box collection of plugins. It pushes the variety of plugins a lot farther, adding such effects as Smoke and Fire. A later collection by Alien Skin is Xenofex, adding even more possibilities for texture creation. I prefer the Eye Candy collection, however, since I must select only one.

http://www.alienskin.com

Xaos Tools' Terrazo

Terrazo is the mother of all tiled-texture plugin applications. If you are looking to create patterned clothes textures for your Poser figures, go no farther. Terrazzo's easy-to-understand interface and optional patterns make it a great Poser asset.

http://www.xaos.com

Virtus' Alien Skin Textureshop

This is another Alien Skin creation, but since they created it for Virtus Corporation, I thought it righteous to slip in here. It is also a pattern creator, one with blends and organic-looking possibilities that make it just right for creating skin and scale textures for Poser figures.

http://www.virtus.com

Andromeda F/X

Andromeda F/X is spread across a number of volumes, each offering unique painting and texturing tools that can help you create texture maps and backgrounds for your Poser work. My favorites are Screens and S-Multi.

http://www.andromeda.com

Photoshop's Internal Effects

Photoshop comes with its own libraries of plugin effects already installed internally. They are listed under several headings: Artistic, Brush Strokes, Distort, Noise, and more. For Poser texture development, I like the Distort options best. My favorite Distortion effects for creating Poser textured fabrics are Ripple, Glass, and Wave.

http://www.adobe.com

RENDERSOFT ILLUSIONAE 2.0 TEXTURE MAKER

RenderSoft Illusionae (Win 95/Win NT) is a powerful texture-generation engine for making realistic 3D textures. It creates textures using an algorithmic approach, manipulating formulae and displaying them in the graphical form. It gives you the freedom to explore the generated textures, and change them dynamically. Because of the mathematical nature of the textures, RenderSoft's powerful engine is able to provide an unlimited number of possibilities. A new bump option, perfect for Poser bump maps, Texturizer, is in place. You can also use image files created in other paint programs as bump maps in Illusionae.

Inclusion of some simple filtering operations for the merge window: Edge Detection, Blur, Directional Blur, Emboss, Sharpen, Brighten/Darken, and Tint. Tiling of the merged image is also possible. You can use this function to see whether the merged image is seamless. Permute the images if you are not satisfied with the current series. What is great about this software is that you keep getting new images that you have not seen before. An unlimited number of images are possible due to mathematical nature of the image generation method.

Render superior quality 3D images. Special algorithms are used to produce photorealistic images. The height of the images can be varied. The 3D bump map of a particular texture can be stored and used on other textures. Different bump options are provided for different effects. Merge different textures together if you are not happy with just one layer of texture. Merge functions available include Average, Addition, Subtraction, Multiplication, Min, and Max. You can even specify the amount of transparency for certain. Save the textures in different sizes and a variety of formats: JPEG, PNG, PCX, TGA, BMP.

http://www.rendersoft.com

Post-Production Editing

METACREATIONS' PAINTER

The one attribute that Painter has that allows it to be listed as a post-production as well as a painting application is its ability to load and save animations. When you load an animation into Painter, it is separated into frames, so that you can paint on each one before saving the animation out again. This means that all of Painter's brushes and effects are animation oriented, as well as being able to address textures and backgrounds for your Poser work. See Figure 17.25.

http://www.metacreations.com

ADOBE PREMIERE

Use Adobe Premiere to stitch your Poser animations together into a longer sequence. The separate segments can be attached start to end, or a transition effect can take you from one segment to another. See Figure 17.26.

http://www.adobe.com

ADOBE AFTER EFFECTS 4

Adobe After Effects sets the standard for adding effects to animations, and hundreds of different effects plugins are available to increase its functionality even further. Many of the animations on this book's CD-ROM were processed through After Effects. If you need to composite your Poser animations to other backgrounds, Alpha, and effects layers to create specific effects sequences, you should think seriously about investing in After Effects as part of your professional tools. See Figure 17.27.

http://www.adobe.com

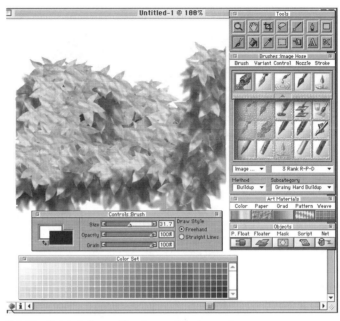

FIGURE   *Painter's Image Hose is one of the best tools you can use to create patterned*
17.25   *textures for Poser backgrounds or clothes prints.*

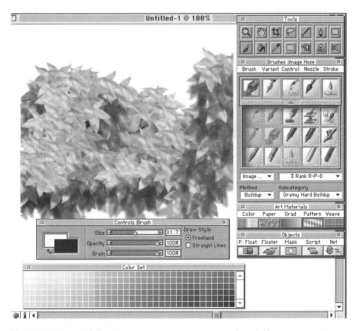

FIGURE   *Using Adobe Premiere, you can piece together different animation sequences.*
17.26

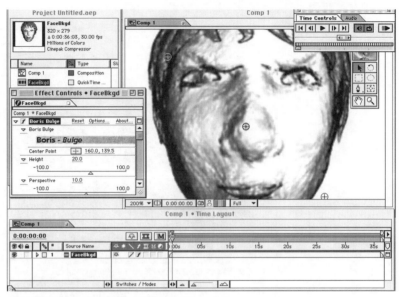

FIGURE *You can apply startling layered effects to Poser output with Adobe After Effects.*
17.27

STRATA VIDEOSHOP 4

VideoShop (Mac) boasts many added functions and options in version 4. VideoShop is related in use to Adobe Premiere, except that it lacks Premiere's extensive external plugin transition effects, but it has a huge library of its own (50 transitions!). VideoShop also allows you to apply any of 35 image effects to footage, including warping, blurring, and a number of other options. You can create edited Movies by combining any number of clips together. VideoShop also features an enhanced audio editing module: TuneBuilder. In addition to incorporating prerecorded sound files, you can create your own soundtrack from scratch. You can also place QuickDraw 3D (3DMF) files in any edited clip. An audio editing feature allows you to instantly reverse the sound track(s), or you can use the CD utility to capture tracks off of an audio CD. See Figure 17.28.

http://www.strata3d.com

COMMOTION

If After Effects is important to your Poser work, than Puffin Design's Commotion is also a must. Commotion adds much more functionality to your postproduction needs, like the ability to play back Poser animations from RAM in real time, and the ability to paint on your sequenced frames. Commotion also

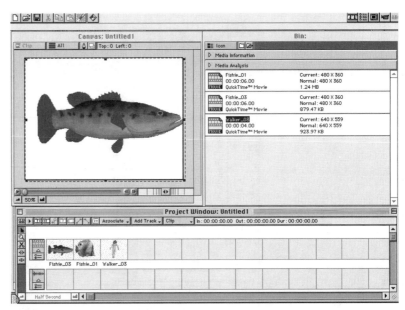

FIGURE *Use Strata VideoShop to composite animations with sound.*
17.28

allows you to use spline masks to composite content layers. Commotion also allows you to apply filters, both its own and QuickTime, over the entire animation, as well as allowing onion skinning and other professional animation effects and processes. See Figure 17.29.

http://www.puffindesigns.com

MEDIA STUDIO PRO

Ulead's Media Studio Pro is a Windows-only application that offers a whole collection of post-production editing capabilities. With Media Studio, you can translate your Poser animations from one format to another, and take advantage of a number of image effects to alter the look of your animations. Media Studio Pro is really a multimedia component package, consisting of an Audio Editor, Video Capture module, and the Video Editor. The Audio Editor has a full mixing console onboard. Just what you need to craft the perfect audio files for your Poser masterpieces. Using the Video Capture module, you can record sequences from your video camera or player direct to hard drive, using your audio interface or card.

http://www.ulead.com

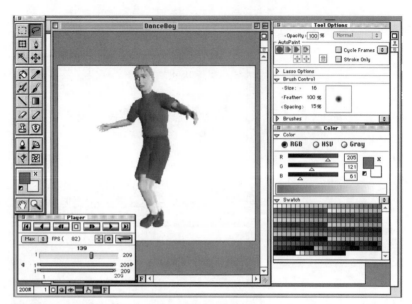

FIGURE *For added professional touches when it comes to digital compositing, explore*
17.29 *Puffin Design's Commotion.*

ANIMATION PAINTING

This class of post-production applications allows you to add painting effects directly to your Poser animation frames. (We've already covered MetaCreations' Painter previously, but remember that it also allows you to load and paint on animated files).

SkyPaint

SkyPaint is a special application that allows you to paint on Panorama files. Panoramas are interactive visualizations that allow you to view an image as if were mapped on a cylinder or sphere, with the viewpoint in the center of the scene. Once a Panorama is stitched together (Bryce has a cylindrical Panorama renderer), it can be posted to the Web or used on a CD for viewers to interactively navigate. Until SkyPaint, there has never been a way to paint on a Panorama after it has been created. SkyPaint comes with a Photoshop plugin that allows you to port the Panorama in sections to Photoshop for painting and effects, and then back to SkyPaint for interactive animated viewing.

  http://www.wasabisoft.com

MediaPaint

Strata's MediaPaint is an awesome package for developing animated effects that can be overlayed on your animation frames. MediaPaint offers you painting and a number of environmental effects. Most 3D applications take a long time to render particle and other effects, used to simulate nature (fire, clouds, smoke, etc.). With MediaPaint, you can paint these effects on your completed animation. This is a way to allow your Poser figures to breathe fire, or to release bubbles underwater.

http://www.strata3d.com

Paint

Discreet Logic's Paint is a interactive vector- and object-oriented painting and animation system. Paint allows you to paint and animate paint strokes, geometry, text, and effects, and it is Photoshop-plugin compatible. One of Paint's biggest assets is its plugin handshaking with 3D Studio Max. This is important if you plan to use Max as your Poser animator, since you can use Paint to develop textures for Poser objects in the Max environment.

http://www.discreet.com

Aura

Aura (Windows only) was created to add animated 2D painting effects to movies, specifically for LightWave and Inspire 3D frames. It can just as well be used to add all sorts of animated f/x to your Poser movies. Aura is a perfect tool for rotoscoping, and allows you to use "Anim Brushes," which are animated sections of the footage that can then be painted down. Aura addresses a number of animation and graphics formats, and can address Poser animations you import. Many of Aura's tools are not duplicated in any other animation paint system, and high-resolution transparency and blending is supported at the pixel level, for very high-end output. Aura supports a number of nonlinear editing boards directly. Since it also writes out Toaster Flyer Clips, Aura is useful for animators planning to animate Poser figures in LightWave.

http://www.newtek.com

3D Painting Applications

3D Painting applications allow you to apply colors, textures, bump maps, and other channel effects directly to your 3D objects, so no special wrapping conventions are needed. For 3D painting to map correctly, the object has to accept UV (Parametric) mapping.

PAINTER 3D

MetaCreations' Painter 3D is a natural choice for most Poser users to gravitate to in terms of 3D painting. It features the painting and texturing options of

Painter itself, so you can even use the Image Hose to create textures for your Poser figures. This is very important if you need to develop Poser texture maps that encompass nature looks, like leaves, clouds, branches, and more. The Celtic mythic figure of the Green Man, for example, can be emulated in Poser by using Painter 3D and the Image Hose. Just load a leaf nozzle into the image hose and create a figure texture of variegated leaves for the figure, head to toe. A lite version of Painter 3D is bundled with Poser 4.

http://www.metacreations.com

4D PAINT

4D Paint from 4D Vision is best used to paint in 3D on 3D Studio Max objects, though you can also import LightWave and OBJ files as well. 4D Paint contains a plugin for 3D Studio Max, so that a selected Max object can be transported directly to 4D Paint. Once there, it can be interactively painted on, and have channel maps (bump maps, transparencies, secularities, etc.) applied, and be shipped right back to 3D Studio Max for rendering.

http://www.4dvision.com

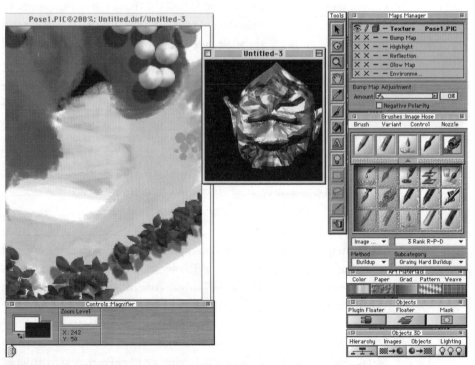

FIGURE *Explore the lite version of Painter 3D bundled with Poser 4 to get the hang of 3D painting.*
17.30

trU-V

Positron Publishing's trU-V is the result of years of exploration and development, centered upon the best way to create textures for 3D objects that show no seams or stretches once an object is rendered and animated. As of this writing, it is 3D Studio Max and LightWave enabled, with more 3D object formats soon to be implemented. trU-V creates a polymap, a stretched-out gridded map that addresses the selected polygonal object, that is then used as a painting reference. After developing a trU-V map, go to 3D Studio Max. Open the Material Editor, select a surface, and add a Diffuse bitmap. Find the trU-V polymap image that was saved out (probably in the TrU-V folder). Select Show Map In ViewPort, and copy the material to the selected object. It should map perfectly, showing the texture map as a series of placed grids. If it look OK, you can port it to any 2D (Painter, Photoshop, etc.) or 3D painting application (like Positron's MeshPaint 3D) from there, creating whatever texture looks you like.

http://www.3dgraphics.com

SURFACE SUITE PRO

This application started out as a 3D Studio Max plugin, and has recently become a standalone 3D texture-creation utility. Though not exactly a 3D painting application like the others mentioned, it does allow you to create seamless textures that wrap around objects. Unique to SurfaceSuite Pro is its use of Control Points to develop seamless textures for objects that show no stretching across complex surfaces, and that can "relax" to mold themselves perfectly to any object that SurfaceSuite addresses. This application also features unlimited layering, so that textures can be developed from a number of sources in a composite. Surface Suite will import 3DS, OBJ, LWO, and DXF models, as well as a number of 2D bitmap formats. It exports 3DS and OBJ files, plus a number of bitmap formats so you can tweak the resulting textures, and it is absolutely perfect for Poser figure texture development.

http://www.sven-tech.com

BVH Motion Capture

Poser's ability to import BVH Motion Files, and to target them to any selected bipedal figure, opens up a number of handshaking possibilities with other applications that create these file formats. This also allows you to collect volumes of BVH Motion File data found in various independently marketed CD volumes.

METACREATIONS' DANCE STUDIO

Dance Studio (Windows only) is a MetaCreations application that can be appreciated as a Poser utility, as well as a fun environment to create mini-music videos. Using Dance Studio, you can select from among a collection of preformatted 3D characters, assigning them a series of dance steps. Then you configure a music track, and set the dancing in motion, saving everything as a movie. Of course, you can use the movie as a Poser background, but more importantly, you can write out the entire dance sequence as a BVH Motion File.

1. Create a Dance Studio Dance (it can be of any length or pattern of complexity).
2. Save the BVH file, naming it whatever you like.
3. Open the BVH file in a Text Editor, and replace the underscore ("_") with a space. Save it out again.
4. Import the BVH file into Poser after you have placed and selected any bipedal figure in the Document. That's it. Sit back and watch your figure dance away in realistic motion.

Although Dance Studio is Windows only, the resulting BVH Motion File can also be used with Poser on the Mac, since a BVH is not platform specific.

CREDO INTERACTIVE'S LIFE FORMS

By Pamela Chow of Credo Interactive, Inc.

Credo Interactive's Life Forms application is an absolute must for Poser users who plan to be doing a lot of work with Motion Data files. Poser, along with many other 3D applications, is able to both read and write Motion Data files. Poser's Walk Designer (see Chapter 14) is an exquisite utility that allows you to create realistic walks and runs, which can then be saved as Motion Data files. But Credo Interactive's Life Forms offers far more extensive Motion Data file editing than Poser, or any other application. What's even better is that Life Form data can be ported directly to Poser. The following information, detailing the Life Forms/Poser connection, was contributed by Credo Interactive.

Poser 4 users can import BioVision motion capture files from motion composition software such as Life Forms, because of the complementary nature of Poser 4 and Life Forms 3. The following tutorial shows you how to bring motion from Life Forms into Poser 4. This tutorial is for any Poser 4 user who wants to use Poser's new BVH motion import feature to bring in animation from Life Forms, a high-end motion composition and editing application.

 *Because Poser models are single-skin meshes, their joints have a more limited range of rotation than models in Life Forms. When the joints of Poser models are over-rotated, the mesh will be distorted. You can still use Life Forms to apply motion data to the Poser models, and then apply Limits and Inverse Kinematics in Poser to reduce or completely remove the distortion. In Life Forms 3 or Poser 4, you can edit the motion data so that the motion does not tear the mesh in Poser.*

What You Need for This Tutorial

- Poser 3 or 4
- Life Forms Studio 3 or higher

For this tutorial we will assume that you are using the Life Forms 3.0 Demo. This demo can be downloaded for free from http://www.credo-interactive. com. Note, however, that the demo version is limited to exporting only five frames of animation.

Animating in Life Forms

Motion editing functions are explained in-depth in the Life Forms User Guide. We'll describe briefly how Life Forms is used for animation.

As a Motion Editor

When you need to make changes to a sequence, you can use Life Forms' graphical timeline to quickly navigate through the animation. Then, use the Range Edit function to apply a relative or absolute rotation to one or more joints. For example, let's say you have a sequence that is perfect for your needs, except that the head should be looking down instead of forward. In Life Forms, this is a simple matter to fix. Simply select all frames and apply an absolute or relative rotation to the head so that it faces the desired position. You can also quickly change the rhythm or timing of a sequence by adding empty frames, and by expanding or compressing a range of frames.

As a Keyframer

- Life Forms is a specialist in Keyframing. When you want to create custom animations from scratch, Life Forms is the tool to use, as it has the following:
  - A Figure Editor for fast and accurate positioning of joints.
  - Simple controls for adjusting location and facing angle of the figure in the Stage window.
  - A graphical Timeline that gives you the ability to navigate through the animation, and expand or contract selected frames.

As a Library of Motions

Life Forms Studio 3 comes with a library of models and motions called Power-Moves. This library contains 120 motion-captured sequences, and over 600 other sequences that you can reuse as is, recombine, or modify, and then port to Poser 4.

For Smart Paste Functions

With Life Forms you can paste one animation in front of, following, or in the middle of another animation. Life Forms automatically recalculates the location values to produce a continuous path. This means that you can quickly assemble a longer animation from short, premade sequences. You can also paste motion sequences from one model to another. The Joint Map editor lets you control how motion data is applied from a source to a destination model.

Setting Up Motion Sequences for Poser

There are two ways to create motion for Poser 4:

- Using motion captured animation
- Keyframing your own animation

Using Motion-Captured Animation

The PowerMoves 1 & 2 library that comes with Life Forms has over 120 Bio-Vision motion-capture (mocap) sequences that you can use. Mocap sequences are recorded from a live actor using motion-sensitive equipment. When you open a mocap file in Life Forms, you will see a BioVision skeleton figure. Its motion is recorded at a frame rate of 30 FPS. This dense motion data produces very realistic movement.

To bring those sequences into Poser 4, simply export the motion-capture animation from Life Forms as a BVH file.

Example

1. Open the motion-captured animation in Life Forms that is contained on this book's CD-ROM in the Credo folder.
   Open this file by choosing File menu > Open. Browse and locate *mt5948 Kick Fly Spin.lfa*. This animation is in the same directory as this document.
2. Export the motion as a BVH file.
   Open the Export dialog box by choosing File menu > Export. Select Bio-Vision BVH file format from the Export Format list. Make sure that all

export option checkboxes are cleared. Click OK. The Demo version of Life Forms only allows you to export five frames but we've included the full BVH export in *mt5948 Kick Fly Spin.bvh* as a sample file for this tutorial.

3 . Import the BVH motion into Poser 4.

Choose File menu > Import > BVH motion. Browse and select Kick Fly Spin.bvh.

4 . Align Arms along the X axis.

dialog box appears. Click along the X axis. Poser will now import and apply the motion to the model selected in Poser.

5. For this animation, we did not choose Use Limits, and no editing was required. See the Poser file: Kick, and the movie file Kick.mov in the same Credo folder.

After the motion has been imported, examine the animation by stepping through the frames. Check to see that the mesh intersects or breaks at various points in the animation. If so, you may try applying Use Limits, and try turning on IK for the arms and leg joints to see if the animation improves. You may also find it necessary to edit several frames in the animation to remove unwanted wrinkles or distortions in the mesh if they occur.

Keyframing Your Own Animation

You can keyframe your own animation using one of Life Forms' Default human models, and then export it to Poser 4. There are four steps in this process.

1. Create the Keyframed animation.
2. Adjust the Frame Rate to 30 f/s.
3. Export the Motion in a BVH file.
4. Port the BVH motion into Poser 4.

To Create a Keyframe:

1. Open a new animation.
   Choose File menu > New Animation to open a new animation.
2. Add a new figure to the animation.
   Choose Figure menu > New Human Figure to insert one of Life Forms' Default human models.
3. Position the insertion point in the Timeline.
   Do this by clicking in any frame in the Timeline.
4. Open the Figure editor window.

Open the Figure editor window by choosing Window menu > Figure Editor. You can also open the Figure Editor window by double-clicking on the figure in the Stage window.

5. Position the joints to create a new shape or pose.
   In the Figure Editor window, drag the joints to create the desired pose. This pose will appear in the Timeline at the insertion point.

6. Complete the animation and improve the timing.
   Repeat this to create the animation you want. Insert empty frames between the keyframes to improve the transition between keyframes.

7. Preview the animation.
   Preview the animation by clicking Play in the Control Panel. You can preview the animation in Rendered mode by opening the Rendered window.

Adjusting Frame Rate Before Export

The default frame rate in Life Forms is 3 f/s. Before exporting animations to Poser 4 as BVH files, you'll need to increase the frame rate to 30 f/s. The following steps show you how to increase the frame rate of keyframed animations to 30 f/s without changing the duration of the animation.

To increase the frame rate to 30 f/s:

1. Note the current frame rate and duration of the animation. Let's take, for example, a frame rate of 3 f/s and duration of 60 s.
2. Choose Control menu > Frame rate. Enter 30 in the Frames/sec field.
3. Notice that the duration of your animation is now 6 s instead of 60 s. You will need to expand the animation to the desired duration. First zoom out of the Timeline as far as possible by using the Zoom bar.
4. Select all the frames by clicking in the gray area to the left of the timeline.
5. Then, position the cursor over the Selection handle until it becomes a double-headed arrow. Now, drag the cursor to the right. Do not release the mouse. While dragging the mouse, keep an eye on the Current Frame box in the bottom-left corner of the Timeline window. This will give you the percentage by which you have expanded the animation. Drag until the animation has been expanded by 1000%, or 10 times.

To Export BVH Files

1. Make the animation you want to export the current animation by clicking in one of its windows.
2. Choose File menu > Export.

3. In the Export Format list, select BioVision BVH.
4. Make sure that all export options are cleared. Then click OK.

To Import BVH Motion Data into Poser 4

1. Choose File menu > Import > BVH motion. Browse and select HipHopC.bvh.
2. Align Arms along the X axis.

A dialog box appears. Click Along X axis. Poser will now import and apply the motion to the model selected in Poser.

3. Several messages will appear, warning you that certain parts are missing. Keep clicking OK until all these messages are closed.

After the motion has been imported, examine the animation by stepping through the frames. You may see the mesh intersect or break in certain frames of the animation. If this happens, try applying Use Limits. You may also try turning IK on for the arms and leg joints to see if this helps.

http://www.credo-interactive.com

Fashion Studio

If clothes for your Poser figures are important to you, and you relish the idea of designing Poser wardrobes, than Fashion Studio will be a necessary component of your Poser toolkit. Fashion Studio is a professional clothing designer's application, with loads of functionality for Poser users. With it, you can fit clothing to a model, and save the results to a DXF file. The clothing can be animated, using gravity, wind, and other factors, in Fashion Studio. To animate it in Poser, however, means computing all of the Bend and Hierarchy Parameters necessary. Fashion Studio imports DXF files, so you have to make sure to save the Poser figures you want to clothe out as DXFs from Poser first, using them as designer models in Fashion Studio. You can download a demo from the Web. See Figure 17.31.

http://www.dynagraphicsinc.com

Media Conversion and Compression

Available now for the Mac, and for Windows, Terran Interactive's Media Cleaner Pro may be the most valuable utility you can own when it comes to compressing your Poser animations in a multitude of display formats. A Poser animation that writes out as a 10MB file can typically be compressed by Media Cleaner down to 2MB or less, with no visible image loss. When you consider

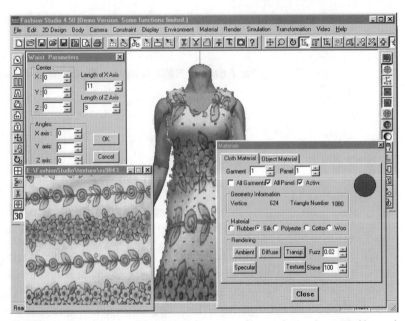

FIGURE *In Fashion Studio, you can design garments that can be saved as DXF files, and*
17.31 *placed on Poser figures.*

the amount of space that can be taken up by multiple Poser animations, you
can see that being able to reduce them in size by 80% or more is quite a savings
of storage space. For Web animations, Media Cleaner includes the Sorrensen
Video Codec, so that your Poser animations download to Web viewers systems
much faster.

Every animated sequence I have created on the computer in the last three
years, whether for broadcast or CD-ROM production, has been sifted through
Terran Interactive's Media Cleaner software. If you have never heard of it before, then pay close attention. Using Media Cleaner (now Media Cleaner Pro
version 4, which I will abbreviate from now on as MCP), you can compress
your animations dramatically while maintaining quality and enhancing playback speed. If you have seen the CDs for any of my books, and have played
some of the demo animations, you are seeing the results of MCP. Many of these
animations weighed in at 30 to 60MB when they were recorded, and were
compressed to between 2 to 5MB after a severe MCP cleaning. MCP allows
you to control every single animation parameter, so you can maintain or sacri-
fice any aspect of the animation for speedier playback and miraculous compression results.

Media Cleaner Pro 4.0 is the only tool that handles all the major formats,
including Apple's QuickTime 4, RealNetwork's RealG2, Microsoft's Windows

Media Technologies, MP3, MPEG, AVI, and others. Media Cleaner Pro's multistandard and cross-platform support drives the digital content creation market forward by providing developers the flexibility to create the highest quality media in any format required. Developers using both Macintosh and Windows can use one tool to easily prepare professional-quality media for delivery on the Web, broadband, CD-ROM, kiosks, presentations, and DVD.

Some of the new features in version 4.0 include cross-platform support, support for more formats, enhanced QuickTime support, RealG2 support, Windows Media technologies support, Lossless format conversion, and professional-quality audio support. For more information, visit the company Web site. See Figure 17.32.

http://www.terran.com

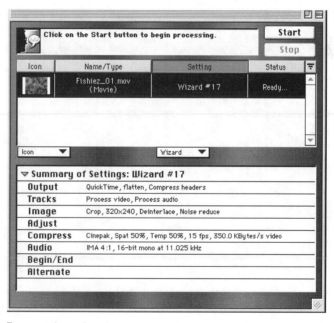

FIGURE *The Media Cleaner Pro interface is a masterpiece of intuitive design and*
17.32 *functionality.*

MetaSynth, MetaTracks, and Xx

There are dozens of music and sound effects creation applications that you can use to develop soundtracks for your Poser movies, but I want to dwell on one in particular for Mac users. It is U&I Software's MetaSynth, from the same developer who created the original Bryce software. MetaSynth is like no other audio software you will ever experience, because it translates graphic images into audio compositions, allowing you a wide selection of digital sampled instruments and a high degree of interactivity. I doubt that you will use MetaSynth to create the next disco top 40 hit, but you can use it to create the most inspiring soundtracks imaginable for animations. You can also combined layered tracks by using MetaTrack, U&I's multitrack recorder and composition system. This is the stuff great soundtracks are made of. If you are MIDI enabled, you can add Xx, U&I's fully variable MIDI composition system. See Figure 17.33. http://www.uisoftware.com.

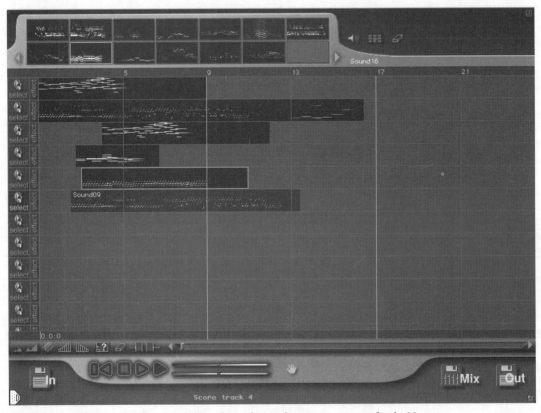

FIGURE *U&I Software's MetaTrack multilayered recording and composition system for the Mac.*
17.33

Content You Gotta Have

The world is flooded with CD-ROMs that offer 3D objects, texture maps, and other content that you can use to make your Poser productions richer. Here are a few that you definitely should consider.

CHRIS DEROCHIE

In Chapter 20, "Hints and Tips from Master Users," you will read a piece by Chris Derochie. Chris is a professional animator with years of experience in the field. One of his present endeavors is the creation of a series of Poser CD-ROMs, loaded with poses, motion files, and other Poser-related material, to be produced quarterly. The first CD-ROM contains 90 animation files of men, women, children, and animals, divided into three different frame rates: 10, 24, and 30 fps. The 10-fps versions are simplified action with low frame counts for game programmers on a tight frame budget. The 30-fps version is much more refined, with more subtlety and higher frame counts for use by everyone; especially animators looking for reference, and people transferring to NTSC video. The 24-fps version is best for feature animators needing reference and for people transferring animation to PAL video, which runs at 25 fps. The CD also contains dozens of facial expressions for men, women, and children. Lighting sets, hand positions, and 75+ poses for men, women, children and animals. The animation and poses for the first CD concentrate on everyday actions and basic game animation.

E-Mail: derochie@tinet.ie

BAUMGARTEN ENTERPRISES

Ed Baumgarten has devoted a lot of time and effort to developing garments and props for Poser figures and environments, and is in the process of releasing his creations on a CD-ROM. You will find a number of his sample objects on this book's CD-ROM in the Baum folder. A descriptive text of his creation methods is also included in Chapter 20. Visit his Web site for more information. See Figure 17.34.

http://www.stewstras.net/baument

SB TECHNOLOGIES

On this book's CD-ROM is a folder with object files and Poser files of a jail cell and a bedroom, all from SB Technologies. You can incorporate either environment in your own Poser scenes, simply by loading them from the CD-ROM. If you like what you see, contact SB Technologies for a list of their other available models and props. See Figure 17.35.

http://www.sbtech.com

CAUTION

Karuna! *The Jail Cell and bedroom Poser files, and all of the OBJ contents, are in the SBTech folder on the CD-ROM.*

FIGURE
17.34
A sample of objects from the Baumgarten Enterprises collection, found in the Baum folder on this book's CD-ROM.

FIGURE   *The SB Technologies Jail Cell Poser environment.*
17.35

REPLICA TECHNOLOGY

Don't miss the Replica Technology Dolphin and Shark collections. The models are exquisite, and can be used as animated props in your Poser or Bryce scenes. Of course, if you're brave enough, you can also create hierarchy files that can be animated directly in Poser. A complete installation will require approximately 65MB of hard disk space (Objects, Scenes, and Textures). This collection was done using LightWave 3D versions 5.0 and V5.5. You can also load the scene files and objects directly off of the CD-ROM. This collection can be loaded by LightWave 3D and Inspire 3D. To get the objects into Poser, you should have a copy of LightWave, Inspire 3D, or another application that can translate LightWave 3D object formats (LWO) into 3DS, OBJ, or DXF files. Inspire 3D can do any of these translations very quickly from the Modeler's Tools/Custom/3D File Exports dialog.

Replica Tech offers a diverse collection of 3D Objects on CD. Most are LWO files, but there are other formats as well. The CDs include The Interior Design Collection, The Wright Collection, The Camelot Collection, The Dolphin Collection Vol. 1, The Dolphin Collection Vol. 2, and The Shark Collection Vol. 1. See Figure 17.36.

http://www.replica3d.com

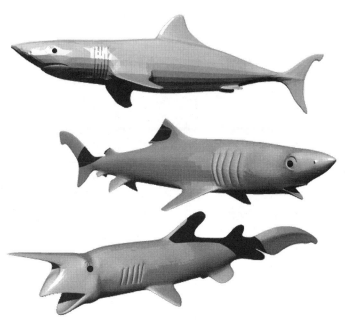

FIGURE *These detailed shark models display the high quality of the Replica Technology*
17.36 *collections.*

ARTBEATS REELS

If you are thinking about using After Effects or another post-production editing application to composite your Poser animations with other content layers, then don't make a move without investigating ArtBeats REEL CD-ROM collections. The REEL volumes contain animated sequences of clouds, water, fire, explosions, and other environmental effects, and can add just the touch of magic you need to your Poser movies.

http://www.artbeats.com

Moving Along   Although we have by no means listed all of the possible applications that can handshake with Poser to enhance your creative endeavors in the chapter, we have presented you with quite a number of hot items to search out. In the next chapter, we'll look at ways you can customize your Poser figure templates to create new texture maps for Poser figures.

CHAPTER

18

CUSTOMIZING TEMPLATES

The Templates used for demonstration purposes in the chapter were created by Robert Saucier, an active member of the MetaCreations Poser List. Mr. Saucier is a Webmaster for a large ERP software company based in Grand Rapids, MI. His high-resolution Poser Templates can be accessed at his Web site. Since they are in high resolution, they allow for much more detail when used to create new textures for Poser figures.

At work, in addition to his Webmastering role, he is also responsible for creating and maintaining presentation material for a small but global part of the company. Poser comes in very handy when process flows are needed. A Poser figure pointing out a step gets a little more attention than just an arrow. As a future project, Mr. Saucier plans to recreate the Poser 2 muscle bump maps for Poser use.

http://www.saucier-pages.com/

File Naming Conventions

When you look in the Templ folder on the CD to retrieve the new Poser Templates, you will see that they are named according to the following conventions:

- P1— Poser 1 map templates
- P2—Poser 2 map templates
- P3—Poser 3 map templates
- P4—Poser 4 map templates
- Px—Map template may be used for one or more of the above
- ZS—Zygote Poser 3 Sampler map templates
- ZA—Zygote Poser 3 Animal Collection map templates

CAUTION

Karuna! *In the following exercises, MetaCreations' Painter 6 is used as the bitmap painting application. You can use another application if you don't have Painter 6, but you'll have to substitute that application's brush and/or texturing capabilities for those mentioned in Painter.*

Creating Textures with Painter

MetaCreations' Painter offers you an almost unlimited number and variety of painting effects with which to paint on Poser Templates.

CREATING A NEW HORSE TEXTURE

In this first exercise, we will walk through the creation of an alternate texture map for the Poser Horse.

1. Open Painter. Load the P3Horse.Tif file from the Templ folder on this book's CD-ROM. This is the hi-res Horse Template created by Robert Saucier.
2. Click the Magic Wand in a white area of the image. Hold down the Shift key, and use the lasso to encircle all of the text lines. Under the Selection menu, go to Invert. All that should be selected now are the actual Templates. See Figure 18.1.
3. Select the Bucket icon, and make sure a black color is selected. Click once inside any of the outlined areas, and all of the areas will be filled with black. See Figure 18.2.

Karuna! *It is important that the outlined marquees remain intact and visible for all painting operations.*

CAUTION

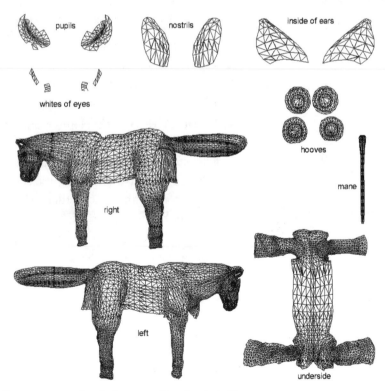

FIGURE *Here's what the beginning Template looks like.*
18.1

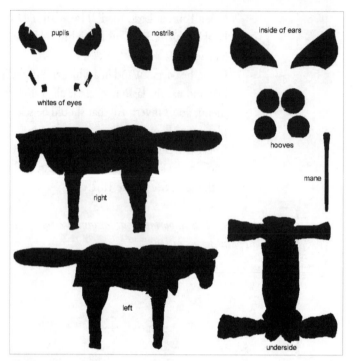

FIGURE *All of the areas are filled with black.*
18.2

4. As you can see, all of the Horse's elements are named on the Template, making it easy to identify what you are painting. Paint the elements as follows with the Airbrush set to Fat Stroke: Pupils black; Whites of Eyes yellowish white; Nostrils black; Inside of Ears light pink inside to dark pink outside, with a black outline; Hooves black; Mane bluish white with streaks of gray-blue; Right and Left Sides, a yellow-white background with gray-blue patches, randomized; Underside should be a mix of gray-white and light blue-gray. Save the template as a texture map in the Textures drawer. See Figure 18.3.

5. Open Poser, and load the Horse from the Animals library. Open the Surface Materials dialog, and load the new Horse texture you just created from the Horse Template. Color all of the Horse elements white so the texture dominates. Pose and render the image, and save to disk. See Figure 18.4.

Repeat the preceding exercise, but this time create a new Horse surface texture that is right for a merry-go-round horse, making the horse and its spots bright primary colors. Use your imagination. See Figure 18.5.

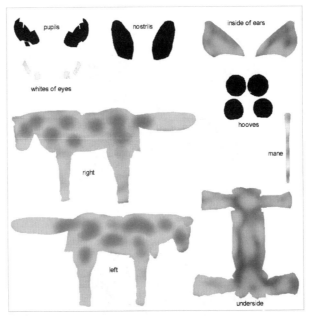

FIGURE *The finished Template painting for an alternate Horse texture.*
18.3

FIGURE *The rendered Horse figure textured with the new dappled map.*
18.4

FIGURE *The brightly colored rendering of a posed merry-go-round horse.*
18.5

You can also use any of Painter's Patterns to create a new Horse texture, like this floral design. See Figures 18.6 and 18.7.

FIGURE *A Painter Floral Pattern is used to map the Horse.*
18.6

FIGURE *In this instance, a Green Textured Glass pattern was used as both a Surface and*
18.7 *a Bump Map.*

THE GREEN MAN

In Celtic lore, it is said that the Green Man exists deep in the woods, granting benefits of the harvest and mysteries of the Earth. The Green Man is the male aspect of Mother Nature, though he has been lost in time. We can bring him back in Poser, at least in a digital world. This exercise especially requires Painter, since we are going to use its Image Hose, a tool found nowhere else.

1. Open Painter, and load the P3ManNude Template from the Templ folder, which will load another of Robert Saucier's detailed maps. See Figure 18.8.
2. Follow the same procedure you used with the Horse to select only the figures outlined surfaces, and not the background or the callout lettering.
3. Use the Fill Bucket to paint everything a light green at the start, making sure the marquee around all of the mapped content remains active.

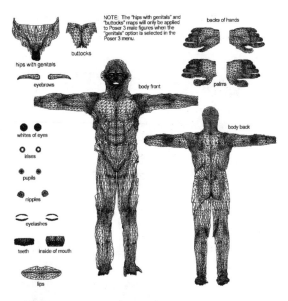

FIGURE   *The P3ManNude Template.*
18.8

Open the Painter Image Hose, and select the English Ivy Nozzle, and set
the Size to 30%. Use the Image Hose to spray this nozzle on the Front,
Back, Hips With Genitals, and Buttocks elements.

4. Use the Airbrush to color other elements as follows: Lips and Irises bright
   red; Teeth yellow; Inside of Mouth dark green; Eyelashes light blue; Nip-
   ples dark blue; Pupils light green. Use a Turbulence Pattern of 30% to
   texture the front and back of the Hands. See Figure 18.9.

5. In Poser, load the Nude Man from the People library. Resize the Head
   with a –14% Taper. Apply the new map you just created to the figure. A
   close-up of the Head should resemble Figure 18.10.

The Green Man is usually pictured with a wreath around his Head, so let's
create one. This will require RayDream Studio.

6. Open RayDream, and place a Sphere in the scene. Squash the Sphere so
   that it is only about 1/4 as high. See Figure 18.11.

7. With the squashed Sphere selected, go to the Deformers tab in the Properties dialog. Select the Spikes Deformer, and set the values as follows:
   Density 6, length 100%, Radius .25, Messiness 100%, Flow and Gravity to 0. See Figure 18.12.

8. Export the Spiked Sphere as a .obj file from RayDream, and import it
   into your Green Man scene in Poser 3. Place it on the head of the figure,

pose, render, and save. Make the Head the Parent of the Wreath. See Figures 18.13 and 18.14.

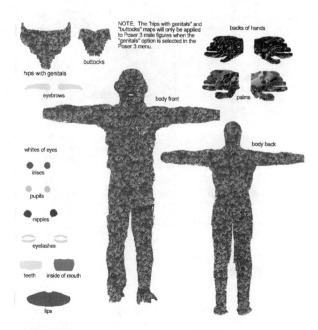

FIGURE **18.9** *The finished Green Man Texture Map created from the P3ManNude Template.*

FIGURE **18.10** *A close-up of the Head of the Green Man.*

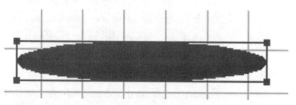

FIGURE **18.11** *Create a squashed Sphere in RayDream.*

FIGURE *The Spiked Sphere looks like a wreath of grass.*
18.12

FIGURE *The posed Green Man with a wreath of spiked grass on his head.*
18.13

FIGURE *A series of Green Man poses, displaying the full texture map.*
18.14

LEISURE SUIT LAMBERT

Let's try one more Template to create a texture variation for a Poser figure, modified in Painter.

1. Load the P3ManBusiness.TIF Template from this book's CD-ROM in the Templ folder. Color the template whatever colors you like, using the previous examples as a guide.

2. Explore the use of Patterns and Weaves to apply designs to the jacket, pants, and shirt.
3. Use an Airbrush with a light gray color to add beard stubble to the face.
4. After applying this map in Poser, get some Sunglasses and a Hat prop from the Zygote Props library, and Parent them to the head. One result of this exploration can be seen in Figure 18.15.

FIGURE *Leisure Suit Lambert wears the highest fashions.*
18.15

CUSTOMIZING THE RAPTOR TEXTURE

The Raptor Template allows you to explore ways that scales and other texture features can be explored. If you are using Painter, then try applying a Paper Texture, and also using the Turquoise f/x Brush to simulate scales. Always apply a Bump Map of the texture to give scales more depth. For one example of another Raptor look, load the texture Raptor2 from the Templ folder on this book's CD-ROM. See Figure 18.16.

FIGURE *A new Raptor look, achieved with the Raptor2 texture map, a variation of the*
18.16 *P3Raptor.Tif Template, included on this book's CD-ROM. Compare this with the default Raptor texture map.*

Karuna! No matter what you do when painting a Template with anything other than solid colors, your figure will display some seams where the Template views meet. You can minimize this artifact by setting the Camera up so that it doesn't see the offending seams. If this is still troubling to you, then you will have to use a 3D Painting application like Painter 3D, 4D Paint, trU-V, or SurfaceSuite Pro. See Chapter 19, "Cameras, Lights, and More Rendering Tips."

Creating Textures with Photoshop

Although it is advisable that you purchase Painter for creating new Poser figure textures because of its infinite creative possibilities, it is more than likely that you already own Adobe Photoshop. Photoshop also offers you tools and techniques for creating Poser texture maps for figures and props. It features a large number of internal painting f/x, which cannot be operated as plugins from other applications, and some of the external plugins you can get for it don't work with anything else.

THE SPOTTED CHIMP OF MARS

In this exercise, we'll use Photoshop to paint on the ZAChimpanzee.Tif template, found in the Templ folder on this book's CD-ROM. Then we'll apply the texture to the Zygote Chimp figure. You will need Poser 3, Photoshop, and the Zygote Animal models to do this tutorial.

1. Open Photoshop, and load the ZAChimpanzee.tif file from the Templ folder on this book's CD. See Figure 18.17.

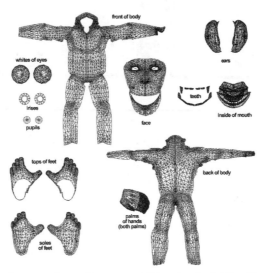

FIGURE *The ZAChimpanzee.tif Template loaded into Photoshop.*
18.17

You'll have to translate the Template from a Bitmap to a Grayscale image to use the Magic Wand in Photoshop.

2. Use the Magic Wand to select just the Chimp's elements on the image, just as you did in the Painter exercises. Then Copy them, and paste so that they are placed on a new Layer (automatic when you use Paste). For now, you can keep the original template as the bottom layer, because it contains the call-outs. Before saving your new texture map, however, you can delete the original Template Layer. Use the Airbrush to colorize the elements of the Chimp's body on the Template. See Figure 18.18.

3. Go to the Filter/Texture menu, and apply a Craquelure texture to the Chimp's front and back, with settings of Crack Spacing 14, Crack Depth 8, and Crack Brightness 9. See Figure 18.19.

4. Select the Chimp's face, and use a Stained Glass Texture effect with a Cell Size of 7, Border Thickness of 1, and a Light Intensity of 1. This adds a mosaic tiled appearance to the face.

5. Now use a solid brush and a yellow color to place yellow dots on the front and back of the image map, trying for a random look. Save the new Chimp texture. See Figure 18.20.

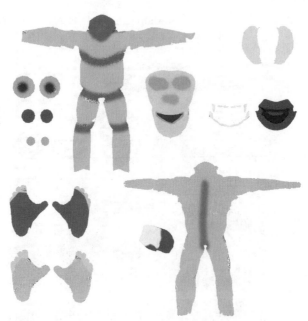

FIGURE *The first step in customizing the Chimp texture, using the ZAChimpanzee.tif*
18.18 *Template in the Templ folder on this book's CD.*

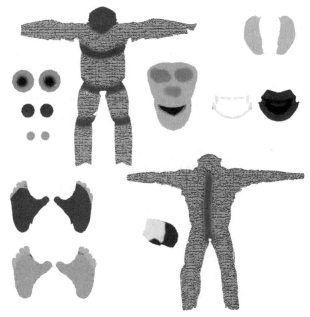

FIGURE *The Craquelure textures is applied to the body elements.*
18.19

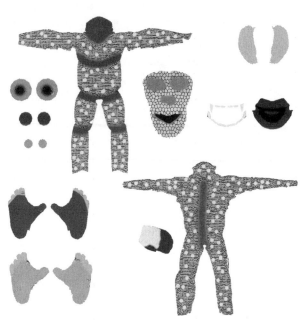

FIGURE *The texture map is now complete, with the spots added.*
18.20

Import the new texture into Poser, and apply it to the Chimp figure. See Figure 18.21.

FIGURE *The Chimp is posed and mapped with the new texture.*
18.21

Mapping a Photographic Face

One of the most frequently asked questions concerning Poser is, "how can I map a real face to a figure?" The answer is that it is not worth the try. Why is this so? Real faces are absolutely never perfectly symmetrical. We have a bilateral brain, and each side controls the opposite side of the face. In a sense, each side of the brain is responsible for sensing the world in a different way, which shows in the difference between the halves of our face. The recognition of a face is based upon its nonsymmetry, which makes even identical twins just a bit different when you look closely. Our two eyes are never on the same horizontal plane, for instance. This has a lot of importance when you consider that Poser heads, those that come with the application, are perfectly symmetrical, which is exactly why they always look a little robotic. Perhaps in a future addition, there will be a specific Parameter Dial for altering symmetry. Until that time, however, we have to alter any photos to match the symmetry of the Poser Head object, fitting the image to the 3D structure. This means that the personality of a photographic face, its asymmetry, must be made symmetrical, and that loses the personality of the photo. At the very best, it can add some skin tones to the Poser Head. On top of that, you have to remove the nose from the image map, because the Poser Figure's nose is a real 3D construct that casts its own shadows.

The best way to get a photographic face is to take the image map and translate it into 3D geometry in a suitable 3D application. This is called Displacement Mapping, where the image actually displaces the geometry of a surface. CyberMesh, which we looked at in Chapter 17, "Handshaking," does this, but the result is more of a mask than a photo. Many 3D applications, like Ray-Dream and LightWave, have a better displacement mapping feature. Then the problem is that unless you spend a huge amount of time developing a hierarchical model of the face that can be controlled with the Parameter Dials in Poser, you won't be able to control the features anyway. For now, it's either develop a complete hierarchical model and associated .phi file on your own, or wait for an advanced version of Poser that offers more of these options.

There is a third option, one that may allow you to get at least a semblance of a Head mapped with a photographic face. Try this:

1. Create an egg-shaped object from a Ball Prop. You will use it to replace the Head of a figure, but don't do that yet.
2. In Photoshop, import a face graphic. Resize its canvas so that the face sits in the middle of a frame 3X the horizontal and 2X the vertical, using the same color as the edge of the face for the canvas backdrop. Blur the edges where the face meets the background. See Figure 18.22.
3. In Poser, Surface Map the face graphic to the Egg. Replace the Head with the Egg. Place Hair on the Egg, and render. You may have to adjust the map a bit, but expect that distortion will be a component of this technique. Actually, the distortion creates interesting caricatures. Save to disk. See Figure 18.23.

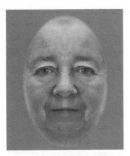

FIGURE *A photo of a face, with the hair cut away, is the main content of a surface map.*
18.22

FIGURE *The completed mapped figure.*
18.23

This technique demands that the face be pretty much front on in the view plane, since there really is no depth to the nose.

Poser Forum Web Ring

For the newest and best creative Poser techniques, stay in touch with the Poser Web Ring.

http://www.iguanasoft.com/poser/ring.html

Moving Along

In this chapter, we've explored a few ways that you can use Painter and Photoshop to create interesting customized textures for your Poser figures. In the next chapter, we'll look at some options for Cameras, Lights, and Rendering.

19

CAMERAS, LIGHTS, AND MORE RENDERING TIPS

In this chapter, we'll look at the Poser 4 attributes whose use and modifications can alter your animations in major ways: Cameras and Lights. We've also added a section called "More on Rendering," adding a few ideas that can make your animations even more interesting.

Cameras

Poser 4 features a number of Camera options that add new ways for you to render and record your output, as well as making your compositions easier to navigate. The standard docs cover the general uses of the Cameras, so we'll look at a few ideas about Cameras that are new, ones that you may find useful in your Poser work.

THE ANIMATING CAMERA

Camera movements create automatic keyframes when the Animating Camera is switched on. It is toggled on or off by selecting the Key icon on the left-hand toolbar. Gray is on, orange is off. When it's on, your Camera movements are recorded as keyframes wherever you're at on the timeline. Leave the Animating Camera off when you are posing a figure, and turn it on after all figures are posed and separately keyframed. This allows you to worry about one thing at a time, and prevents the Camera from animating when all you want to do is to get it to see another view of the scene.

CAMERA LIBRARY ANIMATIONS

Just as you can apply different faces or full poses to alternate keyframes to create an animation, so, too, can you apply different Camera views from the Camera library at different points on the timeline. The best advice is to spend a day or two exploring different Camera angles and perspectives, saving all of those you like to your Camera library. When they're needed, for still positions or keyframes, you'll have many of your favorites to select from.

ANIMATED REFLECTIONS

Here's a neat animation that you can create, showing a person moving in front of a mirror.

1. Select any one of the Poser figures, or even an animal, as your main character, and place it in the center of your Poser document. Turn the Ground Plane on, and adjust the lighting so the figure is well lit. Make the background a light-blue color. See Figure 19.1.
2. Create a 120 frame animation, set to 30 FPS. Make the figure move

FIGURE *This project starts with the placement of a figure of your choice at the center of*
19.1 *your Poser document. This is a Business Suited Male with a Morphed head.*

however you want it to, but for this project, allow its feet to remain in place (you can do this easily by making sure that IK is on for each leg). When you are satisfied with the choreography, render and save the animation.

3. Next, turn IK off for all body parts. Select the figure's Body. Use the Y Axis Parameter Dial to rotate the figure exactly 180 degrees, so its back is facing the Camera. Do not alter any other elements of the figure. See Figure 19.2.

4. Now set the Document Size to the same size as the animation you rendered. See Figure 19.3.

5. You can use your favorite 3D application, or a post-production application to perform the next step. The object is to reverse (flip) the horizontal for the animation you just rendered. I used After Effects for this task. After reading in the animation, I used the Basic 3D Effect, altering the Swivel Radial Dial to read 180 degrees. Then I re-recorded the anima-

FIGURE *The figure is facing away from the Camera.*
19.2

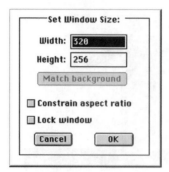

FIGURE **19.3** *Set the size of the Document window to the same size as the animation rendered.*

tion again, so that it would play with everything horizontally flipped. See Figure 19.4.

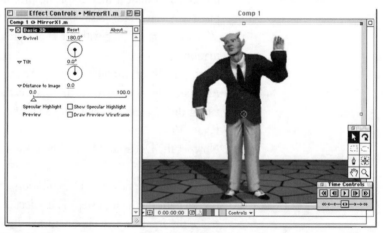

FIGURE **19.4** *If you use After Effects to flip the animation horizontally, access the Basic 3D Effect, and change the Swivel Radial Dial to read 180 degrees. Then record the animation again.*

Why are we flipping the animation horizontally? Because a common mirror flips what is reflected horizontally. Otherwise, the reflection will not match the movements of the figure standing in front of the mirror.

6. After the flipped animation has been rendered, import it into your Poser scene, and use it as a background. Your scene should now look like Figure 19.5.

7. As you can see, the foreground figure is a bit too small. Resize it so that it is a bit larger than the animation; that will now become its reflection. See Figure 19.6.

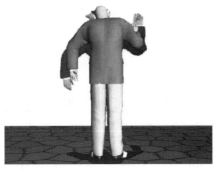

FIGURE *The scene will now look like this, with the flipped animation in back of the*
19.5 *Posed figure.*

FIGURE *The foreground figure is enlarged, and moved a bit to the left, so that both*
19.6 *figure and reflection can be seen clearly. I have also changed the color of the*
jacket, making it lighter, so it doesn't conflict with the reflection of the jacket.

8. Next we have to build a wall, so that it looks like a mirror is inset within
   it. You can either do that in an external 3D application and import it, or
   construct it out of blocks, as I have done in Figure 19.7.

FIGURE *The block wall is created, leaving a hole so that the animated figure shows*
19.7 *through.*

Now animate the whole scene, and you will see the mirrored result. The important thing about the Camera in this project demonstrates how important it is to keep it the same throughout. Otherwise, the reflected animation will look very strange.

CAMERA CLOSE-UPS AND TEXTURES

One thing to consider whenever you do extreme close-ups (zooms) with any Camera is to use just colors for items that are not involved in zoomed views. For items that are involved in zoomed close-ups, use high-resolution textures. This simulates something computer artists call LOD, or Level of Detail. Save detailed textures for items closer to the Cameras. The same holds for shots that picture an action figure with a crowd of onlookers in the background. If you utilize textures for important figures alone, the viewer will see the background figures as hazed out, and without adjusting the Camera itself, you will intimate more depth in the scene.

ON THE INSIDE

There is a strange Camera-associated operation you can perform that is not documented in the Poser 4 manual, and it may be because it is a bit too esoteric for the average Poser user. All of the objects you place in a Document have both an inside and an outside. If you keep zooming in on a selected object or figure, there will come a point at which the Camera is literally "inside" of the construct. In most cases, you will not know it, because it will seem as if you have just passed through the targeted element. This is because most objects in Poser are one-sided polygons, so that the computer does not spend any time rendering their inside faces.

This is not true for the mouth, however, and it's easy to understand why. If the inside of the mouth was constricted from one-sided polygons, then every time the Mouth opened, you would see right through the head. Since this is not exactly the way the real-world presents itself to us, the Mouth and Teeth are made from double-sided polygons for a realistic view.

What does this have to do with the Camera? Simple, it allows us to fly the Camera inside of the Mouth of a figure, so that we can view the world as if we were sitting at the back of a figure's throat. Admittedly, this has limited use, but it may be an effect that you could use when conditions are right. When you place the Camera in the Mouth, you can still manipulate the Mouth openness and other Parameters. This makes the Mouth like a window that can be animated, so you can see whatever is beyond the Mouth in the direction the figure is facing. See Figure 19.8.

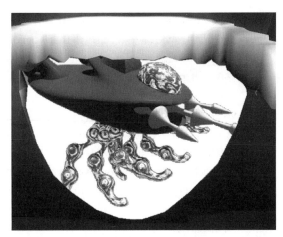

FIGURE *A view from inside the Mouth of a figure shows the back of the Teeth, and*
19.8 *displays the background layer through the mouth opening.*

 *To animate a sequence using the "Inside the Mouth" Camera, make sure Display Settings are used. To create a single image, make a one-frame animation using Display Settings.*

"MILKING" YOUR FOOTAGE

The next time you go to the movies, see how many times the same footage, from different vantage points, is repeated. You can especially watch for this on expensive takes, like explosions, though you may also catch it being used when a character is running, walking, or driving. This is a way that directors often "milk" the footage, and you can take advantage of this same option with your Poser animations.

After all, it may have taken you hours or even days to get everything in your scene set up just as it should be, with all of the tweaked nuances timed correctly. Why should you settle for just one run through of the choreography? Poser's variable Camera options are just what you need to repeat the animation without the kind of repetitive loops that do nothing but bore your audience. Explore these possibilities:

- Render your animation with different Camera types, stitching them together in the post-production process with Adobe Premiere, After Effects, or similar applications. When you stitch them together, use smaller snips from each animation, so that the viewer is always presented with different perspectives for shorter (three seconds per snip) amounts of time.

- Try rendering the same animation from the same Camera using different rendering styles, and then stitch these together. This can lend a very subliminal look to an animation.

- Use different zooms, pans, and rotations to add excitement to an animation. You can do this from one Camera type, by just changing these options with each animation save.

- Cut in views of the face (Face Camera) of your character during an animated sequence that shows the figure in action. This allows the viewer to intuit how that character is feeling about what it is doing.

- Show the same animation from the perspective of each actor involved. If a flower pot is going to fall on an actor's head, show the view from both the actor and the flower pot. Show the actor looking up, and then become the flower pot looking down. Intersperse these views frequently, until the ultimate conclusion. This heightens the tension in a scene. If you have two Poser figures engaged in a karate match, show the view from each of the figures, and then perhaps from someone on the sidelines. You'll only have to choreograph the scene once, but you'll be able to get 10 times the footage out of it.

- Allow your Camera to fly around the action like an insect, weaving in and out. Do this several different ways on a single animated choreography, and stitch them together.

- Use distorted Camera angles to add to user interest, like a view from the ground up that distorts the perspective. Do this in different ways to any single animation.

CAUTION

Karuna! For the quickest way to achieve interesting perspective views, use the Trackball.

- Most importantly, use any or all of these techniques together, adding even more variety (and viewer time) to any animation.

New Lights and Lighting

Here's a collection of hints and tips concerning how lights can be used to enhance and modify your animations.

- If you want your character to be influenced by an explosion in its proximity, use a few keyframes to turn a light's intensity to 1000 or more. This will wash out the details of the figure, so that it will seem like a fiery event has occurred nearby. Use a white light for an atomic flash, a red light for a fiery burst, or a blue-green light when the event is being caused by an extraterrestrial source.

- Do you need a night scene, an environment with no moon or stars, but just your actor(s) moving in the dark? Make sure all three lights are set to pure black or a very deep purple. Then take one light and aim it at the actor(s). Set the other two lights so they shine from above. Set the intensity to 1000. Your scene will show up clearly, but will be cast in deep darkness. To make your character's eyes glow in the dark when using this lighting method, do the following. Turn off all texture for the eyeballs. Set Highlight to full intensity, and select a yellow or yellow-green color. Use a dark blue Ambient color to give the eyeballs a 3D look. This effect is very eerie. You could also use a blood red, giving the eyes a nightmarish glow.

CAUTION

Karuna! *If you are going to use a background image or movie, make sure it is appropriately dark as well, since Poser's lights have no effect on background footage.*

- Use Spotlights of different colors to give your scenes more color depth. This is especially effective when you use complimentary colors on the left and right side of the scene (such as red and green, or blue and orange).
- For a very dramatic lighting effect, use just one light, switching the other two off. You'll be able to control shadows much more effectively by using this method. Turn the light that is activated so that it casts part of the object in shadow. This effect also creates a better 3D depth than multiple lights do. Use this method in conjunction with extreme Camera close-ups. See Figure 19.9.

FIGURE **19.9** *This RayDream flower was created in RayDream, and imported into Poser in OBJ format. Note the detail emphasized by using an extreme zoom Camera with only one light. A Poser head was dropped into the flower center for effect.*

LIGHT LIBRARY ANIMATIONS

Just as you can apply different faces, full poses, or Camera positions to alternate keyframes to create an animation, so too can you apply different light colors and positions from the Lights library at different points on the timeline. The best advice is to spend a day or two exploring different light configurations, saving all of those you like to your Lights library. When they're needed, for still positions or keyframes, you'll have many to select from.

More on Rendering

By Render Options, we can allude to the rendering styles found at the bottom of the Poser 4 interface, or various rendering options found in the Render dialog and other menus. You should be aware of all of these.

ANIMATED SHADOW MAPS

You can use Poser to create content for an Alpha Channel in your favorite post-editing application (like Adobe's After Effects). An Alpha Channel contains only grayscale data, and can be either in black and white or in 256 shades that range from black to white. Pure white prints itself on the channel that the Alpha is placed above, while pure black acts like a drop-out mask. The grays in between act as different levels of transparency, so that the blacker the gray is, the more opaque it is.

Rendering an image or animation using the Silhouette renderer is perfect for creating Alpha Channel information, since it creates a two-color render. If the background is black, and the figure white, only the inside of the figure will allow data to be written over the next layer down in your post-editing composition.

 *If all of these terms seem strange to you, you probably have no experience using a post-editing application. In that case, you can either skip this section and move on, or you can avail yourself of a post-editing application to explore what it can do, and reach a general understanding of these terms.*

Essentially, you would use an Alpha Map to make sure that any effect applied in your post-production software addressed only the Poser figure(s), still or animated. But I have another suggestion for you to explore. Let's say all that you wanted to include on a layer in your composition was a shadow of a figure, perhaps a human, animal, or even a prop. Poser 4 can help you do this, and here's how:

1. Create a Poser animation as you normally would, using any of the tools and techniques required to do the job.

2. Make sure that Ground Shadows are on. Make the Shadow Color White, and the Background Black. Use the Silhouette renderer. All that you should see in the Document is the White Shadow, with everything else being Black.

3. Move the Object or Figure upward along the Y axis. Notice that Shadow Size does not change. Render the animation.

4. Use this animation as an Alpha Shadow mask in your post-production application. Whatever effects are applied to it will only affect the white areas of this Alpha layer, so creating things like shimmering shadows is a snap.

SURFACE ATTRIBUTE COLORS

In the Surface Materials dialog, under the Render menu options, there are three Color selectors: Object Color, Highlight Color, and Ambient Color. There is also a slider that controls Highlight Size. Using different combinations of colors in these three selectors, and adjusting the Highlight Size slider, produces different rendering looks based completely upon these Color qualities. Just as the three global Light Parameters on the main screen alter the overall lighting in a Poser document, so these three Color selectors alter the Light Color components for each targeted element in your scene, by acting as additive colors, almost like color gels for the lights. Table 19.1 shows some suggested combinations, and what they generate. All of these results are achieved by using just one global light set to white, and with Textures set to None.

Once you have explored these color settings with Textures off, try applying a texture over them. You will see that different textures respond in different ways to the same color settings.

RENDER STYLES

More than any other 3D application, Poser 4 makes it extremely easy to alter the rendering styles on your display screen. Pushing the envelope even further, Poser allows you to select any and all of the elements on screen for different rendering styles (Display/Element Style). This makes it easy to render one part of the document as a silhouette, another as a wireframe, and yet another as a shaded render, leading to all sorts of creative possibilities. Here are a few suggested uses that you may want to explore:

- Create a group animation, using several Poser figures. Use the Render Styles to display your primary figure as a shaded model, and all the rest as

Table 19.1 Results of Different Surface Material Light Combinations

Object Color	Highlight Color	Ambient Color	Highlight Slider	Result
Bright Yellow	Black	Black	0%	Yellow Object with Black Shadows Plastic
Bright Yellow	White	Black	100%	Yellow Object with Bright White Highlight over Yellow area and Black Shadows Plastic
Bright Yellow	Dark Blue	Black	100%	Yellow Object with just a touch of blue around the perimeter of the Highlight and Black Shadows Plastic
Dark Blue	Bright Yellow	Black	100%	Blue Object with Yellow Highlight and Black Shadows Metallic
Dark Red	Black	Medium Blue	NA	Pink Object to Purple Shadow tones, resembling sunset reflective surface
Any Color	Any Color	100% White	NA	Completely washes out the object in a flat White Bright Ambience outweighs everything else
White	White	Black	0%	Allows Light Source(s) maximum control over Object Color
1. Dark Red 2. Dark Blue 3. Dark Violet	1. Light Green 2. Light Orange 3. Light Yellow	Black	100%	Using complimentary Object and Highlight Colors with maximum Highlight Size creates Metallic Chromes
Dark Blue	Medium Blue	Light Blue or Light Blue-Green	50-100%	This creates a great water surface color
Black	Bright Red	Black	90-100%	Creates a Dark Red object with a medium-sized Highlight only where the light is shining, making a great Ruby
Dark Green	Light Green	Black	90-100%	This creates a Emerald-like object

wireframes. Render and save to disk. You will notice that the nonshaded figures appear very ghost-like in the animation.

- Create a Poser animation that incorporates just one figure. Use the Shaded Render Style to render the head, and render the rest of the body parts as Silhouettes. Render and save the animation. Import the animation into Painter, which will bring it in as single frames in a stack. Go through the stack and apply a texture or effect to the inside of all of the silhouetted body parts, which is easy since they will all be a single color block. Save out the stack as a new animation, and play it. All manner of magical effects can be applied to Poser figures using this technique.

Color Plate 1: The Pool of Secrets by Shamms Mortier

Color Plate 2: Greening by Celia Ziemer

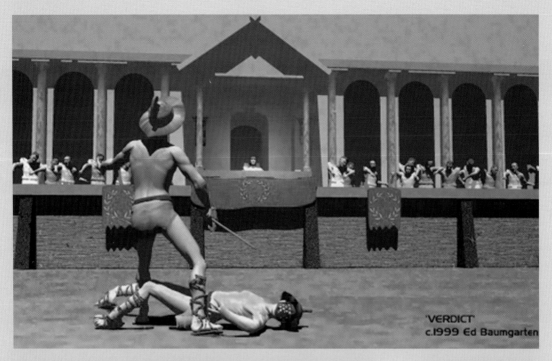

Color Plate 3: **TOP:** *Verdict* by Ed Baumgarten   **BOTTOM:** *Interrogation Room* by Luke Ahearn

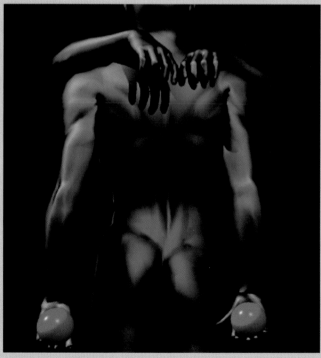

Color Plate 4: **TOP:** *Medusa* by Kuzey Atici   **BOTTOM:** *Hands* by Ken Shumate

Color Plate 5: **TOP:** *Repairs* by Patrick Farley   **BOTTOM:** *Ambush* by Marc Garland McCoy

Color Plate 6: **TOP:** *Triad* by Lisa Boyce **BOTTOM:** *Prince* by Lee Chapel

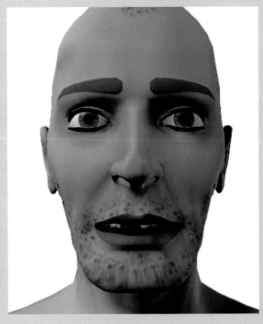

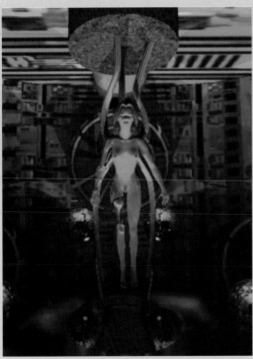

Color Plate 7: **TOP LEFT:** *Baby Sitter* by Janet Glover   **TOP RIGHT:** *Stubble Face* by Rick Schrand
BOTTOM LEFT: *Angel* by Eric Ruffo **BOTTOM RIGHT:** *NY Times Piece* by Ray Sherman

Color Plate 8: TOP: *Junkyard Fairies* by Celia Ziemer
BOTTOM FOUR PANELS: *The Wagoneer* by Shamms Mortier.

- Create a Poser Head that uses a Hidden Line Render Style, except for the eyes. Render the eyes as a Textured Render Style. This looks very bizarre, and when animated, calls extreme attention to the eyes.
- Create an animation that shows a figure interacting with and among several props. Use the full Textured Render Style on the figure, and the Sketch Render Style on the props. This method creates a life-like figure moving in a cartoon world.

There are dozens of other mix-and-match explorations you can make using Render Styles. Take some time to explore as many as possible. See Figure 19.10.

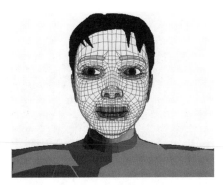

FIGURE   *In this Render Style example, the Hair is rendered in Silhouette, the eyes as*
19.10   *Textured renders, the Head as a Hidden Line, and the lower body as a Sketch.*

CAUTION

Karuna! *Rendering Hair using the Silhouette Style can be much more realistic than using a textured Render. This is because we generally see Hair as a single-color object, except when we zoom in close.*

If you want to use the Render Styles in an animation, just make sure that you reference the Display Settings instead of the Render Settings in the animation dialog.

Moving Along   In this chapter, we have explored a number of ways that allow you to make your animations more interesting, using the capabilities of the Camera, Lights, and the Render Styles. In the next chapter, we'll learn more about Poser from some Master Users.

CHAPTER

20

HINTS AND TIPS FROM MASTER USERS

Whereat defines a Poser Master User? First, a Poser Master User must know Poser from the inside out, having explored not only its tools, but also how to push the tools to the limits. A Master User should also have found ways to bend Poser to his or her personal creative uses, so that the artists and animator's style shines through. Last, I would say that a Master User is also open to sharing his or her discoveries with the wider Poser community, since the master of any tool always takes great pleasure in dispersing that knowledge to others, realizing that knowledge passed on is potentially knowledge deepened. Here then, in every sense of the word, are a few examples of masterful Poser user's words and works.

Chris Derochie

Chris Derochie has been animating since 1984. He has worked on 11 animated feature films, 12 Disney CD-ROMs, and dozens of television series, specials, and advertisements. He was born in Canada and worked in Vancouver as a freelance character animator until 1989. He then moved to Ireland to work at Don Bluth Entertainment for four years. He moved to Australia in 1992, where he worked at Walt Disney Television Australia for two years. He returned to Canada for another two years during which he tried his hand at storyboarding and directing as well as animation. He continued his hobby of encircling the Earth by returning to Ireland in 1996. He works from his home, freelancing for major animation studios and sending his animation to them over the Internet. He uses Poser to plan out difficult scenes, and is presently producing a series of CD-ROMs containing animation, poses, and models for use with Poser.

APPROACHING A SCENE

Text and Images by Chris Derochie

Every animator has his or her own ideas on how to approach or "plan out" their scenes. There is no right or wrong way, but some methods are definitely more effective than others. All of the best approaches share one thing in common: The dominant amount of energy is spent on visualizing and planning rather than animating.

Before you begin any animation or even a single pose, you should take the time to ask yourself these questions: "What is this scene *really* about?" "What is my character' thinking and feeling?" "What do I want the audience to look at in this scene?" "Which part of this scene/pose expresses the meaning of the scene the clearest?" Before you are able to communicate an idea through a scene or pose, you will have to be *very* clear on exactly what your idea is!

If you begin posing or animating before you have a solid idea, the scene will be lifeless and boring. For example, if you were creating a pose of a woman picking up a jug of water without first thinking of what her intentions were for the jug or what she was thinking while picking it up, she will look like a mindless puppet, picking up a jug simply because someone else pulled her strings. See Figure 20.1.

FIGURE   *The woman picks up the jug like a mindless puppet, conveying no human depth.*
20.1

If you posed the scene with the idea that the woman was angry that her husband wouldn't get out of bed, and she intended to dump the water from the jug over her lazy spouse's head, you would find that that thinking changes the way that you would pose every single element of the body, from her face to her fingertips. See Figure 20.2.

FIGURE   *The woman picks up the jug, with an intention to dump the contents on her*
20.2   *husband's head.*

Let's say that her mind is elsewhere; she has lost a child recently and her attention is focused on her grief. Everything she does is lacking in energy as she goes through the motions of her daily routine; if she can even accomplish them at all. You might pose the scene showing her pausing just after she has begun lifting the jug because she hasn't even thought of what she is supposed to be doing with it. She may stay motionless for several seconds before she "wakes up" and continues the action. See Figure 20.3.

FIGURE   *The woman cradles the jug while picking it up, lost in grief.*
20.3

As a final example, we'll say that she has just woken up from a very intense nightmare in which her body was on fire. She rushes over to the water jug, still half dreaming, and dumps the water over her head to extinguish the imagined flames. The extreme tension has to be felt in every part of her pose! See Figure 20.4.

FIGURE   *The woman is still dreaming of fire as she picks*
20.4   *up the jug.*

As you can see from these examples, it's what you make the characters think and feel that is of prime importance, not their positioning. This principle is just as important for animation. Anyone can make characters "move around" on screen, but your characters will only have life if they are seen as thinking, feeling beings. Only then can your audience have any empathy for them. Have you ever watched a film in which the main character was so poorly written that you didn't care if he lived or died? This is because the writer or film-makers didn't allow you to see into the character's personality. You might even see the character as an actor walking around a set, saying his or her lines. How believable would the film be then? It all boils down to this: The action will be determined by what the character is thinking and feeling.

OK, so you've thought the whole thing out, you know exactly what the character is thinking and feeling, (its motivation), now how do you get that Poser figure to look right? This is where talent and experience come in handy! If you haven't spent most of your life as an artist, you'll have to get into a few new habits. You will have to pay close attention to everyone and everything around you; study the world, go people-watching. When you are walking down the street, look at people you pass by and try to figure out what they might be thinking. Then try to observe what it is about how they are moving and holding themselves that made you come to perceive that they were feeling that way. Don't generalize, "He's sad because he's walking slow," or "She's in a hurry because she's walking fast." Try to look at the details that you normally miss or take for granted. For example, you may see a woman talking to a man, and get the impression that she is nervous for some reason.

Get into the details: She's unconsciously fiddling with the zipper on her coat; her gestures are very tense and choppy, yet she keeps smiling at the man that she's talking to; she only gestures when she has to, then she's straight back to her zipper again; she keeps looking around with stiff-necked, darting glances. There may be hundreds of details to see. At this point, you could come up with some possible scenarios to explain her behavior. Perhaps she is attracted to this man and she has finally built up the nerve to speak to him, but she's afraid that she'll run out of things to say or that she will say something stupid. It could be that she is chatting with this guy while her boyfriend could be arriving at any moment. The man may be someone who she hasn't seen in a while, and she just gets very excited and hyper by talking to people. It doesn't matter if you are correct in any way, but you've just built up your own mental library of real-life situations that you can emulate. The next time you need to animate or pose a character in a similar situation, you know the types of actions, gestures, and facial expressions that will get that feeling across.

Another good source is live-action films. Look carefully at your favorite actors in films that you really enjoyed and follow the same analytical procedure. What is it about their performance that gets their thoughts and feelings across so clearly? If you have a video machine with a good freeze frame, you can make your poses match the character on screen. If you have a video camera, you can film yourself, a friend, family member, or even a model. If you have a capture board in your computer, you can then import the video into Poser and use it in the background as reference.

There is one *very* important concept that needs to be understood clearly! Live action and animation are like two very different languages that do *not* translate literally. Think of them as English and Japanese; you know what happens when you try to literally translate them!

The process of taking live-action film and directly tracing it for animation is called "rotoscoping." If you have ever seen a film that was rotoscoped or that had rotoscoping in it, you would notice that it looks sluggish and lifeless. Conversely, if you've seen any of those old live-action TV series about comic book superheroes, you'll notice that they looked like fools in tights moving around in exaggerated ways. They simply can't be transplanted without being converted. For example, if you had a live-action scene of a boxer hitting a punching bag with all of his strength, it would look very powerful in live action. In order to keep that feeling of strength when you translate it to animation, all of the poses must be exaggerated, and the timing must be altered. When the boxer twists his torso and pulls back his fist, you need to go even farther and hold that "anticipation" pose a little bit longer. When he swings through, you need to make the swing faster and lean his body farther forward. As his arm and torso "follow through," you need to swing the arm farther from the body, end in a more extreme pose, and hold it a little longer than in the live action. When you view the animation, it will *feel* the same as the live action, but the actual poses and timing have now been converted.

This strange limitation is the reason that motion capture files never feel right because they are the 3D equivalent of rotoscoping. Although motion capture is used extensively in films and games, it is rarely left in its raw form. Animators usually use the motion capture files as a stepping stone, and refine the scenes by hand.

If you spend more time observing people and building up a mental library of characteristic movements and expressions, you will find it easier to visualize your scenes. By having a clear idea of what you want the character to be thinking and feeling before you pose or animate your scenes, you will find that your work has more life and appeal than ever before.

Martin Turner

FAST AND DIRTY, QUICK AND EASY, SLOW AND PAINFUL: THREE LEVELS OF LIP-SYNCING AND PHONEMES.

Text and images by Martin Turner

Martin Turner is a regular on the MetaCreations Poser List, and has expertise in both the shaping of phonemes and in creating clothing for Poser 4 models. Poser 4 leapt through the light barrier by offering animatable faces and the ability to import and graph sounds. This tutorial gives you a fast-and-dirty way of lip-syncing, and then works through some of the more technical aspects of making speech look good.

Phonemes, a Quick But Important Note

Phonemes are the smallest speech sounds that make a difference to what word is being said. The difference between "tooth" and "truth" is one phoneme—the "r" sound—even though the spelling is quite different. If you are an English speaker, you probably spent considerable time as a child learning how to read and spell English, and discovering that things didn't look the way they sounded. When working with phonemes, you have to forget all that. It is terribly, terribly tempting to look at the way words are written, and try to do your lip-syncing on that basis. The result will simply be wrong. The only way (and even trained phonologists do this) to work out which phoneme you should be using is to mouth it to yourself. So bear that in mind as you work through this tutorial.

HOW FAR TO GO

This tutorial is in three parts: Fast and Dirty, Quick and Easy, and Painful and Slow. How far you go depends on how much realism you need. If your character is being animated from a distance, head half-turned, using sketch shading to give everything a cartoon feeling, then Fast and Dirty is about all you need. It works from the Library palette. If you need more realism, then you still need to work through the Fast and Dirty stuff, but the Quick and Easy, which is about consonants, will give you enough detail to help your character talk sense. If you are looking for the max, then you also need to take into account the Painful and Slow stuff, which is mostly about vowels. There is one step beyond that—useful if you are doing broadcast-quality rendering. That is when you put everything you learned in this tutorial together with careful study of real people speaking, and meticulous use of the Poser tools to get everything just right. For that, you are on your own—in art, as in life, only *you* can take things to the ultimate. No tutorial can do it for you.

Fast and Dirty Lip-Syncing

First, record some speech in your favorite recording application, and save it in a format that Poser understands. For Mac, the format is QuickTime; for Windows the format is AVI.

In Poser, choose File menu>Import>Sound, locate your sound, and import it.

Then open the Graph palette. When you import a sound, you can view it in the Graph window. The green line marks the frame you are on, and the red line marks the changes you have set in the selected value. Poser will also play the sound as you move from frame to frame. This graph shows the word "Excellent," with a little background music before and after. The word begins just before the green line, but notice that the mouth opens first—people usually breathe before they start to speak. See Figure 20.5.

Play the sound through a couple of times, so that you get the hang of which sounds go with the peaks on the graph. Essentially, the short changes in level are consonants, and the long ones are vowels. M and n sounds can be very loud, though, and are longer than most consonants, so watching carefully is the best advice.

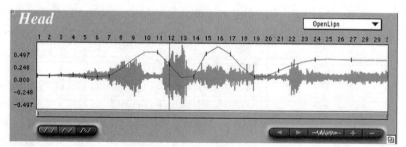

FIGURE **20.5** *The Poser Graph palette.*

Now, keeping the Graph palette open, go to the Libraries palette, take Faces, and select the Phonemes library. The Phonemes in the Faces section of the library is fine for fast-and-dirty lip-syncing, but the results you will get will be very stylized and exaggerated. Unless you are enunciating very carefully, you would never open your mouth like this for "oh." See Figure 20.6.

FIGURE *The Phonemes library.*
20.6

In the Graph palette, move the cursor onto the first sound, and then select the face in the Phonemes library that goes most with that sound. Load it, and then move the cursor on to the next abrupt change in the sound level. As you move the cursor, Poser will "pronounce" the sound to help you. Repeat the process, using the nearest-looking phoneme in the library until you have finished. Tweak the phoneme shapes by using the Parameter Dials for the mouth. People move their faces differently as they speak. The man in Figure 20.6 is nodding. Some people tilt their heads, wince, or lick their lips. Remember that anyone speaking for more than a few seconds will also blink at least once.

Making realistic phonemes will almost always involve setting a number of the dials. Sounds are influenced by what comes before and what comes after. Expression is very much influenced by how the person is speaking and smiling, frowning, or shouting as he or she talks. Work at it until it looks natural.

See Figure 20.7 and 20.8.

FIGURE   *Apply the correct phoneme to the selected figure.*
20.7

FIGURE   *Tweak the Parameter Dials for the mouth as needed.*
20.8

PROBLEMS WITH FAST-AND-DIRTY LIP-SYNCING

What you just achieved—assuming you tried it—should have taught you all you need to know about the Poser technicalities of lip-syncing. It's easy, and fun. But the result you got will look exaggerated and unnatural. To get a smooth, natural look, you need to know some of the basics of phonology, and you need to use the Parameter Dials that go with the face element, rather than the library phonemes.

QUICK-AND-EASY CONSONANTS

Consonants can be grouped by where they happen in the mouth, whether they are voiced or unvoiced, and whether they are fricatives, plosives, nasals, and so forth. It doesn't matter if this doesn't mean anything to you yet—things will become clear when you start mouthing the sounds listed in Table 20.1.

To construct them, you need to forget the Library palette, and go straight to the Parameter Dial controls, which come up by clicking on the figure's head. Apart from that, the process is the same, just using the Parameter Dials instead of the prebuilt phonemes.

Table 20.1: Showing the consonants of English, their phonological descriptions, and how to achieve them in Poser 4. As practice, mouth the sounds with your fingers on your mouth to see how it moves.

Voiced	Unvoiced	Type	Poser Notes: Use These Controls
*Bilabials (with both lips)		Mouth M	
b	p	Plosive	Lips coming together sharply
m		Nasal	Lips remain together longer
w			Lips don't quite meet
*Labiodentals (lips and teeth)		Mouth F	
v	f	Fricative	
*Dentals (tongue on teeth)		Mouth t (Higher values of T)	
th (as in the)	th (as in thick)	Fricative	
*Alveolar (tongue on ridge behind teeth)		Mouth t (lower values of t)	
d	t	Plosive	
z	s	Fricative	
l		Lateral	Mouth 1
n		Nasal	
Palato-alvelar (blade of the tongue near the ridge behind the teeth			Just open the mouth a little, plus mabye some Mouth 1
	sh		
j (edge)	ch	Affricate	
Palatal			
	y		Maybe a little Mouth 1
Velar (back of the tongue on roof of mouth)			
g	k		
Glottal (mouth open, vocal chords narrow)			
	h		

1. Generally, only those at the front of the mouth will show up. I have starred these in the consonant table. The rest will take the sound of the vowel they **precede**. For these consonants, just close the mouth a little and open it wider for the vowel.

2. Voiced and Unvoiced look exactly the same as far as the tongue and lips are concerned. However, the sound graph will show voiced as about half as loud as vowels, while unvoiced will be much quieter.

3. The range that poser offers for "tongue T" and the other controls is much more than the ordinary range of speech. You should experiment with different levels. The louder someone is speaking, the more movement. Women move their lips more than men do (in general). Watch out particularly for Mouth M and Mouth F, where too high values look ridiculous. You will very rarely need to move the Dial as high as 1, even for someone shouting.

4. For quick-and-easy vowel sounds, use a combination of Smile and Open-Lips, except for the O sound, for which you use Mouth O. You should note, however, that in British English the O sound is *not* always made with mouth O, so watch out for this. Vowel sounds are less determined than front-of-the-mouth consonants, so it's less critical to get it right.

5. The only way to be sure a phoneme is correct is to check what it actually looks like when animated—you may need several goes at first. In general, it is better to under-animate than over-animate. If you are doing a particular accent that isn't yours, watch someone who has that accent while he or she is speaking, and remember any particular features.

6. Each person has a different way of moving his or her lips to talk—the most important difference is the amount of lip movement, but people also vary the way in which they open their mouths wider *during* a vowel. It's important to remake your lip movements for every actor/character, rather than using a standard set, because the way people talk is one of the most important aspects of characterization.

PAINFUL-AND-SLOW VOWELS

The Painful-and-Slow section concentrates on vowels. Everybody's vowels are slightly different, and they vary greatly from accent to accent. So, this is just a guide. However, it is much more difficult to spot inappropriate vowels than it is bad consonants.

Six Criteria that More or Less Pin Down Vowels

- The part of the tongue that is raised (front, center, or back)—ignore everything but the front.

- How high the tongue rises toward the palate (high, mid-high, mid-low, low).
- The position of the soft palate (ignore this one—you can't see it).
- The kind of opening made at the lips—various degrees of rounding or spreading.
- Length of the vowel. In phonetic script, this is marked as : for long; hence i: e:.
- Diphthongisation—one vowel after the other. A lot of sounds you think are one vowel are actually two. For instance, in UK southern English (think how Lara Croft talks), "go" is actually *g-uh-oo,* but the *uh-oo* comes so close together you imagine it is one sound. Fifty years ago, and still in other parts of the country, the sound is a straight long *o.* Incidentally, word on the street is that no language has both long and short diphthongs, although Anglo-Saxon (think, JRR Tolkien and CS Lewis) is written as though it does.

Difference in dialect is most likely to be shown in the diphthongs—one dialect might make the *ay* sound as *ah-ee* (which means a mouth movement from smile to no smile in Poser 4), while another might make it as a single sound in the middle of the mouth (just open lips).

What Poser Offers You

- Mouth O = rounding
- Smile = spreading
- Open lips = nonspread, nonrounded
- Tongue L = various degrees of tongue rising at the front and glides

Glides (the yuh sound in "royal") are very important for speech, but given that you'll just want a touch of Tongue L for them, you can probably ignore them.

Do diphthongs as one vowel after the other, if there's a visible difference on your sound graph.

Vowels

The vowels listed in Table 20.2 are UK English (but will be similar for all Englishes). The script is not the conventional IPA alphabet, but should be easier to follow for nonlinguistics people. I am only listing the vowels you can see; for all others, Open Lips, in an amount proportional to the volume of the vowel (but don't be taken in by *m* and *n* sounds, which can be very loud, even though the mouth is closed) will be fine. Remember as you do this that vowels are very idiosyncratic. Experimenting is the key.

Table 20.2: Achieving Specific Vowel Sounds.

Sound	Poser Parameter Dial
"i" in cheese	Smile
"a" as in car	Some Smile (maybe)
"a" as in bad	More Smile
"u" as in put	Some Mouth O
"oo" as in shoot	A lot of Mouth O
"o" as in got	A touch of Mouth O
"aw"	Some Mouth O
"e" as in bay	Open Lips
"e" as in get	Less Open Lips
"uh"*	Only a very little Open Lips (depending on volume)

* "uh" is one of the most commonly occurring sounds in English—almost any vowel that isn't stressed tends to become an "uh" sound. If your lip-sync looks over-animated, it may be because you are using front vowels rather than "uh."

Cecilia Ziemer   **ELECTRIC ART**

Text and images by Cecilia Ziemer

POTTED

The apprehensive Plantman is the Poser 4 Male Nude, slightly distorted on his Y axis and opened for a fast transplant to a pot in RayDream Studio 5.0.2. This is almost misusing the Poser plugin, which shines its best adding scenery to and editing Poser animations.

In a separate file in RDS, I made aerial roots, the fire-can, the pot, and its potting soil, in the Vertex Modeler (the potting soil is the inside shell of a duplicated pot, resized, with the last cross-section filled). Leaves and petals are duplicates of a single-mesh Modeler Leaf, resized, rotated, and perturbed with the Magnet tool.

I opened the Poser scene in RDS and pasted pot, fire-can, petals, and leaves into it, then opened the figure in RDS's Poser Modeler to tweak the Plantman (using Poser's regular tools) into a more vegetative attitude (i.e., translating the feet closer together so they'd fit into the pot), and adjusting angles of the head and hands to prevent foliage interpenetration. See Figure 20.9.

When the Plantman was potted, rooted, and blooming, I put cellular shaders on everything but the firing-can, the pot, and the board holding the

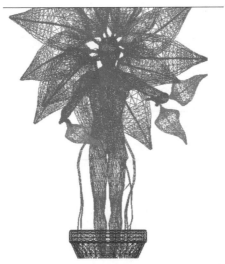

FIGURE   *The Poser scene is composed in RayDream Studio.*
20.9

pot. The atmosphere is 4 Elements Wind; the fire is RadFX fire with a red bulb light hidden in the pot. See Figure 20.10.

FIGURE   *The finished artwork.*
20.10

JUNKYARD FAIRIES

Just so. In fine gardens, fairies are made of gossamer and moonlight, wear silken robes, and dine delicately on dew. These two guys are the other kind: raucous, muddy, deranged, and devolved, wearing shreds of moss and the grime of ages; it's best not to speculate on their diet or pastimes. Only the wings allude to their species.

To make an ugly creature from a handsome Poser model, I started with the Poser 4 Male Nude, gave him Toddler's height, and rescaled him in all directions. The pot belly, combined with the sway-backed flat-footed stance, required a little tapering on most of the torso parts, and some major adjustments of Scale and Joint Parameters for both hip and abdomen to prevent tearing and separating. See Figure 20.11.

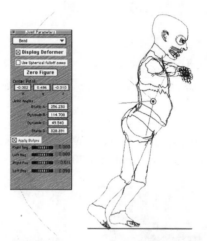

FIGURE *The model is first composed in Poser.*
20.11

By the time the figure was mauled into proper uglification, no body part remained undistorted or with its normal scale. The eyeballs were scooted forward on the Z axis, until they barely cleared the eyelids; a value of –1 on the Worry Dial brought the eyebrows down at the right angle to give the eyes a little shadowing from the top.

The head extension is a Woman's Hair, cropped and remodeled in Ray-Dream Studio 5.0.2; the wings are three objects, also made in RDS. The outline for the membrane and the cross-section shape extruded for the veins were drawn in Adobe Illustrator and imported; these had to be separate meshes for later texturing in Bryce. Lunch is a piece of Skeleton exported from Poser and dismantled in RDS. I exported hair and wing parts from RDS as individual OBJs. See Figure 20.12.

In Poser, the hair is attached to the head as a Prop, and wing-groups are attached as Children of the collar sections. Then I imported the bone and curled

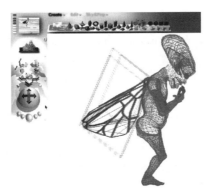

FIGURE   *Parts modified in RDS are imported into Bryce 3D.*
20.12

the hands around it, and bent hands and bone close to the mouth to afford him a good gnaw; I exported it all to Bryce 3D as separate groups for body parts. The second fairy, seated and pondering a large and unshared bone, is the same model, repositioned in Poser and exported. See Figure 20.13.

The hairy-pod-thing is a RayDream cylinder mesh, subdivided, spiked, twisted, and spherized; the branches are RayDream Vertex Modeler branches. The materials are all Bryce procedurals: I made a custom material based on Stucco Noise and applied it to the bodies and hair after ungrouping, then re-

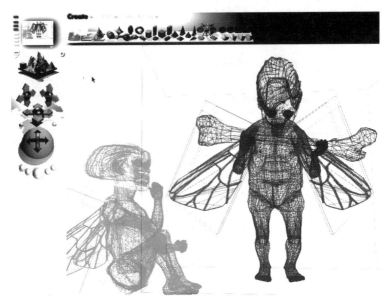

FIGURE   *The final scene is composed in Bryce 3D.*
20.13

grouping without eyes or wings. The eyes are the default "What are You Look-ing At" recolored and with a 50% Ambient setting. See Figure 20.14.

FIGURE   *The final rendering in Bryce 3D.*
20.14

RAGDOLL

The four-armed mud-creature crouched on the pier is the same figure I used for Junkyard Fairies, doubled. With IK unchecked, I positioned the figure in its basic crouch, then added it to the New Figures library. Viewing with the Side Camera, I added the new figure as a second figure; it opened accurately aligned with the first figure.

I moved the second figure downward along the angle of the first figure's spine until the shoulders were clear of the first figure's shoulders. I bent all the arms into position, and made invisible on the first figure (the upper) everything below the chest, and the second figure's head and neck. See Figure 20.15.

Then I attached the "hair" and exported it.

The winged object of contention is the same figure (again), squashed a little shorter, repositioned, and rescaled down to about 50%.

The tentacle is an RDS spiral with a few spikes here and there. This was the first object in the scene, since placement of the other two figures and all the ob-

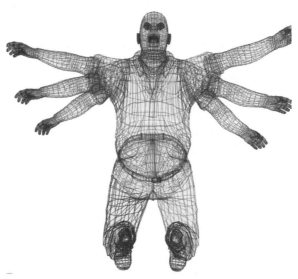

FIGURE
20.15
Here is the process using three figures with only arms and collars visible.

jects floating in water and sagging in air (except the pier) depended on tentacle placement—it had one angle suitable for an ankle grab. Other objects in the image are Bryce primitives, including the kitchen match (these are little guys) for light. The wings were added and scaled down at the last. See Figure 20.16.

FIGURE
20.16
The finished Ragdoll composition.

BONES

See the Bones animation in the QuickTime folder on this book's CD-ROM.

Who knows what's on parade in the depths of the galaxy? Or what strange apparitions and devices Poser's four-handed Camera Translation tool will appear to us in dream? Or what good is a baby and a dismantled skeleton? See Figure 20.17.

The bones for the wheel (originally the Poser skeleton) and the mesh forms of the tail are hierarchy conversions; the baby is a distorted Zygote Infant from the Zygote People disk, with its head replaced.

The "wheel" is one shin with foot attached, adjusted in RayDream Studio's Mesh Form Modeler. I detached the polymeshes on the foot (for a little toe-bending later), naming arches, heels, and toes as they came apart, and elongated the shinbones. This I duplicated in the Perspective window, and one by one, named all the parts of each duplicate, and centered the duplicates around a cylinder. The bones group and the cylinder I exported as separate .obj files. Then I wrote the .phi file in SimpleText, before mesh names flew out of my mind.

Using the leftover cylinder in RDS as a spacing guide, I resized one unemployed shinbone and poked it longways through the cylinder's center, attached

FIGURE   *A Poser composition created from a Baby figure and a dismantled skeleton.*
20.17

two more bones at the ends of the resized bone, then attached a duplicate of the resized bone at the top. Yet another resized duplicate and an enlarged hand makes the seating arrangement; with the center cylinder removed, this bony frame/seat was exported as a solid group. See Figure 20.18.

Now for the snoot-flute player (. . . In Space, no one can hear you practice . . .). After enlarging his belly and feet, narrowing his shoulders, and generally distorting the whole body in Poser, I duplicated him and exported the duplicate to RDS for dismantling in the mesh modeler—all I needed was the head.

With the Magnet tool I distorted the head a little to the back, and pulled some vertices on the top for the head fins. The nose and mouth area I selected and decimated, flattening it further, vertex by vertex. The snoot-flute itself is just a lathed object, fitted to the face at one end and reshaped a little on the other. Head-with-snoot went back to Poser as a prop for head replacement on the original figure.

The tail was modeled in the RDS Vertex Modeler and broken apart in the Mesh Form Modeler. After replacing the head and positioning the hands for snoot-playing, I converted the wheel and tail to Poser models. Snoot-player was positioned in the bony hand and attached as a child object to the frame, as were the cylinder and the wheel. The wheel's center aligned to the cylinder and the whole works is moved by dragging the frame, the easiest part to grab.

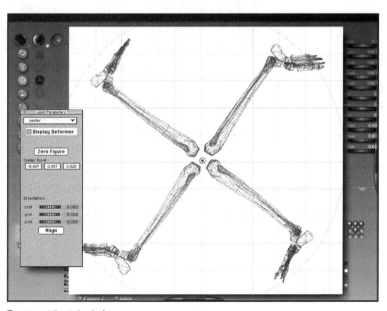

FIGURE *The Wheel object.*
20.18

For animation, the wheel was rotated in 90-degree increments with the toes flexing slightly; the tail swayed, the baby boogied. I set depth cueing on, shadows off, made the background color blue, the foreground gold, and the lights blue and orange; the sky is a Bryce PICT—it has a couple of comets, but they're very hard to see. There's no texture map, only a high ambient setting and reddening for the eyes. See Figure 20.19.

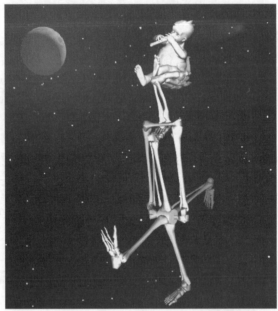

FIGURE *A rendered frame from the Bones project.*
20.19

Roy Riggs

PHI BUILDER

Text and Images by Roy Riggs

Load PHI Builder from the PHI folder on this book's CD-ROM.

PHI Builder v2.1 is a 32-bit Windows application for aiding in the creation of PHI files. PHI files are the means by which you can import your own models into Poser, and set them up so you can actually pose them. This is one of the most exciting new features found in Poser V4.0; unfortunately, it's also one of the hardest things to do. PHI Builder's purpose is to make the creation of your PHI file as easy as possible, and point out any possible problems, so Poser won't encounter any errors when you load it in. If you don't already have PHI

Builder installed, all you have to do is unzip it into your Poser directory. You can check for the latest update at http://edge.net/~fur/index.html.

The first step when making a model for use within Poser is to create your model, or convert your model, into WaveFront's OBJ file format. You should also save your OBJ in its own subdirectory under Runtime\Geometries, because that's what Poser wants. Each piece should be separate from the others; use the existing Poser figures as your guide when splitting them up. This is done in the modeling package of your choice. In my example, I'm using MAX V1.1 with a model of a dancer, provided by CacheForce (www.cacheforce com). See Figure 20.20.

The second step is to create a PHI file, or a Poser Hierarchy file, to tell Poser how to build the joints between each part. Load up PHI Builder, and pick Add OBJ. This will create a default hierarchy, which you will have to rearrange to match your model. See Figure 20.21.

If you have the maintenance patch, this problem should be fixed; otherwise, you'll have to find a way to convert the OBJ file. Now, you might have to manually fix some of the level numbering. PHI Builder's artificial intelligence needs some work, but it's only making guesses based on the name of each part, it's not actually looking at the geometry. You cannot switch into the Tree Editor mode

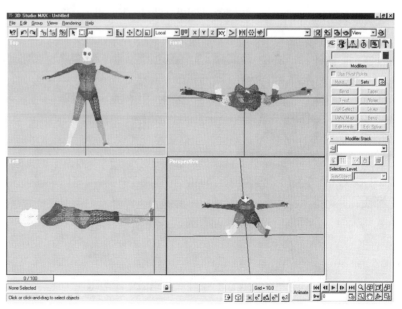

FIGURE   *I've split this figure up in the exact same manner as the models provided with*
20.20   *Poser. It's always a good idea to first import your OBJ into Poser just as a test;*
if that succeeds, you may continue on.

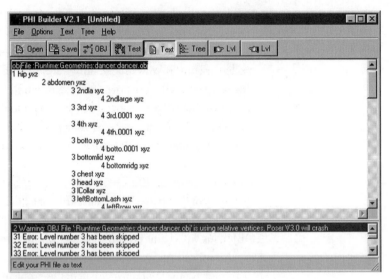

FIGURE
20.21 *This shows that PHI Builder has already noticed a common problem, the OBJ file format exported by MAX is incompatible with Poser V3.0.*

of PHI Builder until you have a syntactically correct PHI file. If you try to switch into the Tree mode, it will automatically verify the PHI file before switching over. Once switched over, you can drag and drop the nodes, and double-click on them to edit them. Figure 20.22 shows the PHI after it's been rearranged.

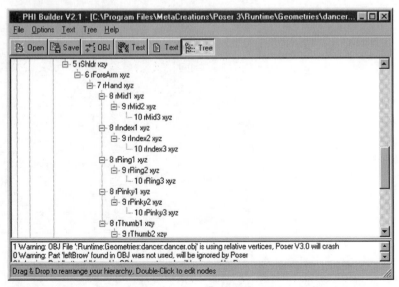

FIGURE *Here's how PHI Builder looks after the rearrangement is completed.*
20.22

Now you'll need to add the IK Chains for your model. If you select the Parent part of your chain, and select the Tree|Add IKChain menu item, PHI Builder will bring up a dialog with the remainder of the tree under the Parent item, and it will have already selected the most likely Child part. All you need to do is supply the name of the IK Chain. See Figure 20.23.

At any time, you can press the Test button, and PHI Builder will test the PHI and OBJ files for problems. Naturally, the File|Open and Save features work as expected. PHI Builder will register itself as the owner of PHI files, so your PHI files will get a little icon in the Explorer window, and you can double-click them to launch PHI Builder, or drag and drop them to the PHI Builder window. Additionally, PHI Builder keeps track of the most recently used PHI files to make switching between them easier. PHI Builder does come with context-sensitive help, but it will not replace MetaCreations' advanced manual.

The third step is to use the File|Convert Hierarchy File menu inside Poser. Poser will read the PHI file, and any OBJ files it includes, to create a .CR2 and an .RSR file to go along with your OBJ. This RSR file basically serves as a compiled version of your OBJ, which Poser can load in faster. If you ever make any changes to your OBJ or PHI file, you MUST delete any previous .RSR files before reconverting the PHI! Hopefully, PHI Builder will have already caught anything that might trip Poser up, and this step should go without a hitch. If you are having problems, make sure the original Poser 2 Man is loaded as default, as this was reported to fix a problem some users were having.

The final step is editing all of the Joint Parameters for your model inside Poser. For more detailed information on this process, read MetaCreations'

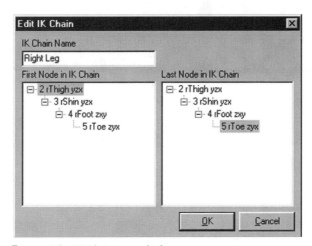

FIGURE *The IK Chain is supplied*
20.23

Advanced Poser Manual. ftp://ftp.metacreations.com/pub/Applications/ Poser/goodies/advanced_techniques.pdf

If you want some more PHI tutorials, try Bushi's Graphics Page at http:// www.spiritone.com/~bushi/

Jackie Lewin

MORPH TARGETS FOR HORSE FORELOCK AND MANE

Text and Images by Jackie Lewin

This tutorial was carried out using 3D Studio Max 2.5, but most of the steps can be duplicated using other 3D modeling software. If you are using 3D Studio Max and do not already have them, you will need to download the excellent Obj2max and Max2obj plugins from Habware at **http://www.habware.at/.**

I will start with the forelock. This is a simple Morph and will demonstrate the stages we will use for the horse's mane. Import the original horsehiP3.obj from your Poser 3 or 4 Runtime/Geometries/ HorseHi, folder into 3D Studio Max. The forelock Morph only requires the head section of the model, so you can either import the head only, or load the whole figure and delete all of the other parts of the horse. See Figure 20.24.

It is extremely important that you do not move or rescale the mesh from its original loading position. If you do, Morph Target will grossly distort the Poser figure and be useless.

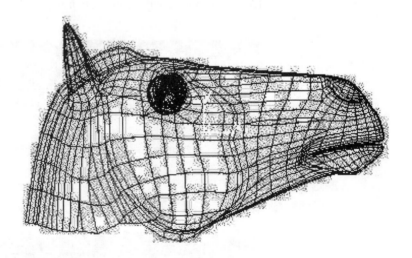

FIGURE *The head of the Horse figure is imported into Max.*
20.24

Add an "Edit Mesh" Modifier to the head section. This can be found by clicking the More button in the Modify panel. You can now edit the individual vertices. Select the vertices. See Figure 20.25.

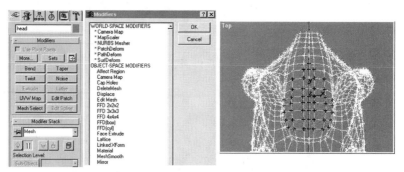

FIGURE *An Edit-Mesh Modifier is added. The vertices are then selected as shown on the*
20.25 *far right.*

Add a 4x4x4 Free-Form Deformation Modifier to the selected vertices (Figure 20.26 left). This can also be found in the Modify/More panel. Activate the lattice by clicking the Sub-Object button in the Modify panel, and select Control Points from the selection box (Figure 20.26 center). Highlight the control points shown in Figure 20.26 right. If your software allows you to lock the points, so that only selected points can be moved, it is useful to do this.

Figure 20.27 shows how I shaped the vertices for the forelock.

Save your file to 3dsmax format so you can return and edit it later. Export the horse head as an .obj file to a directory that you can remember. To apply the

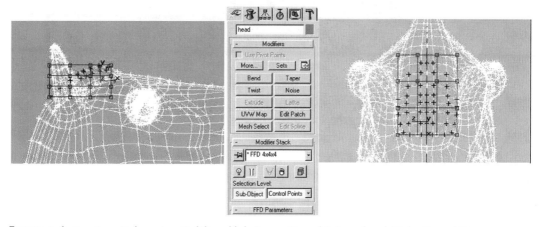

FIGURE *Left: Free Form Deformation Modifier added. Center: Control Points selected. Right: Control Points*
20.26 *highlighted.*

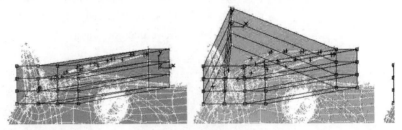

FIGURE *Left to right: The vertices of the forelock are shaped.*
20.27

Morph Target, open Poser and load your horse figure. Double-click on the horse's head. Click Add Morph Target in the Properties window, and locate the .obj file you exported from your modeling program, then click OK. Name the Morph Target, and click OK. A new Parameter Dial will appear. A setting of 1.000 will be equivalent to the modification you made. See Figure 20.28.

FIGURE *The Morph Target reshapes the forelock.*
20.28

THE HORSE'S MANE

Following the same procedure for the forelock, load the horsehiP3.obj file. The parts required are head, upneck, lowneck, and chest. Highlight all four parts and add an Edit Mesh Modifier. Using a side view, select the vertices as shown in Figure 20.29 left and center. Add a 4x4x4 Free Form Deformation Modifier to them, as shown in Figure 20.29 right.

Change to top view. Activate the lattice by clicking the Sub-Object button in the Modify panel, and select Control Points from the selection box. Select the center control points as shown in Figure 20.30.

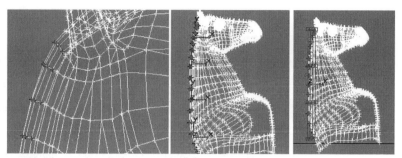

FIGURE   *Free Form Deformations are added to the figure.*
20.29

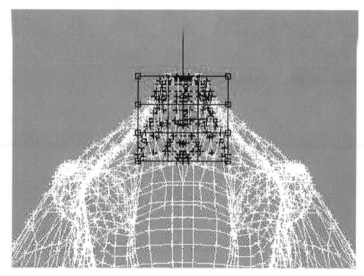

FIGURE   *The center control points are selected.*
20.30

Back in side view, move these points so that your mesh looks similar to Figure 20-30. Save the file.

The deformed vertices will need to be rotated through large angles to produce a convincing mane. Therefore, it is a good idea to spend a little time repositioning some of the vertices so that the mane will look good when texture mapped. You will need to add a second Edit Mesh Modifier so that you can reposition the vertices. Now to turn the mane. Reselect the vertices you have been working on and add a second 4x4x4 Free Form Deformation Modifier to them. Change to front view and move the control points as shown in Figures 20.31 and 20.32.

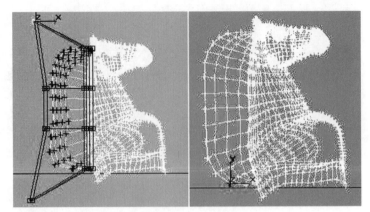

FIGURE *The second Edit Mesh Modifier is added.*
20.31

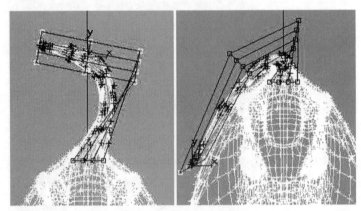

FIGURE *Move the control points as shown.*
20.32

Save your file in Max format.

Deselect the Free Form Deformation modifier by pressing the Sub-Object button. Click outside the mesh to deselect the vertices and selected mesh parts.

You need to export each mesh part as a separate .obj file. To do this, delete the upneck, lowneck, and chest parts, and export the head mesh to your Morph Target directory, and name it something like manehead.obj. Undo the Delete operation in Max and repeat the process for the other parts naming them maneupneck.obj, manelowneck.obj, and manechest.obj.

Hiding the unwanted parts is not sufficient as they will be exported with the visible part, and the Morph Target will not work.

You can now open Poser and apply your Morph Targets to the figure sections. If you look at the mane in the chest area, you can see that it could be improved with a little tweaking. As you saved the file in 3D Studio Max, you can always return and make any fine adjustments if you need to. See Figure 20.33.

FIGURE   *The finished Morphed mane.*
20.33

Stephen L. Cox   ## UVMAPPER
Stephen L. Cox

UVMapper is a utility for texture mapping WaveFront (OBJ) 3D models. You can use it to create texture map templates for models that are already fully texture mapped. This template can then be brought into a 2D paint program such as Photoshop or PaintShop Pro, painted on, and then applied to the model in a 3D rendering program such as Poser or Bryce. If the model has no texture map (UV) coordinates, don't despair! With UVMapper you have the ability to generate texture map coordinates completely to your specification.

UVMapper is available for Windows 95 (or better), and for the Power Macintosh. At the time of this writing, the Mac version is undergoing a complete rewrite in order to make it compatible with the Windows version. There is a Mac version currently available for generating texture map templates, and doing simple mapping. Texture map layout editing is not currently supported. Therefore, the following tutorial is done with the Windows version, and should work with the new Mac version when it becomes available. The Mac version is being ported from the Windows source code by Mr. Steve Martin of Australia.

You can get the latest versions of UVMapper at home.pb.net/~stevecox.

TEXTURE MAPPING A CHAIR WITH UVMAPPER

After launching UVMapper, select File->Load and select the WaveFront model you would like to use. This tutorial uses a chair model named Lch4.obj, which is available on the Sampler 1 CD from Zygote at www.zygote.com. Once the model has finished loading, you will be presented with a list of statistics about the model. Click OK to continue.

Since the model has no texture (UV) coordinates, initially UVMapper starts off with a blank screen. To add texture coordinates to the model, select Edit->New UV Map->Box. Use the default settings: 1024 for map size, Split front/back and Gaps in Map both selected. Press OK. Since the model now has texture coordinates, they are displayed in UVMapper. Box mode texture mapping places the model in a cube and evaluates every facet to see which side of the cube it is primarily facing. The cube is then spread out and laid flat. You can see the top, left, front, right, back, and bottom views of the chair. Each view only contains the facets that are mostly facing in that direction. See Figure 20.34.

Now we're ready to start adjusting the texture map to better suit our needs. Let's start by displaying the texture map colored by material. Materials and groups can be assigned to facets in a model to help make texture mapping easier. Select Edit->Settings and click on Color by Material. Next, select Edit->Se-

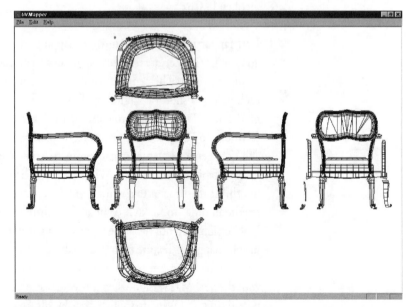

FIGURE *The Chair views.*
20.34

lect->By Material and click on ClothWhite_cushion. This will select every facet that has been assigned that material in the model. The reason for selecting a portion of the model is so that we can remap and move the selection without altering the rest of the model. Select Edit->New UV Map->Planar. Use the default settings with the exception of selecting Y Axis alignment. Now that the selection has been remapped, we need to resize and position it on the map. Maximize the selection by pressing =, shrink it by pressing / on the numeric keypad, and press Shift+y five times to adjust the aspect ratio. Reposition the selection by pressing Page Down to move it to the lower right-hand corner, and finally press Shift+right-arrow and Shift+up-arrow to move it away from the edge of the map. Pressing Enter will save all these changes and clear the selection. See Figure 20.35.

Next, select Edit->Select->by Material and click on ClothGreen_tapestry. Select Edit->New UV Map->Planar, and this time select Z-axis alignment. To resize and position it in the upper right, use the same methods as before. Pressing Page Up will move the selection to the upper right. A listing of all of the hotkeys can be seen by selecting Help->Hot keys.

You can also select portions of the texture map by left-clicking with the mouse, and dragging across them. We will do this to select the next portion of the texture map we want to work with. Left-click and drag the mouse over the top-left cushion from the selection we just remapped.

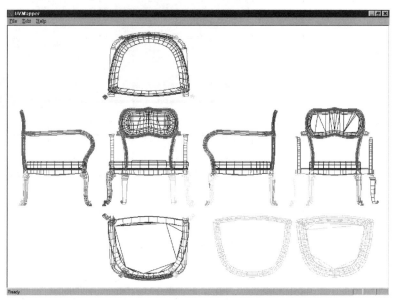

FIGURE   *The second step is taken for creating the new UV Map.*
20.35

Move the selection to the upper left of the texture map. Enlarge it by pressing the * on the numeric keypad. Press Shift+- to decrease it slightly in size. Use the arrow keys to reposition it. You can also left-click on a selection with the mouse and drag it to the new position. Once you have it where you want it, left-click and drag the mouse to select the upper-right cushion.

Resize it and reposition it in the lower-left corner just as we did with the previous cushion. Left-click and drag the mouse to select the two remaining cushions in the top-right corner.

Select Edit->New UV Map->Planar. Use the default settings with the exception of selecting Y-axis for alignment. Resize and position the selection in the upper-right corner. Press Enter to save your changes.

If you like texture maps colored by material, you can save your work now and exit. If you prefer black-and-white texture maps, select Edit->Settings, and click on Black and White. Select File->Save Model to save your work. I recommend that you save the model under a new name so you don't lose the original. At this point, it's a good idea to save the texture map using File->Save Texture Map. This will be the template that you take into your paint program. See Figure 20.36.

FIGURE *The final texture is applied.*
20.36

When applying your new texture map to the model, you must use the updated model you just saved. The texture map will not work with the original model because it has no texture map coordinates.

Your final texture map should look something like Figure 20.37.

FIGURE   *The final chair with the UV Map applied.*
20.37

Rick Schrand

BUMP MAP AND TRANSPARENCY MAP TIPS

Text and Images by Rick Schrand

One of the most anticipated additions to Poser 4 was the ability to create more detailed and complex texture maps for the various models, including transparencies. Prior to this feature being added, to create see-through material or ectoplasmic apparitions or even holes in clothing, you had to import the Poser file into a modeling program, or the rendered character into a program like Adobe Photoshop to get the effect you wanted. Well, that's all history now.

This will be a two-phase tutorial utilizing two different Poser 4 figures: the Male Cowboy Boots (which, by the way, aren't—they're work boots!) and the Male Overcoat. Both of these items can be found under the Figures menu and then selecting the Male Clothing folder.

First, why don't we get our Poser guy ready for a night of two-steppin' by making some fancy boots for him. The boots as they are in the program are fine for working out in the South-40 and slogging through the mud and cow patties, but they sure won't do to go out dancin' with his favorite Posette. So we'll supply him with something of Brooks and Dunn-like quality.

If you haven't loaded the templates into your Poser folder, you can get them (CowBtLTmplt.tif and mensOvercoat.tif) from the Poser Content CD that came with the program. You will be loading them into your paint program. For this tutorial, we'll be using Adobe Photoshop, but the principles all work the same with any suitable bitmap application.

After importing, use the Magic Wand tool to select all the white space around the template, and then choose Inverse to make the template the selected target. Make sure you also deselect the heels on the right unless you want them to be the same color as the boots. Now create a new layer and call it whatever you want. Fill this with whatever color you want your boots to be; in our case, we want them to be gray.

Here comes the fun part. Create a new layer. Using the Lasso tool, draw a licking flame-type outline from the bottom of the boot to about 1/2 or 2/3 of the way to the top. Don't worry about going outside the lines. Your grade won't go down for being sloppy. Anything outside of the colored area will be ignored by the program. Now fill this with a nice, deep red.

Using judicious amounts of filters is paramount to creating a realistic texture in any paint program. With the flame still selected, choose Filter>Noise>Add Noise, select Gaussian, and then set the amount of noise to your liking. If you're using Photoshop 5.x, you can go to Layer>Effects>Bevel and Emboss. Set the parameters for Inside and then whatever depth looks good to you. If you're using an earlier version, there are numerous ways you can create this pillowing look, including through creative lighting effects. After this, select Layer>Blur>Motion Blur and streak the noise. Duplicate the flame, paste it into a layer behind the one we've just been working on, then scale it so it's slightly larger than your original. See Figures 20.38 and 20.39.

To finish off the boots, use the Brush or Airbrush and choose an interesting pattern in the Brushes files and decorate the boot shaft. But leave the center of the shaft alone, because we need to add seams to it. Repeat the process on the patterns to give them some depth. Now duplicate each level or merge these images (not with the boot or background, though), flip them, and move them over to the other side of the boot. After you've saved the file as a PICT (Mac) or BMP (Win) image, it's time to hit the bump-y trail. We need a few seams to make the boot a bit more realistic. First, turn the image into a grayscale. Use the airbrush with a good, soft brush, to create the seams on the shaft and at the base. Use Adjust Levels to accentuate the whites and blacks so there's a good, strong definition between the two. Remember, white creates the bump, whereas black is pretty much ignored. Variations between the two determine intermediate height. See Figure 20.40.

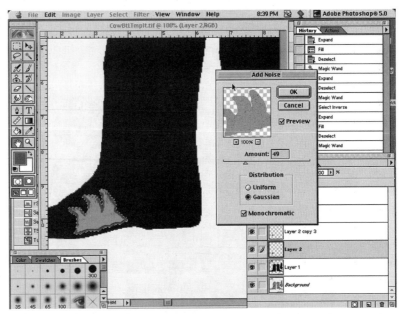

FIGURE *These boots are really H-O-T.*
20.38

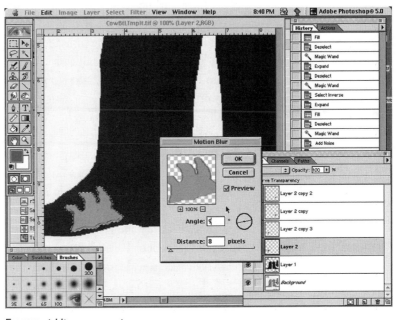

FIGURE *Adding some motion.*
20.39

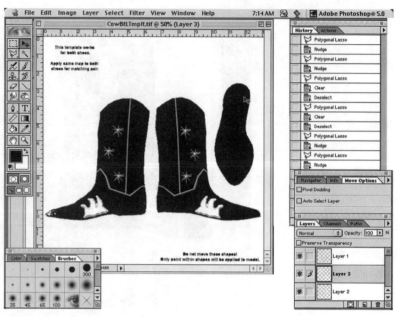

FIGURE *Adding the seams to the boot.*
20.40

To make sure we got the seam bumps we wanted, we used the Bevel and Emboss filters on the seams and on the pattern and flame bumps (Figure 20.41), and then saved the file as a PICT. When brought into Poser, this will automatically be changed to the correct format for the program to read.

Now it's time to see our handiwork. Load the image map and the bump map into Poser, fiddle a bit with the bump intensity (in our case, we put it all the way up), and then see how your design turned out. See Figure 20.42.

With some more effort in Photoshop, we could have added some bumps to simulate the shaft's softer leather, or added more detail to the seams to give the feel of being stitched. We could also go back into the image map and give the seams a different color to stand out a little bit more on the finished product.

But for now, the flames are basically all that would be seen since the Poser dude's pants will cover up the shaft. So, let's move on to creating some transparencies while we're waiting for date time to arrive.

It seems that poor ol' Poser Guy has a problem. It's a bit nippy outside, so he went to the closet to get his overcoat only to find it's in pretty bad shape. How bad? Well, that's up to you. Open the maleOvercoat template in Photoshop and let's repeat many of the steps we took on the boots. Give the coat some color and texture, and then save the file. In our case, we want this poor guy to

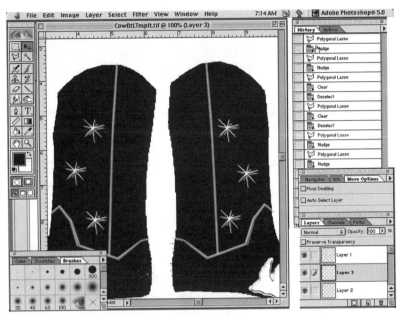

FIGURE *Giving the seams some more depth.*
20.41

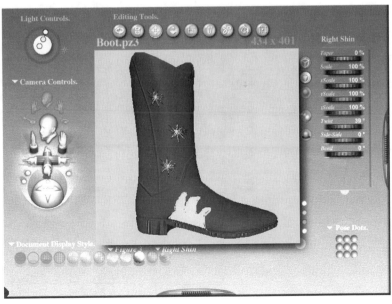

FIGURE *The Boot as it appears in Poser.*
20.42

really be upset, so we plan on ruining a nice, expensive mohair overcoat. (Yes, my great-great-great-great grandfather is the Marquis DeSade!). See Figure 20.43.

Turning the layered image into a grayscale, it's time to do the dastardly act of ruination. First we create a bump map in the same way we did earlier. See Figure 20.44.

With transparencies, as with bump maps, we'll work with whites and blacks; black being what creates the transparencies. Using different brushes and the Lasso Tool, begin ripping shreds from the hapless coat. We even decided to lose a button on the front. See Figure 20.45.

When you bring the transparency template into Poser, you'll be able to set the degree of transparency with the sliders in the middle of the screen. The higher the minimum and maximum values are, the more transparent. So, we put them to their strongest level. See Figure 20.46.

What you'll be able to do as you experiment further with this is literally create loose threads, threadbare areas around elbows and knees where you still see some of the material clinging to life as they get stretched beyond comprehension, and all kinds of effects on clothing and characters that were impossible before in Poser. See Figure 20.47.

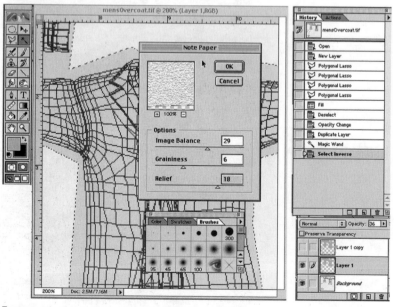

FIGURE *The Overcoat is tweaked in Photoshop.*
20.43

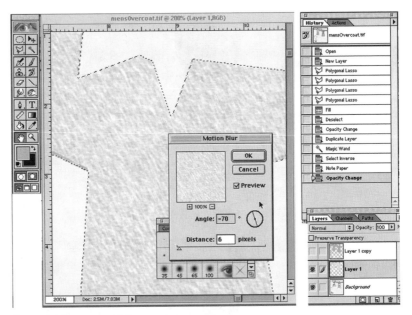

FIGURE *A bump map of the texture is created.*
20.44

FIGURE *Small rips are created for the Overcoat.*
20.45

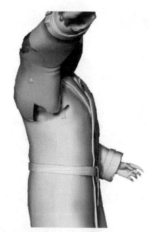

FIGURE *This coat has seen better times.*
20.46

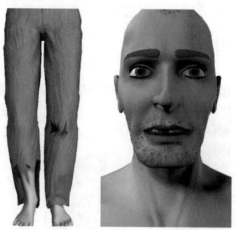

FIGURE *Tears, stubble, and more can be created by using the techniques described here.*
20.47

Morph Manager   Morph Manager is a freeware application written by Mr. X, and copyrighted by Mr. X for Poser 3. It can be distributed freely, but cannot be sold nor be a part of any package that is sold. Although features may be added to it in the future (such as more drag-and-drop functions, prop management, and maybe a morph viewer), the new Hierarchy Editor in Poser 4 covers the same creative ground as this freeware application once did.

http://www.gwz.org/propsguild/

The OBJ File Format

Thanks for this article goes out to an anonymous person on the Poser List.

Poser 4 uses only a subset of the full OBJ file format. The OBJ file format is a text file format, which means you can edit OBJ files in a Text Editor if you like. You may have to convert the end-of-line characters depending on which tools you are reading the OBJ file in from. (For instance, the OBJIMP plugin for 3DS Max will crash when reading in any of the OBJ files that shipped with Poser.) Windows Text Editors may think the files are binary.

The first character of each line specifies the type of command. If the first character is a pound sign, #, the line is a comment and the rest of the line is ignored. Any blank lines are also ignored. The file is read in by a tool and parsed from top to bottom just like you would read it. In the descriptions that follow, the first character is a command, followed by any arguments. Anything shown in square brackets is optional.

a comment line

These are always ignored. Usually the first line of every OBJ file will be a comment that says what program wrote the file out. Also, it's quite common for comments to contain the number of vertices and/or faces an object used.

v x y z

The vertex command, this specifies a vertex by its three coordinates. The vertex is implicitly named by the order it is found in the file. For example, the first vertex in the file is referenced as '1,' the second as '2,' and so on. None of the vertex commands actually specify any geometry; they are just points in space.

vt u v [w]

The vertex texture command specifies the UV (and optionally W) mapping. These will be floating point values between 0 and 1 that say how to map the texture. They really don't tell you anything by themselves; they must be grouped with a vertex in a "f" face command.

vn x y z

The vertex normal command specifies a normal vector. A lot of times these aren't used, because the "f" face command will use the order the "v" commands are given to determine the normal instead. Like the "vt" commands, they don't mean anything until grouped with a vertex in the "f" face command.

f v1[/vt1][/vn1] v2[/vt2][/vn2] v3[/vt3][/vn3] ...

The face command specifies a polygon made from the vertices listed. You may have as many vertices as you like. To reference a vertex, you just give its index in the file; for example, "f 54 55 56 57" means a face built from vertices 54–57. For each vertex, there may also be an associated vt, which says how to map the texture at this point, and/or a vn, which specifies a normal at this point. If you specify a vt or vn for one vertex, you must specify one for all vertices. If you want to have a vertex and a vertex normal, but no vertex texture, it will look like "f v1//vt1." The normal is what tells it which way the polygon faces. If you don't give one, it is determined by the order the vertices are given. They are assumed to be in counter-clockwise direction. If you aren't using vns to specify the normal and you wanted to "flip the normal," you would reverse the order of the vertices. In most 3D programs, if the normal points the wrong way, there will appear to be a hole in the object. Luckily, Poser 3 renders both sides of a polygon, so even if you are editing something in another program that looks like it has holes, they will effectively go away inside Poser (NOTE: I read that somewhere, but haven't personally confirmed that fact.) One more thing, if you ever see a negative v, vt, or vn, that is a relative offset. It means go back that many vertices from where you are now in the file to find the vertex. This is part of the OBJ file spec, but I haven't seen any Poser OBJs that use it.

g name

The group name command specifies a subobject grouping. All "f" face commands that follow are considered to be in the same group.

usemtl name

The use material command lets you name a material to use. All "f" face commands that follow will use the same material, until another "usemtl" command is encountered. For all of the Poser OBJ files I've seen, all "g" commands should be followed by a "usemtl" command. Remember that for vertices, they can be interspersed throughout the file; only the order they appear makes a difference. The faces can also be spread throughout the file, except they must follow the vertices they use and they will be part of whichever group and/or material they follow. That said, most OBJ files follow a consistent layout. Now the "normal" layout of the file will be:

```
# comment about what application generated this file.
# all of the 'v' commands will be listed
v x y z
v ...
```

```
# all of the 'vn' commands will be listed, although most Poser OBJ files
# do not use the 'vn' commands
vn x y z
vn ...
# all of the 'vt' commands will be listed
vt x y z
vt ...
# the object and its material will be set
g object
usemtl material
# all of the 'f' commands are listed
f 1/1 2/2 3/3 4/4
f ....
```

ADDITIONAL ITEMS

If you had two OBJ files and wanted to merge them, you can cut all the "v," "vt," and "vn" commands from the second file and paste them at the end of the first. However, you cannot just copy over the "f" commands, because they will have to have all their vertices offset. I'm thinking there has to be a tool out there somewhere that will do this for you, but I don't know of any. Hair objects with separate pieces like the ponytails that have a hairtie that can be colored separately, are actually a single group. They use additional "usemtl" commands to perform their magic. You can set up the additional material parameters in the .hr2 file (MAC). Example OBJ:

```
v x y z
v ...
g hair
usemtl hair
f 1 2 3 4
f ...
# there is NOT another g command here
usemtl hairTie
f 10 11 12 13
f ...
```

s groupNumber

Poser 2 hair objects sometimes use the "s" command to set a smoothing group. The groupNumber is used to make separate groups. All subsequent "f" commands are in the same smoothing group until another "s" command is encountered. These also have some kind of interaction with vertex normals, but I haven't explored it fully because apparently as of Poser 3, it doesn't use the "s" command anymore.

Moving Along

In this chapter, we have benefited from the viewpoints and work of a selection of Poser masters. In the next chapter, we'll explore the creation of the Poser figures from the standpoint of the developers themselves.

CHAPTER
21

FIGURE DEVELOPERS

I n this chapter, we will take a look at the people responsible for developing the expanding library of 3D figures for Poser. Whether it's anatomically correct humans, animals, or robots, there is no other software that can boast such a rich resource of 3D developers for figure creation and animation.

The Zygote Media Group

The Zygote Media Group has a reputation for creating custom models of the highest quality for clients such as Digital Domain, Pixar, DreamWorks, and Disney Interactive. Zygote brings that same expertise and quality to MetaCreations' Poser 4, one of the most anticipated software releases of 1999. Zygote continues to provide the main model content for MetaCreations' Poser 4, with new animals and new morphable humans that surpass anything provided for Poser to date. Since the release of Poser 3, Zygote has also provided many additional characters, props, and animals optimized for Poser at unbelievably low prices.

    http://www.zygote.com
    poser@zygote.com
    1-(800)267-5170
    1-(801)375-7220

HOW ZYGOTE DEVELOPED THE MODELS FOR POSER 4

As you read the following methods that Zygote used in developing the models for Poser 4, it may help you to create your own Poser models.

History of the Process

At the start of the Poser 3 project, Larry Weinberg (Poser's main programmer at MetaCreations) and Steve Cooper (Poser Product Manager at MetaCreations)

FIGURE   *The Zygote team at work.*
21.1

came and visited Zygote to get to know us and train us on the process of optimizing models for Poser 3. Figuring out the process to get a model prepared and into Poser was a long and difficult challenge. Many issues had to be addressed, at times requiring new tools to be created, and ongoing communication about problems and solutions. Larry Weinberg was our savior on the programming end, answering questions, teaching, and occasionally working those programming miracles he has become known for.

By the time Steve Cooper came back to discuss the new content that we would be providing for Poser 4, Zygote had been creating additional Poser models for about a year. With an expanded Poser team and more experience with the product, we had come up with some ideas on how to improve Poser content and, of course, so had Steve. He told us of the new functionality that was planned for Poser 4, and we discussed ways that we could optimize our models for these new features. During the subsequent process of creating the new content and communicating with MetaCreations, we again added to Zygote's Poser division, and established an assembly-line production method that has worked well for us.

What's Involved in Set Up: A Basic Outline

A. Build the model.
B. Group it for Poser, again for materials, and again for texture mapping.
C. Assign materials.
D. Project the UV texture coordinates for mapping.
E. Lay out and unfold the UV coordinates for mapping, and save out a texture template.
F. Delete all grouping but the Poser grouping.
G. Create morph targets.
H. Create either a hierarchy file to start from scratch, or modify an existing .cr2 file to read in the model to Poser.
I. Adjust the joint parameters until the sun goes down.
J. Test texture mapping, and fine-tune all materials.
K. Save out the model (actually do this along the way, but at the end, create a nice icon).

A. Building the Model

Of course there's a whole science and art to building models, and many programs and methods you can use. If you want to try creating your own Poser content, make sure your model is completely clean with no holes or reversed

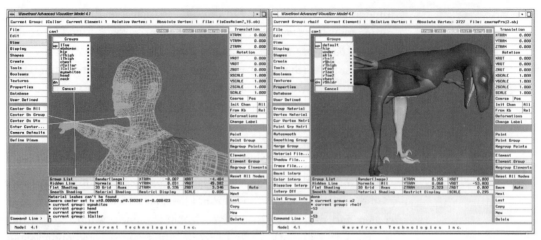

FIGURE *Zygote Poser modeling in process.*
21.2

normals. There is one other note: Five-sided polygons in Poser can drop out, so the mesh should consist of quadrilaterals and triangles. See Figure 21.2.

B. Grouping

When you look at a model in Poser, you can see it is grouped out where it will bend, at the joints. These are the only groups in the .obj file that Poser will handle, and they must be named specifically. The naming of the groups is case sensitive, and a critical element of success in even reading in a model to Poser. A text .cr2 file is created with every .obj file, and the names of groups must exactly match. Naming is also important for Poser's Walk Designer to function properly.

You will also notice when you start working with a model in Poser that different parts of the model are able to have separate changeable colors. These are the materials of the various parts. The model before it was read into Poser, was grouped out for those materials in WaveFront, the materials were applied to the .obj file, and then that material grouping information was removed. As you get ready to paint a texture map for a model, you might take the opportunity to view the default texture map or texture template in a 2D image editor. If you do, you'll see separate sections of the model laid out like an unfolded world map. This means that at some point, the model was grouped out again for these sections of UV coordinate mapping, the coordinates were projected onto the model, and these groups were removed.

C. Applying the Materials

The materials initially applied are just white—color is irrelevant because they will be changed within Poser. The only thing to be concerned with is that each appropriate group has a separate material assigned. Then, even though the groups will be removed, the .obj file still retains the materials information that Poser is able to access.

D. Projecting the UV Texture Coordinates

We have traditionally used WaveFront to project the coordinates of each particular part of a model. When a 2D representation of this projection is opened inside Digits Ní Artís Flesh, all the parts will need to be scaled up and positioned in an orderly fashion. We still occasionally do this, especially for complex, organic models. However, we have recently begun using UVMapper, an excellent freeware utility by Steve Cox, which can project coordinates, scale and situate them, and produce a finished template. Whatever procedure is used for projecting, it must allow for one map of the entire model, with each part represented.

E. Creating a Texture Template

Within Flesh, the UV coordinates can be unfolded. The reason this is done is to minimize the problem of stretching when maps are applied later. A texture map is a 2D image anchored to the mesh by the UV coordinates. With Flesh, UV coordinates can be manipulated apart from the mesh, and affect the placement of the texture. The projections in most cases are simple planar projections, so as you look at the UV coordinates of a human model, for example, you will see a clear image of the head in the middle, but around the edges they overlap each other. (This is because the geometry was going back into space.) These edges need to be pulled out to allow paint to be applied separately to all these polygons along the edges. The coordinates, once they are pulled out and unfolded, are then scaled and placed to maximize the use of space in the map, and in as orderly a fashion as possible. This texture is saved out to serve as a template so that users can paint maps. There are some real benefits to this procedure, but also some drawbacks. Because models are unfolded by hand, so to speak, rather than in some automated and controlled way, it has been difficult for users to match up seams when they want to paint things such as horizontal stripes on clothing. The texture map templates are designed to be painted on within either a 3D or 2D paint package. They can be scaled up to any resolution, and then painted on, and applied as maps to the geometry.

F. Removing Extra Groups

At this point, the model's grouping information will be removed. The model can't have overlapping groups in Poser, so material groups and UV groups will be removed. We found that we needed to save backups at every step of this process, and set up a naming convention so that we would know internally what obj file had been through which steps. This isn't so important if you're only working with one obj file, but when we were setting up multiple models, organization was a life saver. Of course, we learned that lesson the hard way.

G. Creating Morph Targets

Now that the model has been through the UV stage, it's a good time to create the morph targets you need. At Zygote, we create morph targets for Poser models in WaveFront or Mirai. (Again, many different applications can be used to create morph targets, each with its own advantages and disadvantages.) Make sure that the software you use will not reorder the vertices in the .obj file, or the morph you create won't work. When creating morph targets, you must work from the exact data you want to morph. In other words, to create a smile for the Nude Man, the head group geometry must be taken from the Nude Man, the vertices pulled to create the smile, and this new head saved out.

H. Reading the Model into Poser

Once extra grouping has been removed, the model is ready to be brought into Poser. This can be done in a couple of ways: an existing .cr2 file can be used, or a .phi file can be created. Both of these options require the use of a text editor; we use BBEdit on the Macintosh. All the .cr2 files for all the figures in Poser are contained in Runtime: libraries: character. You can open these in text editors to see what they look like. When using the first option (starting from an existing .cr2 file), the names of all the groups in the .obj file will obviously have to match those listed in the .cr2 file. Then there are two locations near the top of the .cr2 file where the reference to the old .obj file needs to be changed. Using an existing .cr2 file can be a great time saver; if the geometry is similar, the blend zones may not need to be adjusted too much. If, however, you want to bring in a figure that is substantially different from anything already in Poser, you will need to start from the .hier file stage. This is a simple file that describes the hierarchy of the groups in the model, which Poser will use to generate a .cr2 file when you choose "convert .hier file" under the File menu. This command brings up a dialog box allowing you to locate the .hier file you've created. The process of creating .hier files and adjusting blend zones is spelled out in the Advanced Poser Techniques manual on MetaCreations' Web site, and has been made much easier with the hierarchy editor in Poser 4. The .obj files that are referenced by either of these methods should be placed in Runtime: Geometries.

When the model doesn't come in the first time, or comes in part way, or causes a crash, you get the happy task of hunting down whatever step it was you overlooked. One important step that often causes problems is naming for the groups. If groups are dropping out once the model is in Poser, it's probably because the group names don't match exactly from .obj file to .cr2 file.

I. Adjusting Joint Parameters

Regardless of which course you used to bring the model into Poser, you will need to adjust its joint parameters. If you started from a .phi file, these blend zones will need to be set up from scratch. I usually work from the inside out on a model, and just methodically set up each zone and test it as much as I can. I might start on the chest region, and set up blend zones for each channel (center, x,y,z, and scale zones). By "set up blend zones," I mean adjust the parameters that Poser created at the joint, so that it works well when the joint bends in its various positions. By looking at the movement in wireframe mode you can see exactly how the geometry is being deformed, which sometimes helps. When you think about how many joints there are on a human, and how many rotation channels there are on each joint, you can begin to see the task ahead of you.

The first step to setting a blend zone is to see that the center point is where you want it. This is typically at the pivot position of a joint, but collars and thumbs can be tricky. (In fact, Zygote is currently working on ways to improve many of these joints.) The "twist" is usually what I set next; this is a simple gradient bar indicating how the body part is going to twist along the axis. Then the remaining two rotation channels are controlled with the "handle bars." These are also straightforward: two handles are green and two are red, the space between the greens and reds is affected by the deformation. So you can move these handle bars around and see how the mesh is affected. There are a couple of general guidelines to bear in mind as you adjust joint parameters. First, set up the zones initially with the model at its zero position, because the zones move in space with the body part. And remember that the Child body part is blending up into the Parent. Sometimes it gets confusing, the blend zones for the thigh should be located up near the hip, not down at the knee (even though it's all the thigh group). This might seem obvious, but you would be surprised how your mind can get turned around. Nothing is more frustrating than working for an hour or two to get a body part working right, move to the next joint, and realize it belongs at the position you thought you just finished. The collars blend into the chest, not the shoulders. The shoulders blend into the collars, and so on. It just helps to keep that hierarchy in mind. An optional but often necessary tool is to set up the spherical fall-off zones. These spheres can be moved and scaled into the desired position (it's often quicker to switch to "bounding box mode" when trying to manipulate the spheres) to affect the bend of the particular channel. Basically, everything inside the green sphere is affected by the rotation, everything outside of the red sphere is unaffected, and everything in between the spheres gradually tapers from the green to the red. It's important to remember that these spheres work *in conjunction* with the handle bars, they do not take the place of the handle bars. Often I'll spent a lot of time manipulating the spheres into all sorts of sophisticated positions with no real improvement at the joint, and then I move the handle bar slightly and the problem gets fixed.

But the spheres do have real purposes, and real effects. They are primarily used for joints where you only want a portion of the geometry to be effected, like a thigh coming into a hip. The hip, in this case, is the Parent of the thigh, but it's actually the Parent of both the right and left thighs. So you would set up spheres such that when the right thigh bends, the hip is only effected in the area over the right thigh, not the area over the left thigh. You can toggle the display mode of the spheres, change them to "lit wireframe" mode, for example, to get a better 3D feel for what they are doing, and where they are placed. Setting up blend zones for a figure can be very time intensive, and there is a subjective nature to it. It's important to test the parameters by bending the parts all around. You might adjust the zones to a certain position, which causes the thigh to look good as it bends forward, but this may screw up the backward bend. It gets particularly difficult when you see how one channel affects another. For instance, a thigh bend might look right when it's bent to a certain degree in X, but combine that with a Y rotation and see what happens. Adjusting the joint parameters often involves making such concessions.

I should mention one feature that is a huge time saver. Notice within Poser under "Figure/Symmetry" there are mirror commands. This allows you to pose a portion of the figure, and then mirror that pose to the other side. When you mirror, you'll be asked whether you want to also copy the joint zones setup. Click Yes, and the joint parameters get mirrored as well as the pose. Spherical zones, handle bars, center points, everything except limits and nonstandard body parts (such as Left Wing, or Right Ear), which will still need to be set manually.

During this blend zone process, because you're moving the body parts all around, it's also a good time to set the limits for each body part. Try to set the limits at the farthest range the motion can take. I haven't mentioned setting up the scale zones; these can get a bit tricky. They basically work as ramps, sort of like the twist. The weird part is that there's a zone going from Parent to Child, and a zone going from Child to Parent, but they are really the same zone. Whichever one you set is the one that is activated and takes effect. I don't really know of any secrets as to how these work, I just set them and start scaling to see if I like what it's doing. The spherical zones can also be helpful on these. The most difficult place for scale zones is going from a Parent that has multiple Children, such as a chest. I usually start at these types of parents and work outward and it seems to work all right.

J. Test Texture Mapping and Fine-Tune Materials

At this point, I would scribble different colors on the texture template to make sure the coordinates are functioning properly and to make sure no part of the model was left out. Once you've verified that the template works, you can take the time to paint texture maps as well. If the model's UV coordinates are messed up, you can just go back to that step, fix the problem, and plug the new and improved .obj file back into the Geometries folder in Runtime. You can use the .cr2 file you've already created with this fixed .obj file. (As long as all the groups still match, there will be no problem.) Default materials can be set now as well. Use the Paint Bucket tool to set the material color, and then by holding down the Command key on a Mac or Control key on a PC, you can set the highlight colors. You can also position the model to work properly with the IK chain, by giving the parts a slight bend in the direction they would need to go, and then selecting Edit/Memorize/Figure.

K. Saving Out

You should save your work periodically throughout this process, of course, but on your last save you'll want to capture a nice icon for the model. The little "plus sign" at the bottom of the library drawer saves the file into the library. Sometimes you'll need to save a file a second time (over the first save) for the icon to show up.

And there you have it. Those are the basics, along with some helpful tips.

ADDITIONAL POSER MODELS FROM ZYGOTE

Ever since the release of Poser 3, we have been bombarded by requests, suggestions, and ideas for new models. We've also had a good reception for the additional Poser products that we've released so far. It's actually quite difficult to determine what sort of content to begin developing, simply because of the wide variety of responses out there. Many people would love to see more clothing and hairstyles for the figures. Others would rather we supply more nude figures and maps. Also, animals are a big hit, and many people have asked us for more. There are many collections and models we plan to create for Poser. We must be careful to maintain profitability, however, and so it's important for us to build models that will have the widest market appeal. The one exception to this rule is, of course, the custom Poser models that we create for clients with specific needs and larger budgets.

In addition to the Poser collections that Zygote initially produced for use within Poser 3 (all of which work with Poser 4, too), we now have some new collections and individually sold Poser models. All of these Poser plugins are available to view and purchase from our Web site via the secure online store, or by phone directly to Zygote Media Group at (800) 267- 5170, or (801) 375- 7220. While we don't have the space here to list all of these products, the following are some of our Poser collections. To preview these and many other Poser models, go to our site at http://www.zygote.com.

FREE Poser Models
Every week we put up a new Poser model on our site for free. These models stay up for a limited time, so be sure to check often.

Sampler For Poser $14.95
A sampling of fun 3D data that will give you a good feel for our high-quality Poser products. This CD includes 15 accessories, 2 figures (the wrestling baby and the alien), 1 animal (a doe), and 5 motion capture files.

Costume Shop $49.95
A selection of clothing, hairstyles, accessories and morphs to add variety to your Poser figures. The collection includes such outfits as cheerleader and warrior, and individual items like cloaks, capes, and weapons.

Animals $99.95
Nine animal models completely texture mapped and ready to animate. We've also included templates so you can customize the texture maps to your heart's content. This CD includes a chimpanzee, cow, zebra, penguin, grizzly bear, buck deer, shark, killer whale, and bass.

Animals 2 $99.95
Here's another collection of animals, including Rhinoceros, Panther, Swordfish, Bee, Octopus, Camel, Panda, Chicken, Crab, and Gazelle.

Motion $89.95

Add motion captured from real people to create life-like poses and animation! Motion capture is the process of digitizing fluid human motions from live actors. These 52 specially prepared BVH motion files from "House of Moves" can easily be applied to Poser figures. Use the motions to move your models to the perfect pose, or for realistic animations. Amazing results made unbelievably simple.

Accessories $29.95

One hundred various models designed to compliment your Poser figures. Decorate your 3D environment with these high-quality objects optimized for use within Poser. All models include texture templates for painting maps.

Super Sampler (Price to be determined)

One hundred and one models total—props (buildings, accessories, weapons, etc.), hairstyles, clothing, etc.

ZYGOTE HISTORY

Zygote's mission is to establish its reputation as the premier provider of high-quality 3D models and related computer graphic products. We maintain a working environment that enhances productivity, creativity, and job satisfaction; and increases company value and profitability each year.

In September 1994, Zygote Media Group began operation. Three leading modelers in the industry—Chris Creek, Roger Clarke, and Eric Merritt—saw an excellent opportunity to capitalize on their skills in the fast-growing 3D modeling market. Zygote Media Group, Inc. is a Utah-based company providing 3D computer models and texture maps for clients mainly in the entertainment industry. The name "Zygote" signifies the first stage of life, just as computer modeling is the first stage of a 3D computer animation. The name also conveys Zygote's main expertise and targeted market niche: building organic shaped models such as humans and animals.

In 1995, Zygote built models for a computer game called "Titanic: Adventure through Time" by Cyberflix, Inc. Since that first custom job, Zygote has produced models for several high-profile clients including "DreamWorks," "Digital Domain," and "Hannah Barbara," Zygote's artists have built models for such feature films as "The Fifth Element" and "Godzilla," as well as a number of television commercials (for clients such as Coca-Cola, Jeep, Orkin, Kool-Aid, and Southwest Airlines), and TV shows (such as the Discovery Channel). Zygote's modeling talents have also been seen in numerous computer games such as those by Dynamix, Inc., and Sierra On-line, Inc. In addition to custom work, Zygote is also involved in creating products for resale, such as our "Stuff for Poser." For more information, go to Zygote's Web site at http://www.zygote.com.

bioMechanix	by Keith Hunter: The Hunyes Publishing Company

How bioMECHANIX Evolved

I founded bioMechanix at Rhythm & Hues Studios while working as head of the modeling department. During the last five years I've worked on my own personal projects in my free time, developing my own design sensibilities. I worked with Larry Weinberg (the creator of Poser) for years at Rhythm & Hues, so it seemed natural that I'd end up contributing some of my work to his latest creation, Poser 4. By accident, I called Larry just before he was finishing Poser 4 and showed him my project. He thought the robots would be ideal for Poser, but since they were mechanical, they'd look a lot better if Poser had reflection mapping. Although it wasn't in his programming schedule, he squeezed in reflection mapping over night! While I was setting up my robots, I mentioned that, once again, it would be really great if we had transparency because of the robot designs. Once again, he had transparency mapping by the next day. One of my robots had pneumatic pumps(shock absorbers) connected to the neck, hips, and shoulders. The problem with this was that if you move the arms head or legs in Poser using Inverse Kinematics, the shock absorbers wouldn't extend and contract automatically because there was no way to properly include them in the hierarchy. Of course there was no room in the schedule to add a feature to fix this, but once again, I had a fix in the next few days. Basically, Larry created something called a point-at. You parent the pump half of the shock to the hip and the rod half to the thigh, then you point the halves at each other. This way, no matter where the hip is in relation to the thigh, the shock will automatically expand and contract. This is the kind of technical expertise and savvy that makes Larry great to work with and Poser such a great product.

At Rhythm & Hues, some of the modeling is done in Alias, but most of the modeling is done with our own proprietary package called AND. It's similar to WaveFront and it has a unique tool set that makes it one of the best polygonal modelers around. Many of the organic creatures we model start off as sculptures that get digitized into the computer. The reason we prefer to sculpt first is because we have clients like Sony and Disney who demand high quality along with the ability to make modifications. We find it's easier and more efficient to get approval from a sculpture than to try to "fix it in the computer." Part of this may be psychological. If you can see and touch a real sculpture, you're more likely to be confident that is looks the way you want. We also model objects directly from blueprints or drawings. Here is how most of the models for the Poser 4 bioMechanix figures were created:

1. Spend anywhere from 10 minutes to a few days designing the model.
2. Scan the drawings into the computer as background reference for building model. Usually a front and side view is enough.
3. Build the model on top of the scanned drawings.
4. Assign groups and materials.
5. Apply, and clean up.
6. Create texture maps.
7. Import into Poser and set up.

As I started working on this project, I realized that there were other modelers in my department like Tom Capizzi, Max Okazaki, and Steve Ziolkowski, who might be interested in contributing models to bioMechanix. They were and they did. I designed and created Helix, H.A.R.D., Brain-Stem, Prime-Evil, Prime-Ordeal. Ziolkowski designed and created Dead Weight, Heavy, Hot Rod, Wedge, Truck. Capizzi designed and created Bad Dog. Okazaki designed and created Type 2 Bike. The interesting thing about the modelers for bioMechanix is that they're not only good modelers, they're also good at lighting, designing, and/or animating. So they can each design models and set up characters. Being in production at a high-quality studio like Rhythm & Hues has given us a unique perspective on how to deliver a film-quality product to the marketplace. BioMechanix is looking forward to further contributions to the Poser community by continuing to make unique, high-quality products.

We have some modelers who can light, and/or animate, and/or direct and/or do production design. Because of this rich diversity, we can grow and shrink our department with production demands. It also means that if you're a modeler at Rhythm & Hues, you'll never get bored or pigeonholed. Many of us go to SIGGRAPH each year to keep current, and sometimes we go to educate the computer community on new computer techniques.

bioMECHANIX NEW FIGURES FOR POSER 4

www.hunyes.com

We have 12 models that you can buy individually or as a set. Each model is $25, or you can buy the whole set for just $100. You can also pick up the comic book and videotape "Prime-Ordeal: Power is Everything!" the project that insured the creation of bioMechanix. You can order these models online with a credit card and download them by FTP, or you can fill out the snail mail form.

There's also a four-minute QuickTime of Prime-Ordeal at the site. See Figures 21.3 and 21.4.

FIGURE **21.3** *A bioMechanix figure takes shape.*

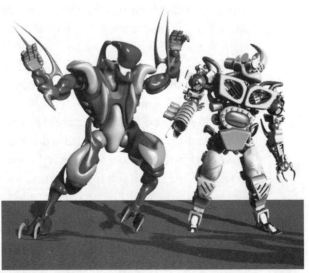

FIGURE **21.4** *The Poser bioMechanix figures are completely articulated, and add an aura of mystery to any scene.*

WhiteCrow 3D

This is the latest developer to join the growing list of Poser figure providers. They have many CD volumes planned for the near future. They also feature a Web site that allows you to download a revolving selection of Poser-ready models.

http://www.zig3d.co.uk

ALIEN POSER PACK 1

Looking like a cross between the "GREY" style alien and "MARS ATTACKS" alien, this figure has a standard body type (undernourished-looking) with elongated arms and short legs. Exaggerated Oversized Hands can hold the amazing variety of props, including FishBowl-style helmet with front plate and neckpiece (deep-sea diver's helmet but exaggerated), Airtank backpack (looks like two diver's airtanks joined together and squared off), a variety of rayguns and scifi-related instruments (comic book style with lots of rounded edges and bright colors). This will be the first in a series of new Poser articulated figure releases. See Figure 21.5.

WHITECROW 3D AT WORK

WhiteCrow3D is a small company based in the UK (Scotland), whose staff come from varied backgrounds, from Graphic Design, Traditional Art, Soft-

FIGURE *The Alien from the new Alien Poser Pack 1 from WhiteCrow 3D.*
21.5

ware Development, and more. Inspired by the beauty around them, the design team tries to envisage new frontiers in 3D graphics and then develop solutions to breathe life into their creations.

WhiteCrow3D develops original character models (some with props, including animals, fantasy, scifi, humanoids, monsters etc.), original Pose Sets for our own creatures and humanoid characters, small themed packs of characters, props, backdrops, textures etc. (all you would need to create an entire scene or animation), individual Costumes & Clothes, individual Props (see our large database of items on our Web site or request a custom model), Vehicles, Architectural Backdrops, Accessories & Slot together Interiors (a range developed to design your own interiors quickly and easily to create realistic 3D backdrops.), BVH motion paths, Poser Morph Targets, Textures, Bump maps, and various Plugins and Tools. All of these can be browsed on the Web page database. If you cannot see what you require, send suggestions or fill out their custom modeling form.

WhiteCrow3D also does animation\film editing, custom modeling, Web site development, and application programming. If you are interested in any of these, see their services page at http://www.poser-props.co.uk.

WhiteCrow 3D uses its own inhouse development tools (they may release these at a later date.) alongside industry-standard packages, including Animation Master, PaintShop Pro, Adobe Photoshop, Poser, Bryce, RayDream Studio, and more. Along with their modeling skills, they also have a good R&D\Concept staff that can develop ideas for most media projects.

A typical project starts with an informal meeting with management, clients, and staff, and shortly after, the following usually takes place:

- Concept stage
- Schedules\deadlines set
- Concept approval
- Low-quality copies are draughted
- Copies approved
- Final creation stage
- Adjustment stage

WhiteCrow3D plans to expand into application development/video/computer graphics for broadcast and game production.

http://www.poser-props.co.uk

The Poser Props Modeler's Guild

If you would like somewhere to send your Poser models, from full figures to props, think about joining the Poser Props Modeler's Guild. You can find them at http://www.gwz.org/propsguild/. See Figure 21.6.

HOW TO JOIN THE GUILD

Just fill out the online registration form and send your Prop. Here is the information you will be asked for:

- Your name (they will not accept free email accounts, due the nature of this site).
- Your true e-mail Address.
- How do you know about them?
- If you know them from a current Member, what is her (his) name?
- If you already have a Web site, what is your URL?
- For IRC meetings purpose: Where do you come from? (your country)
- What 3D file formats can you use (3DS .obj .DXF .cob .max .iob .LWO other)?
- Any additional comments.

FIGURE *The Poser Props Modeler's Guild Web page.*
21.6

RENDER REQUIREMENTS FOR MODELS FOR THE POSER PROPS MODELER'S GUILD

1. All renders are to be 200x150 pixels.
2. Renders will use the supplied backdrop.
3. All Renders must be in .JPG format.

Special note For Bryce 4 Users: Please disable gamma correction to void bright colors.

Poser Characters Showcase Image Parameters

1. All renders are to be 300x300 pixels.
2. Renders will use the supplied backdrop.
3. All renders must be in .JPG format.

Moving Along

In this chapter, we have taken a journey with several of the developers who are creating Poser's extremely realistic figures. In the next chapter, we'll present a collection of advanced projects that you can work through to master all the Poser possibilities.

CHAPTER

22

ADVANCED
POSER
PROJECTS

The following projects represent a recap of many of the things you have learned while working through the tutorials in this book. You will find that they are useful on their own, and also act to reinforce your further creative Poser explorations.

The Carousel

The following exercise can be completed without your having to own the Zygote Poser collection. It will require Poser 4, Photoshop (version 5 or later is best, or another suitable bitmap painting application like Painter will also work) with Kai's PowerTools version 3 plugins installed, and RayDream Studio (version 5 or later is best, or another 3D application like Carrara can be substituted; anything that writes out OBJ files that Poser can read). If you have worked through the tutorials in this book, and have also explored all of the Poser 4 documentation, this project should take you a maximum of about six hours to complete.

HOW TO PROCEED

1. Open Photoshop, and load in the Horse texture.pict from the Poser 4.Runtime/Textures/Poser3 Textures folder. This is the default texture map for the Poser Horse. Using this as our base, we can see how it is treated to texture the default Horse. See Figure 22.1.

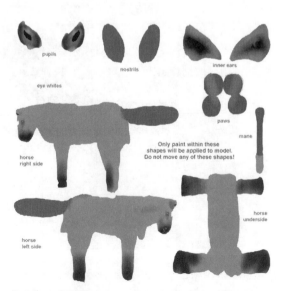

FIGURE *The default texture map for the Poser Horse.*
22.1

2. Use the Magic Wand, and click on the Horse's light brown skin. Go to the Select menu and select Similar. This places a marquee around all of the light browns in the texture map.

3. Go to the KPT 3.0 filters and to Texture Explorer, which will open its interface. See Figure 22.2.

4. Assign a KPT Texture to the selected brown skin areas of the Horse.

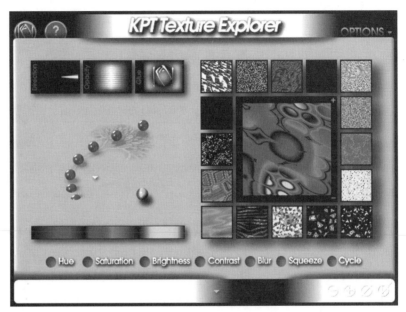

FIGURE *The KPT 3 interface.*
22.2

The preceding step assumes you know how to navigate in the KPT Texture Explorer interface.

5. Repeat this procedure for the gray areas of the Horse texture. Save the result as HorseText2.pict to the same folder. Repeat this entire process until you have created four separate and colorful textures for the carousel. Do not use bump maps, and push the Highlight to the max, since we are looking for enamel painted ponies. See Figure 22.3.

6. From the Top Camera View, rotate and move the horses so that they are in a circular arrangement. See Figure 22.4.

The Main Carousel Structure

We'll create the main structure out of two Poser Cylinders, a Cone, and four Balls. Do the following (see Figure 22.5 as a visual reference to these steps):

FIGURE *Four colorful ponies for our Carousel.*
22.3

FIGURE *The Horses are moved into a circular arrangement, as seen from the top.*
22.4

1. Create Cylinder 1 as the base. Leave some room between the top of the base and the Horse's feet. Size the base so that it covers the area that the four Horses cover (Top View Camera). Reduce the Y dimension of the base to about 1/4 of the Horse height.

2. Cylinder 2 acts as the spindle for the Carousel. Size it so that it pokes through the base, and extends about twice as high as the Horses. Place it in the center of the base, as seen from the Top Camera View.

3. Make the Cone the same diameter as the base as seen from the top. Place it on the spindle, and flatten its Y dimension so it looks more like a canopy.

4. Create four spheres, using Figure 22.5 to reference their size. They should all exist on the same horizontal plane, and be placed over each Horse to be to top of the bar we will soon put through the Horse, so it can move up and down.

5. Parent everything as follows: All four Horse Body elements should have the Base as their Parent. The base references the Spindle as its Parent, as does the Cone. The Balls have the Cone as their Parent.

FIGURE *The basic structure is finished and parented. You may want to add a texture to*
22.5 *the Cone-canopy as was done here.*

Designing and Placing the Poles

You can use simple cylinders for the poles, but I decided to make them a little more complex, using RayDream Studio 5.

1. In RayDream 5, place a Modeling Wizard icon (the Top Hat) in your scene, which opens the Modeling Wizard dialog. Select the Twisted Object/Twisted Column. When it is written to the screen, increase its Y dimension to 44. Save it as a OBJ file, and quit RayDream Studio. See Figure 22.6.

2. Import the Twisted Column into your Poser Carousel scene. Make it tall enough (Y axis) so that it can embed itself in the base a little, go through a Horse, and then embed itself at the top in one of the Balls. When you have accomplished this, save the Twisted Column to the Poser Props library. Now you can add its clones to any scene.

FIGURE *The Twisted Column is designed in RayDream, for use in the Poser scene.*
22.6

3. Place four Twisted Columns through the four Horses as indicated in Figure 22.7, and make the Balls at their tops the Parent objects. See Figure 22.7.

FIGURE *The Twisted Columns are now the poles that allow the Horses to move up and*
22.7 *down.*

Riders

Of course you'll want riders on the Horses. You can select any of the Figures in the Poser libraries for this. Make sure you seat them the way they should be posed, and then make the Horse they're sitting on their Parent object. See Figure 22.8.

FIGURE *Now the Carousel looks interesting, with some different figures riding the*
22.8 *Horses.*

Animating the Carousel

Here are some ideas to explore when you want to animate the Carousel:

- Give all of the riders some movement. It doesn't have to be extensive, but even a waving arm will add viewer interest.
- Make the opposite pair of Horses move up and down in unison. The other two should be down when the selected two are up, and vice versa.
- Adjust the lighting so that you are using different angles. Shadows will mingle, and look more interesting. Also, turn two of the lights down, with an intensity of 60%.
- Select a Camera angle that gives you an interesting perspective. For more interest, shoot the animation two or three times with different angles and close-ups, and then stitch the animations together in an appropriate post-production application.

The Centaur

The Mythic Centaur has always intrigued artists and animators. Walt Disney's Fantasia features a scenario that starred the Centaur as a romantic hero, though many times the Centaur is not depicted so positively. Piccasso uses the Centaur as a stand-in for his own instinctual self. In this exercise, we'll combine two Poser figures to create an animated Centaur.

HOW TO PROCEED

No other applications except Poser are needed to complete this project.

1. Load the Horse and the Nude Male to the screen. Resize the Nude Male to Heroic proportions, and then resize him to 135%. See Figure 22.9.
2. Make the following elements invisible: Horse Upper Neck and Head; Man's Hips, Thighs, Shins, Feet, and Toes. See Figure 22.10.
3. Select the Horse's Lower Neck, and rotate it to –60. Rotate the man so he is facing in the same direction as the Horse. Select the Man's Body, and move him into position over the open Neck of the Horse. Make the Horse's Lower Neck the Parent of the Man's Abdomen. See Figure 22.11.

When you create a composite figure, color both components the same and leave the texture map off. That way, it'll look like one figure and not two. You can also explore using the same texture on both figures, like the Default Ground Texture.

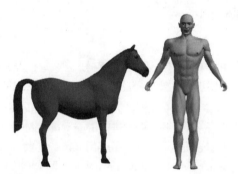

FIGURE *The size of the Horse as compared to the Nude Male should look like this.*
22.9

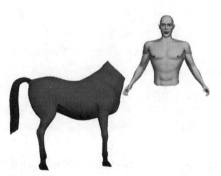

FIGURE *Parts of each figure are made invisible.*
22.10

FIGURE *The Man is placed in position over the Horse's rotated Lower Neck. The man's*
22.11 *Abdomen is Parented by the Horse's Lower Neck. Both are colored the same,*
and mapped with the Default Ground Texture.

4. Resize the Man's Head to 130%, to make it appear more mythic. Place long black Hair on his head. Use another Prop Hair to give him a black beard. See Figure 22.12.

5. The Zygote Props/Weapons has a nice Shield and a Spear. If you have purchased the Zygote collection, you may want to add these elements. Remember to use the Grasp Parameter Dial on the Hand that holds the Spear, and to Parent all Props to the appendage they belong with. See Figure 22.13.

FIGURE *The Head is enlarged, and Hair and beard are added.*
22.12

FIGURE   *The Centaur figure brandishes a Shield and a Spear, and is ready for any*
22.13   *challenge.*

   *Using the new Hierarchy Editor in Poser 4 to turn off the visibility of multiple se-
lections at the same time makes this whole process a lot easier.*

Making Vampire Morphs

To make Morph Targets for any of the Poser 4 figures, you need a modeling
program that will allow you to adjust the individual polygons on the base
geometry of the figure. The three requirements for the modeling program are:
1) They do not scale or transpose (move) the geometry during the import/ex-
port process; 2) They do not add, take away, or restructure the polygons of the
base geometry; 3) They are able to import and export in the WaveFront Obj
format (.obj). For this example, I will be using MetaCreations' RayDream Studio modeler. The process is similar for most of the major modeling packages.
Command names and options may differ.

The first step in making a set of morph targets is figuring out what you want
to accomplish. I want to turn the Poser 4 Nude Male into a classic vampire,
complete with fangs and a series of facial morphs. Having a good idea of a final
character will help you visualize what areas of the geometry you will need to
modify. For this example, I can see that I will have to make the following modifications to the Poser 4 Nude Man's face:

- Fang morphs for upper and lower teeth
- Ear morphs that will elongate and make the ears more bat-like
- A hooked-nose morph
- A morph to give the facial area an emaciated or skull-like look

PREPARING THE BASE FILE

The first stage of any Morph Target is to isolate the part that you want to work on from the whole of the original Poser .obj file.

1. Start RDS and open the following file: C:\Program Files\Metacreations\ Poser 4\Runtime\Geometries\P4NudeMan\blNudeMan_Gen.obj

RDS will bring up the .obj Import window. Under the Create Meshform Objects section of the dialog box, check the dot next to the One for each .obj group. The rest of the options you can leave as the defaults. We want to work on the head for all of the morphs that we will be making, so we need to isolate just the head. To do this, first use the Select all Objects command: Edit→Select all Objects (Ctrl+Alt+A)

2. Now in the timeline window, hold down the Shift key and deselect the head.
3. Once the head is no longer highlighted, press the Delete key or use the Edit→Delete command to get rid of the extra parts.

It is a good idea to save the head object to disk for later use. When the time comes that you want to make another head morph, you can just bring in the file and start right in—no need to repeat the first steps over again if you don't have to. On the Command bar, click File→Save As. This will bring up a dialog box.

4. Select WaveFront (*.obj) in the Save as Type Box and name your file P4NudeMan_Head.obj. This will let you know the figure and body part when you use it again later. Click the Save button.

TEETH MORPHS

For the teeth morphs we will be using the Push/Pull technique of altering the Geometry. You will also get some experience with hiding areas of the mesh to work on inner areas. Now that you have your base file, it is time to get down to the actual making of the Morph Target.

1. In the timeline window, double-click on the Head object. This will bring the head into the Mesh Form Modeler. All of the actual morphing work will be done in the Mesh Form Modeler. Our first morph will be the fang morphs.

You will be looking at a Perspective view of the Head geometry. You will need to change the view to a right-sided view, and increase the magnification on the head so you can get a closer look at the polygons.

2. On the Command bar, select: View→Preset Position→Right (or Ctrl+6). Then select the Magnifying Glass tool and click a few times on the center of the head. My example has the magnification up to 32:1.

3. Because the teeth are an internal feature of the mesh, you will need to hide the outer shell of the head to get to the teeth. (This also works for the tongue and the eyelashes.) Switch to the Arrow tool. Under the Tool Properties tab of the Properties window, you will need to change the Angle of Selection Propagation option from 45 degrees to 180 degrees. This will allow you to select the whole outer shell of the head with one double-click.

4. Double-click on one of the lines at the back of the head. This will select all of the points and lines of the head except for the eyelashes and the inner mouth structure.

5. Now we need to hide the selected polygons so that we can get at the teeth. Select View→Hide Selection on the Command bar. This hides the outer shell from view, leaving only the inner mouth and the eyelashes.

6. Zoom in to 512:1 on the teeth using the Magnifying Glass tool. To work on the top teeth, we will need to hide the bottom teeth and the tongue. This is the same process as hiding the head, so double-click on the bottom teeth, and hide them, and then do it again for the tongue. When you have them hidden, you will be looking at a right-sided view of the upper teeth geometry.

7. You will now select the tips of the teeth that you want to elongate into fangs. Because you are in a side view, if you use the Box Selection tool to select the points of the tooth closest to you, it will also select the points of the other tooth. Switch to the Box Selection tool and select the two points at the end of the third tooth in.

8. Using the Arrow tool, pull downwards with these points selected and it will bring the teeth down into fang-like points.

9. Switch to a front view to see what your fangs look like. View→Preset Position→Front (ctrl+1).

10. From here you can widen them a little by selecting the points on the side nearest to the center of the teeth object and pulling them in closer to the center.

11. Once you get your fangs looking the way that you want them to, it is time to export the Morph Target. File→Save As Under the Save as Type option, select the WaveFront (*.obj) option and name your file P4Nude-Man_UpperFangs.obj. Again, this will help you identify what the morph

is and what it is for later on. Before you save the object, click on the Options button on the right-hand corner of the Save As dialog box. It will bring up the Options dialog. Here you can uncheck the Export Normals and Export UV Values options. Poser 4 does not use them for Morph Targets, and by not exporting them you cut at least 40% off the final size of the Morph Target file. Press the OK button in the Options dialog, and then the Save button on the Save As dialog, and then click through the usual RDS warning dialog box. Congratulations, you have made a fang morph!

The process for the bottom teeth is the same as the top teeth. Close the morph you just made and open up the isolated head file that you saved awhile back. Bring the head into the Mesh Form Modeler and go through the process of hiding the head, upper teeth this time, and the tongue. Make your lower fangs and export them as you did the upper ones. Name these P4Nude-Man_LowerFangs.obj. See Figure 22.14.

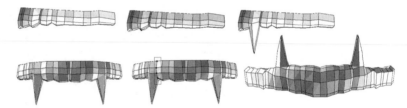

FIGURE *The development of the Teeth Target Morphs.*
22.14

EAR MORPH

The ear morphs will be made with a mixture of the Push/Pull technique and a Tapering technique that thins or thickens an area of the mesh by moving sections of the mesh closer or further apart.:

1. In RDS, open the base head file once again. Import using the defaults and bring the head into the Mesh Form Modeler by double-clicking on it in the Perspective View window. Once you have it in the Modeler, switch your view to the front and zoom with the Magnifying Glass tool so that the head fills most of the window.
2. Using the Box Selection tool, select all of the mesh between the two ears.
3. Hide the selected area of the mesh. View→Hide Selection. And the change the view to the right. View→Preset Position→Right (ctrl+6). Zoom in on the ears a bit, but leave some space at the top to work with.

4. Using the Box Selection tool, select an area on the upper rim of the ear closer to the front. When you have that selected, use the Arrow tool to pull the selection upwards and to the right a little.

5. Using the Box tool again, select the next section of the ear rim. Pull this section about half as far upwards as the first and a little more to the right. You ear should be looking more and more like a vampire's.

6. Skip the next section of ear rim and use the Box tool again to select the one after that. Pull this one out some to the right. The ear should begin to look fluted, almost wing-like.

7. Switch your view to the front again and you will see that the ears look a little bulky from the front.

8. To fix this, select a section of the ear tip and move it closer to the section adjacent to it. This will thin that side of the ear.

9. One by one, keep moving sections of the very tips of the ears until the ear tips are thinner, as shown in the illustration. You can also use this thinning method on other areas of the geometry when making your own Morph Targets. It works great on the face, the nose, the ears, and the hip/abdomen area. Remember that you can also use the technique to make things thicker by spreading the sections out.

Save the ear morphs as you did the teeth morphs, with the same settings. Name this file P4NudeMan_VampireEars.obj. See Figure 22.15.

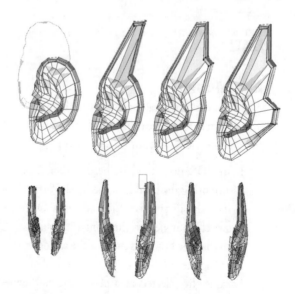

FIGURE   *The development of the Ear Target Morphs.*
22.15

NOSE MORPH

1. For the nose morph, we will be using a Scaling technique to make some of our changes in the mesh. This technique scales the selected mesh areas larger or smaller in one to three dimensions. These same morphs could also be done with the Tapering technique or with the Push/Pull technique.

2. Open your base head file in RDS, and bring the head into the Mesh Form Modeler by double-clicking on the head in the Perspective window. Once in the Mesh Form Modeler, zoom in on the head and switch the view to the right-side view.

3. Select the tip of the nose and the bridge of the nose. This may take several selections while you hold down the Shift key.

4. Once you have the areas selected, we are going to pull them out away from the head by scaling the selected vertices 115% along the Y axis. Use the command Selection→Resize to make your changes. In the pop-up dialog window, increase the Y scale to 115% and apply the change.

5. I think that the nose should be a little lower, so I use the Arrow tool to pull the current selection down a little, making the nose look more beak-like.

6. I also want to thin the nose bridge some, to give the face a more angular look to it. Using the Selection tool, select the outer area of the bridge. Again, it may take you a couple of selections holding the Shift key, to get all of the area that you need.

7. Switch to a front view to see the area that you have selected and to make the scale change.

8. Use the command Selection→Resize to make your changes. In the pop-up dialog window, decrease the X scale to 80% and apply the change. Switch to a right-sided view to see what you have done. The tip of the nose needs to be thinned some, so from the right-side view, select the tip area of the nose. Shift to the front view and resize the selection 80% on the X axis.

9. I would like to add some wrinkles or ridges where the nose bridge meets the eye area. Zoom in on the nose bridge and look at the geometry there. We are going to need to move some of the polygons from the lower nose up so that we have enough material to work with. You may find that you need to do this for other morphs from time to time.

10. Using the Box tool, make a selection of the first group of points that make up the top edge of the nose. Pull these right and up, a little over the level of the rest of the nose bridge. This forms the top of our first wrinkle.

11. Continue to grab these sections and move them up with the others. You will want to alternate the levels of those point sections so that you end up with that ridged look on the upper nose.

12. Switch to the top view again to get another look at what you have done. The nose is still a little wide for my taste.

13. Select the tip area again, this time from the top view. I have decided that I want the nose to be real pointy at the tip. Resize the selection 50% along the Y axis. This will leave you with a pretty sharp-looking nose point.

14. Move to the Perspective view to take a look at the final effect, and then save your morph as P4NudeMan_VampNose.obj using the settings you used for all of the above morphs.

FACIAL MORPHS

For the last set of morphs that we are going to make, we will be using a mixture of the three techniques shown in the other parts. Here we will be making some changes to the cheek and chin area to make our vampire have a sunken-face sort of look that you would expect a vampire to have.

1. Start by opening the Base head file once again, bringing the head into the Mesh Form Modeler, and switching the view to the right side.

2. Using the Selection Box tool, select an area on the cheek that you want to bring out and away from the face. These will be a set of raised cheekbones.

3. Again, use the command Selection→Resize to make your changes. In the pop-up dialog window, increase the X scale to 110% and apply the change.

4. Using the Box Selection tool, select the eyebrow area.

5. Pull the selected area out away from the head and up a little. This will give the face the appearance of having a bony ridge above the eyes, and it will make the eyes look like they are sunken in some.

6. For the last part of this face morph, I want to elongate the chin some. To do this, select, using the Box tool, the chin tip area. Again, it may take several selections while holding down the Shift key.

7. Using the Arrow tool, pull the chin forward a ways, and down slightly. Switch to the front view to see how the chin looks. You will see that the chin is still a little wide.

8. Keeping the same selection, resize the chin on the X axis by 60%. This will give you a nice tight pointed chin. Apply the resize as you have the others.

9. Switch to the Perspective view to get a final look at your new face morph. Save the morph as P4NudeMan_VampireFace.obj using the same method as the other morphs that you have made. See Figures 22.16 and 12.17.

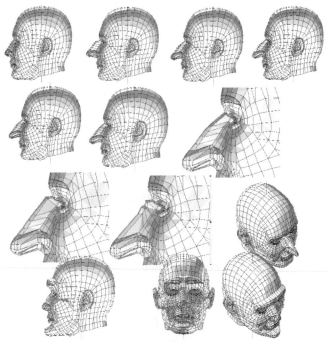

FIGURE *The development of the Nose and Face Target Morphs.*
22.16

FIGURE *The Finished Poser Vampire.*
22.17

APPLYING THE MORPHS

Once you have finished all of your morphs it is time to test them out. Open Poser 4 and bring the P4 Nude Male into your document. Switch to the head camera so you can get a good look at what is going on. Apply your morphs in the standard way, by double-clicking on the head and bringing the new targets in one by one. Give them good descriptive names in case you want to use this character again. Once you have them applied to the character, set them all at 1.0 to see how the morphs look. For my final character I left all of the dials set at 1 except for the vampire face morph, which I turned down to 0.7. I also adjusted the worried eye brow dials and the new Poser 4 long face morph to give him a more sinister look. If you are unhappy with any of your morphs at this point, you can re-open them in RDS and make any changes that you want to. Simply re-save the morph and reapply it.

GENERAL MORPHING TIPS

The three basic rules of morphing:

1. Always use the base geometries of the figures. These can always be found in the Geometries folders. If you don't, you will not get a morph that works properly.
2. Never move or scale the whole body section that you are working on; just scale or move specific areas of the mesh.
3. Never add or delete parts of the geometry.

Most, if not all, problems with morphs can be attributed to not following these three rules, or having a modeling package that alters the object on import or export.

Positive/Negative Morphs:

Morphs can have positive or negative values. If you are having trouble making a morph, you can always make the opposite of the morph you want to make and apply a negative value to the dial when using it.

For example, I need a morph that pulls the ears in closer to the head, but because of the tight spaces I am having problems getting it to work. What I could do is pull the ears out away from the head, and apply that new morph with a negative value. Also you should try all of your morphs on the negative end of the dial just to see the results. Some of these can be very handy when sculpting the figure with morphs.

Morph Target Range Limits

If you have used a lot of morphs, you may have noticed that some of them can only go to 1.0 on the dial, and others can be pushed to 4.0 or 5.0. The difference between the two is that the ones that are limited to 1.0 are morphs that move the geometry in different directions at once (Like the vampire face morph). The higher-ranged morphs usually only move one area in one direction (like a morph that elongates just the tips of the ears). When making morphs, keep this in mind.

Micromorphing

When I am working on a character, I make morphs for one area at a time. If I need the cheeks out, I make a morph just to move the cheeks. If I need them rounded more, I make another morph. This may seem like more work, but if I make two separate morphs, I can use the two to make an almost endless combination of cheek smoothness and bulge. Also, these can be used again to make other characters.

Bryce Beach and River Scenes for Poser Figures

By Sarah Sammis

This tutorial is an expanded version of my Bryce 4 water tutorial, which includes using Poser 4 characters, conforming clothing and custom texture maps, and the importance of scale between Poser character and Bryce terrain. Before you start posing people, decide what sort of scene you want to create.

For this tutorial, I decided to create an illustration for an ongoing project I am working on. I will create a beach on which Princess Grace and her grandfather are meditating at dusk. For this scene, I have already created the Emperor and have him saved as a Bryce .OBP, so I only have to create and pose Grace. Since she will be wearing a version of her grandfather's native costume, I will need to create a custom texture map for the Poser 4 Miniskirt. It helps to create a folder or directory called "water tutorial" or something similar to keep all your files together.

CREATING PRINCESS GRACE IN POSER 4

1. Open up Poser 4 and select the P4 Nude Woman from the Figures: People menu. Click Replace Character, and OK. The default Poser Man will be replaced with the Poser 4 Nude Woman. Select a side view, view from right or view from left. Select the woman's hips as it is the main connecting point for the rest of the body. I prefer to use the dials for posing as

they give a greater control than working directly with character. I used the yTran dial to make the woman sit. Then I selected each of her feet and set the xTran dials to augment the bending of her legs so she would look a little more natural.

2. Next I needed to pose the arms and hands. I chose the Posing Camera to see both hands in relation to the rest of the figure. For the left hand, I selected a hand pose from Hands: Library/Basic Hands. I decided on the Limp pose and then added more of a bend to make it appear to conform to her left knee. When you look at the figure from the Posing Camera, you will notice that her hand is not actually resting on her knee. Since I will be using her in a 3/4 profile, the hand/knee problem won't be an issue. See Figure 22.18.

FIGURE   *The left hand is posed.*
22.18

3. I then posed the face. I used the Blink Dials to close her eyes, the Frown Dial to give her a slightly pouty (contemplative) look. See Figure 22.19. Again, as it will be dusk and her face will be in shadow, an accurate facial pose is not necessary. Now that my pose is complete and I am ready to start adding more figures (the clothes and the poseable hair each count as figures), I will save my file first. It is always a good idea to save your work and to give your changes new names. I usually give my files a name and then a number so I can keep track of where I am in the modeling process.

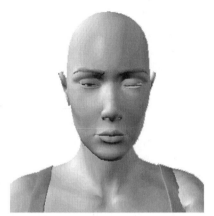

FIGURE *Eye Blinks are adjusted.*
22.19

4. Next I added the Miniskirt to the scene (Figures:Clothing-Female: Miniskirt). When it is first added, it floats above the figure. I went to Figure:Conform to and then a window popped up and I selected conform to Figure 1. Caution: Sometimes the naked figure ends up selected instead of the clothing. If that happens, select the clothing first. The naked figure is always "Figure 1." I then did the same thing with the Halter Top. Then Grace was dressed, her clothing was conformed to her, but she was still bald.

5. Since Grace is a Princess, she should have long flowing hair. The Long ConformCurls serves this purpose nicely (Figures:Clothing-Female: Long Conform Curls). The Long Conform Curls and the Long Curls don't automatically conform to the head like the standard Poser Hair does; it needs to be conformed just as the clothing does. See Step 4. The advantage of the Long Conform Curls is that it is poseable. I selected the base of the hair and used the yTran and zTran Dials to make it flow better down Grace's back. Then I saved the file again. Since I hadn't made any drastic changes, just added clothing, I saved my changes into the original file. If, however, you might want to go back and make changes, give it a new name!

6. Grace is half human, half alien. Since I will be relying for the most part on Poser 4's ability to export Material libraries (.mtl), I did the majority of my custom coloring in Poser 4. Again, since Grace will not be well lit, the amount of detail afforded through using the texture map template that comes with Poser 4 was not needed. Instead, I used the Paint Bucket to give Grace a lavender complexion, green eyes, and a black halter top. Since I will be using a custom map for the miniskirt, I leave it alone.

7. Now I am ready to export Grace. I choose File:Export:Wavefront. A window pops up asking about the number of frames I want to export. I click OK. Now Poser 4 gives me the Hierarchy window. I deselect the ground, and click OK. Poser 4 does not provide a progress bar for exports to WaveFront obj files, so just sit tight and give it a couple of minutes to do its thing. You will know it is done when the menu bar blinks or when your mouse movement actually makes the pop-up windows work.

Grace is now complete. Now it is time to move on to Painter 3d SE (which comes with Poser 4) to create the custom map for her miniskirt (which will serve as a stand-in kilt). One of these days, I will bite the bullet and create a miniskirt-to-kilt Morph Target, but not now. Quit/Exit Poser 4.

PAINTER 3D SE: CREATING THE TEXTURE MAP FOR THE "KILT"

8. Open up Painter 3d. Go to Acquire:Wavefront and then in the open dialog box, find your way back to Poser4:Runtime:Geometries: Poser4Clothes: Skirts:MiniSkirt.obj and click Open. Painter 3D will give you a 3D view of the miniskirt.

9. First I selected a deep blue color using the Color Wheel. Then I selected a large brush and clicked on the center section of the skirt. A texture map options window pops up. Make sure that "implicit" is selected for the mapping type. Then click OK. At this time, select the Texture Map window, and save. It will ask for a name. Name it something like graceskirt.tif, and select tiff as your option. If you want to make changes later, you might want to save it as .rif, which is Painter 3d's native format for maps. Since the skirt is poseable, it has sections. To create one map for the entire skirt, you will have to share the map. Click on another section of the skirt to color it in blue as well. Another Texture Map Options window pops up. This time, you have to check both that "implicit" is selected and that the map is being shared. Then, make sure that graceskirt is selected as the shared map. Click OK. Repeat for all other sections of the miniskirt.

10. Now that all the skirt is painted a deep blue, it is time to add the red spirals that signify the universe in this alien culture. Change brushes to a Detail brush, set it to a small radius and click the Build button. If you forget to do so, Painter will give you an alert box asking you to click the Build button. Once the entire map is covered with red spirals, save the

texture map again and the model. Save the model to your Water Tutorial folder or directory. See Figure 22.20.

Quit/Exit Painter 3d SE.

CREATING THE BEACH SCENE IN BRYCE

11. Create a terrain and click the E to go to the Terrain Editor. See Figure
22.21.

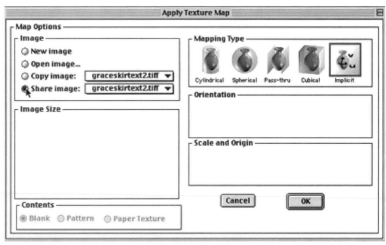

FIGURE *A texture is painted on in Painter 3D.*
22.20

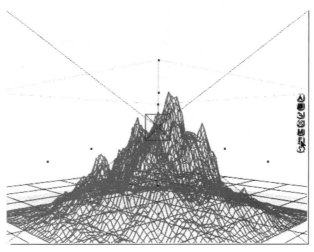

FIGURE *Create a Bryce Terrain.*
22.21

Click New to get a black area to paint your terrain on. If you want greater control of the terrain creation process, you can create your terrain as a grayscale image in Photoshop and import it with the Picture option. For a beach, I created a gradual and curved slope going from white to black, black being the lowest level of terrain and the point where the water will lap onto the beach sand. Playing with erosion and the fractal options (see bryce28.tif) in the Terrain Editor will add character to your terrain. Before you leave, get rid of the excess black area by dragging the bracket on the right upward. This will prevent your terrain from having a square edge. When you are satisfied, click the Check Mark.

12. Your terrain should still be selected. If it isn't, select it. Then duplicate it. This terrain will become your water. Select E to edit your newly duplicated terrain. In the Terrain Editor, choose Invert. Don't be alarmed when your nice black edges turn white and create a horrible-looking border around your new terrain. See Figure 22.22.

What you need to do is paint out the white areas with black and then remove the excess black areas as in Step 11. See Figure 22.23.

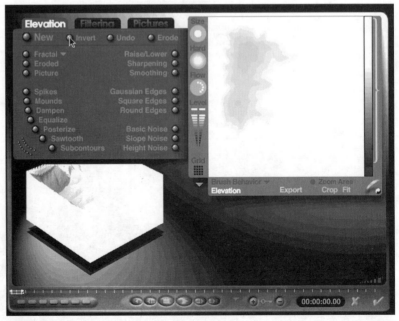

FIGURE *The Beach begins in the Terrain Editor.*
22.22

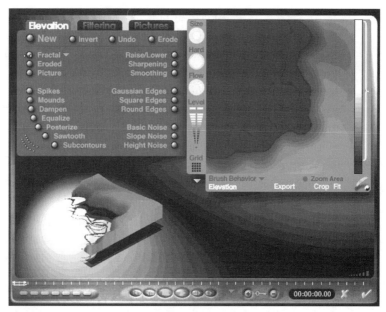

FIGURE *The Beach takes on a recognizable shape.*
22.23

I also suggest lowering the terrain, but the final thickness of the water will be controlled with the Attributes window. When done, click the Check Mark.

13. If you have lowered elevations of the water terrain in the Terrain Editor, your water terrain will be aligned in the X and Z planes but will be floating in the Y plane. Click the A, and then lower the terrain to about 1 to 10 in the Y plane. In this case, I lowered it to 5.

14. Select your beach terrain and give it a sand material (the one from the tutorial works well). Give your water terrain a water material. I like the Foamy Seawater one. It doesn't hurt to change the settings a bit on the presets. Of course, if you have already created a water material that you love, then use it. Since this will be a beach scene and the water will be extending to the horizon, I selected the Ground Plane and gave it the Foamy Seawater material as well. If you were creating a river scene with mountains on the horizon, it would not be necessary to use a water material on the Ground Plane.

15. Select both your beach and water terrain, and click the G to group them. This scene will be a close-up scene with the water lapping the beach. For a good sense of scale between the Poser 4 characters that will be imported and the Bryce scene, it is best to increase the size of the Bryce terrains to

something rather large. I tend to make my terrains around 500×500 in the X and Z planes, and between 50 to 150 tall in the Y plane.

16. Position the camera. Move to the top-down view. The wireframes will give a good idea as to where the coastline is. Select your camera and move it to the coastline. Then return to the camera view and do some fine-tuning of the position. Once you are satisfied with the view, it is time to import your Poser 4 character. If you haven't saved yet, now is a good time. Take advantage of Bryce 4's naming conventions and give it a name that ends in a number. The next time you select "Save As," Bryce will change the number by one higher. So, in my case, I saved it as "Tropicali1," and the next Save As will be "Tropicali2."

17. Go to File:Import Object. (See bryce49.tif) Find your Poser 4 obj file. In my case, it was Grace.obj. Click OK, or press Return. Grace will not import to where you put your camera. Use either the top-down view or the Directors Camera to position her to the bit of coastline you have decided to be your focal point. Another quick way to get her into position is to note the position of the camera from the Attributes window and then to type in similar coordinates for the Poser object.

18. Once you get your Poser object situated on the correct bit of coastline, do a quick render to check your scale. Actually, you can judge the scale by just looking at the wireframes, but sometimes a quick render can drive the point home. Another quick way to check things in full color is to select the Spray Can on the right-hand part of the Bryce screen. Then paint over the area you want rendered, and Bryce will give you a preview of what the render will look like. Sometimes you have to be patient with the Spray Can. Complicated scenes slow down the Spray Can just as they do render times. Your Poser character will probably look like a behemoth on the coastline. You will need to scale down your imported object to be about a third the size of its default import size. A calculator comes in handy for getting the calculations done correctly and quickly. I must admit that most times, I just estimate.

Incorrect estimations can lead to distortions! To change the object's dimensions, go to Select Group: Obj Group 1. This will select your Poser object. I highly recommend renaming the object to something more descriptive. In my case, I renamed her to Grace.

CAUTION

19. Once you have scaled your object down, you will need to reposition it in the Y plane because it will be floating once again. Then use the Spray

Can to check your scale again. Now you should have a tiny person on a large beach. If you want a greater degree of detail, move the camera inward by using the arrows on the left of the Bryce screen.

Zooming in with the Magnifying Glass will cause a fisheye effect. Now that your Poser object is imported, scaled, and positioned, it is time to Save As. If you have put a number at the end of your file name, Bryce should be asking you if you want to save it as version 2.

20. Now that the Poser character, Grace, is positioned, it is time to give her the custom map for her miniskirt to give it a more tribal look. Select Grace from the Select Group drop-down menu. Then click on the green dot between the two arrows to isolate her from the rest of the scene. Click the U to ungroup Grace's various meshes. Next, while holding down the Shift key to select more than one mesh, go to Select Mesh and find the Meshes that are named Right Hip 2, Left Hip 2, and so on. These are the pieces of the miniskirt. Once the entire miniskirt is selected, click the G to group them. Give the new group a clever name like "skirt." Then click the M on the newly created group to go to the Material Editor. On the diffuse row, click A and then click P for Parametric mapping. It will open up the texture map editor. In the left hand box, click "Load" and find the skirt map that was created in Painter 3d SE. In the middle box, click the white circle to delete the Alpha Channel info. Then click the Check Mark to return to the main window of the Material Editor. Click the Check Mark again to apply the new map to the skirt. Then drag your mouse around all of the Poser object to select the entire object, click G to regroup it, and rename it Grace. Then click the red circle between the two arrows to return to the entire Bryce scene.

21. I like to save my imported Poser objects as Bryce obp presets in case I want to use them again. See Figure 22.24.

For this tutorial, I decided to use Grace's grandfather, whom I had created a few weeks before and saved as an obp file. A few notes on the Emperor: He is sporting the Poser 3 women's hair, which has been conformed to his head, and the Poser 4 women's skirt, which was scaled up to about 110 and then conformed to his body. Again, I used the skirt to serve as a kilt. His kilt pattern was created in Bryce 4, but was applied by selecting the skirt meshes as described in Step 20. The Bryce obp will have to be scaled and positioned just as the imported object was.

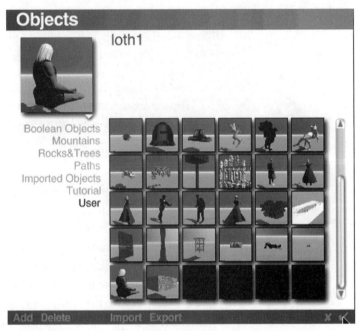

FIGURE   *The Bryce User Objects library.*
22.24

22. I like the palm trees that come with Bryce. I used them in this beach scene. I added them by clicking the arrow next to the create to get the obp preset lists. I went to Rocks and Plants and scrolled through until I found the palm trees. Then I clicked the Check Mark. I then positioned them and scaled them up by doubling all their dimensions. Remember, palm trees grow to be very tall. Unless it is a baby palm tree, don't have the Poser people be the same size as the tree! I created two sets of palm trees, one near Grace and her Grandfather, and one in the distance to give some interest to the image.

23. The last thing I did was to set the Sky Lab to create a nice sunset sort of look. It is a preset that has been slightly changed. Since the light from the sun was no longer illuminating the faces of my characters, I created two omni lights and gave a soft yellow gel to them to take some of the shadow away.

Then I rendered the image. See Figure 22.25.

The palm trees really add to the render time as did the omni lights. I had the machine render while I went to bed.

CAUTION

FIGURE   *The final rendering.*
22.25

Physical Manifestations of Terror

By Janet Glover

CAUTION

Karuna! *Work through this tutorial by applying the expressions described to any face you like.*

Remember when you were a kid, trying to think of really gross things, always attempting to top whatever your friends came up with. Why not make a list of things that are really creepy. It's easy to do, and I did it for this project. Basically, they fall into a few categories:

- Stagnant and slimy things: mucous, slugs oozing things, and slithering movements.
- Opposing and out-of-context characteristics: such as Evil Clowns and "Chuckie the doll." The lovely vacation resort in Stanley Kubricks' "The Shining," and the cute white flesh-eating rabbit in "Monty Python and the Holy Grail." Out of proportion or quantity: Giants, too many body parts or too few: Cyclops, and the insects in movies like "Them," "Arachnids," etc.

- Rough features, gnarly toes and fingers, warts, hairy moles, scars, horns, scales.
- Putrid colors and effects, green/yellows
- Death-like skin, icy vacant stares, hang-jawed drooling mouth, body parts falling off.
- And, of course, the ever popular mix of organic and/or mechanical body parts, such as The Fly, Frankenstein, or the Borg in *Star Trek Next Generation*.
- Automatons: Zombies, Nazi sensibilities.
- Horror expressed in the mundane: Beaurocracy. Examples: "The Castle" Franz Kafka, or the dark comic horror movie "Brazil."

So where am I going with this? What do all of these things have in common? Well it is we: our combined sense of the horrific! We all respond to terror with much the same physical response. It manifests itself in muscular contraction, the outpouring of Adrenaline, and the Fight or Flight response.

Darwin observed that "all people from an Oxford don to an aborigine, express grief by contracting their facial muscles in the same way. In rage, the lips retract and the teeth clench. There are similarities in the snarl and in disgust. All over the world, flirting signals are the same: a lowering of the eyelids or the head followed by direct eye contact. Embarrassed people close their eyes, turn their heads away, or cover their faces. And anger is easily recognizable in all cultures. Such universality indicates that emotions are part of the innate set of adaptations we possess." 1 Robert Ornstein

At first I thought of creating a really gross or evil-looking Poser figure. But then it came to me, why not create the response to terror? Pose a figure that expresses that feeling of a chill running down the spine. That moment of imminent danger, of being paralyzed in terror. A look that tells you something horrible is occurring, just outside the perimeter of the picture. It could be anything your imagination conjures up, which makes it very personal. We all have our own fears and demons.

PROGRAMS USED IN THIS TUTORIAL

MetaCreations' Poser 4, Zygote's Poser People CD, and Painter 3D were used in conjunction to create the following examples. You may use any figure to accomplish this task. You may use any paint program; however, Painter 3D (or Detailer) allows you to paint directly on the model, which helps in isolating the exact position of the wrinkled forehead on the texture map.

First ,let's look at the basic face without any alteration. Load a basic face. This shows a loose, relaxed musculature.

MUSCLES OF THE FACE

There are two major muscle groups that affect the facial expression of terror. They are the *Corrugator* and the *Frontalis*.

The Corrugator is actually a set of two different muscles that always work in conjunction with one another. They are anchored at the bone at the base of the nose, and fan upward between the eyebrows. See Figure 22.26.

The outer pair of Corrugator muscles connect to the skin just above the center of the eyebrow and socket of the eye. They always contract together. These muscles are most active in times of emotional distress, so are essential in the expression of fear, anger, and sadness. They are responsible for vertical frown lines and the development of swollen musculature at the area between the brows.

The Frontalis starts along the hairline near the top of the skull. It covers nearly the entire forehead and connects to the skin around the eyebrows. This is what lifts the brows upward and wrinkles the forehead. The effect of these muscles varies according to the level of stress we are experiencing. There is very little difference between a mildly saddened or angry person and slightly fearful person's face. The characteristics change, however, when the sadness becomes depression, the anger turns to rage, and the fear escalates to terror. Each of these

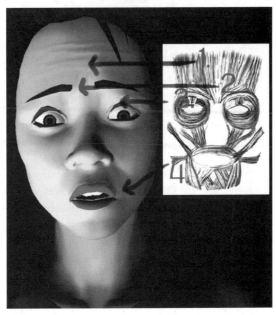

FIGURE   *This illustrates the position of the facial musculature.*
22.26

states is marked by changes in the shape of the mouth and the pull of the eyebrows. See Figure 22.27.

The mouth is undoubtedly the least crucial part of the face of terror. It can make or break the expression of fear, though. The biggest thing to be aware of is the inconsistency between the mouth and the eyes. A dumb grin may help to create a psychopathic look, but won't be convincing as a look of impending doom. The Levator Palpebrae controls the upper lid movement, which gives the appearance of the bulging eyes of terror. It is merely pulling the lid up, exposing more white of the eye.

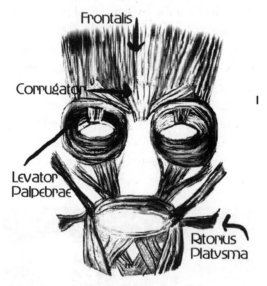

FIGURE *Here is the facial muscle map.*
22.27

The Risorius/Platysma controls the widening of the lower lip, pulling the sides of the mouth to the sides of the face. This results in a nearly horizontal lower lip. This varies according to the levels of tension the person is experiencing. In the first of these examples, notice the mouth of fear. The second example shows great sadness or grief. This occurs because of the action of additional muscles: the Mentalis and Zygomatic Minor. The last example shows anger's effect on the musculature. See Figure 22.28

THE FACE OF TERROR

The lifted brow and widened eyes are a survival response of the body. We become more alert to the danger in our environment, ready to defend ourselves or

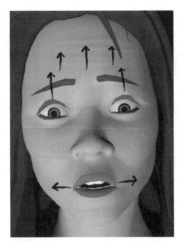

FIGURE   *The direction of the muscle movement of the mouth of terror.*
22.28

find a place to flee. The wider our eyes open, the more fear we are experiencing. As the fear subsides, the entire musculature of the face relaxes.

When we are afraid, our mouths drop open and the lower lip stretches sideways. It is believed that this is to aid in heavier breathing, and in effect, receive more oxygen to the brain. The generally accepted description of the mouth is the D shape, turned on its back. Generally, and depending on the view of the camera as in our situation, the lower teeth are visible.

One of my favorite artists and humanitarians is Kathe Kollwitz. She was quoted as saying, "Beauty is that which is ugly." To you, this may seem rather negative; however, Kathe found beauty in the struggles of the starving, struggling, and working classes of Depression and war era Germany.

"She found meaning and importance in the hands, feet, and hair of the workers, and the suggestions of the physical form beneath their clothing. The bodies shaped by labor remained beautiful to her. Constantly she stressed that art should grip, even shatter, the human heart." See Figure 22.29.

This is one of eight drawings in the series "Parting and Death." It was a study for lithographs completed about 10 years later. As you can see, the mouth demonstrates the sideways D shape, and the wrinkled brow of the Frontalis muscles. It is an excellent example of the face of terror.

RAGE

The raging female has a different set of muscles pulling the sides of the mouth down and out. Her brow is drawn down and toward the bridge of the nose.

FIGURE   *Kathe Kollwitz "Death Clutches a Woman" charcoal drawing, 1923–1924.*
22.29

The eyes can range from wide open to half shut, depending on the level of anxiety experienced. See Figure 22.30.

FIGURE   *This image displays the face of Rage.*
22.30

POSER

Okay, I'll stop with the anatomy lesson and get to the dial setting! Start up Poser 3. I used the "Asian Casual Female," which is available from Zygote. You may use whatever you like, since as we've discussed, this expression is universal. Set up you pose however you wish. Add hair, and set the properties to head. Save and name it. Now you want to select the head and start manipulating the dials. For this, it is best to zoom in real close, use the camera arrows and trackball to position the head in the Camera View. See Figure 22.31.

FIGURE   *The dial settings for the Asian Female.*
22.31

Open lips	0.000
Smile	–0.170
Frown	0.665
Mouth O	0.944 to 1.072 (this is a good range for escalating terror in an animation)
Mouth f	–0.174
Mouth m	-0.916
Tongue t	0.016
Tongue l	–0.177
Rbrowdown	1.219 to 840
Lbrowdown	2.162

Of course, the Left Brow can use the same settings as the right brow; this is my interpretation, faces not being symmetrical.

If the face is symmetrical, it should be the same as the other brow. Even though the Corrugator muscles move together, they are not necessarily equally as strong. Remember how I said the Frontalis moves the whole brow section upward? Well, people can develop weak muscles on one side of the face, or have stronger muscles to begin with. There are numerous conditions that can cause a face to be unequal in muscle condition. One example is Bells Palsy, which weakens the facial muscles, and the drooping of one side of the face.

Rbrowup	0.872
Lbrowup	1.994 (here I go again with the asymmetry)
WorryR	0.771
WorryL	1.236

The Eyes

Now select the eyes. In a terror state, the eyes can seem to pop out. There will appear to be more white showing at the top of the Iris (the colored part of the eye). Using dials, move the eye to positions shown in Figure 22.32. She looks pretty horrified now!

This isn't all we need to do, however. When these muscles contract, they wrinkle up the skin and cause the area above the bridge of the nose to swell up. This can only be achieved by the creation of a separate Bump Map. There are many ways to set this up. For this tutorial, I saved and exported the Poser figure as a Detailer Text file. This allows me to open up the model and the texture map and paint directly on the texture map. I have included the portion of the texture map that has the wrinkles already drawn in for you. Just copy and paste it to the (copy of) texture map you intend to use. Remember, this is only for use in the Bump part of the Render Options. See Figure 22.33.

Complications, of Course

When I decided to write this tutorial, I figured I would forgo the use of the classic Poser Anglo-Saxon model. Using the Asian model from my Zygote Poser People CD would be nice and give some variation to the usual Poser females we generally see. This choice led to an unexpected problem. The texture map is very different for the Asian figure. The placement of the body parts on the texture map is laid out completely different. The facial settings for the Asian Poser just don't work for the basic Nude Female in Poser. I was shocked when I saw how the Terror settings became completely absurd on the Nude Female. Since I knew the majority of readers would not have the Asian model, I

FIGURE *Horror expression, with and without bump applied.*
22.32

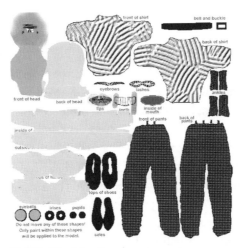

FIGURE *The Asian Female texture map.*
22.33

had to completely redo all of the settings, and redraw the wrinkles Bump Map for the basic model. See Figure 22.34.

FIGURE *The revised look for the non-Asian Poser Nude Female.*
22.34

PAINTER 3D

Start by selecting File/Open image file; in this case, AsianWomCas.tif, or choose the texture map that belongs to the Poser figure you are using. Save it *immediately* as something else. For this, I just added a number to the original name AsianWomCas1.tif. In this way, I have numerical variations in a particular texture map and avoid trying to remember which map goes with which model. Now, select File/Acquire/Detailer text.

The Detailer Text window will open, asking you to locate the *.vtx (text) file that you exported from Poser 4. Next you will be asked to SET VIEW SIZE. For this, I generally use 350 × 350; however, you may need a smaller window if you don't have the system memory. Painter 3D will now show a progress bar, "Now Importing Detailer text, file C:\whatever\nude.vtx." When it's finished, the imported text file will appear in the Model window. Using the Magnifying Glass, zoom into the face. Use the other positioning tools to line it up straight-forward facing you directly. Select the Paintbrush tool and click on the Model window, then the face. A dialog box will ask you to make selections. Parametric, and choose OPEN image. Insert Figure 22.35.

Select the location and the map you have just made a copy of. Now you will be able to start painting directly on the model, and see them interpreted on the map. These marks will be so very slight! That is exactly what you want.

With the Paintbrush tool selected, choose the Pencil from the Brushes window and select single pixel for the size. With a very light touch, draw directly on the model, so that you can position the wrinkles exactly where you want them. It seems that just when every mark is perfect and all is going right, Painter 3D will all of a sudden shoot a long line off in some crazy direction, so be prepared to Edit/Undo these pesky lines and carefully proceed. See Figure 22.36.

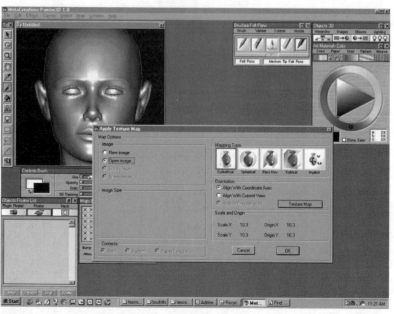

FIGURE   *A dialog will open for you to configure.*
22.35

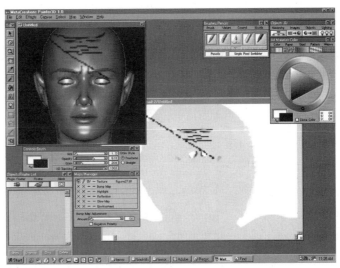

FIGURE   *A crazy line, "Has this happened to you?"*
22.36

Adding the Bump Map

Choose Render menu/Surface Material. In the Bump Map selection box, choose the texture map that you've created with the wrinkled forehead. It will ask if you want to change it to a Bump Map and, of course, you will agree. Play with the strength slider settings, increasing and decreasing the Bump until the height is correct for your scene. See Figure 22.37.

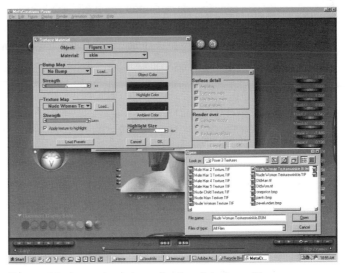

FIGURE   *This image shows the application of the Bump Map.*
22.37

Lighting the Face

Lighting conditions are dependent on numerous factors:

- **Mood:** Decide what you are going to describe. Is this a cadaverous scene that requires the use of a more blue-gray or sickly green lighting, casting pallor on the face of the victim? Or is the figure to be represented in an abyss of oppressive heat, which would call for the more severe red and orange mixes of light? Don't get too caught up in what you think the mood "should" be. Assumptions tend to cancel out the creative impulse. Sometimes the opposite is better than that which we originally conceive. Here is a quote from Dante's *Inferno* to demonstrate:

  "Far across the frozen ice can be seen the gigantic figure of Lucifer, who appears from this distance like a windmill seen through fog, and as the two travelers walk on toward that terrifying sight, they see the shades of sinners totally buried in the frozen water. At the center of the earth Lucifer stands frozen from the chest down..." 4.

We assume that Lucifer should be in a fiery hell, but this demonstrates the opposite.

- **Contrast:** Think about casting shadows on the figure or a backdrop, representing the object of the person's terror. This is better accomplished by exporting the figure to a modeling program, then placing an object between the light and the person. The camera, however, would be between the person and the object casting the shadow. The contrasted darkness of a shadow cast upon the figure can achieve more tension than an additional figure in the scene.
- **Direction:** Uplighting the figure can produce more intense contrast in the features. Shadows and highlights make the bone structure and musculature more visible. If done to extremes, however, the face can look comical, so be careful.

Placing different and striking colors on both sides of the face will make the face glow. See Figure 22.38

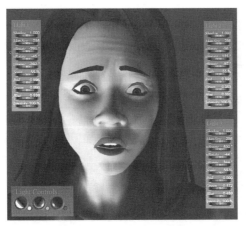

FIGURE   *This image shows the use of red and blue side lighting and settings.*
22.38

- **Intensity:** Do you want this picture to be shockingly stark? Or are you looking for a subtle growing sense of impending doom? Bringing up the intensity of the lights in an animation, either singularly or as a group, can add to the drama. This increases the emotional impact of the work.
- **Selectivity:** When it comes to fear, nothing registers in our minds as strongly as the eyes. Selective lighting of the eyes can be extremely effective in upping the sensation of terror. Think of it as looking in your rearview mirror while driving and seeing just the eyes of terror reflecting back at you. See Figure 22.39.

FIGURE   *The mirror, horror expression in eyes.*
22.39

Here are the settings for the model I used in the mirror lighting example. See Figure 22.40.

Keep these thoughts in mind when you are attempting to create a picture that goes beyond the predictable. We live in a world of imagination, which we as individuals have constructed of our own life experiences. "Our experiences, percepts, memories are not of the world directly but are our own creation, a dream of the world, one that evolved to produce just enough information for

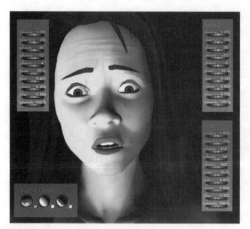

FIGURE *shows settings for golden lighting.*
22.40

us to adapt to local circumstances."1. Our brains act on the adaptations of our earliest ancestors. The same brain wiring that allowed the sensing of danger for our ancestors is still important for our making life and death decisions. But even more, it influences the way our mind perceives, what we find enjoyable, how our thoughts link together into concepts, and even what we hear and see. For some, it influences what they don't see!

ADDENDUM

If you wish to save the light settings you have created. See Figure 22.41.

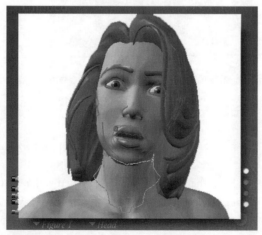

FIGURE *This figure shows the results of the Add (+)selection tool.*
22.41

All you have to do is make sure one of your lights is selected, and the library is open to Lights, create your own folder or add your lights to an existing one. Just click the plus sign, and a thumbnail of your lighting effect will appear. See Figure 22.42.

FIGURE   *The final Face of Terror.*
22.42

BIBLIOGRAPHY AND REFERENCES

The Evolution of Consciousness, The origins of the way we think. Robert Ornstein, Simon & Shuster 1991

The Artist's Complete Guide to Facial Expressions, Gary Faigin, Watson-Guptill Publications 1990

Kathe Kollwitz: Life in Art, by Mina C. Klein & H. Arthur Klein Schocken Books, NY 1972

The Divine Comedy, Inferno, Dante Alighieri (1265–1321)

Moving Along

In this chapter, we have presented a series of advanced Poser tutorials by a selection of Poser masters. If you have followed along, you are now at the master stage yourself, and ready to take on any Poser project. In the next chapter, a number of the color plates are detailed as to their production, giving you even more information on how best to utilize Poser tools and processes.

23 COLOR PLATE DETAILS

rtists learn from other artists. This is as true in the digital age as it was in the ages that preceded it, and will remain true in the future. For that reason, we have crafted this last chapter of the book to allow you to do just that. Taking some of the color plates that appear in the color inserts in the book, the artists will speak in their own voices, telling you things about the ways in which elements of their images were put together, and some of the thought process behind it. As we do this with various color plate selections, be sure to look at the full color image first, so you can get a better idea of what is being described and detailed.

Color Plate 1: The Pool of Secrets

By Shamms Mortier

This is the image that was used for the cover of the Poser 4 Handbook. It depicts a visit to a special hidden pool by a unknown tribe, riding the thought-to-be-extinct Triceratops. See Figure 23.1.

FIGURE *Refer to these key numbers for the following details in the text.*
23.1

1. The Zygote Triceratops was used as the transportation vehicle for these figures. It was posed in two different positions in Poser, and both were exported separately as OBJ files to Bryce 4.
2. The two older male figures are Zygote Abominable Snowmen, colorized to fit the scene. The facial characteristics of this figure are perfect for emulating aboriginal tribesmen. Zygote gave this model away free on their Web site, so it pays to check what they are offering once a week.
3. The tree was a palm tree added in Bryce from the Objects library. It was placed behind the rocks and the mounted rider for a background effect.
4. The female in the scene is the Poser Afro-American Female Nude, though she has white hair like her male counterparts in the scene. The child in the background is the Nude Boy figure, also given a white wig to complete the family group.
5. This fountain is the centerpiece of the picture. It uses a series of posed Bass from the Poser Animals library, all colored gold in Bryce. The head at the top was given character by using the new Poser 4 Racial Morphs. Everything was ported to Bryce as an OBJ file for texturing.
6. Bryce has the most realistic water effects you can find, and the Turbulent water preset was used to map the pool and this stream coming from the fish's mouth. The stream itself is just a boolean arc fashioned from a part of a cylinder in Bryce, and given a 80% transparency.
7. Notice the lovely rippled effects in the water. I wish I could say these were planned, but they were a lucky accident. Of course, I kept adjusting the water parameters until the accident took place.
8. All of these Bryce rocks use altitude mapping. This allows them to have a grass look on the top with rock on the sides.
9. I purposely kept the sky very simple, with just a 20% cloud setting. The scene itself is too complex to allow for a complex sky on top of that. The sky frames the action, and calls attention to the actors and elements.

Color Plate 2: Greening

By Celia Ziemer

The poor woody mannequin sits patiently, day after day, ignored and rejected time and again in favor of the fine human models.. What does it dream in its digital cell? Could it be . . . revenge? See Figure 23.2.

1. I exported a Poser Mannequin's arm to RDS 5.0.2's Meshform Modeler to remove the spheres at the joints, reshape, and pull vertices along the edges to form into leaf lobes. In the Perspective window, I duplicated the

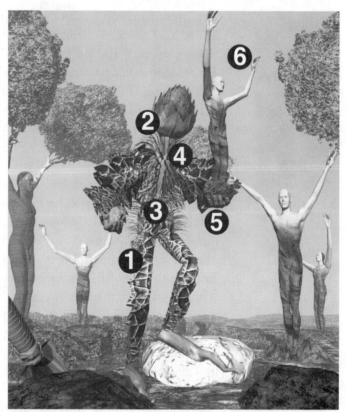

FIGURE *Refer to these key numbers for the following details in the text.*
23.2

arm, opened each in the Meshform Modeler, and deleted the forearm of one, the shoulder of the other. Then I duplicated and mirrored the parts. Next, I applied mapping, exported the four pieces to Poser as Wavefront objects, and added them to the Props library. I did the same with the legs, also removing the spheres at the knees to model the top of the shin and the bottom of the thigh closer together to approach "stalkhood" without spheres to break into the roughness along the leg edges. With new arm and leg parts now in a Prop library, I opened another Mannequin and re-placed the body parts with the ones I redesigned. So far, everything fit, so the file was saved.

2. Next, I made everything invisible but the head and exported it to Ray-Dream Studio as a measuring device for head size. The thistle/artichoke type head was one Meshform object duplicated, rotated, and scaled. It looked too regular, so I passed it through PLAY's Amorphium to draw

out veins and apply little dings here and there, and then it was back to Poser as a Prop where it was used to replace the Mannequin's head. So this far, I had two arms, two legs, and a head to work with.

3. One at a time, the Chest, Abdomen, and Hip elements went to RayDream Studio for Spiking, then back to Poser for body part replacements.

4. Nothing quite fit at first. Ankles, wrists, and neck were still just dark spheres, and the hands and feet were still the Mannequin's hands and feet. I exported the whole figure to RDS, separated groups for body parts, and checked for overhaul. The spheres became Neck, Wrists, and Shins and were extended, and the shoes were pulled into shapes more appropriate to a plant man. I detached and renamed the body parts and deleted the Hands, then applied mapping coordinates while the figure was still in the Meshform Modeler. On finishing this, I exported the figure to Poser and created a new hierarchy.

5. When the hierarchy was converted in Poser, I opened the Right and Left Hands (from the Additional Figures library), scaled them down, and parented them to the forearms. The rooty toes weren't long enough, so they were rescaled along their Z-axes in Poser. After setting joint parameters and putting the figure in a good gardening position, I exported him to Bryce4.

6. The Saplings are the regular Poser male figure. Arms and fingers were scaled up along their X-axes in Poser, (generally, the older the Sapling the longer the arms and fingers). Last, the figures were posed and exported to Bryce for planting and rendering.

Color Plate 3: (Top) Verdict

By Ed Baumgarten (www.baument.com)

The image Verdict was constructed with the old "epic" movies in mind. The gladiators in the image have brought their conflict to its conclusion, and the victor awaits the "verdict" from the emperor. Of course, the crowd has their own opinion about the prospective outcome. This image was constructed using a number of programs: Poser for the figures, 3D Studio Max for the custom models, Bryce for the final render and architecture, and, finally, Photoshop for lighting effects and touch-ups. Numbers in () are numerical tags in picture. See Figure 23.3.

The gladiators would have to have four custom models constructed. They are essentially the same except for their final poses. The models consist of the helmet (1), bottoms (6), sandals (4), and weaponry (5).

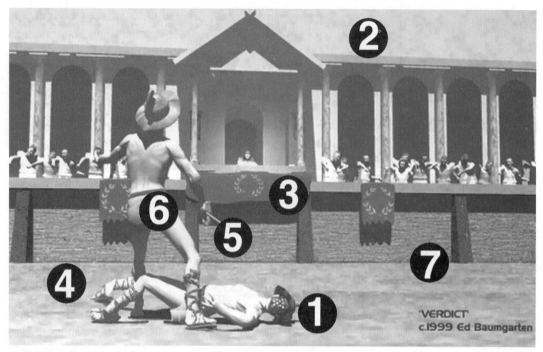

FIGURE *The Verdict.*
23.3

The helmets (1) were constructed in Max using a cylinder stretched to shape for the brim, a sphere booleaned to a cylinder for the vertical portion, and extruded spline shape for the crest. The perforated face shield was made with a box polygon, mesh-edited to shape, and then an array of cylinders booleaned out of it. The face shield then had a bend modifier applied to it for roundness. The parts were all combined, checked against an exported obj of the default Poser Male for scale, and exported as a 3DS file.

The bottoms (6) were constructed from a loft using splines shaped to fit the section of the Male Poser Hip. The resulting loft was then shaped using a free-form deformation modifier to get it to fit the figure. The sandals (4) became a project unto themselves. They consist of two parts each, upper straps and lower straps with sole. The upper straps were constructed by lofting a rectangle spine on a helix spine path. The helix was manipulated to the proper shape (using a Poser Calf as a guide), and then the rectangle lofted around it. The loft was then mirrored to increase the complexity of the straps. The sole of the san-dal was constructed with a spline drawn to the proper shape of the Poser foot and then extruded. The lower straps are more lofted splines. The upper and lower shapes were then mirrored for the opposite foot and exported. Having two parts makes them flex with the ankle.

The sword (5) in the victor's hand was constructed using a stretched rectangle for the blade and a custom g2h map for the hilt. This was then exported as a 3DS object file. Once all of the models were ready, Poser was fired up and the default Male selected as the subject. The helmet, bottoms, and sword were all imported and parented to the head, hip, and hand, respectively. The sandal parts were then imported and parented to their perspective calves and feet.

Working on one subject at a time, the poses were struck for the victor and the loser. I knew I wanted one figure with his sword down and his upturned hand out looking at the crowd. The victim was posed as if at the victor's feet, head turned toward the viewer with his legs contorted. These figures were each exported with their props as .obj files set to have all parts exported separately.

The gallery of crowd figures (18 total) were all constructed using the default Poser Male. A pose was struck with the "thumbs down" attitude. A custom tunic was constructed in Max and imported for the figure. The figure then had his legs and feet hidden (to conserve polygon count, if you don't see it, don't include it) and exported as an .obj file. The figure was then re-posed with minor variations in body and head tilt—different hair etc.—and exported another 17 times. I then fired up Bryce to construct the "set"(2) for the figures. Using rectangle primitive, I built up the foreground wall and pilasters, and the background wall and portcullis. The arches in the background wall were constructed by booleaning a cylinder and a rectangle together, and then booleaning that shape out of the back wall. The columns were custom made in Max and imported.

The hanging banners (3) in the scene were constructed in Max using rectangle shapes, mesh-edited to shape, and then ripple modifiers were applied to give them a wavy appearance. The textures on the banners were painted by hand in Photoshop and applied in Bryce. The background scene then had textures applied to it using standard Bryce textures tweaked a bit in the DTE for the proper noise scale. The Poser figures were imported one at a time, ungrouped, textured, and placed in the scene. This may sound like quite a task since there are 18 background figures, but once you get the hang of it, it's a pretty mindless operation. They were placed in the gallery and rotated/moved to impart a "mob scene" feel.

The gladiators were then imported, textured using the same method as the crowd, and placed in the scene. Once you get that far, it's just a matter of adjusting your camera angles and models to get the perspective you like. I will usually set up three or four different angles using the Save Camera Dots and switch between them until I see what I like. Also when positioning this many figures, the use of the number keys 2 through 4 is essential to get them just where you want them. Once the figures were positioned and the textures adjusted for color, the sun was moved to the proper location, and several fill spots where inserted to highlight the key figures. Several test renders were made at this stage to adjust the lighting. The scene was then given a final hi-res render and exported.

Bringing the render into Photoshop for a little post work, the base of the wall (7) was lightly brushed with green to help blend the wall into the ground, and a light yellow omni-directional light was rendered in to get that "old movie" overtone. The scene was cropped to produce a more "letter box" aspect, titled, and saved.

The bulk of this project was done on a PII 450, Bryce 3 patched and Poser patched. There were no crashes and the total scene creation start to finish was around six hours. The final Bryce file weighed in at around 132MB. The sandals used in this scene can be downloaded from our site at www.baument.com.

Color Plate 4: (Top) Medusa

By Kuzey Atici

1. 3D programs such as Poser and Bryce make it so easy to produce great art. Here, a normal Poser Female figure is transformed into Medusa with the help of a simple prop and the wonderful textures of Bryce4. A straightforward standing pose was used from the Poser library.

2. The snake's head was modeled in Infini-D 4.5 and completed in RayDream Studio 5.02. The good thing about RayDream Studio is that you can have your Poser figure loaded while building the model. Using the figure as a guide, duplicate the original snake until you have enough, and slightly alter each one as you go.

3. Don't be afraid to make test renders of your character; after all, it's the secret to how good your final image will be. Even though I was happy with the snakes, they still didn't look like they were part of the character itself. The smaller hair-like snakes were added to help bring everything together and complete the Medusa character.

4. To avoid that "Poser look," I didn't use any texture maps in Poser itself. Instead, I customized the figure with the use of Bryce 4 textures. Melting Ice from the Rocks & Stones Material library was used for her skin. The lips had the same texture applied, but the color was changed to a dark red in the Deep Texture Editor.

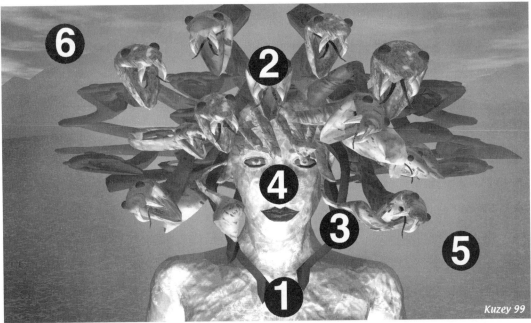

FIGURE *Refer to these key numbers for the following details in the text.*
23.4

5. A Bryce background can sometimes overpower your creation. To neutralize any possible distraction and still have an environment for the figure to live in, a sphere was added and the Smoke Stack texture applied. You can also increase the Fog and Haze settings to get a similar effect.

6. It's worthwhile to customize the sky to suit the type of character and scene you have. Another Interesting Alien sky was used as the base, with the sun color changed to a light yellow. To complete the effect, the time of day was also changed from day to night.

In Closing . . .

We hope you have enjoyed this book, and that your Poser skills have benefited from using it. The real secret to truly mastering Poser, or any artistic process, is to struggle and explore until your own style manifests itself. Keep playing and experimenting, and there is little doubt that your skills will increase as you go. Until the *Poser 5 Handbook* . . . stay creative!

WHAT'S ON THE CD-ROM

The **Poser 4 Handbook's** companion CD-ROM contains elements specifically selected to enhance the usefulness of this book, including:

- New objects from the author and other developers that you can add to your Poser 4 scenes. These are separated in many folders, so explore the CD to discover where they are located.
- Animations from Kuzey Atici, a Poser master artist and animator. You will find these in the Kuzey folder.
- A large collection of animations or Poser scenes and rendering options. These are located in the ANIMS folder.

You must have Apple's QuickTime for either the Mac or Windows to run the animations. Mac users can simply double-click on a QuickTime file to automatically load the QuickTime player. Windows users should open the QuickTime viewer, and load the animation from the File menu.

- Explore the CD-ROM for Mac and Windows demos of Media Cleaner Pro and a Window's version of Motivate's 3D Development system.

B CONTRIBUTOR BIOGRAPHIES

The following is a short list of contributor biographies, received in time for publication in this book.

LUKE AHEARN

Luke is the Lead Designer at Goldtree Games, makers of Dead Reckoning, Cylindrix, and Kingspoint. He writes game industry articles, novels, and lots of game related documentation. Check out his work at www.goldtree.com.

ED BAUMGARTEN

Ed Baumgarten of Baumgarten Enterprises (est. 1988) has been modeling in 3D for many years, offering custom model building for hire to hobbyists and professionals alike. The popular 'Meshes' series of CD model collections is offered for sale via secure E-commerce on his web site along with regularly updated FREE models for download. Well known among the 3D community for unique models for Poser, Bryce and virtually every other 3D modeling program, Baumgarten Enterprises promises to provide the hobbyist and professional, quality models at an affordable price. Be sure to check out their website at www.baument.com for their regular updates!

LISA BOYCE

Lisa is a nurse/graphic artist living in north Texas. She is married and has two children ages 8 and 10, a cat, and a little shih-tzu that controls the entire household. She has taken art and design classes of various sorts on and off for years but as yet has no degree in art. She also works in traditional media (oils and pastels) and textile art (quilting and related handwork).

LEE CHAPEL

Lee first started working with personal computers in 1978, with a couple of computers that used a 6502 processor: the SYM and the KIM. Over the years he has gone through a TRS 80 clone, a Radio Shack Color Computer, various IBM PC clones, and finally to the homebuilt Pentium II 400MHz machine he now uses. During that time he mainly wrote and sold computer games for the various machines he owned, and occasionally accepted special programming requests and acted as a software consultant. He is not a professional artist, but works as a Computer Information Consultant in the Bureau of Air at the Illinois Environmental Protection Agency. He recently started putting his graphics talents into use there by helping with the Bureau's intranet. He first got into 3D graphics around 1996 with the purchase of Vistapro 3. Early in 1998 he spotted Poser 2 and Bryce 3D at reduced prices and decided to purchase and experiment with them. Since then he has added other graphics programs to his collection of graphics software, and upgraded to Bryce 4 and Poser 4. A gallery of some of his better work can be seen on his web site at http://members.aol .com/leec279241.

STEPHEN L. COX

Stephen was the lead programmer on Fantastic Worlds, an add on disk for Sid Meier's Civilization II, assisted in design, laying out many of the scenario editors included in the product. He has also worked for Acclaim Entertainment, where he was the Director of Product Development. At DreamWorks Interactive, he was the Project/Tools Programmer, and assisted in the programming of the Sony PSX version of Jurassic Park II, wrote a code profiler, CD-layout optimizer and sound tools (Windows 95, MFC) for software development on the Sony Playstation. He worked for Sega of America as a Project Programmer, where he designed and programmed all the tools needed for game development on the Sega Genesis, including graphics conversion and animation tools. At Electronic Arts he was a Project Designer/Programmer and wrote a Sega Genesis game based on Electronic Arts' ASIC chip. He has many other credits in addition to this, and has worked on UNIX, Apple II, Atari 800, Commodore

64, Amiga, Macintosh, MS-DOS, Windows 3.x (Win16), Windows 95 (Win32/MFC), Winsock, NES, Super NES, Sega Genesis, and Sony PSX.

JANET GLOVER

Janet is an award winning portrait and landscape painter. She is also a Space Muralist for Abrams Planetarium's Black Light Gallery at Michigan State University. She instituted and provided a therapeutic art program for emotionally impaired children in residential treatment in Detroit, Michigan. Currently; she heads Glover Illustration & Design—www.gloverdesign.com. She is also on the staff of PixArt, managing the 3D section—www.ruku.com She writes for "3D Creature Workshop" and "Mastering 3D Graphics." She is married to Ross, has 3 cats and a German shepherd and resides in rural Michigan in a painters' paradise in the woods.

KEITH HUNTER

Keith Hunter heads the Model Department at Rhythm & Hues Studios. His architectural background makes him a perfectionist when it comes to constructing computer graphic models of characters, buildings, and objects. Keith holds a Bachelor's Degree in Architecture from The Ohio State University and a Master's Degree in Architecture from Harvard University. During his eight years at the studio, he has supervised the model work on *Spawn, Batman & Robin, Speed II, Kazaam, Waterworld, Hocus Pocus, Star Trek, The Experience,* and *Babe,* for which Rhythm and Hues received the Academy Award for Best Visual Effects in 1996. In addition, Keith helped create the models for the famous Coca Cola polar bear commercials and the award-winning "Sea Creatures" in *Seafari,* an MCA theme park ridefilm in Japan.

Tom Capizzi works in modeling and lighting at Rhythm & Hues. He has an extensive background in modeling on shows such as for Captain Amazing's head on *Mystery Men,* or some of the talking animals on *Babe 2.* He also had a hand in lighting on *Mystery Men* and an independent film called *Entrophy* in which he had to make a cat talk.

Max Okazaki is a modeler who helped design some of the vehicles in a film called *Joust.* He has also worked in modeling on projects such as the Coca Cola polar bears and *Babe 2.*

Steve Ziolkowski was a modeler/animator. Steve is highly technical and has written shell scripts to set up characters and procedurally build models. He's been a character animator/animator on projects like *Star Trek, The Experience* in Las Vegas, in which he animated the starship and the Klingon Bird of Prey. He also worked on projects like The "A Bug's Life" theme park attraction at

Walt Disney's Animal Kingdom in Florida, in which he animated many of the bugs. Some of his modeling credits include the submarines in *Seafari*.

JACKIE LEWIN

Jackie is a laboratory technician in charge of an electron microscopy unit. 2D and 3D graphics are her hobbies and she spends much of her spare time creating 3D meshes and short animations. She lives in North London with her partner and two cats.

NICHOLAS MARKS

Nicholas is currently CEO of Free Media Network, which is responsible for sites such as www.freetextures.com and www.3dbay.com. Combined, these sites represent the largest resource of free assets on the internet.

ERIC RUFFO (GHOST)

Eric is a full-time college student who is using Raydream Studio and Poser4 as a hobby. He has used Poser since Version 2, but only started posting his work after Poser3 was released. His current interests in 3D are horror and sci-fi. He enjoys posting his work for others to enjoy and cannot picture doing anything else in his spare time! He is often found lurking online as "Ghost."

RICK SCHRAND

Rick's background runs the gamut from writing to reporting to corporate start-ups. With over 28 years in the broadcast industry, three Emmy awards and numerous former Broadcast Promotion & Marketing Executives (BPME) awards for writing and producing. He has now turned his attention to the world of 3D with his company, GRFX ByDesign, located just outside of Nashville, Tennesee. He has written numerous tutorials for books and for the "3D Creature Workshop" and "Mastering 3D Graphics" sites.

Rick has a Doctorate in English and holds a Bachelors Degree in Broadcast Journalism and Communication. He has worked in both local and national television, including the NBC television network as a publicist. While there he helped create a daytime drama, and was responsible for helping turn another show, *Days of Our Lives*, into the #1 daytime soap. He has been listed in seven Marquis "Who's Who" publications since 1994, including "Who's Who in Entertainment," "Who's Who in America," and "Who's Who in the World."

RAY SHERMAN

For 15 years, Ray was a figurative painter using traditional media: oils, paper collage, and found objects. He exhibited his work throughout the U.S. and

Europe. About 10 years ago he turned to computer graphics, and has been hooked ever since. When Poser was first released, he thought it would be a perfect program with which to rough out his paintings. He found that it was much more than that. He could create images and develop concepts more quickly, and thus, illustration was the natural path to follow. For the last 7 years he has been illustrating for publications such as the *New York Times* and *Newsday*. His work can be seen online at www.raysherman.com.

KENNETH SHUMATE

Kenneth Shumate hails from a long line of southern artists. His cousin John Chumley is well known nationally as a landscape artist in the Andrew Wyeth tradition. His mother, Nancy, was a well known portrait and landscape artist. Kenneth's experience has been in design and commercial art and most recently in digital art. He lives in Atlanta, Georgia. Additional work by him can be seen at his web page. http://www.kennectonline.com

ERIC VANDYCKE

Eric VanDycke is a 26 year old Freelance Graphic/3D artist and collectable toy dealer who lives in rural upstate New York. He has dabbled in painting, drawing, sculpting, ceramics, woodworking, and metalworking before finding his one true love—computer graphics. He is an experienced user of Ray Dream Studio, Poser, Bryce 3D, Rhino, Amorphium, and a handful of other 3D programs. He is currently involved with the Online Poser Props Modeler's Guild, the 3D Comic Collective, and his own site: Traveler's Morph World, in which he makes all of his custom morph targets and characters available for download. Contact him at nimbus@telenet.net.

CELIA ZIEMER

Celia jumped from nonobjective painting and pen and ink drawing to the computer several years ago, finding it was her magic "Anything-Box." She works on both Mac and Windows with 3D Studio Max, Ray Dream Studio, Bryce, Photoshop, Poser 3, Painter 3D, and has lately added Nendo, Organica, and Amorphium to the box. The last two have caused her to back down from a former belief that the only way to model was vertex by vertex. Although she has done right-down-to-the-moss-blooms-on-the-rock-realism for scientific illustration and museum topos, there's a great necessity to roll her own worlds. With 3D, she can climb right in, manipulating the on-screen world of the imagination to tell her story—or watch the story unfold. She loves to mess with your head.

APPENDIX C

VENDOR CONTACT DATA

Here is the contact information for some of the vendors mentioned in the book.

Adobe

After Effects, Photoshop
345 Park Ave.
San Jose, CA 95110
http://www.adobe.com
(408) 536-4292 phone

Charles River Media

Publisher
403 VFW Drive
P.O. Box 417
Rockland, MA 02370
(781) 871-4184

Forge Studios, LTD.

PoseAmation
PO Box 34
Celbridge, Co. Kildare
Ireland

MetaCreations

Poser, Bryce, Carrara, Painter
6303 Carpenteria Avenue
Carpenteria, CA 93013
http://www.metacreations.com

PLAY, Inc.

Amorphium
2890 Kilgore Road
Rancho Cordova, CA 95670
http://www.play.com

Terran Interactive

Media Cleaner Pro
(408) 356-7373
http://www.terran.com

U&I Software

ArtMatic and MetaSynth
http://www.uisoftware.com

WhiteCrow 3D

Poser Collections
WhiteCrow3D
Studio 8, 1 Leonard Place
Kinnoull Causeway, Perth
Scotland, UK PH2 8HL
(UK)+44 07974 617793
http://www.poser-props.co.uk

Zygote Media Group

Poser Collections
One East Center St., Suite 215
Provo, UT 84606
http://www.zygote.com

D POSER WEB RESOURCE SITES

T he following list does not represent all of the Poser-related sites, but a good many of them. The list is growing constantly, so stay tuned to Poser with your Web browser to keep informed.

3D VISIONS

http://www.3dvision03.freeserve.co.uk/resource.htm

3D COMICS

http://www.loston.net/aftermath

- AFTERMATH: The Chosen. 1999's hottest new 3D comic book. Taking the battle between good and evil to new heights of Poser realism!
     http://members.aol.com/omnvstdwnd
     http://members.aol.com/omnvstdwnd
- Extensive use of Poser to illustrate the characters for a superhero shared-world project.
     http://readtome.com
- Uses animated Poser characters to present stories and comedy routines.

AMERICAN VAULTING ASSOCIATION

http://www.horsenet.com/ava/
    Poser content is presently somewhat limited.

BAUMGARTEN ENTERPRISES

http://www.stewstras.net/baument/downloads.htm

POSER FORUM

http://www.poserforum.com/

GEOCITIES

http://www.geocities.com/Nashville/8864
    Full sections on Poser.

LANNIE'S HUGE LIST OF POSER SITES

http://www.probe.net/~lannie/poser.htm

LANNIE'S WEB GRAPHICS

http://www.probe.net/~lannie
    A Poser Resource site for Tutorials, Models, Textures, etc., plus a Poser
Bryce Gallery.

THE MALL

http://www.loston.net/themall/
    Lotsa Poser-related downloads

MIND'S EYE

http://westwood.fortunecity.com/galliano/520/enter.html
    Poser art, comprehensive links list for all things Poser related—other sites,
textures, models, and tutorials.

MOBIUS WEBSITE

http://www.geocities.com/SiliconValley/Monitor/7556/
    Lots of Poser stuff.

PIXART

http://www.ruku.com/poser.html

- Tutorials
  http://www.gloverdesign.com/poser.html
- Custom-built models
  http://www.gloverdesign.com/poser.html
- Tutorial links and custom props

PoseAmation

http://www.the-forge.ie
 Royalty-free animation and much more for use with Posers 3 and 4.

Poser and Poser/Bryce Galleries

http://www.tedbell.com
http://www.lastband.com> www.lastband.com
http://www.chesserstudios.com
http://www.users.globalnet.co.uk/~pcooke/graphics/examples.htm
http://www.fix.net/~pharley/Anthro.html
http://www.widowsweb.com/
http://www.swaity.com/> http://www.swaity.com
http://members.aol.com/leec279241/
http://hometown.aol.com/beyondvr/
http://www.spaceports.com/~helend
http://junior.apk.net/~celimage
http://www.swcp.com/~danm
http://lonewolf.tierranet.com
http://www.piedmontyoga.com
http://www.monkeyyoga.com
http://www.idiom.com/~kalin

PoserMART

http:// www.loston.net/themall
 PoserMART is the world's largest second-hand Poser clothing mall for free
Poser-related downloads, software reviews, chatroom, and more.

Poser Models Integrated Onsite

http://www.tdrphoto.com
 TDR PhotoDesign has only recently begun to incorporate the use of 3D
models using programs such as Poser. Even though most of their clients have
no need for designs that use 3D models, they feel it an unwise move to let the
3D world slip past them.

Poser Props Guild

http://www.gwz.org/propsguild/

PoserWorld

http://www.poserworld.com
 Models and textures etc., etc., for Poser with a specialty of 3D clothes.

ROY'S MAX-POSER PAGE

http://personalweb.edge.net/%7Efur/index.html
    Mapping magician plus.

SCIFI AND FANTASY

http://home.clara.net/pembers/pictures/
    Imaginative science fiction and fantasy pictures made with Poser, Bryce, and
POV-Ray.
    also...
    http://members.xoom.com/dadchamp/
    http://members.xoom.com/dadchamp/

STRIKE A POSE PAGE

http://www.spaceports.com/~helend/Textures/index.html
    Lots of links plus downloads.

TEXTURES FOR POSER

http://www.spaceports.com/~helend/Textures/index.html

TIPS AND HOW-TO'S

http://www.3dartist.com

UVMAPPER

http://home.pb.net/~stevecox
    UVMapper is a texture-mapping utility for Wavefront OBJ files. Can be
used on objects exported from Poser as well as objects to be imported.

XOOM SITE

http://members.xoom.com/dadchamp/">http://members.xoom.com/dad-
champ/
    Dragon is now available. The Xoom site will be slowly built up into a Poser-
only site with the free characters posted there and a picture/movie gallery later
on. RavenStar Video Productions.

ZIMAGE GRAPHICS 3D / WHITECROW 3D

http://www.zig3d.co.uk/
    Poser Prop CDs. High-quality 3D data sets for use in Metacreations' Poser
are now available (Mac and Windows). CDs include the following titles:
Household 1—A collection of furniture and household items; Household 2—

A collection of more furniture and household items; Household 3—A collection of more furniture and household items; Weapons 1—A collection of medieval and historical Weaponry; Computer 1—A collection of computer/technology related items. Each CD contains 100 high-quality original models in PP2 format (Poser Prop files), and all are easily installed using the CD's own auto executable file. They are also giving away a free Poser Prop on every Monday. As well as the Props, they also have several Texture CDs and some already up for you to download at $1 per Texture.

ZYGOTE

http://www.zygote.com

CAUTION

Karuna! *One of the most important sites for tutorials is that of Charles River Media—http://www.charlesriver.com. (Graphics Resource Club) Why? Because that's where this author will be posting monthly tutorials on both Bryce and Poser. Check it out!*

INDEX

A

Additional Figures library list, 72
Adobe After Effects, 372, 374
Adobe Premiere, 372, 373
Advanced Poser projects, 487–529
  Bryce beach and river scenes for Poser
    figures, 505–515
  Carousel, 488–493
  Centaur, 493–496
  making vampire morphs, 496
  physical manifestations of terror,
    515–529
    face of terror, 518–519
    muscles of the face, 517–518
    Painter 3D, 523
      adding the Bump Map, 525
      lighting the face, 526–529
    Poser, 520–523
      complications, 522–523
      eyes, 522
    programs used in tutorial, 516
    rage, 519–520
Alien-looking hands, 78
Alien Skin Textureshop (Virtus
    Corporation), 371
Aliod hand morph, 80–81
Amapi, 356–357, 358
Amorphium, 361–362, 363
Andromeda F/X, 371
Animal animation, 257–276
  animating Poser and Zygote animals,
    270–275
    Bass, 272
    Bear, 272
    Buck, 273
    Cat, 270
    Chimpanzee, 273
    Cow, 273
    Doe, 272
    Dog, 270
    Dolphin, 271
    Frog, 274
    Horse, 271

    Killer Whale, 274
    Lion, 274
    Penguin, 274
    Raptor, 271–272
    Shark, 275
    Wolf, 275
    Zebra, 275
  Eadweard Muybridge, 259–269
    using Muybridge's books, 261–269
  locating Poser Animals, 258–259
Animal models, posing and customizing,
    107–148
  assigning human characteristics to
    animals, 133
  customizing animal models,
    134–144
  deforming animal models, 144–148
    Arcturian Rat, 145–147
    making animatable creatures, 148
    making creatures breathe, 148
  external models, 121–132
    Zygote Animal models, 122–132
  internal animal models, 108–121
Animals, and Walk Designer, 299–302
Animated hand projects, 239–240
Animated reflections, 410–414
Animating Camera, 410
Animation Controller, 223–225
Animation controls, 41, 42, 221–234
  Animation Controls toggle, 41, 42
  Animation menu, 230–233
  control environments, 223–230
    Animation Controller, 223–225
    Animation Palette, 225–230
  Inverse Kinematics, 233
  keyframing, 222–223
  preparatory movements, 234
Animation menu, 34–35, 36, 230–233
  Animation Setup, 230
  Loop Interpolation/Quaternion
    Interpolation, 232–233
  Make Move, 231
  Mute Sound/Clear Sound, 233

    Play Movie File, 233
    Resample Keyframes, 232
    Retime Animation, 231
    Skip Frames, 233
  Animation painting, 376–377
    Aura, 377
    MediaPaint, 376–377
    Paint, 377
    SkyPaint, 376
  Animation Palette, 35, 225–230
    animating to sound, 229–230
    Graphic Display, 228–229
  Animation Setup, 230
  Animation Setup Window, 35
  Antialias Document, 34
  Apply dialog, 293–295
    Align Head To, 295
    Always Complete Last Step, 295
    Transition From Pose, 295
    Transition TO Pose, 295
  Arcturian Rat, 145–147
  ArtBeats REELs, 392
  Articulated hands, animating, 235–242
    animated hand projects, 239–240
      Balinese Dancer, 239
      Pebble Pickup, 239
    hand jewelry, 240–242
      strange hand, 240–241
      Talking Head Ring, 241
      warrior wristband, 241–242
    pre-attached Hands, 236–238
      manually animating a hand,
        237–238
      simple way of animating hands, 238
    Standalone Hands, 238–239
      animating, using Hands library,
        239
      hand posing, 239
    studying the body, 242
  ArtMatic, 369
  Aura, 377
  Auto Balance, 26
  Axial resizing, 63

B

Backgrounds, 180, 191–193
  color gradient, 192
  movies as, 192
  photographic, 192
  single-color, 191
  using digital camera, scanner and
    video camera, 193
Balinese Dancer, 239
Basic Hands, 73
Bass, Zygote
  animating, 272
  customized, 137–138
  posing, 122
Baumgarten Enterprises, 205, 389, 390
Bear, Zygote
  animating, 272
  customized, 138
  posed heads, 123–124
  posing, 122–123
Bend Body Parts, 33
bioMechanix, 480–482
  evolution of, 480–481
  new figures for Poser 4, 481–482
BioVision Motion Capture files, 10–11
Biplane composite Prop, 198–199
Blink, 250–251
Bomber Man, 61–62
Bones animation project, 442–444
Bryce, 353–354
Bryce beach and river scenes for Poser
  creating beach scene in Bryce,
    509–515
  figures, 505–515
    creating Princess Grace in Poser 4,
      505–508
  Painter 3d SE: creating texture map
    for "kilt," 508–509
Buck, Zygote
  animating, 273
  customized, 138–139
  posing, 124
Bump Map, 525
Business Man figure, 60
BVH Motion Capture, 379–385
  Credo Interactive's Life Forms,
    380–385
  MetaCreations' Dance Studio, 380
BVH motion capture data, 11
BVH Motion File, 302–303

C

Camera Controls, 44–45
Camera Controls List, 45
Camera library animations, 410

Cameras, 410–416
  animated reflections, 410–414
  Animating Camera, 410
  camera close-ups and textures, 414
  Camera library animations, 410
  camera view from the inside, 414–415
  "milking" the footage, 415–416
Camera View, 31
Canoma, 354–356
  how it works, 354–356
Carousel, 488–493
  how to proceed, 488–493
    animating the Carousel, 493
    designing and placing poles,
      491–492
    main Carousel structure, 489–491
    riders, 492–493
Carrara, 322, 328, 348, 353
Casual Woman figure, 63
Cat
  animating, 270
  customized, 135
  posed bodies, 109–110
  posed heads, 110, 111
CD, Poser 4 Content, 13–14
CD content collections, 205–207
  Baumgarten Enterprises, 205
  PoseAmation, 206
  WhiteCrow 3D, 206–207
Centaur, 493–496
  how to proceed, 494–496
Change Parent, 27
Cheek Puff Target Morph, 315, 316
Chimpanzee, Zygote
  animating, 273
  customized, 139
  posing, 124–125
  posing hands, 125
  posing heads, 126
ChinJut Target Morph, 315
Color Controls, 41
Color gradient backgrounds, 192
Color plate details, 531–539
  Plate 1: The Pool of Secrets, 532–
    533
  Plate 2: Greening, 533–535
  Plate 3: Verdict, 535–538
  Plate 4: Medusa, 538–539
Commotion, 374375, 376
Composite character animation,
  277–290
  mixed composite combination
    animations, 283–290
  complex composites to animate,
    286–290

rules for using Props with human
  and animal models, 284–286
multiple Composite Poser Models,
  278–281
  Rapskelion, 278–280
  Sharkboy, 280–281
Prop Composites, 281–283
  external Prop creations, 282–283
Composited figures, 149–178
  described, 150
  internal amalgamated composites,
    151–173
    assigning multiple Heads, 166
    creating element content, 167
    cross-species composites, 159–163
    incorporating external forms,
      165–166
    multiple element composites,
      159–163
    riders, 171
    rules for basic element design, 167
    single Prop composites, 151–158
    total figure element replacement
      project, 168–170
    using extra heads and hands, 165
    using Tail, 172–173
  Poseable Clothes, 174–175
  Prop morphing, 176
  spawning Props, 177–178
  using the Hierarchy, 174
Conform To, 25
Content CD, 13–14
Converting the hierarchy, 326, 339
Copy/Paste function, 12
Copy Picture, 24
Corel PhotoPaint, 370
Counting Hand, 73, 74
Cow, Zygote
  animating, 273
  customized, 139–140
  posing, 126–127
Cox, Stephen L., 453–457
Create Full Body Morph, 25
Create Magnet, 27–28
Create Spot Light, 31
Create Walk Path, 26
Create Wave, 29–31
Cross-species composites, 163–165
Customizing hands, 76–79
  alien hands, 78
  making hand elements invisible,
    77–78
  twisting hands, 78, 79
  types of options, 77
  writhing snakes appearance, 78, 79

Customizing human body, 60–65
  Axial Resizing, 63
  Global Resizing, 60–62
    head, 60–61, 62
  tapering, 63–65
  using deformers, 65
Customizing templates. *See* Templates, customizing
Cut/Copy/Paste, 24
CyberMesh, 364–367
  creating a CyberMesh head for Poser, 365–366
  Faces accessory, 367

D

Dance Studio, 380
Data sites, 46
Deformable props, 11–12
Deformations and Ground Plane, 186–187
Deformers, 33
Deforming animal models, 144–148
  Arcturian Rat, 145–147
  making animatable creatures, 148
  making creatures breathe, 148
Delete Figure, 26
Delete Object, 31
Depth Cued, 33
Depth Cueing, 43
Derochie, Chris, 389, 424–429
Digital camera, 193
Display Menu, 31–33
  Camera View, 31
  Bend Body parts, 33
  Deformers, 33
  Depth Cued, 33
  Figure Circle, 33
  Foreground/background Color, 33
  Ground Shadows, 33
  Guides, 33
  Paper Textures, 33
  Paste Into Background, 33
  Show/Clear Background Footage, 33
  Show/Clear Background Picture, 33
  Styles, 31–32
  Tracking, 33
Display Shadows, 43
Document Window, 42
Document Window Size, 36
Doe, Zygote
  animating, 272
  customized, 140
  posing, 127
Dog
  animating, 270

customized, 135–136
posed heads, 113–114
posed models, 110, 112–113
Dolphin
  animating, 271
  customized, 136
  posed heads, 116
  posing models, 114–115
Dome Target Morph, 315
Doorway, 204
Droop Target Morph, 314, 315

E

Ear boat, 199
Earoidz Target Morph, 311
Editing tools, 39
Edit Menu, 23–24
  Copy Picture, 24
  Cut/Copy/Paste, 24
  General Preferences, 24
  Memorize, 24
  Restore, 24
  Undo, 24
External Animal models, 121–132
  Zygote Animals, 122–132
External forms, 165–166
Eyebrow Dials, 88–92, 97
  Left/Right Brow Down, 88–90
  Left/Right Brow Up, 90–92
  Left/Right Worry, 88, 97
Eyebrows, 251–253
  Left/Right Eyebrow Down, 251–252
  Left/Right Eyebrow Up, 252
  Left/Right Eyebrow Worry, 252
Eye Candy (Alien Skin Software), 370
Eyes, 84–87, 249–253, 522
  animating, 249–253
    altering size, 250
    Blink, 250–251
    eyebrows, 251–253
    moving eyeballs out of head, 251
    wink, 250
  size of, 87
Eye Stretch Target Morph, 314

F

Face library keyframing, 254
Face modification methods, 84–87
  eyes, 84–87
Face Pull Target Morph, 316
Faces, creating expressive, 83–106
  emotive power, 84–99
    face modification methods, 84–87
    head parameters, 88–97

Parameter Dial combinations, 97–99
Racial Morphs, 99–106
  alternate Morph targets for faces, 102–106
Faces (InterQuest, Inc.), 367
Facial characteristics, animating, 253–255
  Face library keyframing, 254
  facial distortion animations, 253–254
  size modifications, 253–254
  tapering, 254
Facial distortion animations, 253–254
  size modifications, 253–254
  tapering, 254
Fashion Studio, 385
Figure Circle, 33
Figure developers, 469–486
  bioMechanix, 480–482
  Poser Props Modeler's Guild, 485–486
  WhiteCrow 3D, 483–484
  Zygote Media Group, 470–480
Figure Height, 16–17, 25
Figure Menu, 24–26
  Auto Balance, 26
  Conform To, 25
  Create Full Body morph, 25
  Create Walk Path, 26
  Delete Figure, 26
  Drop to Floor, 26
  Figure height, 25
  Genitalia, 25–26
  Hide Figure/Show All Figures, 26
  Lock Figure, 26
  Lock Hand Parts, 26
  Set Figure Parent, 25
  Symmetry, 26
  Use Inverse Kinematics, 25
  Use Limits, 25
Figures as Props, 201–204
  doorway, 204
  Hand Chairs, 203
  oracle, 204
  statues, 202
  table legs, 203
File Menu, 23
File naming conventions, 394
Flexing a muscle, 79–80
Flying Logos, 215–216
Foreground/Background Color, 33
form•Z, 356, 357
4D Paint, 378
Frog, Zygote
  animating, 274
  customized, 140–141

posing, 127–128
Frown, 94, 246–247
Full Figure Morph, 10, 11

G

General Preferences, 24
Genitalia, 25–26
Geometric Props, 153–155
Global resizing, 60–62
Graph, 36
Graphic Display, 228–229
Green Man, 398–401
Ground Plane, 180–190
    creating patterned, 181–182
    deformations and, 186–187
    oblique abstracted patterns, 182–186
        shadow letters and logos, 184–185
        shadow spotlights, 185–186
    questions and answers about,
        180–181
    reflective and transparent, 187–190
Ground Shadows, 33
Grouping tool, 7, 8
Guides, 33

H

Hair and Hats Props library, 156–157
Hair library, 155–156
Hair models, 12–13
Hair Props, 194–195
    internal Props for hair, 194, 195
    from Zygote Extras Props library,
        194, 195
Hand Chairs, 203
Hand jewelry, 240–242
Hand 'O Heads, 288–290
Hand Puppets library, 74
Hands, posing and customizing, 71–81
    customizing, 76–79
    general rules for posing, 74–75
    Parameter Dial alterations, 76
    using deformers on hand, 79–81
Handshaking, 347–392
    BVH Motion Capture, 379–385
        Credo Interactive's Life Forms,
            380–385
        MetaCreations' Dance Studio, 380
    Fashion Studio, 385, 386
    media conversion and compression,
        385–387
        Terran Interactive's Media Cleaner
            Pro, 385–387
    MetaSynth, MetaTracks and Xx,
        387–388
    post-production editing, 372–377

Adobe After Effects 4, 372, 374
Adobe Premier, 372, 373
animation painting, 376–377
Commotion, 374–375, 376
Media Studio Pro, 375
MetaCreations' Painter, 372, 373
Strata VideoShop 4, 374, 375
RayDream Studio, 348–353
recommended CD content, 388–392
    ArtBeats, REELs, 392
    Baumgarten Enterprises, 389, 390
    Chris Derochie, 389
    Replica Technology, 391
    SB Technologies, 389. 390
3D applications, 353–368
    Amapi, 356–357, 358
    Amorphium, 361–362, 363
    Bryce, 353–354
    Canoma, 354–356
    CyberMesh, 364–367
    form•Z, 356, 357
    Inspire 3D (LightWave Jr.),
        357–359
    Nendo, 364
    Organica, 362–363
    Plant Studio, 368
    Strata Studio Pro 2.5, 359–360
    3D Studio Max 2+, 360–361
    trueSpace 4+, 361, 362
3D Painting applications, 377–379
    4D paint, 378
    Painter 3D, 377–378
    SurfaceSuite Pro, 379
    trU-V, 379
2D f/x plugins, 370–372
    Alien Skin's Eye Candy, 370
    Andromeda F/X, 371
    Kai's PowerTools, 3, 370
    Photoshop's Internal Effects, 371
    RenderSoft illusionae texture
        maker, 371–372
    Virtus' Alien Skin Textureshop, 371
    Xaos Tools' Terrazo, 370
2D painting applications, 368–370
    ArtMatic, 369
    Corel PhotoPaint, 370
    MetaCreations' Painter, 368–369
    Photoshop, 369
Hats, and their modification, 193–194
    composited hats from basic Props,
        193–194
Head
    parameter Dial combinations, 97–99
    parameters, 88–97
        Eyebrow Dials, 88

resizing, 60–61, 62
Help Menu, 36
Hide Figure/Show All Figures, 26
Hierarchies, 8, 9, 321–345
    automated hierarchies, 343
        creating a new Prop figure,
            343–344
    basic hierarchy development,
        322–327
        methods used to develop Poser
            figures, 323–327
        overview, 322–323
        See also Poser figures, developing
    Hierarchy editing tips, 344–345
    primitive Toy Birdoid, 327–343
        Toy Birdoid, making and
            exporting, 328–341
        troubleshooting, 342–343
Hierarchy Editor, 8, 9, 36, 37, 344–345
Hierarchy list, 174
Hierarchy Window, 8
Hints and tips from Master Users,
    423–468
    Chris Derochie, 424–429
        approaching a scene, 424–429
    Martin Turner, 429–436
        lip-syncing and phonemes,
            429–436
    Cecilia Ziemer, 436–444
        electric art, 436–444
    Roy Riggs, 444–448
        PHI Builder, 444–448
    Jackie Lewin, 448–453
        Morph Targets for Horse forelock
            and mane, 448–453
    Stephen L. Cox, 453–457
        UVMapper, 453–457
    Rick Schrand, 457–464
        bump map and transparency map
            tips, 457–464
    Morph Manager, 464
    OBJ file format, 465–468
History of Poser 4, 4
Horse
    animating, 271
    customized, 136–137
    new texture for, 394–398
    posed head, 118
    posed models, 116–117
Human body, posing and customizing,
    47–70
    basic posing, 49–59
    customizing, 60–65
    customizing with deformers, 65
    paying attention, 48

I

IK. *See* Inverse Kinematics
Inspire 3D (LightWave Jr.), 357–359
Interface, Poser 4, 22–46
    Animation Controls toggle, 41–42
    Camera Controls, 44–45
    Camera Controls List, 45
    Color Controls, 41
    Depth Cueing, Tracking, Display
        Shadows, 43
    Document Window, 42
    editing tools, 39
    Library palettes toggle, 39–40
    Light Controls, 45–46
    Memory Dots, 41
    Menu Bar, 22
        Animation Menu, 34–35
        Display menu, 31–33
        Edit Menu, 23–24
        Figure Menu, 24–26
        File Menu, 23
        Help Menu, 36
        Object Menu, 26–31
        Render menu, 33–34
        Window Menu, 35–36
    Parameter Dials, 40
    Selection Lists, 42
    Style buttons, 43
    upgrades, 16
Internal Animal models, 108–121
    Cat, 109–110, 111, 135
    Dog, 110, 112–114, 135–136
    Dolphin 114–116, 136
    Horse, 116–118, 136–137
    Raptor, 118–121, 137
Internal replacement Props, 199–201
    using Taper operation, 200–201
Inverse Kinematics, 233, 279

J

Joint Editing, 344
Joint Editor, 36, 37
Joint Parameters, 326–327
    dialog, 73
Junkyard Fairies, 437–440

K

Kai's PowerTools 3, 370
Killer Whale, Zygote
    animating, 274
    customized, 141
    posing, 128–129

L

Left/Right Brow Down, 88–90

Left/Right Brow Up, 90–92
Left/Right Worry, 88, 97
Leisure Suit Lambert, 401–402
Lewin, Jackie, 448–453
Libraries, 36
Library Palettes toggle, 39–40
Life Forms, 380–385
    adjusting frame rate before export,
        384
    creating a keyframe 383–384
    exporting BVH files, 384–385
    importing BVH motion data into
        Poser 4, 385
    as keyframer, 381
    keyframing an animation, 383
    as library of motions, 382
    as motion editor, 381
    setting up motion sequences for
        Poser, 382
    for smart paste functions, 382
    used for animation, 381
    using motion-captured animation,
        382
Light Controls, 45, 46
Lighting, new options, 8, 10
Lights and lighting, 416–418
    Lights library animations, 418
Lights library animations, 418
LightWave Object (LWO), 357
Lion, Zygote
    animating, 274
    customized, 141–142
    posing, 129
Lips Out Target Morph, 313, 314
Load Morph Target, 27
Lock Actor, 27
Lock Figure, 26
Lock Hand Parts, 26, 72
Logos, 184–185
Long Chin Target Morph, 313
Loop Interpolation, 232–233
Lowface Target Morph, 313

M

Mac screen size, changing, 20, 21
Magnet and Wave Deformers, 7
Make Movie, 231
    dialog, 35, 36
Mannequin, 162–163
Mapping a photographic face, 406–408
Master Uses. *See* Hints and tips from
    Master Users
Material Group Painting, 216–218
    Group Painting factoids, 217–218
Materials, 34

Media Cleaner Pro, 385–387
Media conversion and compression,
    385–387
    Terran Interactive's Media Cleaner
        Pro, 385–387
MediaPaint, 376–377
Media Studio Pro, 375
Memorize, 24
Memory Dots, 41
Menu Bar, Poser 4, 22
MetaCreations
    Dance Studio, 380
    Painter, 368–369, 372, 373
    RayDream Studio, 106, 322, 328,
        348–353
    SREE-D, 17
MetaSynth, 387–388
MetaTracks, 387–388
Micromorphing, 505
Morphing madness, 305–317
    in action, 316–317
    creating Morph Targets, 306
        developing Poser 4 Morph Targets,
            308–310
        materials required, 307
        Target Morph Types, 310–316
Morphman, 105
Morph Manager, 464
Morph Targets, 306
    developing, 308–310
MorphWorld, 104, 105
Motion Capture Files, 11
Mouth, animating, 244–249
    with Mouth controls, 244–249
        combining Open Mouth, Smile,
            and Frown, 247
        Frown, 246–247
        mouth shapes for phonemes,
            247–248
        Open Mouth, 245
        Smile, 245–246
        tongue, 248–249
Mouth, "F," 95, 248
Mouth Letter Structures (O, F, M),
    247–248
Mouth "M," 95, 96, 248
Mouth "O," 94–95, 247
Movies as background, 192
Multiple basic Prop composites,
    161–162
Multiple element composites, 159–163
    Mannequin and Stick Figure options,
        162–163
    multiple basic Prop composites,
        161–162

Multiple element composites *(Cont.)*
  multiple figure composites, 159–163
  multiple Zygote Prop composites, 163
  preparing to create figure composites, 159–161
Multiple figure composites, 159–163
Multiple Zygote Prop composites, 163
Mute Sound/Clear Sound, 233
Muybridge, Eadweard, 259–269
  using Muybridge's books, 261–269
Muybridge Complete Animal and Human Locomotion volumes, 259, 260

N

Nendo, 364
New features, 4–17
  BioVision Motion Capture files, 10–11
  Content CD, 13–14
  Copy/Paste function, 12
  deformable props, 11–12
  enhanced custom textures, 14, 15
  Full Figure Morphs, 10, 11
  Hair models, 12–13
  hierarchies, 8, 9
  interface and speed upgrades, 16
  Magnet and Wave Deformers, 7
  MetaCreations' SREE-D, 17
  new lighting options, 8, 10
  polygonal grouping and picking, 7, 8
  Posable Clothes, 5, 6
  proxy modeling enhancements, 16–17
  Sketch Designer, 5, 6
  transparent and reflecting materials, 8, 9
  Walk Designer, 14, 16
Nostril Target Morph, 312

O

Object Menu, 26–31
  Change Parent, 27
  Create Magnet, 27–28
  Create Spot Light, 31
  Create Wave, 29–31
  Delete Object, 31
  Load Morph Target, 27
  Lock Actor, 27
  Point At, 27
  Properties, 26–27
  Replace Body Part with Prop, 27
  Spawn Morph Target, 27
obj file, 324
OBJ file format, 465–468
OBJ files, 104, 106
Open Lips, 92–93, 245

Open Mouth, 245
Oracle, 204
Organica, 362–363
Ostrich Lady, 63
Out of Body Experience, 294

P

Paint, 377
Painter, creating textures with, 394–403
Painter 3D, 377–378
Paper Textures, 33
Parameter Dials, 40, 63
  combinations, for Head, 97–98
Paste Into Background, 33
Path, 298–299
Pebble Pickup, 239
Penguin, Zygote
  animating, 274
  customized, 142
  posing, 129–130
People Library, 60, 63
People Poses library, 133
phi file, 325, 337
Phonemes, 429
Photographic backgrounds, 192
Photographic face, mapping, 406–408
Photoshop, 369
  creating textures with, 403–406
Photoshop's Internal Effects, 371
Plant Studio, 368
Play Movie File, 233
Point At, 27
Poseable Clothes, 5, 6, 174–175
PoseAmation, 206
Pose Hands libraries, 73
Poser figures, developing, 323–327
  colors and Joint parameters, 326–327
  converting the hierarchy in Poser, 326
  editing obj file, 324–325
  editing the groups, 325
  exporting model from RDS, 324
  importing the model, 323
  naming the parts, 324
  obj text editing, 324
  RayDream Studio, 323
  setting up RDS5 and Poser, 323
  setting up the hierarchy, 325–326
Power Forum Web Ring, 408
Poser Props Modeler's Guild, 485–486
  how to join, 485
  render requirements for models, 486
Poses Library, 53
Post-production editing. *See* Handshaking
Potted, 436–437

Pre-attached Hands, 236–238
Preparatory movements, 234
Prop, defined, 151
Prop Composites, 281–283
  external Prop creations, 282–283
Properties, 26–27
  dialog, 72
Prop morphing, 176
Props, 11–12, 193–204
  building Prop vehicles from internal elements, 195–199
    Biplane composite Prop, 198–199
    ear boat, 199
    wagon, 196–197
  deformable, 11–12
  figures (and partial figures) as Props, 201–204
    doorway, 204
    Hand Chairs, 203
    oracle, 204
    statues, 202
    table legs, 203
  hair Props, 194–195
    internal Props for hair, 194, 195
    from Zygote Extras props library, 194, 195
  hats and their modification, 193–194
    composited hats from basic Props, 193–194
  internal replacement Props, 199–201
    using Taper operations, 200–201
Proxy modeling enhancements, 16–17

Q

Quaternion Interpolation, 232–233

R

Racial Morphs, 99–106
  alternate Morph Targets for faces, 102–106
Ragdoll, 440–441
Rage, 519–520
Raptor
  animating, 271–272
  customized, 137
  customizing texture for, 402
  posed hands and feet, 120–121
  posed heads, 120
  posed models, 118–120
RayDream Studio, 322, 328, 348–353
Carrara, 353
  Free Form Modeler, 349–350
  Mesh Form Modeler, 348–349
    Sphere of Attraction tool, 349
  Poser animating in RayDream, 350

RayDream Deformations, 351–252
  internal deformations, 351–352
    Morph Target Deformations, 351
read-write OBJ files, 348
RDS5, 323, 324, 337
Reflecting materials, 8, 9
Reflection Mapping and Ground Plane,
  187–189
Reflections, animated, 410–414
Rendering, 207–212, 418–421
  animated shadow maps, 418–419
  finished, 209, 210
  Render Styles, 419
  Sketch Designer, 209, 210–212, 213
    commands and options, 211–212
  surface attribute colors, 419, 420
  using Render Styles, 207–209
Render menu, 33–34
  Antialias Document, 34
  Materials, 34
  Render Options, 34
  Sketch Style Render, 34
Render Options, 34
RenderSoft Illusionae 2.0 texture maker,
  371–372
Render Styles, 419
  using, 207–209
Replace Body Part with Prop, 27
Replica Technology, 391
Resample Keyframes, 232
Resize tool, 60, 61, 63
Resizing
  axial, 63
  global, 60–62
Restore, 24
Retime Animation, 231, 280
Rider, 171
Riggs, Roy, 444–448
Rotation Trackball, 44

S
SB Technologies, 389, 390
Scanner, 193
Schrand, Rick, 457–464
Screen size, changing
  on Mac, 20, 21
  in Windows 95/98/NT, 20–21
Selection Lists, 42
Set Figure Parent, 25
s groupNumber, 467–468
Shadow letters, 184–185
Shadow maps, animated, 418–419
Shadow spotlights, 185–186
Shark, Zygote
  animating, 275

customized, 143
  posing, 130–131
Shooting a Cannonball, 287–288
Show/Clear Background Footage, 33
Show/Clear Background Picture, 33
Sign Language hand poses, 73, 75
Single-color backgrounds, 191
Single Prop composites, 151–158
  basic Geometric Props, 153–155
  Hair and Hats Props library, 156–157
  Hair library, 155–156
  single Zygote Prop composites,
    157–158
  Zygote Hat Props, 157
Single Zygote Prop composites, 157–158
Sketch Designer, 5, 6, 36, 38, 209,
  210–212
  commands and options, 211–212
    Auto Spacing, 212
    Background Direction, 212
    Color Blend, 212
    Density, Line Length and Width,
      211–212
    Light 1, 2, 3, 212
    Line Color Randomness, Opacity,
      and Cross Hatch, 212
    Lo and High Brightness, 212
    Objects, Background, Edges, 211
    Over Black/Auto Density, 211
    Presets, 211
    Stroke Head and Tail, 212
    Total Angle and Color Cutoff, 212
Sketch Style Render, 34
Skip Frames, 233
SkyPaint, 376
Smile, 93–94, 245–246
Sound, animating to, 229–230
Spawning Props, 177
Spawn Morph Target, 27
Speed, rendering, 16
Spikes Target Morph, 311, 312
Spotted Chimp of Mars, 403–406
Standalone Hands, 238–239
Starfish of Tails, 173
Statues, 202
Stick Figure, 162–163
Strata Studio Pro, 359–360
  animating a boned Poser figure, 359
Strata VideoShop 4, 374, 375
Style buttons, 43
Styles, 31–32
Surface attribute colors, 419, 420
Surface Materials Window, 8, 9, 34, 35
SurfaceSuite Pro, 379
Symmetry, 26

T
Table legs, 203
Tail, 172–173
  Starfish of tails, 173
Talking Head Ring, 241
Talouse Target Morph, 311, 312
Taperhead, 64
Tapering, 63–65
  face, 254
Taper operation, 200–201
Taper tool, 63
Target Morph Types, 310–316
  Cheek Puff, 315, 316
  ChinJut, 315
  Dome, 315
  Droop, 314, 315
  Earoidz, 311
  Eye Stretch, 314
  Face Pull, 316
  Lips Out, 313, 314
  Long Chin, 313
  Lowface, 313
  Nostril, 312
  Spikes, 311, 312
  Talouse, 311, 312
  Two Horns, 314
  Uplift, 311
  Wide Nose, 312, 313
Templates, customizing, 393–408
  creating textures with Painter,
    394–403
    creating new horse texture,
      394–398
    customizing Raptor texture, 402
    Green Man, 398–401
    leisure Suit Lambert, 401–402
  creating textures with Photoshop,
    403–406
    Spotted Chimp of Mars, 403–406
  file naming conventions, 394
  mapping a photographic face,
    406–408
Terrazo, 370
Terror, physical manifestations of,
  515–529
Textures
  creating
    with Painter, 394–403
    with Photoshop, 403–406
  custom, 14, 15
3D applications. *See* Handshaking
3D Painting applications. *See*
  Handshaking
3D Studio Max 2+, 360–361
Tongue "L," 96, 249

Tongue Parameter Dial, 248–249
    Tongue "T," 249
    Tongue "L," 249
Tongue "T," 95, 96, 249
Tool Control Toggles/Show-Hide Tools, 36
Toy Birdoid, 327–343
    beak, 336–337
    body, 328–329
    converting, 339–341
    exporting model from RDS, 337
    head, 330–331
    legs, 332–333
    making the text (.PHI) file, 337
    neck, 329–330
    recheck object names, 337
    shoulders, 331–332
    troubleshooting, 342–343
    wings, 333–336
Tracking, 33, 43
Transitional walks, 299
Transparency Map, 212, 214–216
Transparency Mapping and Ground Plane, 189–190
Transparent figure textures, 212–216
    Flying Logos, 215–216
Transparent materials, 8, 9
trueSpace 4+, 361, 362
trU-V, 379
Turner, Martin, 429–436
2D f/x plugins. *See* Handshaking
2D painting applications. *See* Handshaking
Two Horns Target Morph, 314

U

Undo, 24
Uplift Target Morph, 311
Use Inverse Kinematics, 25
Use Limits, 25, 73
UVMapper, 453–457
    texture mapping a chair with, 454–457

V

Vampire morphs, making, 496
    applying the morphs, 504
    ear morph, 499–500
    facial morphs, 502–503
    general morphing tips, 504
       micromorphing, 505
        morph target range limits, 505

positive/negative morphs, 504
    nose morph, 501–502
    preparing base file, 497
    teeth morphs, 497–499
Velociraptor, 118
Video camera, 193

W

Wagon, 196–197
Walk Designer, 14, 16, 36, 38, 291–303
    animals and, 299–302
    control dialog, 292–295
       Apply dialog, 293–295
    new options, 14, 16
    parameter combinations, 298
    parameters, 295–297
    Paths, 298–299
    transitional walks, 299
    using BVH Motion Files, 302–303
Wave Deformer parameters, 30–31
    amplitude, 30
    amplitude and frequency noise, 30
    offset, 31
    phrase, 30
    stretch, 30
    turbulence, 31
    wavelength, 31
    wave type, 31
WaveFront, 322
WhiteCrow 3D, 206–207, 483–484
    Alien Poser Pack 1, 483
    company operation, 483–484
Wide Nose Target Morph, 312, 313
Window Menu, 35–36
    Animation Palette (toggle), 35
    Document Window Size, 36
    Graph (toggle), 36
    Hierarchy Editor, 36, 37
    Joint Editor, 36, 37
    Libraries, (toggle), 36
    Sketch Designer, 36, 38
    Tool Control Toggles/Show-Hide Tools, 36
    Walk Designer, 36, 38
Windows 95/98/NT screen size, changing, 20–21
Wink, 250
Wolf, Zygote
    animating, 275
    customized, 143
    posing, 131

Worry, 97
Wristband, 241–242

X

Xx, 387–388

Z

Zebra, Zygote
    animating, 275
    customized, 144
    posing, 132
Ziemer, Cecilia, 436–444
Z Trans Parameter Dial, 251
Zygote Animal models, 122–132, 258
    Bass, 122, 137–138
    Bear, 54, 122–124, 138
    Buck, 124, 138–139
    Chimpanzee, 124–126, 139
    Cow, 126–127, 139–140
    Doe, 127, 140
    Frog, 127–128, 140–141
    Killer Whale, 128–129, 141
    Lion, 129, 141–142
    Penguin, 129–130, 142
    Shark, 130–131, 143
    Wolf, 131, 143
    Zebra, 132, 144
Zygote Extras CD collection, 55
Zygote Hat Props, 157
Zygote Media Group, 108, 121, 470–480
    additional Poser models from Zygote, 477–479
    address, 122
    history of, 479–480
    how Zygote developed models for Poser 4, 470–477
    adjusting joint parameters, 475–477
    applying the materials, 473
    building the model, 471–472
    creating morph targets, 474
    creating texture template, 473
    grouping, 472
    history of the process, 470–471
    projecting the UV texture coordinates, 473
    reading model into Poser, 474–475
    removing extra groups, 474
    saving out, 477
    testing texture mapping and fine-tuning materials, 477